# Daniel Dennett

Author of such groundbreaking and influential books as *Consciousness Explained* and *Darwin's Dangerous Idea*, Daniel C. Dennett has reached a huge general and professional audience that extends way beyond the confines of academic philosophy. He has made significant contributions to the study of consciousness, the development of the child's mind, cognitive ethnology, explanation in the social sciences, artificial intelligence, and evolutionary theory. His work is distinctive in establishing contact with areas such as neuroscience and game theory. This volume is the only collection that traces all these connections and furnishes the nonspecialist with a fully rounded account of why Dennett is such an important voice on the philosophical scene.

Written by a team of international authorities, most of them specialists in the disciplines concerned, this collection will appeal to students and professionals in philosophy, psychology (child, developmental, and evolutionary), neuroscience, computer science, economics, and evolutionary biology. Those who have followed Dennett's recent work also will find material of great interest and originality.

# Contemporary Philosophy in Focus

**Contemporary Philosophy in Focus** will offer a series of introductory volumes to many of the dominant philosophical thinkers of the current age. Each volume will consist of newly commissioned essays that will cover all the major contributions of a preeminent philosopher in a systematic and accessible manner. Comparable in scope and rationale to the highly successful series **Cambridge Companions to Philosophy**, the volumes will not presuppose that readers are already intimately familiar with the details of each philosopher's work. They will thus combine exposition and critical analysis in a manner that will appeal both to students of philosophy and to professionals, as well as students across the humanities and social sciences.

FORTHCOMING VOLUMES:

*Stanley Cavell* edited by Richard Eldridge
*Donald Davidson* edited by Kirk Ludwig
*Ronald Dworkin* edited by Arthur Ripstein
*Jerry Fodor* edited by Tim Crane
*Thomas Kuhn* edited by Thomas Nickles
*Alasdair MacIntyre* edited by Mark C. Murphy
*Hilary Putnam* edited by Yemina Ben-Menahem
*Richard Rorty* edited by Charles Guignon and David Hiley
*John Searle* edited by Barry Smith
*Charles Taylor* edited by Ruth Abbey
*Bernard Williams* edited by Alan Thomas

# Daniel Dennett

Edited by

**ANDREW BROOK**
*Carleton University*

**DON ROSS**
*University of Cape Town*

CAMBRIDGE
UNIVERSITY PRESS

PUBLISHED BY THE PRESS SYNDICATE OF THE UNIVERSITY OF CAMBRIDGE
The Pitt Building, Trumpington Street, Cambridge, United Kingdom

CAMBRIDGE UNIVERSITY PRESS
The Edinburgh Building, Cambridge CB2 2RU, UK
40 West 20th Street, New York, NY 10011-4211, USA
477 Williamstown Road, Port Melbourne, VIC 3207, Australia
Ruiz de Alarcón 13, 28014 Madrid, Spain
Dock House, The Waterfront, Cape Town 8001, South Africa

http://www.cambridge.org

First published 2002

Printed in the United States of America

*Typefaces* Janson Text 10/13 pt. and ITC Officina Sans     *System* LATEX $2_\varepsilon$   [TB]

*A catalog record for this book is available from the British Library.*

*Library of Congress Cataloging in Publication Data*
Daniel Dennett / edited by Andrew Brook, Don Ross.
    p.   cm. – (Contemporary philosophy in focus)
    Includes bibliographical references and index.
    ISBN 0-521-80394-2 – ISBN 0-521-00864-6 (pbk.)
1. Dennett, Daniel Clement.   I. Brook, Andrew.   II. Ross, Don.
III. Series.
B945.D394 D36   2001
191 – dc21       2001037489

ISBN 0 521 80394 2 hardback
ISBN 0 521 00864 6 paperback

# Contents

# Acknowledgments

We would like first to acknowledge the vision of Cambridge University Press and its New York Publishing Director for the Humanities, Terence Moore, for creating the unique series of which this volume is a part. May it make a difference!

Although Dan Dennett has had no part in this volume and indeed has not even seen most of the essays in it, we would like to thank him for two things. First, for the originality and generativity of his thought over the past thirty-five years. Second, for the generosity with which he has helped so many researchers, including many of the contributors to this volume, to find their own way. (Where Dan Dennett has seen a chapter in this volume, it is because the chapter was part of an ongoing research activity of some kind in which he is involved.)

We would like to thank the contributors most warmly. Every essay in the volume is new.[1] It says a great deal, about the author and about Dan Dennett, that some very busy people much in demand in their own right would take the time to prepare a special paper for this volume.

Finally, we acknowledge with gratitude and fondness the indispensable role of our partners, Christine Koggel (Bryn Mawr College) and Nelleke Bak (University of the Western Cape). That they are willing to put up with our various ventures is in no small part because their own professional lives are occupied with just as many ventures of their own.

A. B.
Carleton University, Ottawa, Ontario, Canada

D. R.
University of Cape Town, South Africa

---

[1] A portion of Chapter 10 appeared previously in *Biology and Philosophy* 16:251–60, and is reproduced with permission.

# Acknowledgments

# Contributors

KATHLEEN AKINS is associate professor of philosophy at Simon Fraser University, Canada. Her work focuses on the theoretical problems common to both philosophy of mind/metaphysics and the neurosciences. She is co-ordinator of the McDonnell Project in Philosophy and the Neurosciences, funded by a James S. McDonnell Centennial Fellowship. She is currently working on a book on the physiology and philosophy of colour vision with Martin Hahn.

SIMON BARON-COHEN is Co-Director of the Autism Research Centre, Departments of Experimental Psychology and Psychiatry at Cambridge University. He wrote *Mindblindness: An Essay on Autism and Theory of Mind* (MIT Press/A Bradford Book, 1995).

ANDREW BROOK is professor of philosophy, director of the Institute for Interdisciplinary Studies, and chair of the Ph.D. Programme in Cognitive Science at Carleton University, Canada. He is the author of *Kant and the Mind* (Cambridge University Press, 1994), coauthor with Robert Stainton of *Knowledge and Mind* (MIT Press/A Bradford Book, 2000) and coeditor with Don Ross and David Thompson of *Dennett's Philosophy: A Comprehensive Assessment* (MIT Press/A Bradford Book, 2000).

DOROTHY L. CHENEY is professor of biology at the University of Pennsylvania. She is coauthor with Robert Seyfarth of *How Monkeys See the World: Inside the Mind of Another Species* (University of Chicago Press, 1990).

PAUL M. CHURCHLAND is professor of philosophy at the University of San Diego. He is author of *A Neurocomputational Perspective* (1989), *The Engine of Reason, the Seat of the Soul* (1995), and coauthor with Patricia Churchland of *On the Contrary: Critical Essays 1987–1997* (1998) (all from MIT Press/Bradford Books).

ANDY CLARK is professor of philosophy and cognitive science at the University of Sussex, U.K. He has written extensively on artificial neural networks, robotics, and artificial life. His latest books are *Being There: Putting Brain, Body and World Together Again* (MIT Press/A Bradford Book, 1997) and *Mindware: An Introduction to the Philosophy of Cognitive Science* (Oxford University Press, 2001).

RICHARD GRIFFIN is a research scientist at the Autism Research Centre's Infant-Toddler Lab, Departments of Experimental Psychology and Psychiatry, University of Cambridge. He studied philosophy and psychology at Harvard University, and was a frequent participant in Dennett's philosophy seminars at Tufts University.

DON ROSS is professor of economics and convenor of the programme in philosophy, politics, and economics at the University of Cape Town. He is the author of *Metaphor, Meaning and Cognition* (Peter Lang, 1993) and *What People Want: The Concept of Utility from Bentham to Game Theory* (UCT Press, 2001), and coeditor with Andrew Brook and David Thompson of *Dennett's Philosophy: A Comprehensive Assessment* (MIT Press/A Bradford Book, 2000). He is currently at work on a book on the relationships between economics and cognitive science.

ROBERT M. SEYFARTH is professor of psychology at the University of Pennsylvania and coauthor with Dorothy Cheney of *How Monkeys See the World: Inside the Mind of Another Species* (University of Chicago Press, 1990).

YORICK WILKS is professor of computer science and director of the Institute of Language, Speech, and Hearing at the University of Sheffield, U.K. He has published numerous articles and five books in the area of artificial intelligence and computer language processing, of which the most recent are *Artificial Believers*, coauthored with Afzal Ballim (Lawrence Erlbaum, 1991), and *Electric Words: Dictionaries, Computers and Meanings*, coauthored with Brian Slator and Louise Guthrie (MIT Press/A Bradford Book, 1996). He is editor of *Machine Conversations* (Kluwer, 1999).

Daniel Dennett

# INTRODUCTION

# 1 Dennett's Position in the Intellectual World

*ANDREW BROOK AND DON ROSS*

## 1. DENNETT'S LIFE AND WORK

Over the past thirty years, Daniel Clement Dennett has had a major influence on our understanding of human intentionality and agency, consciousness (and thereby phenomenology and the architecture and neuroscience of consciousness), developmental psychology, cognitive ethology, artificial intelligence, and evolutionary theory. In this introductory essay, we will first give a chronological survey of these contributions and then, starting with Dennett's place in the intellectual history of the last half of the twentieth century, construct an overview of his philosophy. Dennett has played a central role in one of the most significant theoretical revolutions of the past fifty years, the cognitivist revolution. This revolution demolished simple empiricism and put in its stead a view of human action as requiring interpretation in terms of a rich reservoir of cognitive resources and, many argue, evolutionary history. Dennett has played a role in this revolution for thirty-five years now.

Recently, a number of collections have appeared on Dennett's work. This one is different. We are interested in the influence Dennett has had beyond the bounds of academic philosophy. To assess this influence, we have assembled a team of experts who either specialize in one of the areas in which Dennett has had such an influence (Simon Baron-Cohen in developmental psychology, Robert Seyfarth and Dorothy Cheney in cognitive ethology, Yorick Wilks in artificial intelligence) or who, although trained in philosophy, have attained expertise in a discipline beyond philosophy (in alphabetical order: Akins in neuroscience, Brook in cognitive science, Clark in cognitive science, Churchland in neuroscience, Ross in economics and evolutionary theory). We wrote the introduction as much for these contributors as for our readers. Rather than each contributor trying to summarize the aspect of Dennett's work most relevant to his or her contribution, we put together a single common overview for all to share. The various contributors then took this overview as read when they prepared their essays. Thus, the essays should be read together with this introduction.

Although Dennett has deep roots in American pragmatism, he was actually born in Lebanon (during World War II; his father was representing the U.S. government there) and he did his doctorate at Oxford. He is a seasoned world traveller and has spent time in most of the major universities of the Western world (including, he once said with some pride, every university with a philosophy graduate programme in Canada). He did his undergraduate work at Harvard, where, he says, he vigorously resisted his teacher and the most influential American philosopher of the twentieth century, Willard van Orman Quine (doctrines for which he later developed more sympathy) (Dennett 1998, p. 357). His doctoral studies at Oxford were done under the tutelage of the most influential Oxford philosopher of his time, Gilbert Ryle. Dennett received a D.Phil. in the remarkably speedy time of two years in 1965.

Dennett's life has been as stable and unsensational as his work has been brilliant and influential. After a brief stint at the University of California Riverside, he has been at one university ever since, Tufts University in Medford, Massachusetts, a suburb of Boston. He married in university and has been married to the same woman ever since. They have two grown children. He runs a working farm in Maine. (Dennett is said to get some of his best ideas while working the land. Douglas Hofstadter calls this 'tillosophy.') He is an expert high-seas sailor and navigator and an accomplished drummer and choral singer. He is one of a very few philosophers who commands bestseller-sized advances for his books. Dennett once described himself as an ACLU (American Civil Liberties Union) liberal.

Dennett is famous for his generosity to students. A small army of increasingly important young philosophers, psychologists, and even M.D.s have passed through his Centre for Cognitive Studies at Tufts as postdoctoral fellows or visitors. Although Dennett has had a deep influence on thousands of researchers, there are few 'Dennettians.' Unlike many world-class intellectuals, Dennett has never sought to create disciples. His former students are remarkably independent-minded.

Dennett is an accomplished philosophical humourist. He was the main force behind *The Philosopher's Lexicon* (1987d), which consists of 'definitions' of philosopher's names that reflect (or at least spoof) some aspect of their work. The entry for 'Dennett' (not written by Dennett) reads in part: "Dennett, v. To while away the hours defining surnames; hence, *dennettation*, n. The meaning of a surname. 'Every surname has both a meinong and a dennettation.'"

There are many, many sides to Dennett's contributions but one of his most important contributions has been to challenge unexamined orthodoxies. One of his characteristic ways of doing so is to go after comfortable assumptions with what he calls intuition pumps. Here is an example. Pre-reflectively, most of us would think that there is a clear difference between how something tastes to us and how we react to that taste (with pleasure, indifference, disgust, etc.). But consider the case of Mr. Chase and Mr. Sanborn:

> Mr. Chase and Mr. Sanborn both used to like a certain coffee. More recently it has lost its appeal. The reasons they give seem to differ markedly. Chase: "The flavour of the coffee hasn't changed but I just don't like that flavour very much now." Sanborn: "No, no, you are quite wrong. I would still like *that* flavour as much as ever. The problem is that the coffee *doesn't* taste that way any more." (taken from Dennett 1988a)

We are meant to say to ourselves, "Hmmm, maybe this distinction I want to draw between how something tastes and how much one likes the taste does not correspond to a real difference." Then we are meant to generalize the doubt: "Well, if there isn't a clear boundary to be drawn here, what about with other mental states?" – And we are well on our way to shaking up our traditional philosophical conception of the mind as a place populated by a bunch of clearly demarcated mental states.

Dennett is not just a philosophical gadfly. The unsettling intuition pumps, awkward rhetorical questions, and so on, are used not just in the service of iconoclasm (although they are used in the service of iconoclasm). Dennett has a deep philosophical mission, one articulated in his very first book and carried through with verve, ingenuity, and great continuity ever since.

His first book grew out of the work he did with Ryle. It was called *Content and Consciousness* (1969). These two words, 'content' and 'consciousness,' encapsulate much of Dennett's mission. 'Content' refers to the contents of the mind: all the beliefs and desires and values and emotions and hopes and expectations and memories and ... and ... and ... that make up the mental life of all cognitively intact human beings. And 'consciousness' refers, of course, to our consciousness of our world, our mental contents, and ourselves.

In Dennett's view, the correct order in which to examine these topics is content first, then consciousness. (The essays in the current volume might seem to be in the reverse order but they are not. We will explain why later.) To oversimplify mightily, he devoted the 1970s and 1980s to content (with some important forays into consciousness) and the 1990s to consciousness (with some important additional work on content). Mentioning just these two topics may make Dennett's contribution look narrow. It is not. To the contrary, his work on consciousness has led him to study how consciousness evolved, pathologies of consciousness such as Dissociative Identity Disorder (what used to be called Multiple Personality Disorder), whether there is any real difference between how a mental state functions in us and how it feels to us (what the philosophers call, somewhat quaintly, its *qualia* or felt quality), what "selves" might be, methods for studying consciousness, how to model consciousness as a cognitive system, the nature of introspection (the consciousness we have of ourselves and our own mental states), the neural implementation of consciousness, and so on – just about every issue in connection with consciousness that one could think of. And his influence has reached to just about everybody interested in any of these issues.

Similarly with content. His work on mental content has led him to questions about artificial content (AI), the evolution of content, the relationship of content to the environment and brain (neuroscience), content in nonhumans (cognitive ethology), the nature of explanation in psychology and science generally, how content is represented and the different styles of mental representation, the relationship of representations to the brain, how we ascribe mental content to ourselves and others, and so on – all the issues alive in current work on the mind, how it evolved, and its place in the world.

His first major work, as we said, was *Content and Consciousness* (1969). It will figure prominently in the second part of this introduction. His next book was a collection of essays written during the 1970s, *Brainstorms*. This work not only brought together an extraordinarily interesting group of papers on mental content (and four on aspects of consciousness), it helped launch a unique publishing enterprise, Bradford Books. Founded by Harry and Betty Stanton and subsequently absorbed by MIT Press, the Bradford Books insignia has become one of the most important collections of books in philosophy of mind and cognitive science in the English language. Except for some trade books of the 1990s, all Dennett's books since *Brainstorms* have been published under the Bradford insignia (*Brainstorms* has been recently rereleased as a Penguin softcover).

*Brainstorms* begins with the first full articulation of Dennett's distinctive approach to mental content. The approach is called the intentional stance and the paper is called "Intentional Systems." Says Dennett, we can approach something in order to explain it from three stances, the physical stance, the design stance, and the intentional stance. Each has its own advantages and costs, as we will see when we examine some of the details of the approach in Section 2.2. This mode of explanation yields impressive results when we seek to understand people's reasons for what they say and do and in other areas. The best current theory of autism, for example, is that autistic people lack the implicit notion that others are intentional systems, so their ability to adopt this stance to themselves and others is impaired or absent (Griffin and Baron-Cohen). The approach also yields impressive results in cognitive ethology (Seyfarth and Cheney). Although few economists are aware of the connection, the game-theoretic logic that underlies the intentional stance has also become one of the main approaches in economics (Ross 1).

As well as these system-anchoring reflections on content, *Brainstorms* also contained a number of papers on behaviourism and its early cognitivist replacements, a fascinating paper on AI as what you might call philosophy under the discipline of reality (you have to implement your ideas in AI) (Wilks), no less than four papers on aspects of consciousness that presaged a book still fifteen years away, and a number of papers on decision making and responsibility.

It was decision making and responsibility that Dennett turned to next, in an idiosyncratic little book called *Elbow Room: The Varieties of Free Will Worth Wanting* (1984). Beginning life as John Locke Lectures in Oxford, the book advocates a brisk compatibilism between decisions being causally determined and decisions being free in any way that is "worth wanting." For better or for worse, this book has had less influence than Dennett's other books. Interestingly, he is working on a new book on free will as we write (in the middle of 2001). People are awaiting his new thoughts on the matter with great anticipation. (Strictly speaking, *Elbow Room* was not his next book after *Brainstorms. The Mind's I*, edited with Douglas Hofstadter (1981), came in between. It is mainly a collection of works by others, however, so we won't comment on it here, quirky and entertaining though it is.)

The year 1987 saw his second major collection of papers on content, *The Intentional Stance*. Dennett tells us that the first paper in the collection, "True Believers," replaces "Intentional Systems" as his flagship paper. The main difference between the two is that in determining what beliefs, desires, and so on, to attribute to a system, that is, what beliefs, desires, and so on, the system should have, evolutionary considerations now play a much bigger role than they did in the earlier paper (Ross 1). The concern to get clear about the "ontological status" of mental states that was finally put to rest in "Real Patterns" is very much in evidence in Dennett's reflections in the early part of the collection. Two later papers in the collection are on evolutionary theory, including one of the most famous pieces he has ever written, "Evolution, Error, and Intentionality," a paper in which he explicitly and very firmly sets his face against all forms of the idea that mental content can ever be intrinsic to brain states. The volume contains the first full expression of the method for studying consciousness that was to become the centre of a large book on consciousness four years later, in a paper called (enigmatically) "Beyond Belief." There is nothing else in the collection on consciousness. This is firmly a volume about content.

At this point, Dennett left content behind for a while and turned to consciousness. His next book was a huge, sprawling work called *Consciousness Explained (CE)* (1991a). (For Dennett, modesty is a virtue to be kept for special occasions.) *CE* was aimed at a wide audience. For the first time (with the exception of *The Mind's I*), Dennett chose a trade publisher. It would not be the last.

In *CE*, Dennett has two main targets. One is the picture of conscious states that the tradition received from Descartes. This is the idea that there is something to a conscious state, some felt quality, that is unmistakably clear and clearly different from all other properties of mental states (Brook). The other is the picture of the conscious system that the tradition received from Descartes. This is the picture of the conscious system as a kind of screen on which conscious states play before a little homunculus sitting in the middle of the theatre (Dennett calls it a Cartesian theatre), where the conscious states themselves are conceived of as discrete, separately identifiable states, states with, for example, clear stop and start points. Dennett wants to replace the Cartesian picture with what he calls a Multiple Drafts Model (MDM) of consciousness. The MDM treats consciousness as a kind of mental content, almost a matter of programming, a highly controversial point of view (Churchland). The book concludes with a chapter pulling together a picture of the self and a final attempt to beat back two of the more esoteric attempts to make consciousness mysterious, one each by Thomas Nagel and John Searle.

Both Dennett's theory of content and his theory of consciousness require that the brain have certain capacities and structures. It must have the capacity to produce that incredible array of behaviour expressing mental content that we find in ourselves and others. And it must house an MD-type structure, which, Dennett suggests, probably consists in a Pandemonium architecture of some kind (Akins).

Having settled accounts with consciousness, Dennett next took up a task that many had been expecting him to turn to for a long time, evolutionary theory. *Darwin's Dangerous Idea (DDI)* (1995) was also published as a trade book and enjoyed the same phenomenal success as *CE*. Two bestsellers on abstract issues in the philosophy of mind and philosophy of biology in a row is not bad!

In *DDI*, Dennett argues for two main claims:

1. Darwin's theory of evolution is a powerful 'universal acid' for dissolving all manner of intellectual 'skyhooks' and other pseudoscientific props that philosophers (and not just philosophers) have wheeled onto the stage to try to patch up hopeless theories; and yet,

2. Darwin's theory of evolution may deflate the pretensions of many accounts of morality but the ones it deflates are highly problematic in any case. Contrary to those who see Darwin as the destroyer of all morality, however, the theory of evolution leaves one perfectly satisfactory approach to morality and political philosophy untouched, namely, traditional Western liberalism.

In the course of developing his picture of evolution, Dennett tackles the central debates in contemporary evolutionary theory: adaptationism versus the idea that much of evolution has consisted in good tricks developed for one function being coopted for other functions; smooth evolution versus Gould's punctuated equilibrium; the role of genetic drift, climate changes, and other such accidental elements in evolutionary change; and so on. As readers of the *New York Review of Books* will know, some of Dennett's claims on these issues generated a firestorm of controversy. Although it's a little hard to understand why, Dennett found himself accused of being an 'ultra-Darwinian' (whatever that is) and Dawkins's lapdog. Needless to say, he responded with equal vigour and a hot argument ensued (Ross 2).

Among the most important claims introduced in *DDI* is a claim that it is language that makes it possible for us to have our kind of mind, a kind of mind that, by being able to cooperate with other minds and record the results of cooperation for others to build on, can figure out the physics of the universe, find cures for most serious diseases, build Hubble telescopes and Channel tunnels, create artificial speech–interpreters and problem solvers, and so on and so forth. By endowing us with language, evolution has utterly separated us from all cognitive systems that do not have language, where by "language" we mean something that is syntactically articulated and functions by building sentences that are structured compositions of lexical units. This became the basis of his next book, *Kinds of Minds* (1996), an attempt to pull some of his most important ideas about minds in general and our kind of mind in particular together in one place and to say more than was said in *CE* (or anywhere else) on the evolution of our kind of intentionality. How far Dennett wants to go here, whether for example he wants to restrict even consciousness to animals with our kind of language, is not entirely clear (Clark).

Dennett's most recent work (as of the time of writing) is *Brainchildren* (1998), a collection that pulls together a remarkably diverse array of pieces written over the previous decade or so and appearing in various sometimes quite obscure places. The pieces range widely. They include rich philosophical essays such as "Real Patterns" (already mentioned); responses to criticism, especially of *CE*; a strikingly wide group of papers on artificial intelligence and artificial life; and some new papers on animal cognition and consciousness. The collection closes with two occasional pieces, a self-portrait and one of Dennett's few forays into morality, a paper on what the dangers of information technology are and are not. This collection is fun to read – much of it is written in an even more relaxed, polemical style than is usual with Dennett. One of the papers on animal cognition is on animal pain. For interpretationists about mental life such as Dennett, pain poses a special challenge because if anything in mental life just is, just hits us no matter how we interpret it, pain would seem to be it. Dennett does an impressive job of 'downsizing' the range of pains that animals could plausibly be said to feel.

In addition to the books we have discussed, Dennett has written hundreds of papers, critical studies, reviews, proposals, and so on and so forth. He has averaged about ten publications a year for over thirty years!

What does the future hold for Dennett? Well, he is not even at normal retirement age yet, so he is far from the end of his productive life. As we said, a new book on free will is being prepared even as we write. Beyond that, who knows? Dennett has written deep, groundbreaking books on all the topics that he set himself over thirty years ago and has lived in a sea of cut-and-thrust for his whole career as a result. (His public confrontations with John Searle and Jerry Fodor and especially Stephen Jay Gould are the stuff of legends.) But over and over he has shown that he still has new things to say about the topics that matter to him.

This ends the chronological summary of Dennett's corpus. We turn now to the interesting project of fitting the pieces together into a coherent whole. We will start with how the man fits into his time. It is not by accident that Dennett has been so influential. As well as being a brilliant polemicist, he started work at a pivotal point in the study of cognition, the beginning of the cognitive revolution. His own work at the time was an important part of that pivot.

## 2. DENNETT'S PHILOSOPHY

There are a number of ways in which a scholar or scientist can be influential outside their home discipline. One is to have a single large idea. Another is to develop an important new technique. A third is to be so penetrating that just about anything one says on any topic is of interest. It might be supposed that Daniel Dennett's influence beyond philosophy has been of the third kind. His main analytic tool is probably the ingenious rhetorical question, the revealing intuition pump. Dennett's two best-known works outside of professional philosophy, *Consciousness Explained* (1991a) and *Darwin's Dangerous Idea* (1995), seem consistent with this diagnosis. Nonetheless, there is a distinctively Dennettian point of view and its influence has been more important than Dennett's work as a critical gadfly, brilliant and entertaining as the latter often is.

This point of view is clear already in *Content and Consciousness (C&C)* (1969), a blueprint for Dennett's entire corpus. One of the decisive moves in the cognitive revolution was the rejection of empiricism as it existed at mid-century. Dennett was one of those who charted a course beyond this form of empiricism and we will take this issue as our starting point.

### 2.1. Empiricism in Dennett's Time

As we said, Dennett was a student of the iconoclastic Oxford philosopher of mind, Gilbert Ryle, and, before that, of the Grand Admiral of logic and epistemology, W. V. O. Quine. Ryle wrote during the heyday of 'ordinary language philosophy,' the methodological movement inspired by J. L. Austin and given a tremendous boost by a certain (mis)reading of Wittgenstein's *Philosophical Investigations*. Ordinary language philosophers supposed, roughly, that some philosophical problems appear to be insoluble because philosophers misinterpret the language used to state them. Take a notion dear to Dennett's heart, belief. We speak of someone's *believing* that snow is white, and of someone's *believing* in the Loch Ness monster, and of their cat's *belief* that it's suppertime. It is easy to overinterpret these remarks as implying that 'belief' must denote a kind of state or object, as 'gas' does. We then go searching for properties that could gather all and only beliefs into a well-behaved set of such states or objects. Terrible difficulties at once arise. No one (philosophers excepted) ever entertains to themselves the phrase 'snow is white, by gum,' yet most believe that proposition if they believe anything. It is hard to see, however, how a typical person could be said to believe in the reality of the Loch Ness monster unless they *had* sometime entertained the phrase 'Loch Ness monster.' As for the cat, its inability to entertain *any* phrases leaves its status as a believer-of-specific-contents puzzling: Can something have beliefs about suppertimes if, as is likely, it is incapable of believing that supper comes after lunch? Questions like these led ordinary language philosophers to think that something had gone deeply wrong. Typical English speakers seem to use words such as 'belief' without feeling compelled to suppose that cats secretly talk to themselves, or that tiny signs bearing the words 'snow is white' flash inside people's brains from time to time, or other absurdities that their words *seem* to imply.

This example of dissolving a philosophical puzzle is far too crude to represent the work of any actual ordinary language philosopher but it will suffice as an illustration of the method. The crucial move in it is to take the way people express themselves in language as *data*, that is, as a basis for philosophical reflection. However, data can be used in more than one way. In *C&C*, at least initially Dennett started from the same data as ordinary language philosophers but found that they led him to very different conclusions. Dennett never lost his respect for what he learned from his mentors about dissolving philosophical pseudo-puzzles. However, he found in ordinary uses of mentalistic language support, not for bland behaviourism, but for a kind of evolutionary cognitivism, as it is now called. (The kind of evolutionary cognitivism in question is the view that to understand behaviour, we must invoke a rich repertoire of mental states and processes, and that we can best identify the states and processes concerned by viewing the mental as having the shape it has due to natural selection.) Dennett's turn against his philosophical upbringing here was momentous; it marks one of the clearest turning points that we know of in the movement away from simple-minded behaviourism to the current (near)-consensus cognitivism.

Ryle's chief conclusion in *The Concept of Mind* is that philosophical hyper-literalness about the mentalistic idiom had, over several centuries, given rise to an absurd metaphysics of mind. Mentality is not a part of physical objects; physical objects do not hope for things or fear things or believe things. But minds are not parts of objects of any other kind, either. Mental objects no more hope or fear or believe than do physical ones. *People* hope or fear or believe – but, Ryle gives us reason to think, it is not clear that the word 'person' is being used to refer to an object here, certainly not to an object by itself. Ryle demonstrates that ascription of mentalistic predicates to objects is a 'category mistake,' a logical error akin to ascribing a colour to an abstraction ("What colour is the square root of 3?") or contents to a vacuum ("It's chock-full of Nothingness"). Dennett, in *C&C*, summarizes the logical problem involved in applying mentalistic predicates to objects and processes by reference to the concept of *intentionality*. (The concept of intentionality was originally identified by medieval philosophers and reintroduced into philosophy by the nineteenth-century philosopher-psychologist Brentano.) The mental is *about* other states of affairs, whereas physical objects or states of physical objects are not. (Thus, even a good candidate case for mindless about-ness, such as "That tree's rings are about its age," is not one; it means, "That tree's rings *show* its age.") It is a category mistake to take anything having aboutness to be straightforwardly a property of an object of any kind.

It will be objected, "We *do* speak about animate bodies as engaging in activities that are about something; we speak of creatures' activities as directed to achieving goals and goals are about whatever they seek. For example, we say that she is walking *to get to* the store or he is dancing *because* it is fun. And so on. If Ryle is right, how is this possible?" It is possible because we see the motions involved in cases like these as *actions*, that is to say, as expressing reasons for doing things. Reasons for action are not causes, not causes as we usually think of them in the Humean tradition at any rate. Now, how does this distinction between reasons and (usual) causes account for our ascribing goals and other things having intentionality to bodies (i.e., actions) without introducing metaphysical extravagances (mentalistic 'ghosts in the machine,' to use Ryle's phrase)? Answer: Only if we can see how our reasons for doing the actions we do and the undeniably present causes of the bodily motions in which those actions consist relate to one another. In ordinary language, they peacefully coexist. We know that if we wish our arm to go up, then, under normal circumstances, it will go up, but we need not have any explanation of how either the reasons for this action or the causes of the related motion work.

This peaceful coexistence breaks down when we start doing scientific psychology. If all events must have physical causes, then, since beliefs, and so on, are not normal physical causes, the psychological theorist cannot invoke things like beliefs to explain behaviour. At this point, theorists are tempted to go in one of two directions. Either one may *identify* beliefs with states of the body (usually the brain), or one may deny that there are any such things as beliefs. The first path requires abandoning the everyday concept of belief and is otiose, since now the notion of belief is not doing any explanatory work that notions of causes in brain circuitry can't do. Radical behaviourists who denied that minds exist spoke as if they favoured the second option, but they were just adding redundant metaphysical noises to their scientific talk, according to Ryle. That is, radical behaviourists seemed to be saying, "We're not content that it's methodologically unnecessary for us to talk about these things; we insist that they don't exist. We don't need this claim; we just . . . " – what? Hate it when people use alternative language about things like beliefs? It is not among a scientist's responsibilities to be a dogmatic metaphysician. (The *worst* move is to imagine that beliefs *cause* brain-states, for this multiplies entities gratuitously while *still* abusing the everyday concept.)

There is another alternative: logical behaviourism (the term usually applied to Ryle's position). On this view, talk about the causes of behaviour and talk about the reasons for behaviour can coexist because talk about reasons is a way of finding a particular *pattern in* behaviour, not a way of finding the *causes of* behaviour. On this view, scientific psychology and the mentalistic conceptual scheme are taken to have no direct connection to one another; it is only the philosopher's unwarranted assumption that they *must* serve the same functions that forces the postulation of 'the ghost in the machine': an object-like mind that both furnishes reasons for actions *and* is the cause of behaviour.

This happy ecumenicism ceases to be any comfort as soon as someone adds the opinion that science is in the business of describing the world *as it actually is*. In that case, what matters is not whether mentalistic talk is logically compatible with talk about causes of behaviour; all that matters is that science finds no place for such talk. Dennett's other teacher, Quine, explicitly said what Ryle only implied, namely, that mentalistic language describes no facts and is merely a 'dramatic idiom.' Quine marshalled an important point of logical analysis in support of this view. Scientific language, it is generally supposed, ascribes properties to objects (e.g., 'Spacetime is curved'). If so, one ought to be able to interchange coreferring terms within scientific sentences without changing their truth-values. Thus, if "The morning star orbits the sun" is true, then "The evening star orbits the sun" must also be true, since 'the morning star' and 'the evening star' refer to the same object. However, this logical property, called '*substitutability salva veritate*,' does not apply inside many sentences in mentalistic discourse. "Dweezil believes that the morning star orbits the sun" is perfectly consistent with the falsehood of "Dweezil believes that the evening star orbits the sun." In uttering such clauses, one is committed only to someone's intentional state being about something believed in, desired, hoped for, dreaded or whatnot,

not something that exists. By contrast, if one ascribes a property to chairs, one commits oneself to the existence of chairs.

So 'the unicorn in which John believes' refers (if it refers to anything) to what some philosophers call an 'intentional object,' not to an actual animal. Unless, it seems, brain-states can be directly taken to somehow be about intentional objects, sentences describing mental states won't have truth-values that derive in any straightforward way from those of nonmentalistic sentences. For Quine, there is a ready explanation for this semantic peculiarity: Sentences describing mental states do not literally *describe* anything. They are merely what Quine calls a dramatic idiom for something else. In both Quine's eyes and those of his friend Skinner, this analysis buttressed the scepticism of the radical behaviourist about the existence of the mental.

This was the high point of twentieth-century empiricism. Nothing exists, it was thought, except what we can sense using the sensitive surfaces of the body (eyes, ears, nose, taste, touch) and the correlations of these inputs with behavioural outputs. There may in addition be some apparatus connecting inputs to outputs or there may not but it does not matter – no such apparatus would be mental, as the mental has always been understood. Such empiricism pervaded the social sciences and some of the natural ones as well. Anthropologists 'discovered' that humans consist of arbitrary, infinitely variable belief-systems incommensurable with one another. For sociologists, the pressures of class membership caused people to invent value-systems that are merely rationalizations of power. Economists turned their venerable axioms of rationality into summaries of observed choice-behaviour lacking any deeper justification. Political scientists focussed on patterns in voting and other political behaviour. Many biologists emphasized the extent to which species are chains of descent shaped by geological and other environmental accidents. In the case of the biologists, this might have been more spin than substance but the social sciences were dominated by the idea that contingent environmental forces drive all behavioural processes. This was the environment into which Dennett came as a student.

The above description suggests a degree of doctrinal uniformity and simplicity that of course never really existed; but notice that now, thirty-five years later, the picture has no aptness at all. Articles and monographs now pour forth in which social scientists urge their colleagues to concentrate on the universal features of human behavioural patterns shaped by natural selection and fixed in the structures of cognition. Among biologists, the remaining defenders of pervasive contingency as the motor of evolution snarl defensively at 'ultra-Darwinian' adaptationists who depict

Mother Nature as an engineer carving a rationalizable trajectory through design space. Barkow, Cosmides, and Tooby (1992), in their manifesto for evolutionary psychology, aim explicitly at the old empiricism, which they call 'the standard social science model' (SSSM; the phrase is increasingly used as a rallying banner across the disciplines). The foundation of the empiricist SSSM was its concept of mind. In the cognitive revolution against it, Chomsky is the Copernicus. Jerry Fodor and Dan Dennett perhaps fight for the role of Galileo.

Unlike Chomsky and Fodor, Dennett did not overthrow the empiricist concept of mind wholesale. Ryle's analysis is not an inaccurate review of what people *do* in fact say about minds, and Quine's logical semantics remains the single most influential body of work in the field. Dennett showed that we can preserve Ryle's and some of Quine's leading insights while pushing our study of behaviour away from the periphery and deep into the organism.

## 2.2.  The Foundations of Dennett's System

So how did Dennett respond to the radical empiricism of his time? To answer this question, we need to learn more about how he thinks about the mind and explanations of behaviour in terms of mental states. In many of his works, he starts by distinguishing three explanatory stances that one can take toward a complex organism or system. Consider a simple chess-playing computer (a favourite example of Dennett's).

One stance is to explain its current behaviour and predict its future behaviour by understanding how it is built and what the causal processes in it are like. This would give us an extraordinarily detailed, secure explanation of the system but at a severe price – extreme complexity. Not even the programmers who wrote the chess-playing programme could give this kind of explanation of the system. This stance Dennett calls *the physical stance*.

Another stance is to predict and explain the system's behaviour by understanding the design built into it, in this case the programme controlling its operations. Dennett calls this *the design stance*. This stance will produce an explanation much simpler than the first one – all we need to understand is how the system is designed to behave, not all the details of how and how well it implements this design – but the simplicity comes at a price. For our explanations to be any good, the system has to function as it was designed to function – and we have to assume that it is doing so or the design stance is useless to us. Because of this assumption built into them, explanations from the design stance are less secure than explanations from the physical stance.

A third stance is to predict and explain the system's behaviour by treating it as having goals and some capacity to achieve these goals. We can ask, what is the system trying to do, and what means is it adopting in order to do so. For example, we see it move pawns from in front of its queen. We could adopt the design stance and ask, "What rules did the programmers build into the programme to cause it to do this?" Or we can ask, "What is it trying to do? Ah, get its queen out early," and reason, "It knows that it's got to open a path through its pawns in order to do so." This Dennett calls *the intentional stance*.

The intentional stance has the advantage of great simplicity. Instead of worrying about thousands of causal relationships (physical stance) or hundreds of rules, qualifiers, and so on, built into procedures (design stance), all we have to worry about is one little goal, one little desire, to get its queen out early, one little belief, that to do it has to open a path through its pawns, and some fairly simple supplementary beliefs about how to do so in a way that is consistent with the rules of chess and the position of other pieces on the board. A three- or four-line inference and we are there.

Of course, this simplicity comes at a cost: We have to treat the system, not just as having goals and something like beliefs about how to realize its goals (some will already find this too high a cost), but even more important, as having sufficient rationality to figure out, given what it believes, what it has to do to satisfy its goals. And note: These things have to be assumed or the intentional stance does not work, so we cannot use the intentional stance to test these attributions. Thus, the intentional stance buys its simplicity at the cost of accepting assumptions that it can treat a system not just as having mental contents but also a degree of (minimal, self-interested) rationality.[1]

We now introduce a point that is crucial to understanding Dennett's thought. The intentional stance has often been taken to be the centre of his point of view. To read him this way is to miss a rich forest due to paying too much attention to a couple of the trees in it. The intentional stance is just that – a stance. The intentional stance is merely part of an explanatory schema. The really original and interesting part of Dennett's work is found in his view of what the world that underlies that schema is like. What underlies the intentional stance and justifies it as an explanatory schema is a powerful, comprehensive view about the nature of intentionality and the role of natural selection (evolution) in its very coming to be. Dennett's response to the radical empiricism of his mentors, indeed his distinctive contributions as a whole, are to be found in this comprehensive view.

In *C&C*, Dennett sets up a 'philosopher's dilemma,' which we might with hindsight call 'the empiricist's dilemma.' The problem is this. On the one hand, Ryle had shown that the mentalistic conceptual scheme is not trans-latable into the language of mechanisms and Humean causes. Behaviourism thus seems to hold out the only hope for a coherent science of mind, as Ryle had implied and Quine had explicitly said. On the other hand, as Chomsky had already argued in his famous review of Skinner's *Verbal Behaviour* in 1959, behaviourists themselves seem to be stuck with the language of in-tentionality. To take one of Dennett's examples, a behaviourist has not left the ghost in the machine behind if she talks of a rat's *seeking* food, but how can she even begin to understand the rat's behaviour if she does not take it to have goals, a way of grouping stimuli as similar, and so on? (Judgments of similarity require a judgment that 'this a is an F,' which is to say, a net-work of beliefs.) Can Dennett have his cake and eat it, too – can he preserve the intuition that we should work with what we can observe, namely, be-haviour, and yet make room for our rich and, it would seem, vital talk about minds?

The key point, and one that Dennett saw as early as Chapter 4 of *C&C*, is that intentional states are ascribed as a result of an interpretation of relations among behaviour, environment, and dispositions, under the constraint that the target system is sufficiently rational, given its beliefs, to act in ways ap-propriate to reaching its goals. This means that intentional states are not as-cribed to parts of a person, even parts as large as the brain. Intentional states are states of the *whole person*, indeed a person/environment whole. If inten-tional states are complex triangulations of behaviour/brain/environment interactions, then they cannot be reduced to brain-states. So what status do properties of persons and environments as a whole attributed under the constraint of rationality have?

Recently, Dennett (2000) has admitted that his ontological intuitions about intentional states are in "happy disarray." At one stage, he accepted the label of 'instrumentalist,' the view that treats anything unobservable as merely a postulation useful for making predictions of future states given the current states that one is observing. On this view, unobservable states like beliefs and desires have as much reality as things like centres of gravity – and for instrumentalists, that is not very much. (Dennett [1993] recalls this episode of self-labelling with chagrin.) More recently, although not aban-doning his Quinean zeal to reject superfluous entities such as belief and desire circuits in the brain, Dennett has disavowed the label. His certainty that there is *something* real about the patterns we spot using the inten-tional stance along with strong realist intuitions about the things we talk about when we use in particular the physical stance convinced him that 'instrumentalist' was an inaccurate label for his position. The issue has drawn him deeply into debates over the status of 'folk psychology' that have preoccupied philosophers since the late 1970s (1991b). (A term due to Dennett himself, folk psychology comprises our vast storehouse of beliefs, intuitions, maxims, etc., about how motives, beliefs, and perceptions of various kinds will issue forth in other motives and beliefs and in behaviour.) By 1987, the regularities described by folk psychology had become, for Dennett, a 'virtual machine' implemented in the relationships among the distributed neural hardware of the brain, the environment, and behaviour. (His speculative account of the role played by this machine in giving rise to the human 'self' in *CE* has become a crucial aspect of his developed view of agency, as we will see.) Whatever the ontological status of the mental, Dennett views folk psychology and the network of intentional concepts in which its generalizations are couched as irreducible and an indispensable piece of apparatus in the behavioural sciences, probably the majority opinion among philosophers of mind (Clark 1989). Who would have expected, thirty-five years on, that the most stubborn opposition to the 'eliminativists,' as those who look forward to the disappearance (at least from science) of the intentional framework are called, would be coming from the foremost student of Ryle's?

Dennett's attitude to the empiricism in which he was steeped in his philosophical youth is to be found in this tricky business of nailing down the exact ontological status of mental states and events such as beliefs and desires (the 'ontological status' of something refers to whether it exists and if so, what sort of existence it has).

## 2.3. Free-Floating Intentionality and Darwinian Reasons

Dennett's view that intentionality is *attributed* to systems in order to rationalize their behaviour has generated a large body of critical debate centred mainly around two consequences of the claim. First, it suggests that a particular agent's intentional states, including her beliefs and purposes, are not 'up to her,' or even entirely determined by facts internal to her. Second, it raises a question whether ascriptions of intentionality are anything other than arbitrary projections of the ascriber's interpretation. For example, how do we decide that saying a rock has the 'goal' of holding paper in place would be entirely gratuitous, while saying that a bee has the goal of finding honey is not? The intuition seems clear, but we should like to know why. It is not because the rock is incapable of formulating its goal to itself, since the same is true of the bee searching for nectar. Uniquely among philosophers at the time he wrote *C&C*, Dennett finds a solution to both aspects of the problem in Darwin:

> The principles of evolution proposed to explain learning and discrimination in the brain have the capacity to produce structures that have not only a cause but also a reason for being. That is, we can say of a particular structure that the animal has it because it helps in certain specified ways to maintain the animal's existence. It is a structure for discriminating edible from inedible material, or for finding one's way out of danger. (*C&C*, p. 64)

Let us call the reasons thus produced Darwinian reasons. The mature Dennett might have amended one phrase here, changing "maintain the animal's existence" to "maximize its expected number of offspring given its environment," since natural selection 'cares' about an animal's existence only derivatively, and only as long as it continues to have opportunities to replicate. Nonetheless, the passage is remarkable. Spelled out, the approach that Dennett recommends (in 1987b, for example) is to start by asking, What goals ought the organism to have, given its evolutionary history and the possibilities presented by its environment? And what beliefs ought it to have, given its evolutionary history, experience, and cognitive apparatus? We then ask what in this repertoire of goals and beliefs would make what it is currently doing rational in its current environment?

Before we consider this method in its natural (i.e., biological) setting, let us revisit the case of relatively simple artificial problem solvers such as the chess-playing computer discussed above. Where such machines are concerned, goals are relatively transparent, since they provide the justification for the deliberate engineering of the devices. Consider Dennett's (1971) famous example of the thermostat. We may make no scientific error if we refer to the thermostat as *believing* that it's getting colder and *wanting* to warm the room up and therefore *acting* to do so. However, one can convey more information just as briskly by saying that the thermostat was designed to register the temperature of the room and switch on the furnace whenever its mercury drops below a certain predetermined level. There is no *point* – not just given our purposes as explainers but also given the *facts* about the system – in ascribing intentional states to it, and doing so is therefore a scientific error.

As soon as we move to even a somewhat more complicated system such as a chess-playing computer, however, the decision to use the intentional stance is forced. The computer's goal is to win its games. However, there are many ways of trying to do this and all of them must be sensitive to unpredictable contingencies in the trajectory of play. The successful chess programme must therefore be designed so as to be able to formulate subsidiary goals in response to information coming from the world. As a result, its behaviour must be driven by complex interactions of internal informational states. This still does not *force* us to treat the system as intentional. However, as its repertoire encompasses diverse paths to the goal that have little in common except *being paths to that goal*, the regularities in its behaviour become visible only from the intentional stance. This is more than economy of description. Explaining why the computer moved a piece by recounting the history of impulses through its circuits, rather than by noting that it would otherwise have faced checkmate, would fail to support the right counterfactuals; that is, it is not true that the computer would not have moved the piece had its micro-history been different, but it *is* true that it would not have moved the piece had it not been threatened. This is why the intentional stance tracks 'real patterns' (Dennett 1991b) and is not merely the dramatic idiom of radical Quinean empiricism. (We will return to intentional attribution in Section 2.6.)

With the chess-playing computer, we can adopt the design stance or the intentional stance as we choose. Its intentional states are easy to identify: We know they will all be about, and only about, chess. However, the fact that the computer happens to have been designed by engineers with conscious goals in mind is in itself irrelevant to whether its behaviour in fact *does* conform to the intentional patterns associated with chess. How did certain patterns come to be the intentional patterns for chess, the ones that constitute rational strategies, and so on? Suppose that playing and winning chess matches were crucially relevant to some animal's reproductive fitness. Then, in time, natural selection might well hit on the information-processing capacities necessary and sufficient for skilful play. In this case, according to Dennett, it would simply be arbitrary to withhold attributions of intentional states about chess to the animal. That is how patterns get to be intentional ones. Note that the information-processing and problem-solving capacities of actual animals, including humans, are precisely the products of such design pressures. This does not imply any attribution of consciousness to natural selection; you don't need consciousness to achieve intentionality. This conclusion leads Dennett to the doctrine of 'free-floating intentionality,' that is, to the view that intentional contents are not strictly determined by the subjects whose intentions are at issue. Neither the chess-playing computer nor the bee has any concept of its own intentional states, but they have them nevertheless. Rocks, since they are not selected for anything, have none.

This naturalistic grounding of intentionality in Darwinian processes points to a major factual mistake in radical empiricism, the last departure by Dennett from the empiricism of his youth that we will note. Often the production of Darwinian reasons requires complex processes within brains. Not always; intentionality is so free-floating that selection pressures *could* achieve it in systems without complex information-processing capacities. But often is enough; in those cases, any behaviourist form of empiricism has to be wrong.

None of this entails that a system *cannot* become aware of its own pre-programmed goals and, through complex feedback mechanisms, modify them. Clearly, some organisms, especially humans, can override biological goals, including fundamental ones: People sometimes do, for example, decide not to have children. This does not require that some cluster of connections encouraging baby-making be unwired, for there is no such dedicated cluster. Rather, when the disposition to want to reproduce is ascribed to a person, what we are really ascribing is a host of micro-dispositions that tend to a single outcome, namely, reproduction – dispositions to flirt, compete for the attention of prospective mates, find certain people more attractive than others, and so on, together with some relational properties yoking these dispositions to the environment. A conscious decision to use these micro-dispositions for purposes disassociated from reproduction need not (indeed, generally does not) override them. The micro-structures still serve the original Darwinian reasons but the environment is manipulated by conscious choice so that 'normal' processes such as sexual intercourse fail to serve the goals for which they were selected. More simply, while a person can decide not to have sex, they cannot just decide not to want sex; achieving the latter requires, for example, monks to undertake difficult, complex, and not always successful self-reengineering.

Dennett occupied a good portion of the 1970s and 1980s skirmishing with opponents of AI, such as Searle (1984, and then over and over again) and Dreyfus (1979), who objected that whereas computers have merely derivative intentionality, humans and (some) animals have it intrinsically. However, this objection ignores the point of the appeal to Darwinian reasons. Biological systems do not – indeed, as Dennett had stressed in *C&C* (p. 57), could not – arrive in the world as directionless assemblies of cells and then arbitrarily formulate goals for themselves. Young animals are born with a number of generic goals (find reliably dry, warm, nutrient-abundant environments) and highly specific ones (stay close to mother), all engineered by natural selection in service of the only goal to which it can be directly sensitive, maximization of the probability of making more young animals. Hence Dennett's (1987a) prima facie shocking claim that Mother Nature is the only locus of 'intrinsic' intentionality; there are, as Dennett puts it, no other 'unmeant meaners.'

In the 1990s, a major dispute erupted over just how far Darwinian reasons can take us, the so-called Darwin Wars (Ross 2). Gould (1997) and others grouped Dennett together with Dawkins and Maynard Smith as 'ultra-Darwinians.' What is at stake may be no less than a coherent view of humanity's place in nature. Here is what the argument is about: Dennett, like Dawkins, maintains that the way to do biological science (including psychology and linguistics and, we would wish to add, economics [Ross 1]) is to take as one's default assumption that what exists has occurred for Darwinian reasons, and to establish further hypotheses for investigation by asking what the specific Darwinian reasons in question would likely have produced. This is the position referred to in biology and elsewhere as *adaptationism*. Gould and his allies maintain the opposite view, taking as their default assumption that what exists is substantially accidental, and that where one does find Darwinian reasons at work, one should not base further hypotheses on this discovery because the rationale is likely to fail outside of the strict circumstances in which it has been discovered to operate. Consider an example of this last point.

A baboon might luckily kill a human assailant by throwing a dropped spear at him. Since baboons often defend themselves by throwing things, we would say that the monkey intentionally defended itself with a weapon. But if the same baboon shot someone with a pistol, we would say that this was a bizarre accident, rather than generalizing from the precedent of the spear. Note that this judgment turns on what we know about *patterns* in baboon behaviour. A typical baboon simply has had no opportunity for acquiring information about how guns work; and in the absence of any belief that pulling the trigger will deter his enemy, we have no grounds for inferring from the monkey's lucky shot that he desired to fire. However, it is not implausible that if enough baboons observed enough such accidents, they might stumble on the regularity. At that point, we would indeed have intentional marksmonkeys.

The idea that patterns in intentional response are often brought about by copying and other forms of social pressure has been especially significant to Dennett, since if this is not the case then either a highly implausible sort of biological determinism must hold or intentionality is not really free-floating in the case of people. For this reason, Dennett has made extensive use of Dawkins's (1982, 1989) concept of memes. Memes are the cultural analogues of genes, strings of informational code that pass easily from one mind to another, and are thus the basic units on which cultures are built. According to Dennett, they are also the basic units on which individual human personalities, or 'selves,' are built; for selves, as essentially social creations, are expected to be individualized *assemblages* out of a stock of comprehensible pieces, that is, memes. (To see this, compare "He has tastes I don't share: military music and pro wrestling" with "He is crazy. He likes music by artists whose names begin with 'B' and sports that are played in the rain." In the first case, you can understand the person's tastes, although they may seem obnoxious or whatever, but in the second case, you're just baffled. How could anyone have tastes like *those*?

Memes have frequently been the object of derision by philosophers and biologists who deplore careless analogies, since there are many properties (although the exact list is hotly disputed; see Dennett 1995) of genes that memes do not have. We are not sure how one can evaluate the aptness of an analogy except by its fruitfulness. Whether one does or does not approve of the *word* meme, Dennett's point, for which his entire corpus of writings constitutes a sustained argument, remains: Minds are constituted by small semantic units, and the basic semantic units, call them what you like, cannot be deliberately chosen or willed into being. There is, of course, an important sense in which memes *are* human inventions. But what makes an idea a meme, something that may contribute to the self-narrating of many people, is its catchiness, not its content per se. And catchiness is a complex property built on relationships amongst contents, environments (composed most significantly of other memes, which is why intellectual history *is* tremendously important) and biological predispositions. It is thus not a property that is typically within the control of individuals. Here then is another, now social, respect in which intentionality is held by Dennett to be 'free-floating.'

The importance of Dennett's ruminations on these matters cannot be underestimated. They are what have carried his influence well beyond the usual territory of philosophers of mind and psychology. All sorts of things spin off from his approach to intentionality and we will spend the remainder of this introduction exploring some of them.

### 2.4. How Do We Come to Have an Intentional Stance?

If natural selection can give us reasons for action, namely, Darwinian reasons, how do we come by *the ability to recognize and ascribe* these reasons? How do we come by folk psychology, aka the intentional stance? Maybe the turn to Darwin can help us here, too. The learning task involved in acquiring folk psychology is prima facie formidable. Folk-psychological characterizations, we have seen, are system-level rationalizations of processes to whose causal basis the part contributed by the brain is largely concealed. It seems highly unlikely, therefore, that the rich internal logic of folk psychology could have arisen spontaneously in the course of our trying to make sense of our world. Furthermore, if as many suggest folk psychology has not substantially changed in thousands of years – has not even *drifted*, like other large-scale cultural inventions such as poetry or warfare – that, too, suggests that it is not a learned theory of behaviour. The obvious alternative is to suggest that, as many theorists hold to be true of language, it is carried innately. Dennett (1996) offers a speculative history of the evolution of folk psychology consistent with this hypothesis, and a micro-industry within developmental psychology and cognitive ethology is currently arguing for the existence of such a capacity in children (Griffin and Baron-Cohen) and testing the limits of such a capacity in adult primates (Seyfarth and Cheney). Wellman (1990) surveys the child developmental literature, Allen and Bekoff (1997) the animal literature.

The nature and extent of the innate component in folk psychology is still very much an open question. Certainly, some innate dispositions such as a wish to cultivate smiles and hugs from parents and to use language to communicate according to cooperative maxims are necessary for learning *any* social coordination behaviour, including the folk-psychological framework within which we understand such behaviour. However, as McGeer (1996) has argued, it may also be sufficient. Parents treat their children as apprentice members of society before they can talk and everyone around a child is continuously treating everyone else as rational agents. Poverty-of-stimulus arguments (arguments that children encounter very little and relatively degenerate evidence from which to construct a language) provide powerful support for the view that syntax is innate. It is not obvious that a similar argument is available for folk psychology. On the one hand, where organisms with language and a few other innate social dispositions are concerned, adopting the intentional stance may be a solution on which ordinary learning has to converge because there is no other. On the other hand, the best current theory of autism does provide some support for the view that folk psychology, or at least important aspects of its basis, may be innate. The best current theory of autism is that autistic people lack the implicit theory of intentional systems that most of us have, so their ability to adopt this stance to themselves and others is impaired or absent (Griffin and Baron-Cohen). Since this deficit seems to be inherited, the ability to adopt the intentional in those who have it may also be innate.

## 2.5.   A Theory of Consciousness

If Dennett wants intentionality to 'float free,' he faces a challenge. That is not at all how matters *feel* to people. We experience ourselves as consciously directing much of our intentional life; much of the content of one's mental life is felt to be under one's direct and private control. Since Freud, many people accept that they have some beliefs and desires that behave strangely but they are called 'unconscious.' In the realm of consciousness, mental content does not seem to 'float.' It seems to be fixed in the private experience of the conscious self. Most research on consciousness sides with these common intuitions. Dennett cannot. If these intuitions are correct, then Dennett's theory of intentionality is wrong and the ghost remains in the machine. It is thus incumbent on Dennett to conceptualize conscious phenomena in a way that squares with his view of intentionality yet also does justice to common experience. He rose to this challenge with enthusiasm in *Consciousness Explained* (1991a).

For Dennett, the appropriate method to study consciousness is just a special application of the general method of interpretation of behaviour in order to ascribe mental states given to us by the intentional stance. On the new application, we seek to interpret, not what mental states make sense of behaviour, but how things will *seem* to someone given their behaviour. Dennett (1991a, pp. 72–9) calls this *heterophenomenology*, 'hetero' because it is done by another, 'phenomenology' because it seeks to construct how things seem to someone, that is, what their phenomenology is like. When we pay attention to how things seem to ourselves, we are using the same method, interpreting how things must seem to someone given how they are behaving, but, because it is applied to self, not other, and because it uses whatever information is available from the inside, not just behaviour, Dennett calls it *autophenomenology*. However, it is just as much a matter of interpretation and just as much *not* a matter of 'reading off' independently existing features as heterophenomenology.

Conscious states or what many philosophers call *qualia*, the felt quality of things, are thought-experiment heaven. 'Thought experiment' is another name for 'intuition pump' and mounting thought experiments is one of the most characteristic activities of the contemporary philosophers who study consciousness. We find stories about Mary the Colour Blind Scientist, the population of China as a single unified consciousness, inverted *qualia*, absent *qualia* (i.e., zombies – a system functioning like a mind while not conscious), and so on. Dennett fights fire with fire. He tells stories about CADblind computers (systems that can not just generate but also interpret and react to images, yet would still be unconscious on the story of mysterians philosophers such as Nagel and Searle), zimboes (zombies who don't cheat and thus behave *exactly* like us, right down to rich responsiveness to others' behaviour and capacity to monitor and report on their own states), and so on. One of the most famous is the Case of the Lady Remembered with Glasses:

> A short time after seeing a lady who was in fact not wearing glasses, we remember seeing her with glasses. When did the mistake occur? It seems that there should be two possibilities: the lady in question might have been misperceived with glasses or she might have been perceived correctly but, due to a later revision, immediately misremembered.

Dennett calls the first option a Stalinesque option because the way events are portrayed was a show from the beginning, the second an Orwellian option because the initial portrayal was accurate but history almost immediately gets rewritten. And his point is, if you make the time interval small enough, no possible information could decide for one rather than the other of these 'options' – in which case, they are not real options and never were. Put another way, when the error began is something we can stipulate but there is no fact of the matter about it (1991a, p. 125). If so, conscious states are not anything remotely like *qualia* as philosophers have thought of them – discrete, distinguishable 'felt qualities' that we can introspect with perfect accuracy (Brook). Whether there is no such thing as felt qualities at all is another question (Brook 2000).

If the Cartesian picture of conscious states is wrong, what about the Cartesian theatre meant to house these states? Here is the basic problem with it:

> The solitary audience in the theatre of consciousness, the internal decision-maker and source of volitions or directives, the reasoner, if taken as *parts* of a person, serve only to postpone analysis. The banishment of these concepts from our analysis forces the banishment as well of a variety of other self-defeating props, such as the brain-writing waiting to be read, the mental images to be seen, the volitions to be ordered and the facts to be known. (*C&C*, p. 190)

If in addition conscious *states* are not neat, discrete little mental events, then what is the system that has them like? As we said in Section 1, Dennett calls his substitute model the MDM of consciousness. Its main features include:

1. content-fixing processes (particularly judgments). These processes do not generate clearly discrete content-bearing states, however.

2. multiple drafts. These are drafts, versions, of narrative-fragments, and so on, that the content-fixing processes generate.

3. procedures for picking out certain drafts. These procedures select some drafts, deselect others, and tie some of the selected drafts together in a variety of usually loose, sometimes well-integrated ways. The results are temporary 'heads of mind' that Dennett calls *virtual captains*. The virtual captain of the present moment is me; and the story that comes to be told in me in which the succession of virtual captains hang together roughly coherently is the self (or, if you prefer, the Self).

4. probes. Among the procedures for selecting drafts and thereby giving them the cognitive prominence that is consciousness, auto-stimulation by probes into one's current information-bearing states is perhaps the most important.

5. memory storage. These contents, especially ones that take charge and become part of a 'head of mind' of any duration, get remembered; such memory is criterial for consciousness, Dennett insists (1991a, p. 132).

6. implementation. All this could be implemented in something like the old Pandemonium architecture proposed by Selfridge (1959).

In the workspace, packages can come to take charge of the system by commanding computational resources, in particular the system's resources for probing itself and linking what it finds to other information packages and to behaviour. Dennett urges that, unlike the Cartesian theatre, MDM allows for temporal issues in connection with consciousness to be blurry, a matter of interpretation and decision, just as they have turned out to be. Because the MDM sees consciousness as at bottom a matter of content, almost of programming, some theorists have serious reservations about it (Churchland).

When an alliance of information packages controls the self-monitoring and self-expressive capacities of the system, it becomes a short-term 'virtual captain' of the system. Appearances to the contrary, such a virtual captain is what we are talking about when we talk about the Self. Although Dennett has not been entirely clear on this, what links the current virtual captain to earlier virtual captains to produce the sense each of us has of continuing over time is memory, specifically the kind of autobiographical memory in which we remember earlier experiences from the point of view of having them, emotions from the point of view of feeling them, actions from the point of view of doing them. (If we expressed what we remembered, we would say things like, "I remember seeing...," "I remember feeling...," "I remember doing....")

Of the many interesting questions about MDM, here we will ask just one, because it sheds crucial light on Dennett's whole approach to consciousness. What is the status of MDM? Does Dennett see it as a description of what the various phenomena of consciousness consist in, or does he see MDM as a picture of a system that could contain consciousness? This is an important question. On the first alternative, although accepting that consciousness as such exists, Dennett would then be advocating that we eliminate many long-accepted features of consciousness from our theory as not existing – not only would there be no *qualia* of the sort that philosophers have believed in, there would be no unified, conscious subject of experience of the kind assumed by the tradition either. By contrast, on the second alternative all Dennett would be committed to is that the system that implements the various phenomena of consciousness is quite different from what we might have expected. He need not be saying anything about what consciousness itself is like.

This question has been put to Dennett. His response is very interesting:

> Am I an eliminativist? I am a deflationist. The idea is to chip the phenomena of the mind down to size, undoing the work of inflationists who actively desire to impress upon themselves and everybody else just how supercalifragilisticexpialidocious consciousness is, so that they can maintain, with a straight face, their favourite doctrine: The Mind is a Mystery Beyond All Understanding. (2000, pp. 369–70)

Dennett is not merely telling an implementation story. Rather, *by* telling a neurally realistic, uninflated story about what the system that implements consciousness is probably like, he hopes to bring us to see more clearly what the phenomena being implemented must really be like.

It is central to Dennett's picture of consciousness that we can learn about consciousness by inferences from behaviour and other externally accessible evidence. This idea is profoundly disturbing to a number of philosophers, notably Nagel (1974, 1991). Consciousness, according to these philosophers, is essentially subjective and ineffable, and therefore not the sort of thing on which any sort of third-person investigation could shed light. There is some irony in these quarrels between the subjective essentialists and Dennett. In effect, they turn his *conceptual* distinction between the domain of reasons and the domain of causes into a divide between our *epistemological access* to the subjective and the objective and reject all uses of behavioural evidence in studying the internal dynamics of consciousness. Dennett goes far in the opposite direction; not just behaviour but also neuroscience can illuminate consciousness.

There is a social dimension to Dennett's view of consciousness and the conscious self. The intentional stance is a coordinating device, essential for successful life with others. Those who fail to learn it are deemed autistic and children are incited almost from birth to use it to interpret others – and themselves. Applied to self, the intentional stance not only provides one with an account of one's reasons for doing this or that particular action, it provides one with a sense of oneself as a continuing being with a coherent history and unified opening to the future. This narrative sense of self allows for the distinctively human aspect of consciousness, as opposed to the mere discrimination of information and the meta-representation of certain brain-contents to assist in guiding behaviour, and it arises from one taking the intentional stance toward oneself. This self-creating story is also the source of our sense of ourselves as agents, according to Dennett; this idea has not, to put it mildly, achieved universal acceptance. Notice that Dennett's account of the genesis of selves is possible only if people do *not* have direct access to the informational states of their brains, and thus must predict and explain their own behaviour using the same resources as are available to third parties.

## 2.6.  Uses of Dennett's Methods

Dennettian method in behavioural science has three main parts. First, we need a rigorous and disciplined way of formulating models of agents as rational interactors. This move is very much like game-theoretic micro-economics (Ross 1). We then apply 'reverse engineering,' using whatever knowledge we can gather about the constraints under which selection occurred (biological, cultural, or both, as the case may warrant) to frame hypotheses about differences between the behaviour of the 'ideally' rational agents identified in the first move and the actual products of real histories.

As well as leading to a highly original theory of consciousness, this methodology yields fruit in fields far removed from traditional philosophy. We have already mentioned one: autism research. As we said, the best current theory of autism is that autistic people lack the implicit theory of intentional systems that most of us have, so their ability to adopt this stance to themselves and others is impaired or absent (Griffin and Baron-Cohen).

Another is cognitive ethology. In Section 2.2, we illustrated the application of the intentional stance using computers and other artefacts. In fact, reflection on our ways of understanding artificial systems is not the best way to explore the methodology of intentional stance reasoning. In computers, goals are fairly obvious, since devices are engineered precisely to achieve certain goals. The challenges facing the intentional stance are clearer in cognitive ethology, specifically the kind of cognitive ethology in which researchers use the intentional stance to construct models of animal minds on the basis of their behaviour. Natural observation alone will generally not suffice so researchers must mount experiments. Where subjects have language, experimental design is massively facilitated by the fact that subjects can be asked questions. If we want to know whether a subject is discriminating certain information along a particular dimension, we need merely ask her to perform a (typically verbal) task that requires that discrimination.

Where nonhuman animals and human infants are concerned, however, we cannot do that. In these cases, we must carefully work out a battery of probable Darwinian reasons at work; we could not probe animal minds by *any* means if we had no idea as to what sorts of things they pay attention to and why. Suppose, for example, that one is studying baboons. Since we know that their social structures are matrilineal, we may reasonably expect that males, at least before they are integrated into a troop, face the problem of getting females to pay attention to them. Now, suppose we are wondering whether the rare fights between males are motivated by intent to intimidate, drive away, or harm the rival, or are bouts of showing-off designed to impress females. It would of course be suggestive if we passively observed that males fight only when females were looking, but merely suggestive. After all, females are almost always around in baboon society, and might be expected to have their attention drawn to loud squabbles regardless of whether these were being held for their benefit. Alternatively, perhaps male baboons do not get sufficiently excited, in general, in the absence of females to have their tempers riled to combat pitch. We need a Dennettian probe here, perhaps as follows. While males are fighting or displaying at each other, we might distract the females with something the males cannot see, thus encouraging the females to look away from the combatants but perhaps leading the latter to believe that the females have simply lost interest in their fracas. Do the males, at this point, go on fighting or break off and try to recruit attention? Of course, such an experiment could not be definitive, but no experiment, in any field, ever is. Do enough work of this sort, however, in sequences arranged to permit consilience, and one can gradually build a convincing picture of some aspects of the animal's *persona* (Seyfarth and Cheney; see also their 1990). (Note that we could not even interpret this imaginary experiment unless we have grounds for nonarbitrarily assigning beliefs and desires to the baboons.)

We have already mentioned that game-theoretic micro-economics makes moves very much like those in the first part of Dennett's method, though few economists are probably aware of any connection between their work and Dennett's. This parallel may have far-reaching implications (Ross 1).

And what about computers? We just said that computers are not the best way to illuminate the intentional stance, but what about the reverse? Is the intentional stance useful in artificial intelligence research? This is a complicated question that we will merely mention here. (Wilks gives a somewhat pessimistic assessment.)

## 2.7. Two General Worries

There are at least two big, systemic worries that have been expressed about Dennett's work. One starts here. In (1988b), he provided a commentary on lessons for philosophers of mind derived from his experiences in Kenya with Seyfarth and Cheney. These may be summarized as follows. Much philosophy in the empiricist tradition has been forced by its starting assumptions to conclude that languageless animals cannot have minds (except metaphorically), since minds are taken to be constituted by propositional attitudes and propositions must be tokened by sentences that express their content. (For a sophisticated defence of this view, see Davidson 1975.) In *C&C*, Dennett rejects this conclusion on the following grounds.

The basis of the intentional stance is, as we have seen, the fact that internal cognitive states of some organisms and artefacts produce patterns in information tracking, manipulation, and behaviour-control that can be identified only from the stance. But since particular ascribed intentional states need not, indeed generally do not, map onto discrete states of the brain or brain and behaviour, the absence of sentential tokens need not disqualify a creature from being a genuine bearer of intentional states. What could Seyfarth and Cheney have been investigating? The answer cannot be merely vervet *behaviour*, since they did not need their experiments to investigate behaviour; they could simply observe that. And they were certainly not studying vervet *brain-states*. They tell us that they are studying the *minds* of the monkeys, 'how they see the world,' and that is the only remaining candidate.

In (1996) and elsewhere, however, Dennett has argued with great persuasiveness that language is central to our kind of mind. He has been known to speculate, presumably not entirely serious about the exact number, that a mind with a language like ours will be twenty thousand times more intelligent than one without. For one thing, minds with language can learn from work that has gone before and been written up. For another, while minds without language are largely restricted to learning by trial-and-error, which can be lethal if you pick the wrong trial, minds with language can 'let their hypotheses die in their stead,' to use Karl Popper's memorable phrase. So where does Dennett stand on the relationship of mindedness and language? The issue requires an essay all to itself to resolve (Clark).

A second general worry about Dennett's approach is nicely displayed in a dialogue between Churchland and Ramachandran (1993) and Dennett (1993). The worry is that the intentional stance and its application by way of Darwinian and other reasons for action seems to impose an a priori interpretation on the facts, rather than letting the facts 'speak for themselves.' The dialogue centres on the interpretation of so-called filling in phenomenon in visual (and other) perception.

As you stare at a visual scene, you could be questioned (by others or by yourself) about billions of bits of information available to you – about relative depths, sizes, positions, colours, edges, shades, angles, grains, contours, or complex combinations of these – and you could respond correctly more or less at once and without reflection. When you so respond, obviously you are not consulting a stored mental copy of the scene. For one thing, your brain lacks the requisite storage capacity, for the recursive-combinatorial power of our shared descriptive capacities pushes the informational carriage toward infinity ("the bush behind the tree six feet away from the rock parallel to the fence running past the creek"). Furthermore, your eyes are at any time receiving information from, and likely have *ever* received information from, only a fraction of the total scene on which you can report. You cannot report on a particular flower or bug in your visual field until someone or something directs your attention to it. By contrast, you can close one eye without a hole popping into the field of the opposite eye's blind spot and the scene remains a stable array despite the continuously darting saccades of your eyes. In general, what you are literally transducing is a jumping, patchy, gap-filled sequence of partial scenes and when your brain presents this as a single, stable scene, it is evidently doing a great deal of 'correcting.' In what does this 'correcting' consist?

Much of the literature implicitly suggests that the brain constructs a coherent scene by producing mental models in which areas corresponding to unexamined regions of the external space are *filled in* by extrapolation from features of the examined regions. Thus, if you are looking at an expanse of plaid wallpaper, your brain might construct a representation of a uniformly plaid image by 'painting' the entire representation of the wall plaid based on the assumption that the surface of the wall is uniform. However, Dennett argues, this 'painting' metaphor is a residue of the Cartesian theatre, and must be unpacked in a way that does not involve reference to an inner presentation or observer. The brain need be troubled only by *actually observed* discontinuities. If it expects no information from unobserved regions, it need register *nothing* about them. If consistency is the system's default assumption, then when a subject is probed, or probes herself, she will *judge* that the wall is 'all plaid' without examining it further.

Churchland and Ramachandran argue that the experimental evidence is against Dennett here. They present a number of experiments that suggest that how things appear to subjects depends on the brain's having supplied nontransduced content in a way that requires that nontransduced regions have been 'filled in,' rather than merely ignored. More generally, they complain,

> Part of the trouble with Dennett's approach to the various filling in phe-
> nomena is that he confidently prejudges what the neurobiological data at
> the cellular level will look like. Reasoning more like a computer engineer
> who knows a lot about the architectural details of the device in front of him
> than like a neurobiologist who realizes how much is still to be learned about
> the brain, Dennett jumps to conclusions about what the brain does not need
> to do, ought to do, and so forth.... While Dennett's idea ... may seem to
> have some engineering plausibility, it is really a bit of a priori neurophysi-
> ology gone wrong. Biological solutions, alas, are not easily predicted from
> reasonable engineering considerations. What might, from our limited van-
> tage point, have the earmarks of sound engineering strategy, is, often as not,
> out of kilter with the way Nature does it. (Churchland and Ramachandran
> 1993, p. 42)

Dennett in his reply acknowledges that the evidence *might* force the con-
clusion that his conclusions are wrong. However, he does not budge with respect to the soundness of his method. It is, he says (Dennett 1993, 209), "a good way to think – risky, but a fine way of generating hypotheses [though] I might sometimes forget to admit, in the thrill of the chase, that these hunches need confirmation (and hence court disconfirmation)" (Akins).

This stand-off, more generally the relationship of Dennett's whole ap-
proach to neuroscience, is far from resolved. Moreover, it is related to the stand-off between Dennett and Gould with respect to adaptationism that we examined earlier. We have argued that biological and social science could not get anywhere without *some* suppositions about Darwinian reasons. So perhaps all that Churchland, Ramachandran, and Gould are saying is that Dennett lets the intentional stance do too much work. But how much is *too* much? Clearly we need inferences from the 'logic' of evolution and current

behaviour-in-environment. Equally clearly, we need all the help we can get from actual palaeontological and other history, neuroscience, and so on. Dennett has provided a powerful motive for theoreticians to get to work on sorting out the right balance. Indeed, he has done some of the needed work himself (1987c).

This concludes our introduction to the intentional stance and the philosophical system that Dennett has used it to generate. For the rest of the book, it will be taken as read.


## 3. TO COME

The essays to come explore the many areas beyond traditional philosophy in which Dennett's work has had an important influence. Brook and Churchland explore Dennett's contributions to consciousness studies, which now reach well beyond academic philosophy to include experimental psychology, AI, and neuroscience. (The first group of essays being about consciousness does not violate Dennett's dictum that one should start with content, then take up consciousness because the introductory essay just completed gives a full account of Dennett's picture of mental content.) The second group of essays explores applications of the intentional stance in three very different domains. Griffin and Baron-Cohen explore Dennett's contributions to developmental psychology and specifically our understanding of autism, Seyfarth and Cheney to cognitive ethology, and Ross to how one might understand economic theory. Next Clark and Akins explore the two interesting worries about Dennett's work that were just introduced, the one about the relationship between language and his theory of content (also his theory of consciousness) (Clark) and the one about the rationalizing a priorism of the intentional stance and the facts as revealed by contemporary neuroscience (Akins). Finally, Wilks explores Dennett's role in artificial intelligence research and Ross takes up his contributions to evolutionary theory and examines some of the deeper issues underlying the Darwin Wars of the 1990s.

The essays in this volume fall into two categories. Where, on the one hand, the nature of a given influence is fairly straightforward but the influencing theory is complicated or possibly problematic, authors focus on the influencing theory. This is true of Brook, Churchland, Akins, and Clark. Where, on the other hand, the details of how Dennett has influenced a field are interesting in their own right, authors focus on the nature of the influence. This is true of Griffin and Baron-Cohen, Seyfarth and Cheney,

Wilks, and Ross's second paper on the Darwin Wars. Ross's first paper has a foot in both camps.

### Note

[1] Breaking explanation down into a series of nested kinds of explanation, ordered by the size of the basic unit of explanation (beliefs and desires, designed functions, physical components) became a major organizing strategy throughout cognitive studies generally in the 1970s. The version that came to dominate cognitive science goes like this. First, describe how a system is behaving, what tasks it is performing (often done using the intentional stance). Then ask: What procedures, etc., would allow a system to do these things (an application of the design stance). Finally ask: How are these procedures, etc., implemented in the brain or the brain and its environment? (This is not exactly the physical stance, which would study the brain by itself, not how material of other stances is related to it, but is related to the physical stance.)

### References

Allen, C., and M. Bekoff (1997). *Species of Mind*. Cambridge, MA: MIT Press /A Bradford Book.

Barkow, J., L. Cosmides, and J. Tooby, eds. (1992). *The Adapted Mind*. New York: Oxford University Press.

Brook, A. (2000). Judgements and Drafts Eight Years Later. In Ross et al. 2000.

Chomsky, N. (1959). Review of Skinner, *Verbal Behaviour*. *Language* 35:26–58.

Churchland, P. S., and V. Ramachandran (1993). Filling In: Why Dennett is Wrong. In B. Dahlbom, ed., *Dennett and His Critics*. Oxford: Blackwell, 28–52.

Clark, A. (1989). *Microcognition*. Cambridge, MA: MIT Press /A Bradford Book.

Davidson, D. (1975). Thought and Talk. In S. Guttenplan, ed., *Mind and Language*. Oxford: Oxford University Press, 7–23.

Dawkins, R. (1982). *The Extended Phenotype*. Oxford: Oxford University Press.

Dawkins, R. (1989). *The Selfish Gene* (2nd edition). Oxford: Oxford University Press.

Dennett, D. (1969). *Content and Consciousness*. London: Routledge.

Dennett, D. (1971). Intentional Systems. *The Journal of Philosophy* 68:87–106.

Dennett, D. (1984). *Elbow Room: The Varieties of Free Will Worth Wanting*. Cambridge, MA: MIT Press/A Bradford Book.

Dennett, D. (1987a). *The Intentional Stance*. Cambridge, MA: MIT Press /A Bradford Book.

Dennett, D. (1987b). True Believers. In Dennett, 1987a.

Dennett, D. (1987c). Three Kinds of Intentional Psychology. In Dennett, 1987a.

Dennett, D., ed. (1987d). *The Philosopher's Lexicon, 8th edition*. American Philosophical Association Publication.

Dennett, D. (1988a). Quining qualia. In A. Marcel and E. Bisiach, eds., *Consciousness in Contemporary Society*. Oxford: Oxford University Press, 42–77.

Dennett, D. (1988b). Out of the Armchair and into the Field. *Poetics Today* 9:205–21.

Dennett, D. (1991a). *Consciousness Explained*. Boston: Little, Brown.

Dennett, D. (1991b). Real Patterns. *The Journal of Philosophy* 88:27–51.

Dennett, D. (1993). Back From the Drawing Board. In B. Dahlbom, ed., *Dennett and His Critics*. Oxford: Blackwell, 203–35.

Dennett, D. (1995). *Darwin's Dangerous Idea*. New York: Simon and Schuster.

Dennett, D. (1996). *Kinds of Minds*. New York: Basic Books.

Dennett, D. (1998). *Brainchildren*. Cambridge, MA: MIT Press/A Bradford Book.

Dennett, D. (2000). With a Little Help From My Friends. In Ross et al. 2000.

Dennett, D., and D. Hofstadter, eds. *The Mind's I*. New York: Basic Books.

Dreyfus, H. (1979). *What Computers Can't Do* (2nd edition). New York: Harper and Row.

Gould, S. J. (1997). Darwinian Fundamentalism. *New York Review of Books* 12/6/97.

McGeer, V. (1996). Is "Self-Knowledge" an Empirical Problem? Renegotiating the Space of Philosophical Explanation. *Journal of Philosophy* 93(10):483–515.

Nagel, T. (1974). What is it Like to be a Bat? *Philosophical Review* 83:435–50.

Nagel, T. (1991). What We Have in Mind When We Say We're Thinking. *Wall Street Journal* 11/7/91.

Ross, D., A. Brook, and D. Thompson, eds. (2000). *Dennett's Philosophy: A Comprehensive Assessment*. Cambridge, MA: MIT Press /A Bradford Book.

Ryle, G. (1949). *The Concept of Mind*. London: Hutchinson.

Searle, J. (1984). *Minds, Brains and Science*. Cambridge, MA: Harvard University Press.

Selfridge, O. (1959). Pandemonium: A Paradigm for Learning. *Symposium on the Mechanization of Thought Processes*. London: HM Stationary Office.

Seyfarth, R., and D. Cheney (1990). *How Monkeys See the World*. Chicago: University of Chicago Press.

Wellman, H. (1990). *The Child's Theory of Mind*. Cambridge, MA: MIT Press /A Bradford Book.

# CONSCIOUSNESS

D aniel Dennett has made important contributions to consciousness studies in a number of areas. The two essays to follow explore some of them: Andrew Brook explores his attack on traditional notions of conscious states and specifically on the philosophers' notion of *qualia*, and Paul Churchland offers some fairly critical commentary on Dennett's proposal for what should replace the Cartesian theatre picture of the conscious system, namely, the Multiple Drafts Model (MDM). In addition, two essays to come later have important discussions of Dennett's work on consciousness. Andy Clark discusses it in the context of the general problem of Dennett's views on the relationship of language to different kinds of minds and Kathleen Akins discusses it in the context of a consideration of the relationship of neuroscience to Dennett's picture of mental contents as a whole. Before reading Brook and Churchland, it would be a good idea to return to the Introduction and reexamine the overview of Dennett's work on consciousness given there.

Dennett's attack on *qualia*, that is, on the traditional picture of what the felt qualities of represented items are like, has a number of strands. He attacks specifically philosophical claims about *qualia*, for example, that they are ineffable and directly introspectible. He attacks the idea that the felt qualities of representation are so radically distinct from other aspects of representations that we could, for example, have the other aspects with no *qualia*, that is to say, no consciousness. (Philosophers tend to call such a creature a zombie.) And he attacks an idea at the bottom of all such claims, the idea that conscious states are discrete, separable, determinate states of some sort, states that could be 'read off' a system passively. Andrew Brook sorts these different claims out and, using the case of pain, asks how well Dennett's proposed alternative stands up to the evidence.

The MDM takes consciousness to be a kind of programming, one result of the brain manipulating mental contents in certain ways. Paul

Churchland, one of the world's most important researchers into the relationship of neuroscience and philosophy, sees serious problems in this whole approach. First he attacks the idea that consciousness has anything to do with memes (for the notion of a meme, see the Introduction). Then he attacks the idea that brains get consciousness by any process of manipulating memes or anything else to do with representations. As Churchland sees it, brains have ample architecture to be conscious all by themselves. He concludes with a look at what kind of dynamic parallel system the conscious brain might be.

# 2 The Appearance of Things

*ANDREW BROOK*

## INTRODUCTION

Broadly speaking, Dennett has made two contributions to research on consciousness, one negative and one positive. The negative contribution is a root-and-branch attack on some of philosophers' favourite fantasies about consciousness, inverted spectrum and absent *qualia* (zombie) fantasies in particular, and the notion that underlies these fantasies, the notion that conscious states have a discrete, directly introspectible, separable felt quality (which is what philosophers call *qualia* and what would be absent if *qualia* could be absent). The positive contribution is to introduce the Multiple Drafts Model (MDM) of how consciousness might be achieved by a brain.

These two contributions have had different fates. The attack on *qualia* and related fantasies has been enormously influential, in part because it follows in a long line of scepticism about the traditional ways of thinking about this topic, a tradition including, among philosophers, the later Wittgenstein, Dennett's teacher Gilbert Ryle, John Austin, and Wilfrid Sellars. Psychologists such as Tony Marcel and Bernard Baars and medical neuroscientists such as Marcel Kinsbourne are examples of leading researchers whose work is done in the light of Dennett's critique. Indeed, one can hardly pick up any leading journal of consciousness studies such as the *Journal of Consciousness Studies* or *Consciousness and Cognition* without finding Dennett's name mentioned somewhere. The influence has not been easily won and the ground is still contested. Ringing rejections of Dennett's arguments still appear and he answers them in papers with ferocious titles such as "The Unimagined Preposterousness of Zombies" (1995a). Thought experiments still appear purporting to show that *qualia* are remarkable, in fact utterly extraordinary phenomena. Such rearguard actions notwithstanding, many consciousness researchers are now convinced that deep incoherencies lie buried in the traditional notion of conscious states.

By contract, MDM has not been widely taken up by consciousness researchers. Indeed, many researchers remain indeed more than a bit perplexed by it, in part because Dennett has not yet filled it out very completely, the hundreds of pages of (1991) notwithstanding. In this essay, we will examine Dennett's attack on *qualia*. In the next essay, Paul Churchland will take up MDM.

The attack on *qualia* may appear to be of rather local interest, an intercine battle among philosophers of consciousness. It is not. At its most general, the notion of *qualia* is the notion of things seeming to be like something, feeling like something. The term '*qualia*' is the term for the feature of certain states in virtue of which, to use Nagel's (1974) well-known phrase, it is like something to have them. Related terms include the 'felt quality' and the 'phenomenal quality' of states. Most consciousness researchers believe that things seeming to be some way to someone is a central part of what it is to be a conscious state. Indeed, a standard way of pinning down consciousness is to say that conscious states are states that it is like something to have. The central intuition is this. If a state (or event or . . . ) does not seem like anything to me, then I am not conscious of it. I could be in various forms of informational access to the thing but if it is not like something to have it, I am not conscious of it and it is not a conscious state. Consciousness requires that something seem like something.

The condition called blindsight illustrates the link. Blindsight patients cannot see objects in a certain, often quite large part of their visual field. Ask them what they are seeing there and they will say, "Nothing." However, if you ask them to guess what is there, they guess with far better than chance accuracy. If you ask them to reach out to touch whatever is there, they reach out with their fingers and thumb at the right distance apart to grasp objects that are there. And so on (Weiskrantz 1986). Clearly, these patients have some kind of informational access to what is in front of them. Equally clearly, it is not like anything for them to have this informational access. For this reason, we say that they are not conscious of what is there. This link between consciousness and it being like something to have something also applies to what it is to be a conscious being: It is plausible to say that a being for whom nothing seems like anything will not be a conscious being. This link between *qualia* and consciousness is what gives the former much of their interest.

Note that it is not obvious how far this link takes us. In particular, seeming to be like something might be only a necessary condition of consciousness, not also a sufficient condition. Or, an alternative worry, seeming to be like something might be *so* closely linked to the notion of consciousness that the 'explication' of one in terms of the other is really just to move in a tight little circle. Certainly this much is true: To say that a conscious being is one for whom things seem like something is to say almost nothing about *what it is* to be a conscious being, what it is to be a subject of conscious experience. Nonetheless, it is the link between *qualia* and consciousness that gives the former their interest.

We will begin with Dennett's demolition of *qualia*, then examine the model of consciousness that he wants to replace them with.

## HOW THE IDEA OF *QUALIA* ARISES

If Dennett is right about *qualia* (1988, 1991), then the inverted spectrum and zombie (absent *qualia*) thought-experiments so beloved of many contemporary consciousness researchers should not be taken seriously. Inverted spectrum stories go like this: Whether or not it ever happens, it could happen that what appears red to me appears green to someone else without this difference showing up in our cognition or behaviour in any way: We draw the same inferences from what we are seeing, use the same words (where I say 'red,' the other person says 'red'), and so on. Zombies' stories are stories about beings who are not conscious, yet who are cognitively and behaviourally just like us, so like us that nobody could tell: Again, they draw the same inferences from what they see as we would, use the same words we would use, and so on. The qualification that the other is cognitively and behaviourally just like us in both cases is crucial, as we will see.

Here are some illustrations of what philosophers have in mind when they talk about *qualia*. When we feel pain, the sensation does various things to us, for example makes us cry out, jump back, or whatever – and the sensation *feels* like something, indeed feels painful, awful, and so on. When I see a round coin from an angle, the coin, though still round, *appears* to be oblong. When I read a passage in Kant, however clear the prose may appear to others (!), it *seems* quite unclear to me. '*Qualia*' is the philosophers' term for these feelings and appearings and seemings. (Note: It may seem obvious that the causal processes resulting in crying out and jumping back and the felt quality are two different things. Tempting thought this intuition is, I recommend that it be viewed with scepticism, at least for the time being. Give the *whole* causal picture and maybe it would contain *qualia*. Who knows? No one knows what the whole causal picture might be like.)

Chalmers's well-known (1995) distinction between what he calls the easy problem and the hard problem of consciousness is another illustration of what *qualia* are supposed to be like. When something seems to be a certain way to us, the representation in which it seems that way can play two roles in our cognitive economy. First, the representation (or the contents of the representation) can connect inferentially to other representations (if the stick appears to have two straight parts with a bend in the middle, this will preclude representing it as forming a circle), to belief (if the stick appears straight with a bend in it, I will not form a belief that it bends in a circle), to memory (I can compare this stick as it appears to sticks I recall from the past), and to action (if I want something to poke into a hole, I might reach for the stick). It would seem, however, that so long as I am *representing* the stick in the appropriate way, it is irrelevant whether I am *aware* of the stick or not. My representation could do these jobs for me just as well even if I were not aware either of the stick or of my representation of it. But, second, I am also *aware* of the stick – it does *appear* to me in a certain way.

This distinction between the cognitive role of representations and something appearing to me in them seems to lead to two problems. Chalmers calls them the easy problem and the hard problem. The easy problem is to understand the inferential and other roles of such states. The hard problem is to understand how, in these states or any states, something could appear as something to me, how certain stimulations of the retina, processing of signals by the visual cortex, application of categories, and other referential and discriminatory apparatus elsewhere in the brain can result in an *appearing*, a state in which something *appears* a certain way. Chalmers says that the easy problem is easy because it is simply the problem of the nature and function of representation in general, while the hard problem is hard because it appears to be sui generis, quite unlike any other problem about cognition that we face. If the first problem is easy, I'd hate to see what a hard one is like, but there do seem to be two distinct issues here and the issue of how anything can appear to us at all does seem to be special. One aspect of this specialness is well captured by Levine (1983). *Qualia* present an explanatory gap that cognitive functioning does not present: We cannot begin to imagine a mechanism that would give us any account of what kind of neural or neural/environmental mechanism would and must result in *qualia*.

In order to understand Dennett's attack on *qualia*, there is one more thing that we need to put in place. '*Qualia*' is not only a generic name for the felt qualities of things. The term carries a specific view of what the phenomena in question are like. Roughly, the view is that *qualia* come one to a representation. *Qualia* may or may not represent anything themselves – there is a controversy about this – but they come with representations, roughly, one per representation, and representations are themselves real, discrete, isolable states of the mind/brain. Thus, if I perceive a car going past on the street, that perception is a real, discrete, isolable state of me and there will be a closely related state, which is the car *seeming* to me to be going down the street. It is this picture of *qualia* that Dennett goes after. When things seem to us to be a certain way, he asks, what is the process that yields this result really like? One of Dennett's terms for *qualia* pictured as something given with representations, roughly one to a representation, where representations are themselves real, discrete, and isolable is 'Seemings.' To mark the fact that Dennett is going after a certain picture, I will use the term 'Seemings' for the target of his attack. As a reminder that 'Seemings' is a technical term, I will capitalize it.

## THE NATURE OF SEEMINGS

Dennett has two kinds of problems with Seemings. First, he thinks that the notion gives a completely wrong picture of something seeming to be like something. Indeed, some of the suggestions that flow from the notion may well be incoherent, subtly disguised nonsense. And he raises important questions about whether anything answering to the notion of a Seeming exists. A lot of theorists share Dennett's point of view on the first issue. Even some of those who agree with him here think that he goes too far on the second issue.

Scepticism about the existence of Seemings can easily be taken to be scepticism about the existence of consciousness as such. In Dennett's case, that would be a major mistake. He believes that consciousness exists; he just thinks that nothing resembling Seemings has anything to do with it. Put in jargon that has become commonplace among philosophers, he is an eliminativist about Seemings (and says he is [1988, note 2]), but he is not an eliminativist about consciousness. Eliminativism is the view that if there is no room for talk about a certain kind of thing in scientifically respectable discourse, we should hold that things of that kind do not exist. Dennett says exactly the opposite about consciousness. He insists that conscious states are real. He says, for example,

> Conscious experiences are real events occurring in the real time and space of the brain. (1994a, p. 135)

And,

> Sensory qualities are nothing other than the dispositional properties of cerebral states to produce certain further effects in the very observers whose states they are. (1994b, p. 146)

Of course, this leaves open the question of what it is that *makes* a state conscious. All Dennett is committed to so far is that it is not in virtue of having a Seeming. This combination is puzzling: Does Dennett want to say that conscious states do not have a property of something seeming a certain way? We will return to this puzzle.

How exactly does Dennett deny that Seemings exist? The question needs to be handled carefully: Dennett does not deny, indeed insists, that various things *seem* to us to have various features. The question is: In addition to the thing appearing, is there another state of affairs, the appearing of the thing? Certainly there seems to be. With pain, if the cause of our crying out is real, so, it would seem, is the hurting. With the round coin, if the coin is real, so, it would seem, is some state which is its appearing oblong to me. With Kant, if his prose is real, so, it would seem, is some state which is its appearing unclear to me. And so on. Not at all, says Dennett. While things certainly appear to people in various ways, the idea that there are states that are these appearings, states that are Seemings, is a philosopher's myth. Appearances (!!) perhaps to the contrary, there are no such states.

> "I'm denying [that Descartes' real seemings] exist." (1991, p. 363)
> [The category of] the way things actually, objectively seem to you [is a] bizarre category. (p. 132)
> There is no such phenomenon as really seeming – over and above the phenomenon of judging in one way or another that something is the case. (p. 364)
> There is no such thing [as] actual phenomenology. (p. 365)

What Dennett is after might be put like this. Sentences such as, "It seems to me that the coin is oblong," are often true but even when they are, sentences such as, "There exists a state of affairs, the seeming of oblongness" would not follow and would not be true.

This strain in Dennett's thought derives from the work of the later Wittgenstein, especially the part of his *Philosophical Investigations* (1953) that has come to be called the Anti-Private Language Argument (see especially remarks §§243–314). Dennett's work on these topics frequently refers to Wittgenstein and Dennett acknowledges the influence (1991, p. 463). As we said, Ryle (1949), Austin (1962), and Sellars (1963) have developed similar analyses.

With these preliminary remarks about the existence of Seemings in place, let us turn now to Dennett's claim that many pronouncements made on behalf of them are incoherent, subtly disguised nonsense. Recall the distinction we made between having informational access to something and being conscious of it. In the latter, it is like something to me to have access to the thing. This distinction has played a large role in recent thinking about consciousness – for example, it is behind Chalmers's distinction between the easy and the hard problems of consciousness, as we just saw – but there is a danger lurking in it. It risks making conscious access or what Flanagan (1992) calls *experiential* access look too different from informational access. We should not rule out the possibility that conscious or experiential access is simply *one kind* of informational access. The alternative, thinking of the two as very different, almost forces us to the view that consciousness and the stuff of consciousness, Seemings, have some strange and wonderful properties.

Historically, it has been claimed that (the features of) Seemings are ineffable (i.e., indescribable), intrinsic (i.e., knowable independently of knowing how the state relates to other states), private (i.e., directly knowable only by the person who has them), and directly introspectible (i.e., consciousness of them does not involve inference or interpretation). Dennett focuses his 1988 attack on these claims and presents powerful reasons to reject all of them. I won't rehearse those arguments here because one could reject all these claims about what Seemings are like and yet continue to maintain that such states exist, that is, that there are real, discrete, isolable states that it is like something to have, states in which something seems to be like something. Dennett goes further in (1991). In different places in that work, he confronts two of recent consciousness studies' favourite thought experiments. They are about *inverted spectra* and *absent qualia (zombies)*. If inverted spectra and zombies are impossible, it is hard to see how Seemings of any sort could exist. We will focus on Dennett's attack on these thought experiments.

The idea that inverted spectra are possible is very old, going back at least to Locke (1690). It goes like this. Experience of colour could be inverted, so that the way red things look to me might be the way green things look to you. Moreover, the states in which such things appear to me could be inverted in this way without anything else changing. I could still call the same states of the world 'red' as you do, apply colour wheels and additive and subtractive rules for colour the same way you do, and so on. There would be no way to tell but the situation is possible. If this situation is possible, the Seeming aspect of our cognitive states must be radically isolated from how those states function in the cognitive economy. If so, Seeming states must have very sharp boundaries: clear start and stop points, thoroughgoing separation from other similar states, and complete independence of perceptual and memory inputs and ensuing behaviour. There are serious empirical reservations to be raised about how much of the inverted spectrum story can coherently be told (Hardin 1988; Palmer 1999), but we will let them pass. Before it could take on the empirical problems, it would first have to overcome some serious conceptual challenges.

The idea of absent *qualia* or zombies (philosophers' zombies, not the real ones in Haiti) is the idea that a being could lack all consciousness without anything else changing. Where for us it is like something to engage in information processing activities, beings are possible in which such information processing takes place, right down to detailed self-reporting of how things seem and feel to him or her, with no consciousness at all. There would be nothing it is like to be that creature or to have its representations. As with inverted spectra, the claim is again made that states of consciousness are so isolated from perception, memory, behaviour, and the rest of the cognitive system that it could be impossible to tell.

Dennett urges that both notions are incoherent. The thought-experiments that purport to support them do not lay out genuinely imaginable scenarios. I think that for the most part he is right. Like Wittgenstein and his teacher Ryle, Dennett proceeds against his targets by amassing details, in his case awkward thought experiments (he calls them *intuition pumps*). By contrast, I want to focus on getting the overall shape of his case clear.

As I see it, Dennett's central claim is that the two notions share a common assumption. They both assume that we know what a Seeming is like. We need such a clear conception to know what an inverted Seeming or a complete absence of Seemings would consist in. Wittgenstein once expressed the following worry about such assumptions: "We talk of processes and states and leave their nature undecided. . . . But that is just what commits us to a particular way of looking at the matter" (1953, §308). Dennett's most important conclusion, it seems to me, is that no property of any cognitive state or process in isolation could be a property of something seeming a certain way. Something coming to seem a certain way is a result of a complex cognitive process, not a property there to be 'read off' individual cognitive states. If so, the notions of inverted spectra and zombies are not coherent.

Dennett goes after our assumption that we know what a Seeming would be like in (1988), then turns to the notion of inverted spectra specifically in (1991). Here are some of the thought experiments that Dennett amasses against the general assumption. I hate cauliflower. A magical doctor comes along and reverses this revulsion so that cauliflower now tastes great to me. Does it taste the same after the procedure as before? When I first tasted beer, I thought it tasted like swamp water (a common experience). Later, beer came to taste very nice. Did the taste continue the same or has it changed? One of my favourites is Dennett's case of Mr. Chase and Mr. Sanborn. Mr. Chase and Mr. Sanborn both used to like their company's coffee. Recently, it has lost its appeal. The reasons *sound* very different. Chase: "The flavour of the coffee hasn't changed but I just don't like that flavour very much now." Sanborn: "No, no, you are quite wrong. I would still like *that* flavour as much as ever. The problem is that the coffee *doesn't* taste that way any more." (All these thought experiments are derived from [1988].)

These intuition pumps point to a single idea: Common sense intuitions to the contrary, in these cases we *do not* have any clear idea what a change or lack of change in a Seeming would consist in. In an older terminology, we do not have criteria for Seeming identity. We do not know what the difference would be between two Seemings being exactly similar and being different (or for when we are encountering the same Seeming again and when we are encountering a new Seeming, though this second gap is less important here). If we do not know what it would be for a Seeming of one kind or a Seeming of another to be present, we do not have a conception of a Seeming that we could apply to anything.

### Seemings and Verificationism

It may be useful at this point to say something about verificationism and the argument just given. 'Verificationism' is close to being a term of abuse for many philosophers. If an argument is verificationist, that by itself is a knockdown reason for rejecting it. Whatever the merits of this attitude (and they are probably few), it is not often enough noticed that two very different kinds of move attract this epithet. One urges that if we cannot verify some claim, there is a problem with it. The other is much stronger. Starting from the idea at the heart of verificationism as it was originally articulated early in the twentieth century, the idea that the meaning of a term is simply our method for verifying the correctness of its applications, it urges that if we cannot verify the application of a term, the term lacks meaning.

The move made using Dennett's intuition pumps about cauliflower and beer is clearly not verificationist in the first sense. True, we cannot verify whether cauliflower or beer continues to taste the same, but that is a consequence of the problem, not the problem. Think of the asteroid just visited by a space vehicle. I cannot verify whether there is a fully furnished apartment in the middle of it. However, I know exactly *what would have to be the case* for there to be such an apartment. And *that* is what is missing in the stories that Dennett tells. We do *not* know what would have to be the case for beer to continue to taste the same as one got used to drinking it and came to enjoy it, if one suddenly went from hating to liking cauliflower, and so on. The problem, just to hammer the point home, is not that we cannot *determine* sameness or difference here. It is that we have *no idea* what state of affairs sameness would consist in and what state of affairs would constitute a difference. In short, we don't know what we are talking about.

Nor is Dennett's move verificationist in the second sense, the sense built on the idea that the meaning of a term is our method of verifying the correctness of its applications. This idea yields the 'duck' principle: "If it looks like a duck and waddles like a duck and quacks like a duck, then it is a duck." Or, at the very least, in the absence of evidence to the contrary, we should accept that it is a duck. So: If a creature makes all the judgments about how things seem to it that we would make, we should conclude without further ado that things seem to it as they seem to us. Once again it is clear that this is *not* the move that Dennett is making here. He does make a similar move on occasion, a point to which we will return, but that is not the move he is making here. The move he is making here, again, is to urge that, in the situations he imagines, we have *no idea* what state of affairs sameness or difference would consist in. It is rather like asking whether the universe is right side up or upside down (an example of Dennett's [1991, p. 462]). The problem is not that we do not know how to verify which option is right. It is much worse than that. We have no idea what facts, what states of affairs, would constitute either option.

### Inverted Spectra Undetectable by Others

With these preliminaries, let us turn to the inverted spectrum. Again Dennett relies on intuition pumps. I put on colour inversion glasses and the colours that things seem to have are inverted. A few days later, everything seems normal again. Do colours again seem to me as they do to others or do they continue to seem different but I have compensated somewhere later in processing? I wake up after an operation and colours seem inverted. But there are two possibilities: Perhaps my perceptual system is now processing colour information differently; or perhaps my memory system identifies as green results of colour-processing that it used to identify as red. Based simply on how things seem to me, can I – can anyone – determine which has happened? (Note that the determination has to be based simply on how things seem to me because appealing to neurophysiology or anything else here won't help. We would first have to map the differences in how things seem onto neurological or other differences – and our problem is that we don't know what the difference between them seeming one way and seeming another way would consist in.)

Here is a particularly telling story. It is from (1991, p. 395). Suppose that a particular shade of blue reminds you of a car in which you had a bad accident and so is a colour to be avoided. Your colour spectrum is inverted. At first things are fine. The things that used to look blue to you now look yellow and you do not react to them. However, you adapt to the inversion. (Evidence for this is that you again call 'blue' the shades of colour that others call 'blue,' fit these shades into a colour wheel the way others do, and so on.) Suddenly you start avoiding the things that you again call blue *and it is because they remind you of the car in which you had the bad accident.* That is to say, the shade of colour in front of you strikes you as the same as the shade of colour of the car as you remember it. Does the shade of colour in front of you and/or the remembered colour of the car now seem to you as yellow seems to others or as blue does? Here one is inclined to say, "Given that everything, *everything*, is exactly as it would be if the colour in both cases appeared as blue does to others and indeed to her own preinversion self, what could appearing as yellow does in others *consist in*? What state of affairs could be the state of affairs of either colour appearing as yellow?" Certainly this appearing-as-yellow is a "wheel which plays no part in the mechanism" (Wittgenstein 1953, §271) and that is enough to make it at least very difficult to gain any sense of what such a state could consist in.

There is strong resistance to this claim that we do not know what the difference between an inverted and a noninverted Seeming would be like in supposed colour-inversion-with-perfect-adaptation situations. "Surely it is a perfectly straightforward matter of fact whether something seems red or seems green to someone!" Well, no, it is not. Is the difference between an inverted and a noninverted Seeming to be detectable, even by the person whose Seeming it is, or not? If it is not detectable by anyone, then it is hard to see how we could have any notion of what state of affairs inversion would consist in and what state of affairs noninversion would consist in. If it is detectable, then, since ex hypothesi the difference is not detectable outside the person, it has to be the person his- or herself who could detect it. Could it be detectable by the person him- or herself?

Suppose the person who has the putative inversion is Kanta. If Kanta can detect a change here, there would have to be three possibilities:

– her Seemings have changed and she can spot this.

– her memory has changed, so that when she identifies her current Seemings by reference to other remembered Seemings, her current Seemings *appear* to have changed when they have not.

– she is simply making a mistake, misidentifying what her Seemings are like, so that even though her current Seemings have not changed and her memories have not changed, she gets it wrong what her current Seemings are like.

All of these situations would lead her to *believe* that her Seemings have changed, even though in two of the three cases she would be wrong. Now, based solely on how things seem to her, does she know – does she have any conception – of what one of these three situations rather than either of the other two would consist in? (Again, she cannot go outside how things seem to her without having a way to map how things seem onto this other thing – and for that she would have to make just the distinctions among different situations of seeming that we are discussing.)

Something is amiss. For Kanta to detect that the colours of things suddenly seem different to her, she has to call up the right memory (Wittgenstein 1953, §265). But *based solely on how things seem to her,* what would the difference between calling up the right memory and a wrong one consist in? Checking that a putative memory is right or wrong requires that there be something independent against which to check it, independent of both the putative memory and the introspective context of it, something such as archives and artefacts. There is nothing independent against which to 'check' whether a Seeming has been correctly identified, misremembered, or misidentified. If so, the whole idea of a check or an identification here is a myth.

Another indication that something has gone wrong: These three supposed possibilities all require a *really* peculiar notion – that how something seems could be different from how we judge it to seem. In Dennett's view, the category of "the way things actually, objectively seem to you [is a] bizarre category" (1991, p. 132).

Our results so far. In the imagined scenario where we have to rely solely on how things seem to Kanta, we do not know what it would be for the way colours seem to her to have been inverted. If you tell me that this tomato could seem green to Kanta when it seems red to everyone else without this affecting her behaviour, we have no answer to questions such as: What would count as it seeming *green* to her? Why not pink, or purple, or the taste of cayenne? Note: This is not a problem about what she can or cannot verify. It is a problem about what the relevant phenomena would consist in, whether anyone can verify anything about them or not. We have *no idea* what the difference between seeming one way and seeming the other would consist in.

So what is going on when we notice and say how something seems to us? If when we express a sensation or other mental state in words, we are *not* identifying the sensation as an instance of what those words describe, if, more generally, when we determine how things seem to us in our conscious states, this is not a result of reading an appearance off the conscious state, then what is going on? Dennett's suggestion is this. When I determine how something seems to me, this is a judgment: "There is nothing more to phenomenology . . . than judgment" (1991, p. 366; see also p. 364). When I react to shades of what are in fact blue in the same way as I react to the colour of the car that crashed, I am judging that the colours are the same. When I say that beer does not taste the same to me as it did the first time I tasted it, I am judging that the tastes are different. That is what it is for colours and tastes to seem a certain way to me and there is no further fact of the matter about how they seem. Our question now is: judgment of what? And done in what context?

Something like this. When I decide how something seems to me (how cauliflower or beer tastes, whether two colours seem the same, how clear a passage of Kant is), this judgment is based on the history and context I am in and what I go on to say and do. So: I start from how things are apt to seem given my environment (cauliflower or beer in the mouth, the reading of a passage of Kant, and everything else that I know about the context). I then take into account the relevant history and the behaviour that en-sues, especially the words. Am I inclined to reach for more cauliflower? Am I reacting to the colour in front of me as similar to the colour of the car that crashed? Am I finding crisp, insightful interpretations of the pas-sage? I could also check to see how others are reacting to me. And so on. Taking things like this into account via some cognitive process that aims to achieve a good equilibrium among them, things come to seem a certain way to me. That is all that seeming to me consists in. I am not 'reading off' quasi-perceptible qualities of some hidden inner state because there are no such properties.

Although initially counterintuitive, Dennett's picture yields nice ex-planations of some puzzling phenomena. One of them is the *Capgras delusion*. People caught in this delusion are convinced that their relatives and friends have been replaced by visually, aurally, . . . exactly similar impostors.[1] Dennett says that it should send shockwaves through philosophy (1996, p. 111). The Capgras delusion is said to result from lesions in the visual recognition system at a stage where visual images "connect with" feelings of familiarity (Ellis and Young 1990). On Dennett's account, what is going on is that some result of visual processing, who knows what, has set off a process of interpretation at that point that results in people these patients are perceiving seeming to be impostors. A very natural explanation of an otherwise very puzzling phenomenon.

So what is going on when we use language in connection with how something seems to us? Here we can draw on another idea of Wittgenstein's. (Dennett makes use of this idea, too, but elsewhere in [1991], not in the part concerned with *qualia*.) If what we have said is right, when we express how something seems to us in words, we are *not* identifying some state of affairs in us whose content is that thing seeming that way (Wittgenstein, 1953, §290). Indeed, something like this *has* to be true if determination of how things seem to us is a matter of judgment taking into account context. If expressing how something seems to us were a matter of identifying some state of affairs in us as the Seeming, any such judgment would have been preempted. Well, if using words in connection with how things seem is not using them to identify something, then what is gong on? Wittgenstein tells us that when conscious states are brought about in us, we are simply trained to react with words, in particular, to express the state in words. If so, words replace other ways of expressing what is going on in us consciously (1953, §244). If, as seems evident, crying out in pain is not identifying a sensation as a particular kind of sensation, why should saying "Ouch, that hurts" be?

Dennett's way of capturing the difference we are after here is to say that we do not *report* how things seem to us, we *express* it (1991, pp. 303–9). Expressing something is not a process of picking out a state of affairs and ascribing properties to it. Indeed, for Dennett the way we express something can actually be part of what *creates* how something seems to us. Dennett is very fond of Forster's saying, "How do I know what I think until I see what I say?" (cited in 1991, p. 245). In this, Dennett goes further than Wittgenstein did. So far as I know, Wittgenstein did not explore the possibility that expressing something may be part of what makes the expressed what it is.

Even when judgment does enter, as it does when, taking history, context, and ensuing behaviour into account (plus anything we might happen to know about what is going on in the brain), we judge how a situation will seem to someone, the judgment is not picking out something and attributing properties to it. The judgment is constructing or reconstructing a picture of what the equivalent process of judgment in the agent will have yielded. Dennett calls these judgments *heterophenomenology* when they are of how things will seem to others, *autophenomenology* when they are of how things seem to oneself.

To conclude this section: If our analysis is right, an inverted spectrum could not be coherently described. Note that this is not because inverted spectra could not happen for some empirical reason. It is because we cannot make *sense* of the idea. We cannot even state what would have to happen for a colour spectrum to be inverted without the change showing itself in behaviour. Next, absent *qualia*, zombies.

### Undetectable Zombies

We have laid a lot of the groundwork and can move more quickly. Many commentators have taken Dennett's attack on the possibility of zombies to be verificationist so let us start by returning to that issue. For Dennett, verificationism is not a boogeyman. He wouldn't like to be thought of as the village verificationist (on the model, presumably, of the village idiot) but he doesn't mind the idea that he is an urbane verificationist (1982, p. 355). A verificationist argument, again, is one built on the principle that the meaning of a term is simply our method of verifying the correctness of its applications and strongly suggests the 'duck' principle. If a creature acts like us and talks like us and makes judgments (or 'judgments') about itself like us and in all other relevant ways behaves like us, we should accept that it is like us, including that it is conscious like us. To be sure, some of Dennett's arguments rely on verificationism. One such argument is the argument from zimboes (1991, pp. 310–11).

Zimboes are zombies but zombies that don't cheat. Dennett says that many invocations of zombies do cheat. They present zombies on the model of the real zombies of Haiti – creatures dim-witted, slow-moving, no longer possessed of a will of their own. Here it is easy to say that zombies lack some-thing we have. But this is cheating. Philosophers' zombies are supposed to behave *just* like us and still lack consciousness. So let us imagine zombies that fill this bill: zimboes. Zimboes are lively and animated, talk about how they feel about the kids, curse when they smash their thumb with a hammer, toy with fine comparisons among different bits of what they remember from Kant's transcendental deduction, talk in fine detail about the vividness, clarity, accuracy, and so on, of their experiences, how they feel when they are with someone they love or someone who enrages them – in short, they behave in all the ways that we do. Says Dennett, it is far from obvious that we can imagine *these* creatures nonetheless lacking all consciousness.

This move is clearly verificationist. Whatever its merits (and it would be rash to say that it has none), Dennett offers something better. In virtue of what does a state become a conscious state for Dennett? In virtue of its being like something to have it or it being the basis of something coming to seem like something. But what is it for it to be like something to have a state, for something to seem like something? For Dennett, it is for those states and events, in the context in which they occur and with the behaviour that ensues, to be the basis of judgments of certain kinds. *And that is all there is to consciousness, full-blown phenomenal consciousness.* If so, once we have the full panoply of context, inner (= brain) goings-on, and ensuing behaviour and all of this can be judged a certain way, that is it – there is nothing left to be missing. If so, when the brain of a being with a similar history to ours is reacting as ours would in a given context and it is behaving as we would, including making the same autophenomenological judgments as we would, an absence of *qualia* is not even a possible state of affairs. This, I think, is Dennett's strongest argument against the possibility of zombies, far stronger than the verificationist ones.

This also resolves a puzzle that we left hanging earlier, the puzzle that for Dennett, conscious states lack the property of something seeming a certain way to someone. The resolution is simple: Something seeming a certain way is an interpretation. This interpretation turns the related brain-state into a conscious state but it is not a property of the brain-state, not the brain-state by itself at any rate. "Didn't you quote Dennett," it will immediately be objected, "saying that 'conscious states are real events occurring in the real time and space of the brain'?" Yes, we did. But in virtue of what are these states conscious? The answer, we just said, is: in virtue of being judged to seem like something to someone. If so, then the states can be perfectly real while what makes them conscious is interpreted a certain way. This is a radical view. However, so is the most viable alternative to it: that consciousness is an organic property of brains (Churchland 1999).

If we are right, Dennett's view of inverted spectrum and absent *qualia* stories in which all the relevant behaviour remains the same but something fundamental about conscious experience changes or is absent, is that they cannot be coherently told. If I am right that this account has a lot going for it, Dennett has made a signal contribution to contemporary consciousness studies.

## Hard Cases

A crucial feature of Dennett's story is that what it is like to have or be in states in the brain is never given with or determined by the state itself. Like every philosophical theory, Dennett's theory faces some hard cases. For his account, the hard cases are pains and simple pleasures and other body-rooted sensations. What a pain or a simple pleasure feels like is not, on the face of it, a matter of interpretation. Whacking my thumb will hurt and a glass of cold water on a hot day will feel good no matter how I interpret these situations or my experience of them. More complicated feelings can be most unwelcome and yet resist all efforts to interpret them away, as when I desperately want not to feel bored to tears by someone but still feel bored to tears.

Let us focus on pains. Here is a passage by Dennett on its close companion, suffering:

> Suffering is not a matter of being visited by some ineffable but intrinsically awful state, but of having one's life hopes, life plans, life projects blighted by circumstances imposed on one's desires, thwarting one's intentions. . . . The idea of suffering being somehow explicable as the presence of some intrinsic property is as hopeless as the idea of amusement being somehow explicable as the presence of intrinsic hilarity. (1991, p. 449)

I don't know about the awfulness of suffering being ineffable or intrinsic – indeed, I am not even sure what these terms mean – but the idea that suffering is merely a matter of judgment does not seem right. However, let us grant it. Dennett distinguishes suffering and pain rather sharply (1995b, p. 352). Let us grant this, too. Now, what about pain? What does Dennett have to say about it?

No theory of *pain* as thwarted projects is going to do. If I hit my thumb with a hammer, what I feel will not be a gloomy sense of a reversal in my life fortunes! Indeed, a short, sharp pain like that will probably have no implications for my life fortunes (beyond the five minutes it takes the pain to fade). Yet it still hurts. Dennett himself offers an exactly parallel example (1995b, p. 352). So what does he want to say about pain?

He has given two accounts of pain recently. One puts pain squarely on the interpretation side of the interpretation/physical realization split.

> Are pains real? They are as real as haircuts and dollars and opportunities and persons, and centers of gravity. (1991, p. 460)

A motley collection but (almost) all matters of interpretation – remember how Dennett views the reality of persons (I am not sure what haircuts are doing here). He seems to push the pain-as-judgment line in (1995b), too, even thought he explicitly talks about short, sharp pains there.

The case of morphine suggests that no such account will work. As Dennett himself has articulated very nicely (1978a), morphine acts against pain in a peculiar way. Subjects claim that it does not remove the sensation of pain – but the pain no longer hurts. (Subjects say things like, "I still have the pain but it no longer hurts!") That is to say, it seems to the subject that the pain is still there – but a feeling-state characteristic of pain is not, namely, the hurting, the awfulness. This example would seem to cut against any reduction of pain to judgment decisively. Yet, like the short, sharp pain, again it is Dennett's own example.

To respond to this objection, Dennett (private correspondence) has urged that how things seem to a subject is not definitive (except for how things seem to the subject). Moreover, there *is* a difference of judgment before and after: As we just saw, the subject *judges* her situation after the morphine to be different from her situation before. All true – and important. There is more judgment involved in even sharp, emotionally uncomplicated pain than many have thought. But! First, if even a difference as large as the difference between what I judge a feeling to be like and whether it hurts does not count, if even excruciating sensations come out as judgments, what is the force of the claim that all phenomenology is judgment? There is a risk in an 'all' claim like this. Is Dennett reducing phenomenology to judgment – or merely bending the notion of judgment out of shape, merely turning it into another name for phenomenology? What is being denied? What would a conscious state that was not a judgment *be like*? (This move should appeal to Dennett.)

I don't think that this worry is real. The claim that all phenomenology is judgment includes, for example, a claim that how something seems is never given by a brain or representational state by itself. Dennett is not simply redefining 'judgment.' But there is a weaker worry. What is it about some judgments, descriptions, in virtue of which they hurt, while others don't? Absent an answer to this question, we have not made much progress with pain (or, *mutatis mutandis*, any other state in which what it is like to have it seems to be given by the state).

The interpretationist approach leaves us with a pretty bloodless account of pains. At one point in his long campaign to wean us away from the traditional theory of Seemings, Dennett suggests that the traditional notion needs something like pseudo-pigment, an illusory substance that he calls figment (1991, p. 346). I am inclined to turn this move around. Dennett attempts to give us an account of pains but what he ends up with seem to be – fains.[2] Fains may make us act like they're pains and even thwart our intentions like they're pains (to the extent that pains do thwart our intentions) but they're not awful to have, so they're not pains. (This is one place where looking like us and "quacking" like us is *not* enough for being like us.)

Dennett is perfectly well aware of what pain is like, of course. Early in (1991, pp. 25, 60–4) and in more recent writings (1998, pp. 174, 280), he speaks eloquently about it. Part of the problem may be a nasty lurking dilemma. As Dennett says, any account of what the awfulness of pain consists in must, in some way, break it down into elements that are not themselves awful to have. If your analysis merely breaks it into elements that are themselves awful, you haven't analyzed the awfulness (1991, p. 64). (Compare Fodor on propositional content: "if it is something, then it is something else" [1985, p. 9]). This creates a prima facie dilemma: If you keep the awfulness, it will be at the cost of giving no analysis of it; but if you analyse the awfulness, it will be at the cost of losing "the thing itself, . . . the pain in all its awfulness," as Dennett has his alter ego put it (1991, p. 64). Over the years, Dennett has gone both ways. In (1978a), the awfulness is essentially unanalyzed and Dennett focuses on how the awfulness and whatever it is that we are aware of as pain could be connected to the brain. In (1991), he tries to say something about what pain, including its awfulness, might consist in – and loses the awfulness. Nasty.

Very recently, Dennett has been working his way towards a much less interpretationist approach to pain. In (1991), he treats pain as like belief and perception, a result of interpretation. In the new approach, he is beginning to treat pain as like events on whose reality he himself insists, namely, events in the brain. On this view, certain brain processes would simply *be* awful to have – would obliterate concentration, cause nausea, disappear with analgesics, etc., etc. What would the difference be between, say, an obsessive thought that causes you to suffer but does not hurt and what you feel when you are kicked in the shin? In the latter case, there is,

> a variety of *further* neuromodulator releases and neural firings that are apt to provoke/enable (1) identificatory judgments about a location, . . . (2) intensified involuntary muscle spasms. . . . That's what the difference is,

I think, between cognitive events that hurt and those that don't. (2000, p. 369)

There is a lot to commend this view. Most pains are not intentional, that is, are not about anything, and treating them as real brain events seems preferable to treating them as having the reality of blighted hopes, dollars, centres of gravity, and so on.[3] Moreover, we can accept this view of pain and still keep most of what Dennett wants to say about auto- and heterophenomenology and pain. Exactly what kind of pain one is feeling and what implications it has for one's life could still be a matter of judgment, as unforced by and not a property of brain-state reality as the result of any other auto- or heterophenomenological judgment. A pain can be awful, indeed truly horrendous, without us having any precise view of what kind of pain it is. In fact, we would end up exactly where morphine patients say they are: "I still have the pain" (autophenomenological judgment) "but it no longer hurts" (the awful-feeling brain-state has been altered). And we retain both blighted hopes and short, sharp pains.

This account of what I feel when I hit my thumb would be an application of Churchland's (1999) claim that consciousness is an organic property of brains to the special case of pains (and relevantly similar experiences). Whatever the merits of this view as a general theory of consciousness, it is a promising line to take about pain and the like. Here, at least, what it is like to be in a state *does* seem to be dictated by biology, not by acts of interpretation.

## THE REALITY OF SEEMINGS

Dennett argues more than that what it actually is for things to seem a certain way to us does not support philosophical fantasies about *qualia* as Seemings. He argues that no such thing exists. I want to make a few quick comments on this issue.[4] If the rest of what we have said is correct, here is what we have established concerning existence. The phenomenon that we call seeming to be like something is not remotely as philosophers have conceived it, not remotely like a Seeming. Not only is it not ineffable, intrinsic, private, it is not a property of an individual representational state or event by itself at all. Rather, it is a complex relational property, a property moreover that is purely an artefact of hetero- or autophenomenological *judgments*, judgments about how something seems given context, history, brain, and behaviour. Is this to be real property or not? So long as we are clear on the facts, we can, to use a phrase of the philosopher Elizabeth Anscombe's, say what we like.

Dennett thinks it better, given that these artefacts have virtually none of the properties traditionally ascribed to Seemings, to say that there is no such thing as Seemings. My own preference is to go the other way. Briefly, here is why. Even leaving aside the hard cases (pain, etc.) and sticking to judgment, which is what is supposed makes a state conscious on Dennett's account, judgements certainly exist *and it is like something to make them*. Nor does Dennett deny either point. If so, judgments have two of the traditionally crucial properties of *qualia*. Moreover, when we are not playing thought experiment games, when history, context, brain response and ensuing behaviour line up as they normally do, we can say, and say not just determinately but very precisely, how things seem to us. All this is enough for me to conclude that states in which something seems a certain way exist. One can agree with Dennett that "inner sensations stand in need of outer criteria" (Wittgenstein) without having to say that 'inner sensations' and other states and events that it is like something to have do not exist. To be sure, one can go either way on the existence issues: The states at issue here are totally different from the way the tradition has thought them to be. Since these states do exist, my preference is to say that Seemings exist.

To conclude: Dennett's account of what conscious states are really like is one of the major contributions to consciousness research of recent decades. There are a great many aspects of it that we have not even touched on. Dennett maintains, for example, that many temporal questions about conscious states – questions about when a state started or ended, when some change occurred – are as ill-formed as the questions we examined earlier about how something would seem in various inverted spectrum situations. These are the questions that give rise to the Stalinesque and Orwellian pseudo-options discussed in the introductory essay. For the rich details of the issues left undiscussed here, there is probably no substitute for reading (1991) itself. Fortunately, it is one of the most engaging and accessible books ever written by a major philosopher.[5]

### Notes

[1.] If these patients were good verificationists of the kind that critics try to foist on Dennett, this situation should be a contradiction in terms. If the people they see really are *indistinguishable* from their friends and loved ones, then on the 'duck' principle these patients should take these people *to be* their friends and loved ones. These patients are not verificationists of that stripe – and neither is Dennett.

[2.] I owe this lovely neologism to Chris Viger.

[3.] I owe this view in a way to Don Ross – in a way because it first occurred to me when he was once trying to convince me that pain is firmly on the other side of the real-state-of-the-brain/artefact-of-interpretation divide. He now shares my view that it can straddle the divide.

[4.] I have pursued this issue and others in more detail in Brook 2000.

[5.] Thanks to Dan Dennett, Don Ross, and Rob Stainton for many helpful comments. Stainton started off thinking that almost everything in this essay is wrong and despite my best attempts, still thinks so.

## References

Austin, J. L. (1962). *Sense and Sensibilia.* Oxford: Oxford University Press.

Brook, A. (2000). Judgements and Drafts Eight Years Later. In Ross, Brook, and Thompson 2000.

Chalmers, D. (1995). Facing Up to The Problem of Consciousness. *Journal of Consciousness Studies* 2(3):200–19.

Churchland, P. M. (1999). Densmore and Dennett on Virtual Machines and Consciousness. *Philosophy and Phenomenological Research* 59:763–78

Dennett, D. (1978a). Why You Can't Make a Computer That Can Feel Pain. Reprinted in Dennett, 1978b.

Dennett, D. (1978b). *Brainstorms.* Montgomery, VT: Bradford Books

Dennett, D. (1982). Comments on Rorty. *Synthese* 59:349–56.

Dennett, D. (1988). Quining Qualia. In A. Marcel and E. Bisiach, eds., *Consciousness in Contemporary Society.* Oxford: Oxford University Press, 43–77.

Dennett, D. (1991). *Consciousness Explained.* New York: Little, Brown.

Dennett, D. (1994a). Real Consciousness. Reprinted in Dennett, 1998.

Dennett, D. (1994b). Instead of Qualia. Reprinted in Dennett, 1998.

Dennett, D. (1995a). The Unimagined Preposterousness of Zombies. *Journal of Consciousness Studies* 2(4):322–26.

Dennett, D. (1995b). Animal Consciousness: What Matters and Why. Reprinted in Dennett, 1998.

Dennett, D. (1996). *Kinds of Minds.* New York: Basic Books.

Dennett, D. (1998). *Brainchildren.* Cambridge, MA: MIT Press.

Dennett, D. (2000). With a Little Help from My Friends. In Ross, Brook, and Thompson 2000.

Ellis, H. D., and A. W. Young. (1990). Accounting for Delusional Misidentification. *British Journal of Psychiatry* 157:239–48.

Flanagan, O. (1992). *Consciousness Reconsidered.* Cambridge, MA: MIT Press/A Bradford Book.

Fodor, J. (1985). Fodor's Guide to Mental Representation. Reprinted in Fodor 1990.

Fodor, J. (1990). *A Theory of Content and Other Essays*. Cambridge, MA: MIT Press/ A Bradford Book.

Hardin, L. (1988). *Colour for Philosophers: Unweaving the Rainbow*. Indianapolis, IN: Hackett Publishers.

Levine, J. (1983). Materialism and Qualia: The Explanatory Gap. *Pacific Philosophical Quarterly* 64:354–61.

Locke, J. (1690). *An Essay Concerning Human Understanding*. New York: Dover, 1959.

Nagel, T. (1974). What Is It Like to Be a Bat? *Philosophical Review* 83:435–50.

Palmer, S. (1999). Colour, Consciousness, and the Isomorphism Constraint. *Behavioral and Brain Sciences* 22(6):939–89.

Ross, D., A. Brook, and D. Thompson. (2000). *Dennett's Philosophy: A Comprehensive Assessment*. Cambridge, MA: MIT Press/A Bradford Book.

Ryle, G. (1949). *The Concept of Mind*. London: Hutchison and Co.

Sellars, W. (1963). Empiricism and the Philosophy of Mind. In his *Science, Perception and Reality*. London: Routledge and Kegan Paul

Weiskrantz, L. (1986). *Blindsight: A Case Study and Implications*. Oxford: Oxford University Press.

Wittgenstein, L. (1953). *Philosophical Investigations*. G. E. M. Anscombe, trans., G. E. M. Anscombe and R. Rhees, eds. Oxford: Blackwell Publishers.

# 3 | Catching Consciousness in a Recurrent Net

## PAUL M. CHURCHLAND

Dan Dennett is a closet Hegelian. I say this not in criticism, but in praise, and hereby own to the same affliction. More specifically, Dennett is convinced that Human Cognitive Life is the scene or arena of a swiftly unfolding evolutionary process, an essentially cultural process above and distinct from the familiar and much slower process of biological evolution. This super-added Hegelian adventure is a matter of a certain style of *conceptual* activity; it involves an endless contest between an evergreen variety of conceptual *alternatives*; and it displays, at least occasionally, a welcome *progress* in our conceptual sophistication, and in the social and technological practices that structure our lives.

With all of this, I agree, and will attempt to prove my fealty in due course. But my immediate focus is the peculiar *use* to which Dennett has tried to put his background Hegelianism in his provocative 1991 book, *Consciousness Explained* (1991).[1] Specifically, I wish to address his peculiar account of the *kinematics and dynamics* of the Hegelian Unfolding that we both acknowledge. And I wish to query his novel *deployment* of that kinematics and dynamics in explanation of the focal phenomenon of his book: consciousness. To state my negative position immediately, I am unconvinced by his declared account of the background process of human conceptual evolution and development – specifically, the Dawkinsean account of rough gene-analogs called 'memes' competing for dominance of human cognitive activity. And I am even less convinced by Dennett's attempt to capture the emergence of a peculiarly human consciousness in terms of our brains' having internalized a specific complex *example* of such a 'meme,' namely, the serial, discursive style of cognitive processing typically displayed in a von Neumann computing machine.

My opening task, then, is critical. I think Dennett is wrong to see human consciousness as the result of a unique form of 'software' that began running on the existing hardware of human brains some ten, or fifty, or a hundred thousand years ago. He is importantly wrong about the character of that background software process in the first place, and he is wrong again to see consciousness itself as the isolated result of its 'installation' in the human brain. Instead, I shall argue, the phenomenon of consciousness is the result of the brain's basic *hardware* structures, structures that are widely shared throughout the animal kingdom, structures that produce consciousness in meme-free and von-Neumann-innocent animals just as surely and just as vividly as they produce consciousness in us. As my title indicates, I think the key to understanding the peculiar weave of cognitive phenomena gathered under the term 'consciousness' lies in understanding the dynamical properties of biological neural networks with a highly *recurrent* physical architecture – an architecture that represents a widely shared hardware feature of animal brains generally, rather than a unique software feature of human brains in particular.

By contrast, Dennett and I share membership in a small minority of theorists on the topic of consciousness, a small minority even among materialists. Specifically, we both seek an explanation of consciousness in the *dynamical* signature of a conscious creature's cognitive activities, rather than in the peculiar character or subject matter of the *contents* of that creature's cognitive states. Dennett may seek it in the dynamical features of a 'virtual' von-Neumann machine, and I may seek it in the dynamical features of a massively recurrent neural network, but we are both working the 'dynamical profile' side of the street, in substantial isolation from the rest of the profession.

Accordingly, in the second half of this essay, I intend to defend Dennett in this dynamical tilt, and to criticize the more popular content-focused alternative accounts of consciousness, as advanced by most philosophers and even by some neuroscientists. And in the end, I hope to convince both Dennett and the reader that the hardware-focused recurrent-network story offers the most fertile and welcoming reductive home for the relatively unusual dynamical-profile approach to consciousness that Dennett and I share.

## 1. EPISTEMOLOGY: NATURALIZED AND EVOLUTIONARY

Attempts to reconstruct the canonical problems of epistemology within an explicitly evolutionary framework have a long and vigorous history. Restricting ourselves to the twentieth century, we find, in 1934, Karl Popper (see also 1972 and 1979) already touting experimental falsification as the selectionist mechanism within his expressly evolutionary account of scientific growth, an account articulated in several subsequent books and papers.

In 1950, Jean Piaget published a broader and much more naturalistic vision of information-bearing structures in a three-volume work assimilating biological and intellectual evolution (see also Piaget, 1965 and 1970). Thomas Kuhn's 1962 classic painted an overtly anti-logicist and anti-convergent portrait of our scientific development, and proposed instead a radiative process by which different cognitive paradigms would evolve toward successful domination of a wide variety of cognitive niches. In 1965, and partly in response to Kuhn, Imre Lakatos published a generally Popperian but much more detailed account of the dynamics of intellectual evolution, one more faithful to the logical, sociological, and historical facts of our own scientific history. In 1972, Stephen Toulmin was pushing a biologized version of Hegel, and, by 1974, Donald Campbell had articulated a deliberately Darwinian account of the blind generation and selective retention of scientific theories over historical time.

From 1975 on, the literature becomes too voluminous to summarize easily, but it includes Dawkins's specific views on memes, as scouted briefly in *The Selfish Gene* (1976) and more extensively in *The Extended Phenotype* (1982). In some respects, Dawkins's peculiar take on human intellectual history is decidedly better than the take of many others in this tradition – most important, his feel for both genetic theory and biological reality is much better than that of his precursors. In other respects, it is rather poorer – comparatively speaking, and once again by the standards of the tradition at issue, Dawkins is an epistemological naif, and his feel for our actual scientific/conceptual history is rudimentary. But he had the wit, over most of his colleagues, to escape the biologically naïve construal of theories-as-*genotypes* or theories-as-*phenotypes* that attracted so many other writers. Despite a superficial appeal, both of these analogies are deeply strained and ultimately infertile, both as extensions of existing biological theory and as explanatory contributions to existing epistemological theory. (An insightful perspective on the relevant defects is found in Hooker 1995.) Dawkins embraces, instead, and despite my opening characterization, a theories-as-*viruses* analogy, wherein the human brain serves as a host for competing invaders, invaders that can replicate by subsequently invading as-yet uninfected brains.

While an improvement in several respects, this analogy seems stretched and problematic still, at least to these eyes. An individual virus is an individual physical thing, locatable in space and time. An individual theory is no such thing. And even its individual 'tokens' – as they may be severally embodied in the distinct brains they have 'invaded' – are, at best, abstract *patterns* of some kind imposed on preexisting physical structures within the brain, not physical *things* bent on making further physical things with a common physical structure.

Furthermore, a theory has no internal mechanism that effects a literal self-replication when it injects its own genetic material into the interior of a successfully highjacked cell. And my complaint here is not that the mechanisms of self-replication are different across the two cases. It is that there *is no* such mechanism for theory-tokens. If they can be seen as 'replicating' at all, it must be by some wholly different process. This is further reflected in the fact that theory-tokens do not replicate themselves *within* a given individual, as viruses most famously do. For example, you might have $10^6$ qualitatively identical rhinoviruses in your system at one time, all children of an original invader; but never more than one token of Einstein's theory of gravity.

Moreover, the brain is a medium selected precisely for its ability to assume, hold, and deploy the conceptual systems we call theories. Theories are not alien invaders bent on subverting the brain's resources to their own selfish 'purposes.' On the contrary, a theory is the brain's way of making sense of the world in which it lives, an activity that is its original and primary function. A bodily cell, by contrast, enjoys no such intimate relationship with the viruses that intrude on its normal metabolic and reproductive activities. A mature cell that is completely free of viruses is just a normal, functioning cell. A mature brain that is completely free of theories or conceptual frameworks is an utterly dysfunctional system, barely a brain at all.

Furthermore, theories often – indeed, usually – take *years* of hard work and practice to grasp and internalize, precisely because there is no analog to the physical virus entering the body, pill-like or bullet-like, at a specific time and place. Instead, a vast reconfiguration of the brain's $10^{14}$ synaptic connections is necessary in order to imprint the relevant conceptual framework on the brain, a reconfiguration that often takes months or years to complete. Accordingly, the 'replication story' needed, on the Dawkinsean view, must be nothing short of an entire theory of how the brain *learns*. No simple 'cookie-cutter' story of replication will do for the dubious 'replicants' at this abstract level. There are no zipper-like molecules to divide down the middle and then reconstitute themselves into two identical copies; nor will *repeating* the theory, by voice or in print, to another human do the trick. Simply receiving, or even memorizing, a list of presented *sentences* (a statement of the theory) is not remotely adequate to successful acquisition of the conceptual framework to be replicated, as any unprepared student of classical physics learns when he desperately confronts the problems set on his final examination armed only with a crib-sheet containing flawless copies of the Newton's Gravitation Law and the Three Laws of Motion. Knowing a theory is not just having a few lines of easily transferable syntax, as the student's inevitable failing grade attests.

The poverty of its 'biological' credentials aside, the *explanatory payoff* for embracing this virus-like conception of theories is quite unremarkable in any case. The view brings with it no compelling account of where theories originate, how they are modified over time in response to experimental evidence, how competing theories are evaluated, how they guide our experimental and practical behaviors, how they fuel our technological economies, and how they count as representations of the world's hidden structure. In short, the analogy with viruses doesn't provide particularly illuminating answers, or any answers at all, to most of the questions that make up the problem-domain of epistemology and the philosophy of science.

What it does do is hold out the promise of a grand consilience – a conception of scientific activity that is folded into a larger and more powerful background conception of biological processes in general. This is, at least in prospect, an extremely *good* thing, and it more than accounts for the "aha" feelings that most of us experience on first contemplating such a view. But closer examination shows it to be a *false* consilience, based on a false analogy. Accordingly, we should not have much confidence in deploying it, as Dennett does, in hopes of illuminating either human cognitive development in general, or the development of human consciousness in particular.

Despite reaching a strictly negative conclusion here, not just about the theories-as-viruses analogy, but about the entire evolutionary tradition in recent epistemology, I must add that I still regard that tradition as healthy, welcome, and salutary, for it seeks a worthy sort of consilience, and it serves as a vital foil against the deeply sclerotic logicist tradition of the logical empiricists. Moreover, I share the background conviction of most people working in the newer tradition – namely, that, in the end, a proper account of human scientific knowledge must somehow be a proper part of a general theory of biological systems and biological development. However, I have quite different expectations about how that integration should proceed. They are the focus of a book-in-progress, but the present occasion is focused on consciousness, so I must leave their articulation for another time. In the meantime, I recommend Hooker's "nested hierarchy of regulatory mechanisms" attempt – to locate scientific activity within the embrace of biological phenomena at large – as the most promising account in the literature. (For a review of Hooker's book and its positive thesis, see Churchland 1999b.) We now return to Dennett.

## 2. THE BRAIN AS HOST FOR THE VON NEUMANN MEME

If the human brain *were* a von Neumann machine (hereafter, vN machine) – literally, rather than figuratively or virtually – then the virus analogy just rejected would have substantially more point. We do speak of, and bend resources to avoid, 'computer viruses,' and the objections voiced above, concerning theories and the brain, are mostly irrelevant if the virus analogy is directed instead at programs loaded in a computer. A program *is* just a package of syntax; a program *can* download in seconds; a program *can* contain a self-copying subroutine; and a program *can* fill a hard drive with monotonous copies of itself, whether or not it ever succeeds in infecting a second machine.

But the brains of animals and humans are most emphatically *not* vN machines. Their coding is not digital; their processing is not serial; they do not execute stored programs; and they have no random-access storage registers whatever. As fifty years of neuroscience and fifteen years of neuro-modeling have taught us, a brain is a different kettle of fish entirely. That is why brains are so hopeless at certain tasks, such as multiplying two twenty-digit numbers in one's head, which task a computer does in a second. And that is why computers are so hopeless at certain other tasks, such as recognizing individual faces or understanding speech, which task a brain does in even less time.

We now know enough about both brains and vN computers to appreciate precisely why the brain does as well as it does, despite being made of components that are a million times slower than those of an electronic computer. Specifically, the brain is a massively parallel vector processor. Its background understanding of the world's general features (its conceptual framework) resides in the slowly acquired configuration of its $10^{14}$ synaptic connections. Its specific understanding of the local world here-and-now (its fleeting thoughts and perceptions) resides in the fleeting patterns or vectors of activation-levels across its $10^{11}$ neurons. And the character of those fleeting patterns is dictated by the learned matrix of synaptic connections that serve simultaneously to transform *peripheral* sensory activation vectors into well-informed *central* vectors, and ultimately into the well-orchestrated *motor* vectors that produce our bodily behavior.

Now Dennett knows all of this as well as anyone, and it poses a problem for him. It's a problem because the virus analogy that he intends to exploit, as discussed above, requires a vN computer for its plausibility. But the biological brain is not a vN computer. So Dennett postulates that, at some point in our past, the human brain managed to 'reprogram' itself in such a fashion that its genetically endowed 'hardware' came to 'load' and 'run' a peculiar piece of novel 'software' – an invading virus or meme – such that the brain came to *be* a 'virtual' vN machine.

But wait a minute. We are here contemplating an explanation – of how the brain *came to be* a virtual vN machine – in terms that make clear and literal sense only if the brain was *already* a (literal) vN machine. But it wasn't. And so it couldn't become *any* new 'virtual' machine – and a fortiori not a virtual vN machine – in the literal fashion described. Dennett must have some related but metaphorical use in mind for the expressions 'program,' 'software,' 'hardware,' 'load,' and 'run.' And, as we shall see, for 'virtual' and 'N machine' as well.

As indeed he does. He knows that brains are plastic in their configurations of synaptic connections, and he knows that changing those configurations produces changes in the way the brain processes information. He is postulating that, at some point in the past, at least one human brain lucked/stumbled into a global configuration of synaptic connections that embodied an importantly new style of information processing, a style that involved, at least occasionally, the sequential, temporally structured, rule-respecting kinds of activities seen in a typical vN machine.

Let us look into this possibility. What is the actual potential of a massively parallel vector processing machine to 'simulate' a vN machine? For a purely feedforward network (Fig. 3.1*a*), it is zero, because these cannot

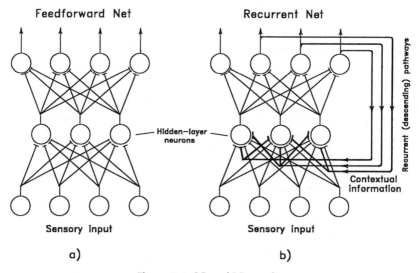

**Figure 3.1** Neural Networks

execute the temporally *recursive* procedures essential to a program-executing vN machine. To surmount this trivial limitation, we need to step up to networks with a *recurrent* architecture (Fig. 3.1*b*), for as is well known, this is what permits any neural network to deal with structures in time.

Artificial recurrent networks have indeed been trained up to execute successfully the kinds of explicitly recursive procedures involved in, for example, adding individual pairs of *n*-digit numbers (Cottrell and Tsung 1993) and distinguishing grammatical from ungrammatical sentences in a (highly simplified) productive language.

But are these suitably trained networks 'virtual' adders and 'virtual' parsers? No. They are *literal* adders and parsers. The language of 'virtual machines' is not strictly appropriate here, because these are *not* cases of a special purpose 'software machine' running, qua program, on a vN-style universal Turing machine.

More generally, the idea that a machine, any machine, might be programmed to 'simulate' a vN machine in particular makes the mistake of treating *vN machine* as if it were itself a *special*-purpose piece of software, rather than what it is, namely, an entirely *general*-purpose organization of *hardware*. In sum, the brain is not a machine that is capable of 'downloading software' in the first place, and a vN machine is not a piece of 'software' fit for downloading in any case.

Accordingly, I cannot find a workable interpretation of Dennett's proposal here that is both nonmetaphorical and true. He seems to be trying to both eat his cake (the brain becomes a vN machine by downloading some software) and have it too (the brain is not a vN machine to begin with). And these complaints are additional to and independent of the complaints of the preceding section, to the effect that Dawkins's virus analogy for cultural acquisitions such as theories, songs, and practices is a false and explanatorily sterile analogy to begin with.

There is an irony here. That fact is, if we do look to recurrent neural networks – which brains most assuredly are – in order to purchase something like the functional properties of a vN machine, we no longer *need* to 'download' any epigenetically supplied meme or program, because the sheer hardware configuration of a recurrent network already delivers the desired capacity for recognizing, manipulating, and generating serial structures in time, right out of the box. Those characteristic recurrent pathways are the very computational resources that allow us to recognize a puppy's gait, a familiar tune, a complex sentence, and a mathematical proof. Which *particular* temporal structures come to dominate a network's cognitive life will be a function of which causal processes are perceptually encountered during its learning phase. But the need for a virtual vN machine, in order to achieve this broader family of cognitive ends, has now been lifted. The brain doesn't need to import the 'software' Dennett contrives for it: Its existing 'hardware' is already equal to the cognitive tasks that he (rightly) deems important.

This moves me to try to reconstruct a vaguely Dennettian account of consciousness using the very real resources of a recurrent physical architecture, rather than the strained and figurative resources of a virtual vN machine. The dynamical profile approach cited at the outset of this paper is the way I will choose to do so. But first I must motivate its pursuit by evoking and dismantling its principal explanatory adversary, the content-focused approach.

## 3. CONSCIOUSNESS AS SELF-REPRESENTATION: SOME PROBLEMS

One strategy for trying to understand consciousness is to see it as a species of *representation*, a species distinguished by its peculiar *contents*, specifically, the current states or activities of the *self*, the current states or activities of the very biological-cum-cognitive system that is engaged in such representation. Consciousness, on this view, is essentially a matter of self-perception or self-representation. Thus, one is conscious when, for example, one's cognitive system represents stress or damage to some part of one's body (pain), when it represents one's empty stomach (hunger), when it represents the postural configuration of one's body (hands folded in front of one), when it represents one's high-level cognitive state ("I believe Budapest is in Hungary"), or when it represents one's relation to an external object ("I'm about to be hit by an incoming snowball").

Kant's doctrine of inner sense in *The Critique of Pure Reason* is the classic (and highly a priori) instance of this approach, and Antonio Damasio's new book, *The Feeling of What Happens*, provides a modern (and neurologically grounded) instance of the same general strategy. While I have some sympathy for this approach to consciousness – I have defended it myself in (1995), pp. 73–5, 119–20, 179–80 – the present essay is aimed at overturning it and replacing it with a specific alternative. Let me begin by voicing the central worries – to which all parties must be sensitive – that cloud the self-representation approach to consciousness.

There are two major weaknesses in the approach. The first is that it fails, at least on all outstanding versions, to give a clear and adequate account of the inescapable distinction between those of our self-representations that are conscious and those that are not. The nervous system has a great many subsystems that continuously monitor a wide variety of visceral, hormonal, thermal, metabolic, and other regulatory activities of the biological organism. These are representations of the self, if anything is, but they are only occasionally a part of our consciousness, and some of them are *permanently* beneath the level of conscious awareness.

One might try to avoid this difficulty by stipulating that the self-representations that constitute the domain of consciousness must be representations of the states and activities of the brain and nervous system proper, rather than of the body in general. But this proposal has three daughter difficulties. Prima facie, the stipulation would *exclude* far too much, for hunger, pain, and other plainly conscious somatosensory sensations are clearly representations of various aspects of the body, not the brain. Less obviously, but equally problematic, it would falsely *include* the enormous variety of brain activities that constitute ongoing and systematic representations of other aspects of the brain itself – indeed, these are the bulk of them – but which never make it into the spotlight of consciousness. We must be mindful, that is, that most of the brain's representational activities are self-directed and lie well below the level of conscious awareness. Finally, the proposed stipulation would wrongly *exclude* from consciousness the brain's unfolding representations of the world beyond the body, such as our visual awareness of the objects at arm's length and our auditory awareness of the whistling kettle. One might try to insist that, strictly speaking, it is only our visual and auditory *sensations* of which we are directly conscious – external objects being only indirect and secondary objects of awareness – but this move is false to the facts of both human cognitive development and human phenomenology, and it leads us down the path of classical sense-datum theory, whose barrenness has long been apparent.

A special *subject matter*, then, seems not to be the essential feature that distinguishes conscious representations from all others. To the contrary, it would seem that a conscious representation could have any content or subject matter at all. The proposal under discussion would seem to be confusing *self*-consciousness with consciousness in general. The former is highly interesting, to be sure, but it is the latter that is our current explanatory target.

The self-representation view has a second major failing, which emerges as follows. Consider a creature, such as you or me, who has a battery of distinct sensory modalities – a visual system, and auditory system, an olfactory system – for constructing representations of various aspects of the physical world. And suppose further that, as cognitive theorists, we have some sub-stantial understanding of how those several modalities actually work, as devices for monitoring aspects of external reality and coding those aspects internally. And yet we remain mystified about what makes the representa-tions in which they trade *conscious* representations. We remain mystified, that is, at what distinguishes the conscious states of your visual system from the genuinely representational but utterly unconscious representa-tional states of a voltmeter, an audio tape recorder, or a video camera. Now, if our general problem is thus to try to understand how *any* representational modality ascends to the level of conscious representations, then proposing a proprietary representational modality whose job it is to monitor phenom-ena *inside* the skin, rather than outside the skin, is a blatant case of *repeating* our problem, not of solving it. Our original problem attends the inward-looking modality no less than the various outward-looking modalities with which we began, and adding the inward modality does nothing obvious to transform the outward ones in any case. Once again, leaning on the *content* of the representations at issue – on the *focus, target,* or *subject matter* of the epistemic modality in question – fails to provide the explanatory factors that we seek. We need to look elsewhere.

## 4. THE DYNAMICAL PROFILE APPROACH

We need to look, I suggest, at the peculiar *activities* in which some of our representations participate, and the special computational context required for those activities to take place. I here advert, for example, to the brain's capacity to focus attention on some aspect or subset of its teeming poly-modal sensory inputs, to try out different conceptual interpretations of that selected subset, and to hold the results of that selective/interpretive activity in short-term memory for long enough to update a coherent representa-tional 'narrative' of the world-unfolding-in-time, a narrative thus fit for possible selection and imprinting in long-term memory.

Any cognitive representation that figures in the dynamical/com-putational profile just outlined is a recognizable candidate for, and a pre-sumptive instance of, the class of *conscious* representations. We may wish to demand still more of such candidates than merely meeting these quick four conditions, but even these four specify a dynamical or functional pro-file recognizable as typical of conscious representations. Notice also that this profile makes no reference to the specific *content*, either semantic or qualitative, of the representation that meets it, reflecting the fact, agreed to in the last section, that a conscious representation could have any content whatever.

However, appealing to notions such as attention, interpretation, and short-term memory may seem to be just helping oneself to a handful of notions that are as opaque or problematic as the notion of consciousness itself, unless we can provide independent explanations of these dynamical notions in neuronal terms. In fact, that is precisely what the dynamical properties of recurrent neural networks allow us to do, and more besides, as I shall now try to show.

The consensus concerning information processing in artificial neural networks is that their training history slowly produces a *sculpted space* of possible representations (= possible activation patterns) at any given layer or population of neurons (such as the middle layer of the networks in Fig. 3.1*a* and *b*). Such networks, trained to discriminate or recognize instances of some range of categories, $C_1, \ldots, C_2$, slowly acquire a corresponding family of 'attractors' or 'prototype wells' variously located within the space of possible activation patterns. That sculpted space *is* the conceptual framework of that layer of neurons. Diverse sensory-layer instances of those learned perceptual categories produce activation patterns within, or close to, one or other of these 'preferred' prototype regions within the activation space of the second layer of neurons.

Purely feedforward networks can achieve quite astonishing levels of discriminatory skill, but beyond a welcome tendency to 'fill in' or 'complete' degraded or partial perceptual instances of the categories to which they have been trained, they are pretty dull and predictable fellows. (For a more detailed discussion of this intriguing feature of network function, see Churchland 1995, pp. 45–6, 107–14). However, if we add recurrent or descending pathways to the basic feedforward architecture, as in Fig. 3.1*b*, we lift ourselves into a new universe of functional and dynamical possibilities.

For example, information from the higher levels of any network – information that is the result of somewhat earlier information processing by the network – can be entered as a supplementary 'context-fixer' at the second layer of the network. This information can and does serve to 'prime' or 'prejudice' that neuronal population's collective activity in the direction of one or other of its learned perceptual categories. The network's cognitive 'attention' is now preferentially focused on one of its learned categories at the expense of the others. That is to say, the probability that that focal prototype category will be activated, given any arbitrary sensory input, has been temporarily raised, relative to all of its categorical alternatives.

Such an attentional focus is also movable, from one learned category to another, as a function of the network's unfolding activation patterns or 'frame of mind' at its higher neuronal layers. Such a network has an ongoing *control* of its topical selections from, and its conceptual interpretations of, its unfolding perceptual inputs. In particular, such a network can bring to bear, now in a selective way, the general background knowledge embodied more or less permanently in the configuration of its myriad synaptic connections.

A recurrent architecture also provides the network with a grasp of *temporal* structure as well as of spatial structures. A feedforward network gives an invariant, one-shot response to any frozen 'snapshot' pattern entered at its sensory layer. But a recurrent network can represent the changing perceptual world with a continuous *sequence* of activation patterns at its second layer, as opposed to a single, fixed pattern. Indeed, what recurrent networks typically become trained to recognize are temporally structured *causal sequences*, such as the undulating pattern of a swimming fish, the trajectory of a bouncing ball, the loping gait of a running predator, or the grammatical structure of an uttered sentence. These phenomena are represented, at the second layer, not by a prototypical *point* in its sculpted activation space (as in a feedforward network), but by a prototypical *trajectory* within that space. Thus emerges a temporally structured 'narrative' of the world unfolding in time.

The recurrent pathways also bestow on the network a welcome form of short-term memory, one that is both topic-sensitive and has a variable decay time. For the second layer is in continuous receipt of a selectively processed 'digest' of its own activity some $t$ milliseconds ago, where $t$ is the time it takes for an axonal message to travel up to the third layer and then back down again to the middle layer. Certain salient features of the middle-layer activation patterns, therefore, may survive many cycles of network activity, as a temporarily stable 'limit cycle,' before being displaced by some other limit cycle focused on some other perceptual category.

Since the network's behavior is now a continuous function of both its current perceptual inputs and its current dynamical (i.e., activational) state, we are looking at a genuine dynamical system with the capacity to display behaviors that are strictly unpredictable, short of our possessing infinitely accurate information about all of the interacting variables. That is to say, the system's future behavior will often be reliably predictable for very short distances into the future, such as a few seconds. And the gross outlines of some of its future behaviors may be reliably projected over periods of a day or a week (such as falling asleep each night and eating meals fairly regularly). But in between these two extremes, reliable prediction becomes utterly impossible. In general, the system is too mercurial to permit the prediction of absolutely specific behaviors at any point in the nonimmediate future. Thus emerges the spontaneity we expect of, and prize in, a normal stream of conscious cognitive activity.

That spontaneity is a direct reflection of the operation of the recurrent pathways at issue, which operation yields another important feature of this architectural addition. With active descending pathways, input from the sensory layer is no longer necessary for the continued activity of the network. The information arriving at the middle layer by way of the descending pathways is entirely sufficient to keep that population of neurons humming away in representational activity, privately exploring the vast landscape of activational possibilities that make up its acquired activation space. Thus is day-dreaming made possible, and night-dreaming, too, for that matter, despite the absence of concurrent perceptual stimulation. Accordingly, and on the view proposed, the dynamical behaviors characteristic of consciousness do not require perceptual inputs at all. Evidently our unfolding perceptual inputs *regulate* those dynamical behaviors profoundly, unless one happens to be insane, but perceptual inputs are not strictly necessary for consciousness.

It is further tempting to see the selective *deactivation* of those recurrent pathways – leaving only the residual feedforward pathways on duty – as the key to producing so-called delta (i.e., deep or nondreaming) sleep. For in such a selectively deactivated condition, one's attention shuts down, one's short-term memory is deactivated, and one ceases entirely to control or modulate one's own cognitive activities. Functioning recurrent pathways are utterly essential to all of these things. The feed*forward* pathways presumably remain functional even in deep sleep, because certain special perceptual inputs – such as an infant's voice or a scratching at the bedroom window – can be recognized and serve quickly to awaken one, even if those perceptual stimuli are quite faint. This is a simple job that even a feedforward network can do. Even an unconscious creature needs an alarm system, and the residual feedforward pathways provide it. But when morning breaks, the recurrent pathways come back on duty, and the peculiar dynamical profile of cognitive activities detailed above gets resurrected. You regain consciousness.

I will leave further exploration of these matters to another time, when I can better tie the story to the actual microanatomy of the brain. (A first attempt appears in Churchland 1995, pp. 208–26. That discussion also locates the explanation of consciousness in particular within the context of intertheoretic reductions in general.) You now have some sense of how some central features of consciousness might be explained in terms of the dynamical properties of neural networks with a recurrent architecture. I close by returning to Dennett, and I begin by remarking that, details aside, the functional or molar-level portrait of consciousness embodied in his multiple-drafts and fleeting-moments-of-fame metaphors is indeed another instance of what I have here been calling the dynamical-profile approach to understanding consciousness. But he painted his portrait first, so it is appropriate for me to ask if *I* may belatedly come on board. I hope to be found a worthy cognitive ally in these matters. Even so, I present myself to him with a list of needed reforms. The virtual vN machine and all of the metaphors associated with it have to go. They lead us away from the shared truth at issue, not toward it.

At one point in his book, Dennett himself registers an important doubt concerning the explanatory payoff of the virtual vN machine story.

> But still (I am sure you want to object): all this has little or nothing to do with consciousness! After all, a von Neumann machine is entirely unconscious; why should implementing it – or something like it: a Joycean machine – be any more conscious? I do have an answer: The von Neumann machine, by being wired up from the outset that way, with maximally efficient informational links, didn't have to become the object of its own elaborate perceptual systems. The workings of the Joycean machine, on the other hand, are just as 'visible' and 'audible' to it as any of the things in the external world that it is designed to perceive – for the simple reason that they have much of the same perceptual machinery focused on them. (1991, 225–6)

Dennett's answer here is strictly correct, but it doesn't count as an *explanation* of why our Joycean/virtual-vN machine rises to consciousness while the real vN machine does not. It fails because it is an instance of the 'self-perception' approach dismantled above in Section 3. Inward-looking perceptual modalities are just as problematic, where consciousness is concerned, as is any outward-looking perceptual modality. The complaint here addressed by Dennett is a telling one, but Dennett's answer won't stand scrutiny, and it represents an uncharacteristic lapse from his 'dynamical profile' story in any case.

The Dawkinsean meme story has to go also, and with it goes the idea that humans – that is, animals genetically and neuroanatomically identical with modern humans – developed or stumbled on consciousness as a purely cultural addition to our native cognitive machinery. On the contrary, we have been conscious creatures for as long as we have possessed our current neural architecture. Furthermore, the contrast between human and animal consciousness has to go as well, for nonhuman animals *share* with us the recurrent neuronal architecture at issue. Accordingly, conscious cognition has presumably been around on this planet for at least fifty million years, rather than for the several tens of thousands of years guessed by Dennett.

I do not hesitate to concede to Dennett that cultural evolution – the Hegelian unfolding that we both celebrate – has succeeded in 'raising' human consciousness profoundly. It has raised it in the sense that the *contents* of human consciousness – especially in its intellectual, political, artistic, scientific, and technological élites – have been changed dramatically. Old conceptual frameworks, in all of the domains listed, have been discarded wholesale in favor of new frameworks, frameworks that underwrite new forms of human perception and new forms of human activity. Nor do I think we are remotely done yet, in this business of cognitive self-reconstruction. Readers of my 1979 book (see especially Chapters 2 and 3) will not be surprised to hear me suggesting still that the great bulk and most dramatic increments of consciousness-raising lie in our future, not in our past.

But raising the contents of our consciousness is one thing – and, so far, a purely cultural thing. *Creating* consciousness in the first place, by contrast, was a firmly *neurobiological* thing, and that must have happened a very long time ago. For the dynamical cognitive profile that constitutes consciousness has been the possession of terrestrial creatures since at least the early Jurassic. James Joyce and John von Neumann were simply not needed.

### Note

[1] I first addressed Dennett's account of consciousness in (1995), pp. 264–9. A subsequent two-paper symposium appears as Densmore and Dennett 1999, and P. M. Churchland, 1999a.

### References

Campbell, D. (1974). Evolutionary Epistemology. In P. A. Schilpp, ed., *The Philosophy of Karl Popper*. La Salle: Open Court, 413–63.

Churchland, P. M. (1979). *Scientific Realism and the Plasticity of Mind*. Cambridge: Cambridge University Press.

Churchland, P. M. (1986). *Matter and Consciousness*, rev. ed. Cambridge, MA: MIT Press/A Bradford Book.

Churchland, P. M. (1995). *The Engine of Reason, The Seat of The Soul*. Cambridge, MA: MIT Press/A Bradford Book.

Churchland, P. M. (1999a). Densmore and Dennett on Virtual Machines and Consciousness. *Philosophy and Phenomenological Research* 59(3):747–67.

Churchland, P. M. (1999b). Review of *Reason, Regulation, and Realism. Philosophy and Phenomenological Research* 58(4).

Cottrell, G. W., and F. Tsung. (1993). Learning Simple Arithmetic Procedures. *Connection Science* 5.

Damasio, A. (1999). *The Feeling of What Happens: Body and Emotion in the Making of Consciousness.* New York: Harcourt Brace.

Dawkins, M. S. (1976). *The Selfish Gene.* Oxford: Oxford University Press.

Dawkins, M. S. (1982). *The Extended Phenotype.* San Francisco: Freeman.

Dennett, D. (1991). *Consciousness Explained.* Boston: Little, Brown and Co.

Densmore, S., and D. Dennett. (1999). The Virtues of Virtual Machines. *Philosophy and Phenomenological Research* 59(3):747–67.

Elman, J. L. (1992). Grammatical Structure and Distributed Representations, in S. Davis, ed., *Connectionism: Theory and Practice. Vancouver Studies in Cognitive Science, Vol. 3.* Oxford: Oxford University Press, 138–78.

Hooker, C. A. (1995). *Reason, Regulation, and Realism: Toward a Regulatory Systems Theory of Reason and Evolutionary Epistemology.* Albany: SUNY Press, 36–42.

Kuhn, T. (1962). *The Structure of Scientific Revolutions.* Chicago: University of Chicago Press.

Lakatos, I. (1965). Falsification and the methodology of scientific research programs. In I. Lakatos and A. Musgrave, eds., *Criticism and the Growth of Knowledge.* Cambridge: Cambridge University Press, 91–195.

Piaget, J. (1950). *Introduction a l'epistemologie genetique.* Paris: Presses Universitaires de France.

Piaget, J. (1965). *Insights and Illusions of Philosophy.* New York: Meridian Books.

Piaget, J. (1970). *Genetic Epistemology.* New York: Columbia University Press.

Popper, K. (1934). *Logik der Forschung.* [Published in English as *The Logic of Scientific Discovery.* London: Hutchison, 1980.]

Popper, K. (1972). Conjectures and Refutations. In his *Conjectures and Refutations.* London: Routledge & Kegan Paul.

Popper, K. (1979). *Objective Knowledge: An Evolutionary Approach.* Oxford: Oxford University Press.

Toulmin, S. (1972). *Human Understanding.* Princeton, NJ: Princeton University Press.

# USES OF DENNETT'S METHOD

Recall from the Introduction that the intentional stance is a stance from which we explain action in terms of the beliefs, desires and other representational states of the actor, where the explanation consists in ascribing representational states that make the action at least roughly and minimally rational, given those beliefs and desires and so on. (By 'roughly' we mean that not all the actions need be completely rational and by 'minimally' we mean minimal self-interested rationality – given what the actor wants and believes, it would have been in the actor's interest to adopt the course of action, i.e., it would have been rational for the actor to believe that that action has a reasonably good chance of getting it what it wanted.)

The intentional stance has proven to be a powerful approach in a number of fields of endeavour. Here we will examine three. Major research has been done in developmental psychology on when and how children develop the ability to assume the intentional stance to themselves and other beings. There is a general though hotly debated presumption behind a lot of this work that to adopt the intentional stance, children must acquire a 'theory of mind' – a theory that explains the behaviour they observe by reference to beliefs, desires, and other mental states of the behaver. (A common name for this theory, one mentioned in the Introduction, is 'folk psychology.') One outgrowth of this research into the child's acquisition of the intentional stance is a rich, deep-running theory of autism, one that has proven to have enormous predictive and explanatory power. The theory is that autistic children have major deficits in their ability to take up the intentional stance to themselves and others, deficits in their ability to see bodies as animated by minds. Richard Griffin and Simon Baron-Cohen explore this application of the intentional stance. Baron-Cohen has been the leading figure in this research for over two decades.

Another application of the intentional stance has been to the explanation of the behaviour, especially the noise-making and social behaviour, of animals who do not have a syntactically structured language, the nonhuman primates in particular. Two of the foremost cognitive ethologists, Robert Seyfarth and Dorothy Cheney, have used this approach with great success in their work on vervet monkeys and other animals in the wild. Their essay explores the ways in which they have used the intentional stance in their research.

Dennett's method for explaining behaviour has applications to human social behaviour, too. Since it starts from the implications of evolutionary theory for psychology, it is not compatible with the so-called standard social science model (see the Introduction). Instead, Don Ross argues, it puts a kind of economics at centre stage in the explanation of social behaviour. This is because economics properly understood is an implementation of Dennett's intentional systems theory. Dennett distinguishes this intentional stance approach from what he calls 'sub-personal cognitive psychology,' the investigation of the actual causal processes behind behaviour. ('Sub-personal' because these processes are seldom available to introspection or observation by others.) While the latter may play a role in the explanation of social behaviour, Ross argues that economics (when economic method is properly understood) is crucial to such explanations. This leads him to suggest new roles for analytic sociology and narrative history.

# 4

## The Intentional Stance: Developmental and Neurocognitive Perspectives

*RICHARD GRIFFIN AND*
*SIMON BARON-COHEN*

Nowhere in the psychological sciences has the philosophy of mind had more influence than on the child development literature on what is generally referred to as children's 'theory of mind.' Developmental journals may seem to be an unlikely place to find Brentano, Frege, and Dennett alongside descriptions of referential opacity and the principle of substitutivity, but it is not at all uncommon in this literature. While the many problems and complexities of the propositional attitude literature are still hotly debated by philosophers, and often ill understood by scientists working in this area, a great deal of empirical progress has already been made. We have Dan Dennett to thank for this extraordinary dialogue between these disciplines.

One of the reasons for Dennett's influence among developmental psychologists and other scientists is his accessible prose. He writes not only for his expert colleagues but also for those of us working on problems of the mind who haven't grown up with the language of *de re/de dicto* distinctions, notional worlds, or intensions-with-an-s. Despite his efforts, however, many confusions linger. The ascendance of cognitivism and the computational theory of mind, combined with our strong intuitions about folk psychology, has led many investigators to favourably discuss Dennett's 'intentional stance,' yet model the competence in ways akin to Fodor's language of thought, despite the apparent incompatibility of these programs. Indeed, scientists are often seen as easy targets by philosophers, who have spent years with their noses deep in these muddy issues. Dennett himself has played the role of 'philosophy police' on many an occasion, but instead of declaring the problems off limits to scientists, he invites participation and promotes informed empirical investigation.

The peer commentary following Premack and Woodruff's (1978) "Does the chimpanzee have a theory of mind?" set the stage and introduced the flavour of the debates surrounding the characterization of systems as 'mindreaders' versus 'behaviour-readers.' Dennett's (1978) commentary laid out some of the difficulties in making this distinction and offered some empirically friendly suggestions aimed at teasing apart mindreaders from behaviour-readers. A key component absent from Premack and Woodruff's experiments was a measure of false-belief attribution, and moreover, false-belief attribution in a novel situation (to rule out an explanation in terms of experienced regularities and other fodder for the behaviourist's cannon). Dennett illustrated one suggestion, suitable for young children, with a scenario in which Punch had a mistaken belief about the location of Judy. Wimmer and Perner (1983) modified the scenario slightly, and a cottage industry of experiments with young children was born.

The result most investigators found was that, before the ages of four-and-a-half, or so, children do not consistently predict the behaviour of someone by taking into account their false-belief. It was a striking finding. Variations on the task abounded, as did replications, and understanding false-belief came to be seen by many as the sine qua non of a representational theory of mind. To understand that a mind represents, one must understand that a mind can misrepresent, and that the misrepresentation (false belief) will cause the believer's behaviour. Wellman et al.'s (2001) meta-analysis of false-belief tasks underlines just how important this notion has become to the literature, as it includes 571 conditions, even in the face of the strict inclusion criteria imposed by the authors.

The extensive focus on this task is due not only to its status as the mindreading watershed but also to the fact that the subtlest experimental manipulations will often produce striking differences in young children's performances. What shouldn't be missed, however, is that understanding other minds doesn't suddenly appear to children six months prior to their fifth birthday. Adults have memories of childhood, although it is quite uncommon for those memories to be the momentous discovery that people have minds. It simply doesn't happen that way as many of our folk psychological mechanisms are already fully operational.

In this essay, we review developments in infancy research and cognitive neuroscience. We follow each selective review with a critical analysis, in an attempt to show how thinking in these fields follows or diverges from Dennett's influential intentional stance. We close by attempting to incorporate some of these findings into Dennett's larger program of explaining our kind of mind. First, however, we attempt to clarify some of the differences between the intentional stance, folk psychology, and theory of mind, as we see them.

## FOLK PSYCHOLOGY, THE INTENTIONAL STANCE, AND THEORY OF MIND

Folk psychology (FP), the intentional stance (IS), and theory of mind (ToM) are often used interchangeably. While this is most often fine for the empirical researcher, there are subtle but important differences.

(a) Theory of mind is a phrase generally limited to the animal or person's ability to represent themselves or others as having intentional, content-bearing, representational states (e.g., believing that p, or knowing that q, etc.). So we would say that a child or a chimpanzee has a theory of mind when we want to say that the child or the chimpanzee knows that others have beliefs and desires, for example, which play a causal role in behaviour.

(b) Folk psychology (also sometimes called belief-desire psychology, naïve, or intuitive psychology, or commonsense psychology) includes theory of mind, but it also includes emotions, qualitative or phenomenal states, traits, dispositions, and empirical generalizations about behaviour (e.g., "People who are overtired are generally irritable").

(c) The intentional stance is Dennett's take both on how we predict behaviour using intentional constructs (the 'craft') and on what intentional states really are. The terms belief and desire are borrowed from folk psychology but they are given a technical meaning. Dennett considers beliefs and desires logical constructs (*abstracta*) rather than theoretical posits (*illata*), which are assumed to have a physical existence. This latter notion is more akin to folk and even scientific thinking about intentional states. Thus, according to the intentional stance, beliefs and desires are not reducible to brain-states. The theory assumes that the belief-desire profile of the system is holistic, so beliefs/desires can not be attributed in isolation. Instead, new beliefs and desires are predicted from the previous belief-desire profile of the system. Moreover, the theory assumes that system under analysis functions optimally and rationally, and it is a black box theory, since the physical instantiation of these intentional states is irrelevant to the theory's predictive efficacy. In this way, the theory is normative, and shares much with game theory or decision theory. Any system whose behaviour can be predicted by the intentional stance is considered an *intentional system*.

In practice, in psychology, all three of these terms (ToM, FP, and IS) have been used interchangeably. The difference between attributing a propositional attitude to another and representing (in the brain) that attribution in the *form* of a propositional attitude is sometimes overlooked in the ToM literature, although this difference is precisely what Dennett is trying to illuminate. He calls what we actually do in folk psychology *the craft* and contrasts this with how we talk about what we do, which he calls *the ideology* (Dennett 1991). For Dennett, the IS as he has laid it out *is* the craft, and our intuitive notion of beliefs and desires as in the head somewhere is no more than false ideology. His technical spin on these terms serves to separate the intentional stance from commonsense psychology. In the two literatures we review in this essay (infancy, and the brain basis of mentalistic ascription), we hope to show how advances in cognitive science are illuminating additional aspects of the craft of folk psychology.

## THE DEVELOPMENT OF THE INTENTIONAL STANCE

Although it isn't until children are around four years old that they can predict behaviour based on a false belief (in a novel situation) (Wimmer & Perner 1983; Wellman et al. 2001), many researchers are prepared to grant much younger children a theory of mind despite this obvious shortcoming. One reason is that children are using so-called simpler mental state terms such as *want, pretend, know,* and *think,* in quite sophisticated ways, soon after they learn to speak (Barstch and Wellman 1995).

An argument more in the style of philosophy provided by Leslie (1987) is based on the two-year-old's abilities to understand the propositional attitude of pretence. Because having a theory of mind is generally thought of as being able to represent representations (qua representations), Leslie posits a meta- or M-representation system with a 'decoupler' mechanism to serve this function. In order for the child to pretend, he or she must be able to hold simultaneous representations on-line without confusing the two (e.g., the banana is a telephone and the banana is a banana). This ability, according to Leslie, involves the same distinction as that between propositional attitudes and propositional content, as it is the computation of the relation:

> agent (e.g. the child) + an attitude (e.g., pretending) + a primary representation (the object being manipulated – e.g., the phone) + secondary representation (decoupled in nature – e.g., the phone as a banana).

Two-year-old children appear to be capable of drawing pretend consequences from pretend assumptions. For instance, Harris (1993) found that two-and-a-half-year-old children can distinguish between a pretend and a real outcome from a pretend or real assumption (e.g., that chocolate would be wet/dry after having pretend/real tea poured on it). This kind of reasoning, if laid out in rules consisting of embedded conditionals (e.g., If A, then if B, then C), appears to be the same kind of reasoning necessary to pass the false-belief task (Frye, Zelazo, and Palfai 1995), which the same children won't pass for almost another two years. Moreover, these data show that young children can overcome an apparent bias to reason only about what (they think) is real in the world.

Additional evidence of an early theory of mind comes from a series of studies where eighteen-month-old children are claimed to infer the intentions and goals of an actor who fails in their attempt to carry out an action (e.g., pulling apart miniature dumbbells) (Meltzoff 1995). In these studies, children are more likely to complete the actor's unfulfilled goal than to spontaneously perform those actions; nor do the children complete the failed actions when they are performed by a machine, presumably because the children do not attribute intentions to the machine. Moreover, fourteen- to eighteen-month-old children will imitate an unfulfilled goal if the action is marked linguistically as purposeful (e.g., "Let's put this on here. There we go!") but not if it is marked as accidental (e.g., "Let's put this on here. Whoops!") (Carpenter et al. 1998).

Several recent theories of language development suggest that understanding the intentions of the speaker is a key component in word learning (Tomasello 1999; Bloom 2000). Eighteen-month-olds will not map novel words onto an object they are looking at when they hear a word, but instead map the word onto the object the *speaker* is looking at (Baldwin 1995). Additionally, eighteen-month-olds will map novel verbs ("Can you fep the ball?") onto intentional but not accidental actions, even if they have never seen the completed action. That is, if they witness an experimenter attempting to 'fep' something but failing, they infer that 'fep' refers to the action required to fulfill the actor's intended goal (Tomasello and Barton 1994).

A number of important behaviours emerge around the child's first birthday, which similarly invite an interpretation of infants as having a simple theory of mind. These include the onset of communicative gesturing (such as declarative pointing), gaze following, or social referencing. All of these come under the heading of joint or shared attention. In these situations, infants alternate their gaze between the adult's eyes and facial emotional expression and an object or event to help determine their course of action or to share information. For instance, a parent's facial expression can influence whether a twelve-month-old will cross a visual cliff (Sorce et al. 1985) or whether a ten-month old will interact with a stranger (Feinman and Lewis 1983). In all these cases, the argument is that the infant is coding the adult's mental state of attention to, or emotion about, a state of affairs.

Likewise, Repacholi and Gopnik (1997) found that when fourteen-month-old children are asked, "Can I have some food?," they will give an experimenter crackers rather than raw broccoli, despite the fact that the experimenter had just expressed interest in the broccoli (e.g., by smiling and saying "Mmm") and disgust at the crackers (e.g., by looking at the crackers, putting on a 'disgust' face, and saying "Yuk!"). Eighteen-month-olds, by contrast, will give the experimenter the broccoli. From this it seem that, by eighteen months, infants can set aside their own desire (for crackers) and recognize the adult's different desire (for broccoli).

An interesting experiment from Johnson, Slaughter, and Carey (1998) teased apart some of the potential cues that will elicit gaze monitoring in children and found that of central importance was contingent interaction. Johnson et al. found that twelve-month-old infants will reliably follow the gaze of a faceless animal-like object provided that the object reacted contingently with them. These children would also follow the gaze if the object had a face alone, but they would not follow the object's gaze if the object was faceless and did not interact contingently, even if it produced the same self-generated behaviours as in the contingent condition. Infants only a few months old interact contingently with caregivers, and become distressed when this interaction is interrupted (Field et al. 1986). Moreover, if shown a contingently interactive adult on a video monitor, infants will respond with greater positive affect than toward a noncontingent video (Hains et al. 1996). Contingent interaction seems to be one important cue the infant searches for as a sign that the object opposite them is both animate and an agent capable of seeing/attending.[1]

Fodor (1987) once quipped that young children get smarter and smarter as experimental techniques improve. Indeed. We now know that infants in the first few months of life have considerable knowledge about the properties of physical objects. For instance, they know that objects remain cohesive and bounded as they move (principle of cohesion), that their motion is continuous and that they continue to exist and move even if occluded from view (principle of continuity), and that objects effect each other only on contact (principle of contact) (Spelke and Van de Walle 1993; Baillargeon 1995). These core principles constrain reasoning about physical objects and infants show surprise when they are violated. However, the constraints of the third principle – the principle of contact – do not hold for *animate* objects.

Animate objects move in the absence of contact, as in self-initiated movement, and such movements may indeed be affected by distal events, through communication or perception for instance.

Schlottman and Surian (1999) used a launching event paradigm (Michotte 1963) to test whether infants perceive causation-at-a-distance with animate objects. They followed a method used by Leslie and Keeble (1987), who showed that six-month-olds were capable of perceiving 'contact' causality, but added the variable of *nonrigid movement* to the simple shapes which served as stimulus items in these studies. Instead of rigidly moving along a stable trajectory, these shapes elongated from squares into rectangles and back again, resulting in a 'caterpillar-like' motion. Results confirmed that, if given these cues of animacy, nine-month-olds do indeed perceive causation-at-a-distance. Other experiments have used different paradigms to test if younger infants are capable of appreciating this principle though the results are less clear (Spelke et al. 1995).

Studies with infants between three- and six-months-old show that by this age, children are able to distinguish between different kinds of motion, such as 'biological' motion and random motion (Bertenthal 1993; Rochat et al. 1997). Although an appreciation of goal-directedness wasn't looked at in these studies, Woodward (1998) claims to have shown *goal-attribution* in five-month-olds. By habituating five-month-old infants to a hand reaching for one of two objects, Woodward found that the babies looked longer when the hand reached for the object not previously obtained, regardless of its position. She concluded that the infants were not encoding the structural elements of the display (e.g., movement to the left or to the right), but were instead encoding the goal of the actor's reach. The claim is strengthened by a condition where the infants did not look longer when the hand was replaced by a metal rod. The rod condition helps to rule out an explanation in terms of a conditioned response (or at least one formed during the habituation phase). It also suggests, like the Meltzoff study, that these children will not attribute goal-directedness to objects that lack cues of animacy.

Perhaps the best evidence of goal-detection in infancy comes from a set of habituation/dishabituation studies by Gergely and colleagues (Gergely et al. 1995; Csibra et al. 1999). In these studies, computer animated circles are shown moving along various trajectories and overcoming obstacles in order to achieve a goal (e.g., to contact the other circle). In one study (Gergely et al. 1995), infants were habituated to either a ball jumping over a barrier and contacting the other ball (experimental group), or to a ball jumping along the same trajectory with the barrier to the right of both circles (control group). The barriers were removed for the test conditions and both groups were shown two conditions: one in which a ball moved in a straight line to contact the other ball (direct), and another in which the ball jumped along the same trajectory as in the habituation phase (indirect).

The experimental group looked longer at the indirect condition, despite the fact that they were habituated to the same trajectory, while the control group looked equally long at both. The authors interpret these results as showing that these infants attributed to the ball the goal of contacting the other ball. They also argue that the infants were not surprised by the direct condition because it was in complete accordance with achieving that goal, that is, it was expected. The indirect condition was surprising to the experimental group because it was not the best way of achieving the goal, indeed, it was irrational, and infants assume that goal-directed agents are rational. Those familiar with Dennett's position will note the familiar rationality assumptions introduced here. The authors see this as well, as is evident by their title "Taking the intentional stance at twelve months of age."

## PROBLEMS OF INTERPRETATION

Can a twelve-month-old infant really take the intentional stance? Before we evaluate the interpretations of some of the above experiments, we should look a bit more closely at what Dennett's stance entails. As discussed in the Introduction to this volume, Dennett provides some 'rough and ready' principles for intentional attribution that are very difficult to fit into a developmental picture as successful intentional attribution relies on many interdependent and interconnected abilities. For instance, he tells us that:

1.  A system's beliefs are those it ought to have, given its perceptual capacities, its epistemic needs, and its biography.
2.  A system's desires are those it ought to have, given its biological needs and the most practicable means of satisfying them.
3.  A system's behaviour will consist of those acts that it would be rational for an agent with those beliefs and desires to perform. (1987, p. 49)

On this picture, intentional interpretation is a package deal, with desire attribution relying on belief attribution and vice versa, all bound up with assumptions of rationality, which, again, are dependent on belief and desire attribution. Psychologists are interested in explaining all of the abilities, but the data suggest that they do not come to the child as a package, nor are they all dependant on each other. How can an infant take the intentional stance while knowing next to nothing about an agent's/system's perceptual capacities, biological/epistemic needs, and biography? In terms of understanding perceptual capacities, children have a quite uneven developmental profile, and even two- and three-year-olds are unclear about how information is obtained through various sensory modalities, even seeing (Gopnik and Graf 1988; Pratt and Bryant 1990). Knowledge of various biological functions comes later still (Keil 1992: Carey 1995), and biographies, insofar as knowledge of them is necessary for successful and unique intentional interpretation, may take a good deal of life experience and learning, and depending on the problem, may not be available even to adults.

Yet when Dennett lays out these principles he is setting the guidelines for success with various and possibly unique intentional interpretations, that is, for flexible interpretation and prediction of intentional systems with different belief-desire profiles. While the vast majority of six-year-olds can not take the intentional stance on the Republican party or the Roman Catholic church, they do pretty well with people, so we can expect the core mechanisms to be in place, with success on these other systems dependant largely on experience. But developmentalists are interested in explaining how children *develop* a belief-desire psychology. The assumption of rationality and the implementation of normativity may be central to an older child's or adult's intentional stance but psychologists are generally wary of granting these reasoning and/or conceptual abilities to preschoolers or infants. Nonetheless, as reviewed above, many psychologists would like to grant young children an understanding of 'simple mental states' such as desires, goals, intentions, attention, and perception (for a review see Johnson 2000).

### Desires, Goals, and Intentions

Philosophy tells us that desires, goals, and intentions, unlike beliefs, are neither true nor false, they are either fulfilled or unfulfilled. One cannot have a false desire, goal, or intention. Psychologists have borrowed this notion to support the claim that these states may be conceptually simpler for young children in that they don't require positing an attitude toward the truth of a proposition (or state of affairs). But philosophical accounts do not permit desires, goals, and intentions to guide actions alone because they are insufficient, in and of themselves, to carry out actions, and hence must be mediated by beliefs about the world (Bennett 1978). Thus, if we are to grant the young child a notion of desires, we'll need to supply a concept importantly analogous to belief to support the child's predictive capabilities, at least until the concept of belief becomes more adult-like, as it gradually does between two and five years of age.

Leslie's (1994) critique of Wellman's (1990) 'drive' theory of desires exemplifies the difficulty in characterizing this early competence. Wellman would like to give the infant a theory of desires without giving him or her proposition-like knowledge. He contends that an infant represents another person's internal drive toward an object without the ability to embed the object into a proposition. For instance, the infant can only represent the other person as 'wanting' an apple, say. But as Leslie points out, Wellman's attempts to subvert the full propositional attitude notion of desire has a major flaw: It is almost useless in terms of predicting behaviour. On this formulation, Wellman's infant may be able to predict that someone 'wants' an apple, but it does not allow the infant to predict what that person will do with the apple (i.e., she cannot represent the notion that the person wants to eat the apple, for instance). Leslie suggests that instead of dropping the propositional content (or state of affairs), Wellman should drop the attitude, formulating the representation as "ACTING to bring about [a state of affairs]" (p. 139), thus avoiding the referentially opaque nature of propositional attitudes. Leslie prudently leaves it open as to whether these representations are instantiated in propositional (language of thought) form.

It is unclear whether replacing WANTS with ACTS, ATTEMPTS, TRIES, or some other apparently nonmentalistic term will serve our purposes; this typically behaviourist move has seldom worked before. Leslie's amendment to Wellman's account, while it replaces desire and (putatively) its philosophical baggage, requires that the infant is capable of representing a more complex future state of affairs, or if you will, the goal of the actor. Leslie sees no problem with this and notes that a representation of a future state of affairs is also assumed in the violation-of-expectancy procedures in the physical knowledge tasks described above. However, no one argues that the infant is attributing a goal or desire to these inanimate objects (to emerge from the occluder for instance, or to come to rest on the ground after a fall). Very young children appear to have expectations about event outcomes but having an expectation is not the same thing as attributing a desire, goal, or intention to another. The important step from expectations of outcomes into the domain of psychological reasoning may lie with the attribution of causes to those events, as characterized by the difference between expecting that an agent will do such and such and attributing as causal the agent's *intention* to do such and such, for instance. But this is no small step, and while a careful use of language may help to clarify what sort of competence we are looking for, it may draw neat lines that bear little relation to the actual psychological mechanisms supporting that competence. This is always the danger when employing folk concepts in a scientific psychology.

In our everyday language, the terms desire, intention, and goal are often used interchangeably. If we are told that "someone intends to do $x$," it seems fair to paraphrase the statement as "someone has the goal of doing $x$," and vice versa. Here the terms refer to something like a plan, which we naturally take to be in the head. So if a researcher claims that an infant detects another's goals, it is natural to think that they likewise detect intentions. Put another way, it seems strained to say that someone has the goal of doing $x$ but does not intend to do $x$. Nevertheless, most infancy researchers would like to avoid this conflation, and use goal-detection to refer to the infant's ability to detect that an agent's behaviour is directed at or about an object (including other agents) or a state of affairs. Thus, because the mechanisms underlying this competence are claimed to detect aboutness relations, they are claimed to detect a basic intentionality. The same may be claimed for the cluster or joint or shared attention behaviours, as well as the instances of social referencing mentioned above.

It could certainly be argued that these attributions are not mentalistic at all, but a logical argument alone is not much use at this stage of the game. What is important is to show, empirically, what a proposed mechanism *does*. If a researcher or theorist claims that an infant represents another's goals, for instance, then it needs to be shown what the child can *do* with this representation. If, in addition, the young child's competence is best characterized by lower-level learning mechanisms, such as correlation or contingency detection, then there may be no work left for a representation of another's goals to do. In such a case, it would be the researcher who is taking the intentional stance rather than the child. (We discuss the point in more detail in the section on cognitive neuroscience.)

### Bringing Rationality into the Picture

The studies by Gergely et al. (1995) and Csibra et al. (1999) provide the best evidence of the kind of goal-attribution mentioned above, but it should be clear by now that this competence is not the intentional stance proper. To be fair, the authors know quite well that infants are not taking the intentional stance, and suggest instead that infants take a *teleological stance* (Gergely and

Csibra 1997; Keil 1994), a nonmentalistic, noncausal, precursor to the intentional stance that interprets actions as goal-directed. The authors are not prepared to grant infants knowledge of beliefs, desires, or intentions, but claim that they are capable of interpreting actions as occurring *in order to* achieve something.

The authors see rationality assumptions as a set of constraints on the evaluation of multiple alternatives.[2] These constraints are suggested to play *the very same functional role* in the teleological stance as does rationality in the intentional stance. So what role does rationality play in the intentional stance? It is a background assumption that constrains hypotheses as to how an agent will act given its belief-desire profile. Irrational agents are unpredictable from the intentional stance so the rationality assumption is, in a sense, forced on us. The assumption is quite implicit, however, and it is unlikely that there is any explicit representation of this sort when we predict behaviour.

Thus, when Gergely and Csibra consider rationality a 'property' attributed to actions (not agents), they may be forcing the notion to do more work than necessary. Constraints on reasoning in any domain are important but there are cheaper and easier ways to get them. A free constraint on multiple hypotheses (expectations may be more accurate) is the child's limited ability to represent multiple ways for A to get to B, for instance. Additional constraints on goal-directed action can also come from core principles in the domain of folk physics, for example, that agents can not pass through solid objects, that agents' motion is continuous, that agents remain bounded when moving, and so on. Even a principle akin to 'agents move in the shortest path toward their targets' need not bring in rationality and may even be learned by example. Gergely and Csibra (see also Csibra and Gergely 1998) introduce an important issue here by looking for and proposing constraints in this domain, which will no doubt differ in important ways from constraints on physical and mechanical reasoning. Although rationality assumptions may be too much too soon, the principles that the infant is using to constrain expectations of goal-directed behaviour will indeed be similar to the rationality assumptions inherent in the intentional stance, implicit as they may be.

An interesting analog between the transparency of belief and the transparency of rationality may serve to highlight the similarities and differences between these rationality assumptions. Just as beliefs only come into focus when there is a conflict or discrepancy of some sort, so, too, with rationality. Young children do quite well predicting behaviour without the concept of belief or rationality because (a) most beliefs are true, and children's knowledge of what (they think) is real in the world is an adequate substitute for the concept of belief – that is, most beliefs are shared between the interpreter and interpretee, and (b) natural selection builds (relatively) rational agents, and hence most behaviour is rational. In this way, rationality only comes into focus when a behaviour is found to be inexplicable. The belief-desire profile of the system in question is crucial, however, in that the interpreter may update this profile to make sense of the behaviour (e.g., in the case of false belief or impaired perception). If no amount of revising renders the behaviour intelligible, then the system is deemed irrational, and hence unpredictable from the intentional stance.

## Developmental Summary

Dennett has been criticized both for setting the 'mindreading' bar too high (Johnson 2000) and too low (Premack and Premack 1997). While it is true that Dennett suggested the false belief task as a measure of teasing apart first-order intentional systems from second-order intentional systems, he never suggested that it was the only evidence. Indeed, in 1983, just as the child's ToM literature was beginning, Dennett made the following prediction:

> It will turn out on further exploration that [young children] will exhibit mixed and confusing symptoms of higher-order intentionality. They will pass some higher-order tests and fail others; they will in some regards reveal themselves to be alert to third-order sophistications, while disappointing us with their failure to grasp some apparently even simpler second-order points. No crisp, 'rigorous' set of intentional hypotheses of any order will clearly be confirmed. (1983/1987, p. 255)

We took the liberty of inserting 'young children' into that passage – Dennett was actually referring to higher nonhuman animal – but the change is perfectly consistent with his program. Immediately following this passage he writes, "I expect the results of intentional interpretations ... of small children to be riddled with the sorts of gaps and foggy places that are inevitable in the interpretation of systems that are, after all, only imperfectly rational" (p. 255). We now have almost twenty years of data on the topic and Dennett's prediction has been borne out. The literature on children's early intentional interpretation is foggy indeed, but this is not due to a failure to replicate, it is due to an uncertainty about what one is committed to when introducing propositional attitudes into their characterizations of young children's abilities.

While Dennett's prediction may appear to be pessimistic, it is not at all; it simply follows from his theory. Dennett is often seen by scientists as an authority on propositional attitudes and this has led some to believe that he actually buys the classical cut. This is far from the case. Not one in the habit of sugar-coating, he writes, "The large and well-regarded literature on propositional attitudes . . . is largely a disciplinary artefact of no long-term importance whatever, except perhaps as history's most slowly unwinding unintended *reductio ad absurdum*" (1994, p. 241). His distrust of this literature, and in clean qualitative leaps in general, relates directly to a central question in our literature: When does the child first have a theory of mind? There will be no clean cut between intentional and nonintentional phenomena, and indeed, the same phenomena may be described using various levels of description. What is important is what we gain or lose in terms of prediction within these levels. This is why he invites scientists to take the intentional stance, while at the same time warning us of its pitfalls. Thus, the mindreading bar can be set as high or as low as we like, as long as we remember that "what counts as mindreading is a less important question than the question of how such an apparent mindreading competence might be organized" (Dennett 1996, p. 124).

## THE COGNITIVE NEUROSCIENTIFIC BASIS OF THE INTENTIONAL STANCE

We turn now to a brief review of the burgeoning literature on the brain basis of mental state attribution. A belief-desire psychology is not a simple process and many brain regions have been suggested to underlie the broad competence. We will concentrate only on the regions of considerable interest at present, which consist of the medial prefrontal cortex (paracingulate cortex, PCC), the superior temporal sulcus (STS), the temporal parietal junction, and the orbitofrontal-amygdala-temporal circuit. We concentrate first on the phylogenetically older substrates involved in social perception and cognition, and later on studies that look directly at theory of mind in humans.

## SOCIAL PERCEPTION AND COGNITION

### Superior Temporal Sulcus

Woodward's (1998) results with five-month-old children suggests that they are capable of encoding the goal of an actor's reach. Although Woodward doesn't appeal to this literature in the discussion of her findings, there is quite a bit of evidence from single-cell recording in monkeys that neurons in and around the superior temporal sulcus, as well as the inferior frontal cortex, are sensitive to various goal-directed reaching motions.

Perrett and colleagues have studied 'hand action' cells in the ventral areas of the STS region and have discovered several interesting response properties. For instance, many of these cells respond better to particular kinds of actions, such as reaching, grasping, picking, tearing, and so on. This responsiveness generalizes across the objects being acted on, across various visual perspectives, and across several spatiotemporal trajectories of the actions (e.g., different speeds and distances). Furthermore, the responsiveness of these neurons is greater when the actions are goal-directed (Perrett et al. 1989).

Cells in the inferior frontal cortex complement the STS cells and code both visual and motor components of these actions. These cells, called 'mirror neurons' have the interesting property of firing not only when the monkey witnesses an action on an object, but also when the monkey executes an action on that object, hence the 'mirror' rubric. Unlike the STS cells, the mirror neurons will continue to fire in the dark and during forced delays in reaching. Other cells in the STS region help to avoid a potential confusion over who is acting, firing only when another acts. These 'other' cells respond continually and can not be habituated, even after long exposure to predictable (rhythmic) actions (Emery and Perrett 2000). The STS region contains other neurons that fire preferentially to head direction and eye direction, both of which have been proposed as dedicated mechanisms in the mindreading competence (e.g., shared attention and eye direction detection; see Baron-Cohen 1995; Puce et al. 1998).

The perception of biological motion has also been attributed to regions in and around the STS. In addition to the perception of various hand actions and head and eye direction described above, movements of the entire body activate cells in this region. A series of Positron Emission Tomography (PET) and functional Magnetic Resonance Imaging (fMRI) studies found activation in posterior STS and anterior superior temporal gyrus to meaningful motions such as walking, dancing, and throwing (Bonda et al. 1996; Grossman et al. 2000). These studies used point-light displays, where lights are attached to various body parts of actors filmed in total darkness. Humans readily interpret meaningful motion from point lights alone (Johansson 1973).

These areas are dorsal and anterior to V5, the homologue of monkey V5/MT, which is specialized for the detection of motion more generally.

Damage to V5 can selectively damage the ability to perceive motion and we might expect that damage to these regions could selectively impair the recognition of biological motion. Such a case has recently been reported (Cowey and Vaina 2000). Interestingly, just the opposite has also been found: a motion-impaired patient with damage to V5 was able to interpret the point-light displays as meaningful, while at the same time unable to determine whether various objects were moving (Vaina et al. 1990; see also McLeod et al. 1996).

A potential explanation for this strange finding may come from studies on *implied motion*. Increased regional cerebral blood flow (rCBF) is found in V5 and in the STS when participants are shown still photographs of implied motion (e.g., stills of someone in the act of throwing a discus or stills of hands acting on objects) (Kourtzi and Kanwisher 2000; Senior et al. 2000). Thus, the intact STS regions may have been sufficient to interpret the point-light displays as meaningful if received in a form analogous to still-frames, despite the lack of continuous motion.

### Orbitofrontal-Amygdala-Temporal Circuit

The obitofrontal-amygdala-temporal circuit has been implicated in several models of social cognition in monkeys, apes, and humans (Brothers and Ring 1992; Baron-Cohen 1995; see Adolphs 1999a for a recent review). These areas share reciprocal feedforward and feedback connections and their proper functioning is to a large degree interdependent. Monkeys with lesions in these areas develop compulsive behaviours with objects, especially via oral examination; they present with unusual tameness, social isolation and avoidance, and appear to lose the ability to mark the emotional significance of stimuli (e.g., picking up snakes) (Kluver and Busey 1939; Myers et al. 1973). We concentrate below on the role of the amygdala and orbitofrontal/ventromedial (OFC/VM) cortices in this circuit.

The amygdala has been implicated as playing a causal role in autistic spectrum conditions (Baron-Cohen 2000). In a task requiring subjects to attribute social information (intentions) based on information from eyes alone, individuals with Asperger syndrome (a mild form of autism) perform worse than controls (Baron-Cohen et al. 1997) and an fMRI version of this task revealed significantly less amygdala activation in the individuals with Asperger syndrome (Baron-Cohen et al. 1999)

The amygdala has a well-known role in fear conditioning in animals and can trigger flight mechanisms even before many features of the stimulus are recognized (Ledoux 1996). Several recent imaging studies with normal subjects and studies with individuals with damage to the amygdala point to an important role for the amygdala in the recognition of emotional expressions, particularly fearful faces (Adolphs 1999b; Young et al. 1995). Patients with bilateral amygdala damage have a tendency to judge faces as far more 'approachable' and 'trustworthy' than do controls (Adolphs et al. 1998). Thus, the majority of research on the amygdala converges on its important role in the processing of fearful and dangerous stimuli. The amygdala may have a more general function however, in the modulation and allocation of processing resources when a stimulus is ambiguous, regardless of valence (Whalen 1999).

Complementing the amygdala, single-cell recording studies have shown that cells in the inferotemporal cortex respond preferentially to information about faces, such as identity, social status, emotional expression (Young and Yamane 1992) and, along with cells in the amygdala, are found to be active during scenes of complex social stimuli (Brothers et al. 1990).

The role of the OFC/VM regions in social cognition has been discussed extensively by Damasio (1989, 1994; Damasio and Anderson 1993), who argues that the OFC/VM aspects of the frontal lobe act as 'convergence zones' and have a special role in coordinating the marking of the emotional significance of events. This marking consists of a circuit which includes amygdala, various limbic and cortical structures, and uses the body (state of the soma) as a 'sounding board,' in effect, against which to base decision making. Patients with damage to orbital and ventromedial regions may lose the ability to use the state of the soma as a value marker for potential outcomes, resulting in the odd and often inappropriate social behaviour observed in patients with prefrontal damage.

While damage to these areas may have no effect on standard measures of intelligence, patients with OFC/VM lesions often have difficulty with planning and on reasoning tasks involving 'hunches' and social scenarios. For instance, a series of studies have shown that OFC/VM patients perform poorly on gambling tasks, where choices are determined by emotional hunches in the face of incomplete information. Normal subjects learn to maximize gains by combining statistical contingencies with the value of the payoff over time, though no explicit reasoning appears to be involved (Bechara et al. 1997). Variations on the Wason deductive reasoning task that involve familiar or social information, but not those requiring abstract reasoning, are also difficult for OF/VM patients. Correct reasoning on these tasks relies on deciphering threats, promises, and so on, against a backdrop of knowledge of social contracts. Thus, these regions may subserve what Cosmides and Tooby (1992) refer to as a 'cheater detection module';

a cognitive adaptation crucial for the maintenance of an evolutionary stable strategy of social exchange.

## THEORY OF MIND STUDIES

### Brain Injury

There have been only a handful of studies directly concerned with mental state attributions in adults with acquired brain injury. Nonetheless, some striking findings have emerged: To date, only patients with right hemisphere damage (RHD), but not the left (LHD), have shown ToM deficits (Happé et al. 1999; Stone et al. 1998; Griffin et al., in preparation).

Varley and Siegal (2000) tested an LHD severe aphasic on first-order and second-order ToM tasks and found no deficits despite the subject's almost total lack of language. Stone et al. (1998) tested LHD and bilateral orbitofrontal patients on first and second-order ToM and social faux pas tasks. Neither group had difficulty on the first-order and second-order tasks, though the bilateral orbitofrontal patients had difficulty on the social faux pas measure. Finally, Happé, Brownell, and Winner (1999), in the first direct comparison between the groups, tested both RHD and LHD patients on a series of ToM stories and cartoons. The RHD but not the LHD group were found to have a selective impairment in ToM reasoning. This result was recently replicated and extended by Griffin and colleagues, and a closer analysis revealed that RHD patients did not differ on first-order ToM attributions, but only on second-order ToM and in their ability to detect deception. Only one of these patients had damage to the orbitofrontal regions, the right amygdala, and the right temporal lobe, although she performed as well as normal age-matched controls on the ToM measures.

RHD patients have well-known difficulties in the expression and perception of emotion, difficulties interpreting nonliteral language, and difficulties using context for inferential purposes, deficits that are shared with the autistic spectrum (Brownell et al. 2000; see also Happé et al. 1999, Table 1, and Sabbagh 2000, for a longer catalogue of shared impairments). Indeed, while the developmental language delays that accompany autism were originally taken to suggest deficient LHD function, the nature of the impairments, such as deficits in prosody, social use of language, and inability to read facial expressions, is more suggestive of impairments following RHD (Prior and Bradshaw 1979). Shields et al. (1996) tested a group of children with autism and a group with semantic-pragmatic disorder on a battery of tasks sensitive to left and right hemisphere injury. Both groups performed better on the LHD battery relative to the RHD battery, leading the authors to suggest that semantic-pragmatic disorder is part of the autistic spectrum, and implicating a link with RHD dysfunction.

### Neuroimaging Studies

A series of ToM imagining studies using stories, wordless cartoons, and moving geometric shapes have found peaks of activation in many different areas, although a rough pattern is starting to emerge. Nearly all of these studies have noted selective activation in areas in and around the medial prefrontal cortex (PCC) at the border of the anterior cingulate. Whether this activation is lateralized to the left or the right may depend on whether the stimulus items are language- or visual-based, with visual-based stimuli resulting in more rightward activation, although a proper meta-analysis has yet to be done (Brunet et al. 2000; Fletcher et al. 1995; Gallagher et al. 2000; Castelli et al. 2000).

Additionally, selective activation in the temporoparietal junction (at the border of the STS) has been found in several of these studies (Baron-Cohen et al. 1999; Castelli et al. 2000; Gallagher et al. 2000). The studies on biological motion mentioned above also fall within this region (Bonda et al. 1996; Puce et al. 1998), although very few of the materials in these studies involved motion. The concept of implied motion may again be useful in interpreting these results, although Gallagher et al. take their results to indicate more, suggesting that the temporoparietal junction "is sensitive not merely to biological motion but, more generally, to stimuli which signal intentions or intentional activity."

Allison et al. (2000) suggest that the putative coding of intentions discussed by Gallagher et al. is also true for an STS cell that responds to downward flexion of the head, a sign of submission in primates. They write "such gestures are probably *intended* by the viewed monkey to signal submission, and are probably interpreted as such by the viewing monkey" (emphasis ours). There is no evidence that this cell responds to the intention to be submissive, as opposed to the downward (ventral) flexion of the head, but the seduction of discovering the 'intention' cell appears to be too much to resist.

Dennett recommends that we employ the IS to provide the ideal against which to test explanations. There is no reason to employ it, however, if a lower level strategy is more predictive and the IS description adds nothing. The characterization of neuronal cell assemblies involved in social perception such as those discussed above, are good cases where several levels of description may be useful. Dennett (1989) provides one such example from Braitenberg's (1984) discussion of the bilateral symmetry detectors common in animal vision systems. These mechanisms do detect bilateral symmetry, and a description at this level is more predictive of the features of stimulus items that will trigger their response than, say, their ability to detect *that some other organism is looking at me* (p. 109). But the existence of such a mechanism would be confusing unless it is looked at as a quick and dirty discriminatory mechanism that detects this kind of evolutionarily important data. The intentional characterization provides the ideal and an explanation of what the device is for. With this information, we can make assumptions about the cost-effectiveness of the mechanism. Moreover, a symmetry detection description, while more predictive about the parameters of the mechanism, will miss the rationale for its triggering of fight, flight, and other mechanisms. Dennett might be amused by the unabashedly intentional title of a paper on the analysis of social signals at the cell level, "Someone is looking at me, something touched me, something moved!" (Perrett et al. 1990).

## The Medial Prefrontal Cortex/Paracingulate Cortex

The medial prefrontal cortex, bordering on the anterior cingulate, has been the central region of discussion in the ToM imaging literature. This region has been activated in several studies using different materials and has been significantly more active than control conditions. Frith and Frith (1999) optimistically suggest "that a brain system dedicated to mentalising can be localized" (p. 1693) and point to the areas bordering the anterior cingulate and medial prefrontal cortex (PCC) as the locus of the mechanism that represents the mental states of self and other. They point to other imaging studies which invite similar interpretation of the PCC as the mindreading centre, such as the reporting of one's emotions, speech and response monitoring, self-generated thoughts, and the perception of pain and tickling (Lane et al. 1997; Rainville et al. 1997; Blakemore et al. 1998; Carter et al. 1998; McGuire et al. 1996; Frith and Frith 1999; see also Castelli et al. 2000, Table 4).

Frith (1996) cites Dennett's IS and immediately thereafter suggests that the distinction made between propositional attitudes and propositional content similarly applies to prefrontal and posterior cortices respectively, with the prefrontal cortices representing the attitudes and posterior cortices representing various contents. Frith contends that prefrontal cortices subserve the 'X believes that,' or the 'Y intends that' representations while the content, the Ps, Qs, and Rs, are housed in posterior, mostly temporal, cortices. The same is true for determining one's own mental states, where prefrontal cortices remain active representing 'I believe that,' while the proper content is elicited from posterior regions. This is a misreading of Dennett, who has been arguing for most of his life that propositional attitudes are not in the head.

An appeal to the non-ToM imaging literature, which is far larger, may help clarify some of the confusion. In a review of 107 PET studies reporting activation in this region, Paus and colleagues (1998) argue that task difficulty is the best predictor of paracingulate activation. This region is closely associated with the anterior cingulate, which has been implicated in lexical retrieval, semantic encoding, and monitoring of action (Posner and Dehaene 1994). Similarly, Duncan and Owen's (2000) recent review argues that this region (which they call the dorsal anterior cingulate) is recruited for diverse cognitive demands, such as response conflict, novelty, number of elements and time delays, and perceptual difficulty. They suggest that this region has a specialized function: In concert with mid-dorsolateral and mid-ventrolateral cortex, it is specialized for the solution of diverse cognitive problems, that is, it is specialized for hard problems. Activity in this region increases when errors due to response competition are likely (Carter et al. 1998).

With this in mind, we can see where Frith's analogy between propositional attitudes and propositional content arises. The tasks cited above involve the inhibition and monitoring of competing elements and hence elicit these regions in the same way that tasks in many domains other than ToM elicit similar regions. The PCC remains active and serves to elicit or inhibit competing responses, or as it were, competing contents. It is a loose analogy, to be sure, and perhaps a misleading one. If the PCC is activated for the reasons described above we should not see this activation on simple or well-rehearsed ToM scenarios. This is an empirical question.

The neuroimaging and adult lesion literature tends to lack a developmental perspective. It is one thing to learn a skill and another thing to perform that skill after it is well learned. The fact that our faculty of folk psychology is so well rehearsed should lead us to expect that much of it becomes automatized, at least insofar as the causal stories we tell about everyday behaviour (e.g., "He brought his umbrella because he thought it was going to rain"[3]). Hence the multi-step tasking characteristic of the frontal lobes and the various task demands mediated by the PCC may not be necessary in simple or well-rehearsed ToM reasoning, although these regions will be quite important in the development and proper functioning of the ability to make more difficult mental state attribution tasks. It is also possible that some of these regions are biological adaptations for complex social problems and have been co-opted for novel problems, although this literature can not speak directly to these questions. Finally, it is important to note that no coherent patient ever loses the ability to supply mental state descriptions, even if their damage is to MPFC/PCC, although their facility with determining the reasons and causes of behaviour may be affected by damage to a number of substrates underlying our folk psychology. The nature of the deficit will depend not only on the functional role of the damaged substrate(s) but also on the task demands.

There are several other interesting threads in this literature, such as the activation of the right middle frontal gyrus and precuneus in imaging studies on both metaphor comprehension and ToM, suggesting possible shared substrates for alternative readings and weak associations, which may explain why RHD patients have trouble with nonliteral speech and ToM (Bottini et al. 1994; Brownell et al. 2000). Moreover, bilateral temporal pole activation has been found in ToM studies and in studies on sentence and narrative comprehension, pointing to a potential story-telling component in these tasks (Happé et al., in preparation; for more on the brain and ToM, see Baron-Cohen et al. 2000). The information processing biases of various brain regions are becoming clearer almost daily and a picture of the brain's role in parsing the social world and constructing mentalistic narratives as a tool for prediction and explanation is beginning to emerge.

### Cognitive Neuroscience Summary

Although we have interspersed commentary and criticism throughout the above section, there are a few other points that may serve to highlight the differences between the empirical research in this area and the IS. The main tension lies with concerns about reducing mental states to brain-states, specifically regarding claims about cause. Many in philosophy, Dennett included, subscribe to a form of externalism, according to which contentful states are seen as relational properties, and are identified by reference to entities outside the brain. Thus, if content ascriptions are extrinsically relational, then they can not refer directly to the local, causal, nexus in the brain. The features of the cause must be local to the causal interaction. We treat the mind as a semantic engine, yet when we look at the brain all we see is a syntactic engine, where the shape and orthography of neurons and neurochemicals are intrinsically causal, and it's hard to see how to get semantics out of syntax.

A reductionist sees semantics as reducible to the brain's syntax, whereas a nonreductionist, such as Dennett, sees them as different levels of description. Dennett does not eschew representational talk; on the contrary, he invites it, provided that we don't treat representational states as brain-states. These different levels usually describe different phenomena, and one should be abandoned in favour of another only if one proves more successful at describing/predicting the same phenomenon. Thus, representational talk is fine if it is seen in nonreductive, functional terms.[4]

## BIOLOGICAL MECHANISMS AND CULTURE

In this essay, we have concentrated largely on phylogenetically older abilities that underlie the intentional stance proper. We have paid little attention to a central feature of the IS and of folk psychology more broadly – language. While Dennett considers the intentional stance the craft of folk psychology, there is much more to the craft than laid out in his rough and ready principles of intentional attribution, as we hope to have shown. Chimpanzees and other primates navigate their complex social landscapes quite impressively, despite the absence of a generative language ability, and we can expect to share many of the mechanisms that allow for this prowess. Their absence of language, however, and their inability to trade reasons and causal stories about behaviour severely limits their predictive and explanatory capabilities.

Our culture of story-telling allows us to anchor what Dennett calls "free-floating rationales." Free-floating rationales are reasons for behaviours that are not explicitly represented in the organism but implicit when looking at the design of the larger system. For instance, while we can see the rationale for a piper plover's feigning of a broken wing, the piper plover can not. There are reasons not only for the broad behaviour but also for the functional design of the mechanisms that carry out the behaviour. Dennett (1996) wishes to explain not only how we developed the ability to see these reasons, but how they came to be "captured and articulated in some of the minds that evolved," so that they become the agent's *own* reasons.

Dennett doesn't expect that a novel, species-specific, mental organ is responsible for our ability to see these rationales or to detect higher-order intentional patterns. Instead, he looks for a more parsimonious route and stresses the role of culture in anchoring these rationales, both within and outside the head. His view is a combination of hardcore evolutionary psychology along the lines of Cosmides and Tooby (1995, 1997) and socio-culturalism along the lines of Vygotsky (1979), positions that are often seen as diametrically opposed. For Dennett, intentionality is not specific to humans nor is it the mark of the mental, but it already exists in organisms built by natural selection to detect and exploit their various niches. In turn, natural selection builds systems that detect these (already intentional) systems, such as bilateral symmetry detectors ("someone is looking at me") or the neuronal ensembles that pick up on eye direction, head direction, goal-directed reaching, and emotional expressions in relation to objects or events in the world (social referencing).

We may share the mechanisms mentioned above with our primate cousins, but for them and for infants, the rationales for these mechanisms are free-floating and invisible. The Vygotskyan flavour of Dennett's view has to do with an outside-in move in the composition, revision, and endorsement of the reasons for our behaviour. This can be put in terms of the notion of 'memes' (this term was introduced in the Introduction). The memes of folk psychology exist in the cultures into which we are born, and our biological constitution renders us the perfect hosts for their instantiation and dissemination. The same is true for the memes of science, some of which are replacing the folk memes, although we are less suitable hosts for these in that we were not designed to break up the world in many of the ways illuminated by science. The process of composition, revision, and endorsement is dynamic, and exists between individuals, the memes of their culture and time, and the state of the world. In this way, the rationales for even our own behaviour – for example, that it is guided by our own goals and intentions – moves from the outside-in.

Dennett sees the pressures of communication in our species as forcing us into declaring categories ("Are you going to fish or cut bait?") and in turn, creating the illusion of more definition of content than actually exists (see also McFarland 1989). These declarations are born from a tangled, competing web of neural circuitry, but the victorious declarations serve to convince us that our behavioural tendencies are controlled by explicitly represented goals – or intentions. Dennett calls this a form of *approximating confabulation* – carving nature in places where there are no salient joints – and compares it to checking off an answer in a poorly designed multiple-choice exam. If "none of the above" is not an option, we're forced to settle for the nearest miss. In this way, representations of intentions enter in a backhanded way.

Almost immediately after children begin talking, they create narratives of their actions (e.g., "now I go up," "now I sit here"), no doubt creating the illusion of clear-cut intentions, but these narratives also serve to change their cognitive and intentional profiles. They quickly develop a list of options and reasons to justify their own behaviours and to predict what others will do. By the time they leave preschool, they are quite adept folk psychologists indeed. Exhaustively charting the many changes between the detection of biological motion in infancy and the ability to tell socially respectable causal stories of behaviour in primary school has occupied lifetimes of research and will occupy many more. While many important details are still unknown, the bigger picture is starting to come into focus.

Folk psychology is intuitive but the intentional stance, despite the many similarities to FP, is not. It is difficult for many to accept the notion that beliefs and desires are not reducible to brain-states, that is, that they are not in the head. It is less difficult to accept the fact that it is beneficial to abstract away from the messy and often irrelevant details of a complex system when attempting to predict and explain its behaviour. This is what science attempts to achieve and this is why Dennett invites science to take the intentional stance. He polices his own theory, however, and is the master of what he calls "killjoy" hypotheses that deflate the intuitive intentional characterization with lower-level explanations. Dennett is not sending mixed messages, he is simply promoting good science. Dennett is a champion of science, although he is well aware of many of the potential minefields that philosophy has charted, such as reducing meaning to the syntax of the brain, a particularly troubling problem for those of us who freely talk about representation. Yet, instead of declaring the field impassable, like many in philosophy, Dennett is handing out maps of how to navigate this potentially treacherous course.

### Acknowledgments

The authors were funded by an MRC Program Grant during the period of this work. The first author was additionally funded by a fellowship from the Cambridge Overseas Trust. We thank Chris Viger, Chris Westbury, and Chris Ashwin for helpful comments on an earlier draft.

### Notes

[1.] Hood (1998) has shown that infants as young as five months old use another's eye direction alone to direct their attention.

[2.] It is not entirely clear what role rationality plays for the Gergely and Csibra model. Rationality, to them, is a "core inferential principle (the principle of rationality)," a "property" that is attributed to actions, and a constraint on evaluation of multiple alternatives (1997, pp. 223–32).

[3.]Moreover, it is quite doubtful that the brain follows the putatively important philosophical distinction between the following explanations: "He *wants* to go to the bathroom" and "He *has* to go to the bathroom." That is, we should not expect the first of these explanations to be supported by the ToM substrates and the latter to be supported by non-ToM substrates.

[4.]An example may help to clarify how functional talk is not causal talk. A physicist would say that heating a gas causes it to expand, and could provide laws that would make this prediction. A biologist would say that heating a mammal causes it to sweat, and that the *function* of sweating is to keep the animal's temperature constant. The physicist would never say that the function of the gas expanding was to keep its temperature constant, even though that is precisely what happens. Thus, functions are effects, not causes, and can not be seen from the physical stance alone. A claim such as "the heart pumps *in order to* circulate the blood" is teleological, not causal, because effects do not bring about their causes.

## References

Adolphs, R., D. Tranel, and A. R. Damasio. (1998). The Human Amygdala in Social Judgment. *Nature* 393(6684):470–4.

Adolphs, R. (1999a). Social Cognition and the Human Brain. *Trends in Cognitive Science* 3:469–79.

Adolphs, R., D. Tranel, S. Hamann, A. W. Young, A. J. Calder, E. A. Phelps, A. Anderson, G. P. Lee, and A. R. Damasio. (1999b). Recognition of Facial Emotion in Nine Individuals with Bilateral Amygdala Damage. *Neuropsychologia* 37(10):1111–17.

Allison, T., A. Puce, and G. McCarthy. (2000). Social Perception from Visual Cues: Role of the STS Region. *Trends in Cognitive Sciences* 4(7):267–78.

Astington, J. W., P. L. Harris, and D. R. E. Olson. (1988). *Developing Theories of Mind*. New York: Cambridge University Press.

Baillargeon, R. (1993). The Object Concept Revisited: New Directions in the Investigation of Infants' Physical Knowledge. In C. E. Granrud, ed., *Visual Perception and Cognition in Infancy, Carnegie Mellon Symposia on Cognition, Vol. 23*. Hillsdale, NJ: Erlbaum, 265–315.

Baillargeon, R. (1995). Physical Reasoning in Infancy. In M. S. Gazzaniga, ed., *The Cognitive Neurosciences*. Cambridge, MA: MIT Press.

Baldwin, D. (1995). Understanding the Link between Joint Attention and Language. In C. Moore and P. Dunham, eds., *Joint Attention: Its Origin and Role in Development*. Hillsdale, NJ: Erlbaum, 131–58.

Baron-Cohen, S., H. Tager-Flusberg, and D. Cohen, eds. (1993). *Understanding Other Minds: Perspectives from Autism*. Oxford: Oxford University Press.

Baron-Cohen, S., H. Ring, J. Moriarty, B. Schmitz, D. Costa, and P. Ell. (1994). Recognition of Mental State Terms. Clinical Findings in Children with Autism and a Functional Neuroimaging Study of Normal Adults. *British Journal of Psychiatry* 165(5):640–9.

Baron-Cohen, S. (1994). How to Build a Baby that Can Read Minds: Cognitive Mechanisms in Mindreading. *Cahiers de Psychologie Cognitive/Current Psychology of Cognition* 13:513–52.

Baron-Cohen, S. (1995). *Mindblindness: An Essay on Autism and Theory of Mind.* Cambridge, MA: MIT Press.

Baron-Cohen, S., T. Jolliffe, C. Mortimore, and M. Robertson. (1997). Another Advanced Test of Theory of Mind: Evidence from Very High Functioning Adults with Autism or Asperger Syndrome. *Journal of Child Psychological Psychiatry* 38(7):813–22.

Baron-Cohen, S., H. Ring, S. Wheelwright, E. Bullmore, M. Brammer, A.Simmons, and S. Williams. (1999). Social Intelligence in the Normal and Autistic Brain: An fMRI Study. *European Journal of Neuroscience* 11:1891–8.

Baron-Cohen, S., H. Tager-Flusberg, and D. Cohen, eds. (2000). *Understanding Other Minds: Perspectives from Developmental Cognitive Neuroscience.* Oxford: Oxford University Press.

Baron-Cohen, S. (2000). The Cognitive Neuroscience of Autism: Implications for the Evolution of the Male Brain. In M. Gazzaniga, ed., *The Cognitive Neurosciences, 2nd ed.* Cambridge, MA: MIT Press.

Bartsch, K., and H. M. Wellman. (1995). *Children Talk about the Mind.* New York: Oxford University Press.

Bechara, A., H. Damasio, D. Tranel, and A. R. Damasio. (1997). Deciding Advantageously before Knowing the Advantageous Strategy. *Science* 275(5304): 1293–94.

Beeman, M., and C. Chiarello. (1998). *Right Hemisphere Language Comprehension: Perspectives from Cognitive Neuroscience.* Mahwah, NJ: Lawrence Erlbaum.

Bennett, J. (1978). Some Remarks about Concepts. *Behavioural and Brain Sciences* 1:557–60.

Bertenthal, B., ed. (1993). *Infants' Perception of Biomechanical Motions: Intrinsic Image and Knowledge-Based Constraints.* Hillsdale, NJ: Erlbaum.

Blakemore, S. J., D. M. Wolpert, and C. D. Frith. (1998). Central Cancellation of self-produced Tickle Sensation. *Nature Neuroscience* 1(7):635–40.

Bloom, P. (2000). *How Children Learn the Meaning of Words.* Cambridge, MA: MIT Press.

Bonda, E., M. Petrides, D. Ostry, and A. Evans. (1996). Specific Involvement of Human Parietal Systems and the Amygdala in the Perception of Biological Motion. *Journal of Neuroscience* 15:3737–44.

Bottini, G., R. Corcoran, R. Sterzi, E. Paulesu, P. Schenone, P. Scarpa, R. S. Frackowiak, and C. D. Frith. (1994). The Role of the Right Hemisphere in the Interpretation of Figurative Aspects of Language: A Positron Emission Tomography Activation Study. *Brain* 117:1241–53.

Braitenberg, V. (1984). *Vehicles: Experiments in Synthetic Psychology.* Cambridge, MA: MIT Press.

Brothers, L., B. Ring, and A. Kling. (1990). Responses of Neurons in the Macaque Amygdala to Complex Social Stimuli. *Behavioural Brain Research* 41:199–213.

Brothers, L., and B. Ring. (1992). A Neuroethological Framework for the Representation of Minds. *Journal of Cognitive Neuroscience* 4(2):107–18.

Brownell, H., H. Gardner, P. Prather, and G. Martino. (1995). Language, Communication, and the Right Hemisphere. In H. S. Kirshner, ed., *Handbook of Neurological Speech and Language Disorders, Vol. 33*. New York: Marcel Dekker, 325–49.

Brownell, H., R. Griffin, E. Winner, O. Friedman, and F. Happé. (2000). Cerebral Lateralization and Theory of Mind. In S. Baron-Cohen, H. Tager-Flusberg, and D. Cohen, eds., *Understanding Other Minds: Perspectives from Developmental Cognitive Neuroscience*. Oxford: Oxford University Press, 306–33.

Brunet, E., Y. Sarfatil, M.-C. Hardy-Baylé, and J. Decety. (2000). A PET Investigation of the Attribution of Intentions with a Nonverbal Task. *NeuroImage* 11(2):157–66.

Carey, S. (1995). On the Origin of Causal Understanding. In D. Sperber and D. Premack, eds., *Causal Cognition: A Multidisciplinary Debate. Symposia of the Fyssen Foundation*. New York: Clarendon Press/Oxford University Press, 268–308.

Carpenter, M., N. Akhtar, and M. Tomasello. (1998). Fourteen- Through 18-Month-Old Infants Differentially Imitate Intentional and Accidental Actions. *Infant Behaviour and Development* 21(2):315–30.

Carter, C. S., T. S. Braver, D. M. Barch, M. M. Botvinick, D. Noll, and J. D. Cohen. (1998). Anterior Cingulate Cortex, Error Detection and the Online Monitoring of Performance. *Science* 280:747–9.

Castelli, F., F. Happé, U. Frith, and C. Frith. (2000). Movement and Mind: A Functional Imaging Study of Perception and Interpretation of Complex Intentional Movement Patterns. *NeuroImage* 12:314–25.

Cosmides, L., and J. Tooby. (1992). Cognitive Adaptations for Social Exchange. In J. H. Barkow and L. Cosmides, eds., *The Adapted Mind: Evolutionary Psychology and the Generation of Culture*. New York: Oxford University Press, 163–228.

Cosmides, L., and J. Tooby. (1995). From Function to Structure: The Role of Evolutionary Biology and Computational Theories in Cognitive Neuroscience. In M. S. Gazzaniga, ed., *The Cognitive Neurosciences*. Cambridge: MIT Press, 1199–210.

Cosmides, L., and J. Tooby. (1997). Dissecting the Computational Architecture of Social Inference Mechanisms. *Ciba Foundation Symposium* 208:132–56; discussion 156–61.

Cowey, A., and L. Vaina. (2000). Blindness to Form from Motion Despite Intact Static Form Perception and Motion Detection. *Neuropsychologia* 38(5):566–78.

Csibra, G., and G. Gergely. (1998). The Teleological Origins of Mentalistic Action Explanations: A Developmental Hypothesis. *Developmental Science* 1:255–9.

Csibra, G., G. Gergely, S. Biro, O. Koos, and M. Brockbanck. (1999). Goal Attribution without Agency Cues: The Perception of 'Pure Reason' in Infancy. *Cognition* 72:253–84.

Damasio, A. (1989). The Brain Binds Entities and Events by Multiregional Activation from Convergence Zones. *Neural Computation* 1:123–32.

Damasio, A. R., and S. W. Anderson. (1993). The Frontal Lobes. In K. M. Heilman and E. Valenstein, eds., *Clinical Neuropsychology, 3rd ed.* New York: Oxford University Press, 409–60.

Damasio, A. R. (1994). *Descartes' Error: Emotion, Reason, and the Human Brain.* New York: Grosset/Putnam.

Davidson, D. (1980). *Essays on Actions and Events.* Oxford: Clarendon Press.

Decety, J., and J. Grezes. (1999). Neural Mechanisms Subserving the Perception of Human Actions. *Trends in Cognitive Science* 3(5):172–8.

Dennett, D. C. (1978). Beliefs about Beliefs. *Behavioural and Brain Sciences* 1:568–70.

Dennett, D. C. (1987). *The Intentional Stance.* Cambridge, MA: MIT Press.

Dennett, D. C. (1989). Cognitive Ethology: Hunting for Bargains or a Wild Goose Chase? In A. Montefiore and D. Noble, eds., *Goals, No-goals, and Own Goals: A Debate on Goal-directed and Intentional Behaviour.* London: Unwin Hyman.

Dennett, D. C. (1991). Two Contrasts: Folk Craft Versus Folk Science, and Belief Versus Opinion. In J. Greenwood, ed., *The Future of Folk Psychology: Intentionality and Cognitive Science.* Cambridge: Cambridge University Press, 135–48.

Dennett, D. C. (1994). Dennett, Daniel C. In S. Guttenplan, ed., *A Companion to the Philosophy of Mind.* Oxford: Blackwells, 236–44.

Dennett, D. C. (1996). *Kinds of Minds: Toward an Understanding of Consciousness.* New York: Basic Books.

Dennett, D. C. (1998). *Brainchildren: Essays on Designing Minds.* Cambridge, MA: MIT Press.

Duncan, J., and A. Owen. (2000). Common Regions of the Human Frontal Lobe Recruited by Diverse Cognitive Demands. *Trends in Neurosciences* 23:475–83.

Elman, J. L., E. Bates, M. H. Johnson, A. Karmiloff-Smith, D. Parisi, and K. Plunkett. (1996). *Rethinking Innateness: Connectionism in a Developmental Framework.* Cambridge, MA: MIT Press.

Emery, N. J., and D. I. Perrett. (2000). How Can Studies of the Monkey Brain Help Us Understand 'Theory of Mind' and Autism in Humans? In S. Baron-Cohen, H. Tager-Flusberg, and D. Cohen, eds., *Understanding Other Minds: Perspectives from Developmental Cognitive Neuroscience.* Oxford: Oxford University Press, 274–305.

Feinman, S., and M. Lewis. (1983). Social Referencing at 10 Months: A Second Order Effect on Infants' Responses to Strangers. *Child Development* 54:878–87.

Field, T., N. Vega-Lahar, F. Scafidi, and S. Goldstein. (1986). Effects of Maternal Unavailability on Motion-infant Interactions. *Infant Behaviour and Development* 9:473–8.

Fletcher, P. C., F. Happé, U. Frith, S. C. Baker, D. J. Dolan, R. S. J. Frackowiak, and C. D. Frith. (1995). Other Minds in the Brain: A Functional Imaging Study of 'Theory of Mind' in Story Comprehension. *Cognition* 57(2):109–28.

Fodor, J. A. (1976). *The Language of Thought.* Brighton, Sussex: Harvester.

Fodor, J. (1987). *Psychosemantics: The Problem of Meaning in the Philosophy of Mind.* Cambridge, MA: MIT Press.

Frith, C. (1996). Brain Mechanisms for 'Having a Theory of Mind.' *Journal of Psychopharmacology* 10(1):9–15.

Frith, C., and U. Frith. (1999). Interacting Minds: A Biological Basis. *Science* 286:1692–5.

Frye, D., and C. Moore. (1991). *Children's Theories of Mind.* Hillsdale, NJ: Lawrence Erlbaum.

Frye, D., P. D. Zelazo, and T. Palfai. (1995). Theory of Mind and Rule-based Reasoning. *Cognitive Development* 10(4):483–527.

Gallagher, H. L., F. Happé, N. Brunswick, P. C. Fletcher, U. Frith, and C. D. Frith. (2000). Reading the Mind in Cartoons and Stories: An fMRI Study of 'Theory of the Mind' in Verbal and Nonverbal Tasks. *Neuropsychologia* 38(1): 11–21.

Gergely, G., Z. Nadasdy, C. Csibra, and S. Biro. (1995). Taking the Intentional Stance at 12 Months of Age. *Cognition* 56:165–93.

Gergely, G., and G. Csibra. (1997). Teleological Reasoning in Infancy: The Infant's Naive Theory of Rational Action. A Reply to Premack and Premack. *Cognition* 63(2):227–33.

Gopnik, A., and P. Graf. (1988). Knowing How You Know: Young Children's Ability to Identify and Remember the Sources of their Beliefs. *Child Development* 59:1366–71.

Griffin, R., H. Brownell, O. Friedman, E. Winner, J. Ween, and F. Happé. (in preparation). Theory of Mind and the Right Cerebral Hemisphere: Issues of Modularity, Executive Function, and Central Coherence.

Grossman, E., M. Donnelly, R. Price, D. Pickens, V. Morgan, G. Neighbor, and R. Blake. (2000). Brain Areas Involved in Perception of Biological Motion. *Journal of Cognitive Neuroscience* 12:711–20.

Hains, S. M. J., and D. W. Muir. (1996). Effects of Stimulus Contingency in Infant-Adult Interactions. *Infant Behaviour and Development* 19(1):49–61.

Happé, F., H. Brownell, and E. Winner. (1999). Acquired 'theory of mind' impairments following stroke. *Cognition* 70(3):211–240.

Happé, F., H. L. Gallagher, N. Brunswick, P. Fletcher, U. Frith, and C. Frith. (in preparation). Brain Activity Associated with Extracting the Meaning from Verbal and Non-verbal Narratives.

Harris, P. (1993). Pretending and Planning. In S. Baron-Cohen, H. Tager-Flusberg, and D. Cohen, eds., *Understanding Other Minds: Perspectives from Autism.* Oxford: Oxford University Press, 228–46.

Heider, F., and M. Simmel. (1944). An Experimental Study of Apparent Behaviour. *American Journal of Psychology* 57:243–59.

Hood, B. M., J. D. Willen, and J. Driver. (1998). Adult's Eyes Trigger Shifts of Visual Attention in Human Infants. *Psychological Science* 9(2):131–4.

Johansson, G. (1973). Visual Perception of Biological Motion and a Model of its Analysis. *Perception and Psychophysics* 14:202–11.

Johnson, S., V. Slaughter, and S. Carey. (1998). Whose Gaze Will Infants Follow? The Elicitation of Gaze-Following in 12-Month-Olds. *Developmental Science* 1(2):233–8.

Johnson, S. (2000). The Recognition of Mentalistic Agents in Infancy. *Trends in Cognitive Sciences* 4:22–8.

Karmiloff-Smith, A. (1992). *Beyond Modularity: A Developmental Perspective on Cognitive Science*. Cambridge, MA: MIT Press.

Keil, F. C. (1992). The Origins of an Autonomous Biology. In M. R. Gunnar and M. Maratsos, eds., *Modularity and Constraints in Language and Cognition*. The Minnesota Symposia on Child Psychology 25. Hillsdale, NJ: Lawrence Erlbaum, 103–37.

Keil, F. C. (1994). The Birth and Nurturance of Concepts by Domains: The Origins of Concepts of Living Things. In L. A. Hirschfeld and S. A. Gelman, eds., *Mapping the Mind: Domain Specificity in Cognition and Culture*. New York: Cambridge University Press, 234–54.

Kluver, H., and P. Bucy. (1939). Preliminary Analysis of Function of the Temporal Lobe in Monkeys. *Archives of Neurology* 42:979–1000.

Kourtzi, Z., and N. Kanwisher. (2000). Activation in Human MT/MST by Static Images with Implied Motion. *Journal of Cognitive Neuroscience* 12:48–55.

Lane, R. D., G. R. Fink, P. M. L. Chau, and R. J. Dolan. (1997). Neural Activation during Selective Attention to Subjective Emotional Responses. *Neuroreport: An International Journal for the Rapid Communication of Research in Neuroscience* 8(18):3969–72.

Ledoux, J. E. (1996). *The Emotional Brain: The Mysterious Underpinnings of Emotional Life*. New York: Simon and Schuster.

Legerstee, M. (1994). Patterns of 4-Month-Old Responses to Hidden Silent and Sounding People and Objects. *Early Development and Parenting* 3(2):71–80.

Leslie, A. M. (1987). Pretence and Representation: The Origins of 'Theory of Mind.' *Psychological Review* 94:412–26.

Leslie, A. M., and S. Keeble. (1987). Do Six-Month-Old Infants Perceive Causality? *Cognition* 25(3):265–88.

Leslie, A. (1994). ToMM, ToBy, and Agency: Core Architecture and Domain Specificity. In L. Hirschfied and S. Gelman, eds., *Mapping the Mind: Domain Specificity in Cognition and Culture*. New York: Cambridge University Press, 119–48.

McFarland, D. (1989). Goals, No-goals, Own Goals. In A. Montefiore and D. Noble, eds., *Goals, No-goals, Own Goals: A Debate on Goal-Directed and Intentional Behaviour*. London: Unwin Hyman.

McGuire, P. K., D. A. Silbersweig, and C. D. Frith. (1996). Functional Neuroanatomy of Verbal Self-monitoring. *Brain* 119(3):907–17.

McLeod, P., W. Dittrich, J. Driver, D. Perrett, and J. Zihl. (1996). Preserved and Impaired Detection of Structure from Motion by a 'Motion-Blind' Patient. *Visual Cognition* 3(4):363–91.

Meltzoff, A. (1995). Understanding the Intentions of Others: Re-enactment of Intended Acts by 18-Month-Old Children. *Developmental Psychology* 31:838–50.

Michotte, A. (1963). *The Perception of Causality*. Andover: Methuen.

Myers, R. E., C. Swett, and M. Miller. (1973). Loss of Social Group Affinity following Prefrontal Lesions in Free-ranging Macaques. *Brain Research* 64:257–69.

Paus, T., L. Koski, Z. Caramanos, and C. Westbury. (1998). Regional Differences in the Effects of Task Difficulty and Motor Output on Blood Flow Response in the Human Anterior Cingulate Cortex: A Review of 107 PET Activation Studies. *Neuroreport: An International Journal for the Rapid Communication of Research in Neuroscience* 9(9):R37–R47.

Perrett, D. I., M. H. Harries, R. Bevan, S. Thomas, P. J. Benson, A. J. Mistlin, A. J. Chitty, J. K. Hietanen, and J. E. Ortega. (1989). Frameworks of Analysis for the Neural Representation of Animate Objects and Actions. *Journal of Experimental Biology* 146:87–114.

Perrett, D., M. Harries, A. Mistlin, J. Hietanen, P. Benson, R. Bevan, S. Thomas, M. Oram, J. Ortega, and K. Brierley. (1990). Social Signals Analysed at the Single Cell Level: Someone is Looking at Me, Something Touched Me, Something Moved! *International Journal of Comparative Psychology* 4: 25–55.

Posner, M. I., and S. Dehaene. (1994). Attentional Networks. *Trends in Neurosciences* 17(2):75–9.

Pratt, C., and P. Bryant. (1990). Young Children Understand that Looking Leads to Knowing (So Long As They Are Looking Into a Single Barrel). *Child Development* 61:973–83.

Premack, D., and G. Woodruff. (1978). Does the Chimpanzee Have a Theory of Mind? *Behavioral and Brain Sciences* 1:515–26.

Premack, D. (1988). How to Tell Mae West from a Crocodile. *Behavioral and Brain Sciences* 11(3):522–5.

Premack, D. (1990). The Infant's Theory of Self-propelled Objects. *Cognition* 36(1):1–16.

Premack, D., and A. J. Premack. (1995). Intention as Psychological Cause. In D. Sperber, D. Premack, and A. Premack, eds., *Causal Cognition: A Multidisciplinary Debate*. Oxford: Clarendon Press, 185–99.

Premack, D., and A. Premack. (1997). Motor Competence as Integral to Attribution of Goal. *Cognition* 63:235–42.

Prior, M., and J. Bradshaw. (1979). Hemispheric Functioning in Autistic Children. *Cortex* 15:73–81.

Puce, A., T. Allison, S. Bentin, J. C. Gore, and G. McCarthy. (1998). Temporal Cortex Activation in Humans Viewing Eye and Mouth Movements. *Journal of Neuroscience* 18:2188–99.

Rainville, P., G. H. Duncan, D. D. Price, B. Carrier, and M. C. Bushnell. (1997). Pain Affect Encoded in Human Anterior Cingulate But Not Somatosensory Cortex. *Science* 277(5328):968–71.

Repacholi, B. M., and A. Gopnik. (1997). Early Reasoning about Desires: Evidence from 14-and 18-Month-Olds. *Developmental Psychology* 33:12–21.

Rochat, P., R. Morgan, and M. Carpenter. (1997). Young Infants' Sensitivity to Movement Information Specifying Social Causality. *Cognitive Development* 12:537–61.

Sabbagh, M. (2000). Communicative Intentions and Language: Evidence from Right-Hemisphere Damage and Autism. *Brain and Language* 70(1):29–69.

Schlottmann, A., and L. Surian. (1999). Do 9-Month-Olds Perceive Causation-at-a-Distance? *Perception* 28(9):1105–13.

Senior, C., J. Barnes, V. Giampietro, A. Simmons, E. T. Bullmore, M. Brammer, and A. S. David. (2000). The Functional Neuroanatomy of Implicit-Motion Perception or 'Representational Momentum.' *Current Biology* 10(1):16–22.

Shields, J., R. Varley, P. Broks, and A. Simpson. (1996). Hemispheric Function in Developmental Language Disorders and High-level Autism. *Developmental Medicine and Child Neurology* 38(6):473–86.

Sorce, J., R. Emde, J. Campos, and M. Klinnert. (1985). Maternal Emotional Signalling: Its Effect on the Visual Cliff Behaviour of 1-Year-Olds. *Developmental Psychology* 21:195–200.

Spelke, E., and G. Van de Walle. (1993). Perceiving and Reasoning about Objects: Insights From Infants. In N. Eilan, W. Brewer, and R. McCarthy, eds., *Spatial Representation*. New York: Blackwells, 132–61.

Spelke, E., A. Phillips, and A. Woodward. (1995). Infants' Knowledge of Object Motion and Human Action. In D. Sperber, D. Premack, and A. J. Premack, eds., *Causal Cognition: A Multidisciplinary Debate*. Oxford: Clarendon Press, 44–78.

Stone, V., S. Baron-Cohen, and K. Knight. (1998). Frontal Lobe Contributions to Theory of Mind. *Journal of Cognitive Neuroscience* 10:640–56.

Tomasello, M., and M. E. Barton. (1994). Learning Words in Nonostensive Contexts. *Developmental Psychology* 30(5):639–50.

Tomasello, M. (1999). Having Intentions, Understanding Intentions, and Understanding Communicative Intentions. In P. D. Zelazo and J. W. Astington, eds., *Developing Theories of Intention: Social Understanding and Self Control*. Mahwah, NJ: Lawrence Erlbaum, 63–75.

Vaina, L. M., M. Lemay, D. C. Bienfang, and A. Y. Choi. (1990). Intact 'Biological Motion' and 'Structure from Motion' Perception in a Patient with Impaired Motion Mechanisms: A Case Study. *Visual Neuroscience* 5(4):353–69.

Varley, R., and M. Siegal. (2000). Evidence for Cognition without Grammar from Causal Reasoning and 'Theory of Mind' in an Agrammatic Aphasic Patient. *Current Biology* 10(12):723–6.

Vygotsky, L. (1979). *Mind in Society*. Cambridge, MA: Harvard University Press.

Wellman, H. (1990). *The Child's Theory of Mind*. Cambridge, MA: MIT Press.

Wellman, H. M., and K. Bartsch. (1994). Before Belief: Children's Early Psychological Theory. In C. Lewis, ed., *Early Understanding of Mind: Origins and Development*. Hove, Sussex: Lawrence Erlbaum, 331–54.

Wellman, H. M., D. Cross, and J. Watson. (2001). Meta-analysis of Theory of Mind Development: The Truth about False-belief. *Child Development*, 72,3:655–84.

Whalen, P. (1999). Fear, Vigilance, and Ambiguity: Initial Neuroimaging Studies of the Human Amygdala. *Current Directions in Psychological Science* 7:177–87.

Wimmer, H., and J. Perner. (1983). Beliefs about Beliefs: Representation and Constraining Function of Wrong Beliefs in Young Children's Understanding of Deception. *Cognition* 13:103–28.

Winner, E., H. Brownell, F. Happé, A. Blum, and D. Pincus. (1998). Distinguishing Lies from Jokes: Theory of Mind Deficits and Discourse Interpretation in Right Hemisphere Brain-damaged Patients. *Brain and Language* 62(1):89–106.

Woodward, A. L. (1998). Infants Selectively Encode the Goal Object of an Actor's Reach. *Cognition* 69:1–34.

Young, M. P., and S. Yamane. (1992). Sparse Population Coding of Faces in the Inferotemporal Cortex. *Science* 256:1327–31.

Young, A., J. Aggleton, D. Hellawell, M. Johnson, P. Broks, and J. Hanley. (1995). Face Processing Impairments After Amygdalectomy. *Brain* 118:15–24.

Zaitchik, D. (1991). Is Only Seeing Really Believing? Sources of the True Belief in the False Belief Task. *Cognitive Development* 6(1):91–103.

Zelazo, P. D., J. W. Astington, and D. R. Olson, eds. (1999). *Developing Theories of Intention: Social Understanding and Self-control*. Mahwah, NJ: Lawrence Erlbaum.

# 5 | Dennett's Contribution to Research on the Animal Mind

### ROBERT M. SEYFARTH
### AND DOROTHY L. CHENEY

## INTRODUCTION

On a warm spring evening, just as the sun is going down, at the edge of a small, muddy pool of water in Panama, a male frog (*Physalaemus pustulosus*) gives its advertising call, onomatopoetically described as a "whine" followed by a "chuck" (Ryan 1985). Almost immediately, several things happen. In the mud nearby, a smaller male of the same species, who has been calling with a whine alone, adds a chuck to his call (Rand and Ryan 1981). Simultaneously, a nearby female who had ignored the male giving a whine alone now becomes active. The female orients toward and then approaches the male giving the lower-pitched chuck (Ryan 1980, 1985). Ten feet overhead, a bat (*Trachops cirrhosus*) that has been circling the pond hears the frogs calling and dives down, flying directly at one of the calling males.

The evolution of calling in *Physalaemus* is now well understood. Male calling appears to have been favoured by natural selection to repel rivals and to attract females, while simultaneously minimizing bats' ability to locate their prey. The strongest frequency of a male *Physalemus*' whine-plus-chuck falls neatly within the range of the best hearing frequencies of males and females of the same species (Capranica 1977). The male's call seems to have evolved in tandem with the auditory system of its intended listeners. Male *Physalemus* are more likely to begin vocalizing if they hear a neighbouring male give a whine-plus-chuck than if they hear a whine alone, and more likely to vocalize if the calling male is closer than if he is farther away. Males also give more acoustically complex calls as the number of calling males nearby increases (Ryan 1985). Females are attracted to the calls of males, and given the choice will approach whine-plus-chucks in preference to whines alone, and lower-pitched chucks in preference to higher-pitched chucks (Ryan 1985).

Calling by male *Physalemus* is also costly, however, because it reveals the frog's location to predatory bats. Presumably in response to predation pressure, natural selection has shaped the acoustic properties of *Physalaemus* whines so that they are as difficult as possible for bats to locate (Ryan, Tuttle, and Rand 1982). Frogs add chucks to their whine because the chucks make them more attractive to females (Ryan 1980), but adding chucks also makes the frogs easier for bats to locate (Rand and Ryan 1981). Over evolutionary time, hard-to-find frogs and super-sensitive bats have engaged in an evolutionary arms race, and despite the frog's best ventriloqual efforts, some bats nonetheless manage to find their prey.

In evolutionary terms, calling by male *Physalemus* seems to have evolved with the goal of communicating to potential rivals and mates, while at the same time communicating as little as possible to bats. But these "goals" are poorly understood, because for all their value evolutionary explanations reveal little about the proximate mechanisms that underlie communication between a frog and its rivals, mates, or predators. Does the frog's call produce its adaptive outcome because the caller "wants" to repel rivals or attract mates? When we describe the caller's behaviour as "goal directed," do we really mean that callers have a plan and monitor the outcome of their actions? Does the frog's call achieve its result because nearby individuals acquire information when they hear it (a female thinks "Ah! There's a male to mate with, and a nice big one, too!")? Or are listeners' responses just immediate, unthinking reactions to a particular stimulus?

The case of the bat is particularly instructive because, once again, the evolutionary tradeoffs are clear but the proximate mechanisms are not, and there is a striking difference between the "interests" of caller and recipient. From the frog's perspective, communication with bats is simply an unintended consequence of behaviour that has evolved to deter rivals and attract mates. Although the frog has no "goal" of communicating to the bat, communication occurs all the same, as bats take advantage of a lucky accident and extract useful information from a signal that evolved for entirely different reasons. But does this mean that, when a bat hears a whine-plus-chuck it "thinks" (or "conjures up images of") a tasty frog even before it sees its prey? Or should we conclude more cautiously that the bat has, in the past, simply been reinforced for seeking food whenever it hears a particular sound?

## SCIENTIFIC BACKGROUND

Beginning with the pioneering work of Niko Tinbergen, Konrad Lorenz, and Karl von Frisch, ethologists have sought to explain the behaviour of animals in terms of evolution, ontogeny (or development through the life cycle), and proximate causal mechanisms. The evolution of calling by male frogs, for example, might be studied by comparing the reproductive success of males that do and do not call. Since the former mate more often and produce more offspring that survive and reproduce, a reasonable hypothesis argues that present-day frogs call at high rates because, over evolutionary time, natural selection has favoured genes that predispose a male to call over genes that do not. The ontogeny of calling might be studied by raising young frogs in different auditory environments to see how experience affects their behaviour. Vocalizations in some species of animals are relatively fixed in the genome and are unaffected by any variation in auditory experience. In other species, such as songbirds, however, normal calling occurs only if the individual receives specific auditory input during a particular period of development. And the proximate mechanisms that prompt a male to call might be studied by measuring or altering circulating hormone levels, through single-unit recordings from cells in different brain regions, or by presenting a male frog with different stimuli (a male or female, for instance) to see which elicits the strongest response.

Each approach to the study of behaviour is valid and important in its own right, and explanations at one level of analysis neither presuppose nor constrain explanation at another (Tinbergen 1963). For example, evidence that calling by male frogs has evolved to attract females tells us nothing about the proximate mechanisms involved. A female's attraction to a male's call could be mediated by hormone levels, neurotransmitter activity, or by an individual female's preference for a particular individual. Females could be attracted to any auditory stimulus between 50 and 60 Hz, or they might be more selective, approaching only the calls of a male from their own species, or only the calls of an individual male with whom they have interacted before.

Although Tinbergen advocated simultaneous research on behaviour at all levels of analysis, during the 1950s and 1960s the scientific study of animal behaviour began to fragment along intellectual lines. European ethologists studied animals in their natural habitat with a view to understanding the evolution of behaviour under different ecological conditions, while North American comparative psychologists focussed their work almost entirely on laboratory rats and pigeons with a view to understanding the causal mechanisms that underlay their behaviour. Research by Europeans emphasized the evolution of different "fixed action patterns," each adapted to life in a different habitat, while North American psychologists – dominated by Skinner – searched for general laws of behaviour that would apply to any species under any ecological conditions.

In the late 1960s and early 1970s, several investigators attempted to integrate these two views. Robert Hinde's (1966, 1970) textbook *Animal Behaviour: A Synthesis of Ethology and Comparative Psychology* tried to combine European and North American research on underlying mechanisms; Peter Marler's and W. J. Hamilton III's (1966) textbook *Mechanisms of Animal Behaviour* tried to place research on mechanisms in an evolutionary context. Two major publications, *Constraints on Learning* (Hinde and Stevenson-Hinde 1973) and *Biological Boundaries of Learning* (Seligman and Hager 1972) offered new evidence that learning in different species is itself shaped by evolution.

The development of a new, synthetic view of evolution and behavioural mechanisms was, however, overtaken in 1975 by the publication of E. O. Wilson's *Sociobiology*. Wilson's view of the proper study of behaviour was quite different from Tinbergen's. In his introduction, he states: "The conventional wisdom also speaks of ethology, which is the naturalistic study of whole patterns of animal behaviour, and its companion enterprise, comparative psychology, as the central, unifying fields of behavioural biology. They are not; both are destined to be cannibalized by neurophysiology and sensory physiology from one end and sociobiology and behavioural ecology from the other" (1975:6). Quoting the geneticist R. C. Lewontin (1972), Wilson continues: "Natural selection of the character states themselves is the essence of Darwinism. All else is molecular biology."

In its most extreme form, Wilson's view seemed to be that scientists should not waste time trying to disentangle the many different proximate mechanisms – neural, hormonal, learning, or cognitive – that might underlie behaviour, because all of these explanations were destined, in the end, to be reduced to molecular biology. What really was important, and what students of animal behaviour should focus on to the exclusion of all else, was behaviour's evolutionary consequences. In their search for functional explanations, behavioural ecologists were free to treat the intervening proximate mechanisms as a black box, contents uninteresting.

In sum, by the late 1970s, scientists interested in the evolution of human and animal cognition found the intellectual landscape rather bleak. On one side were Skinnerians, who believed that all behaviour was governed by simple laws based on experience and reinforcement. For these scientists, the mental lives of animals were unimportant because an animal's thoughts, beliefs, or knowledge could not be studied systematically and because the mind, at least in nonhuman animals, was assumed to play no active role in structuring knowledge or causing behaviour (e.g., Skinner 1957, 1974). On the other side were behavioural ecologists, whose exclusive focus on evolutionary consequences led them away from the study of proximate mechanisms, even in cases where they described behaviour in provocative, cognitive terms. Consider the case of the scorpion fly (*Hylobittacus apicalis*). In this species, mating only occurs if a male can offer the female a dead insect, which is consumed by the female during copulation (Thornhill 1981). Male scorpion flies use three different behaviours to obtain prey: They may catch their own, steal prey from another male by force, or they may approach a male who already has a dead insect, mimic the behaviour of a female, receive the insect as a gift, and then fly away. Dawkins and Krebs (1978) described the third strategy as "deceptive" in order to emphasize its manipulative quality: Communication is not always characterized by mutual co-operation (see also Krebs and Dawkins 1984). In so doing, however, they took pains to assure readers that provocative terms like deception and manipulation, borrowed from studies of humans, should not be taken too seriously. "It should be clear that we [do] not use the term 'manipulation' to imply conscious thought or intention by the actor, but merely to describe a hypothesis about evolutionary selection pressures on signals. Although a bee orchid (*Ophrys apifera*) may manipulate the behaviour of bees in such a way that the orchid benefits (by pollen transfer) and the bee does not (it attempts to mate with an inappropriate object), no one would seriously suggest that orchids have conscious intentions!" (Krebs and Davies 1993, p. 371).

## THE INTENTIONAL STANCE

In Dan Dennett's first encounter with the study of animal behaviour (1983), he took a radically different position. Like Dawkins, Krebs, and their colleagues, he recognized that a scorpion fly – or a frog, a vervet monkey, or even an orchid – could in theory achieve its objective through many different means. Unlike these behavioural ecologists, however, he was intrigued to know which mechanism had been favoured by natural selection. When the male scorpion fly mimicked a female, was this simply an innate, genetically fixed reaction to the sight of another male carrying a dead insect? Or was there an element of true, human-like deception involved? Most likely the answer lay somewhere between these two extremes. How should we quantify the difference? And if we could quantify the difference, how might the scorpion fly differ from the orchid and the monkey?

Like Skinner, Dennett was interested in mechanisms, but unlike the most radical behaviourists he was entirely open to the possibility of "cognitive" mechanisms – that is, mechanisms in which an animal's mental operations have true causal power, both in structuring what the animal perceives and in determining what it does. This is not to say that Dennett supported a return to the casual anthropomorphism of nineteenth-century naturalists like Romanes (1882). Instead, like many scientists trying to chart a course between the Scylla of Skinner and the Charybdis of Wilson and Dawkins, he hoped to combine experimental rigour with an open-mindedness to the possibility that the mental lives of animals might be studied scientifically. In 1983, Dennett applied his views on intentionality (1971, 1978a, 1978b) to research on the predator alarm calls of East African vervet monkeys (*Cercopithecus aethiops*).

Vervets live in groups of eight to thirty individuals, including several adult males, adult females, and their offspring. They sleep in trees at night and forage on the ground or in trees during the day. Throughout their range, they are preyed on by a variety of different predators, including leopards, eagles, and snakes. Each predator elicits an acoustically different alarm call, and each alarm elicits a different, adaptive response. When the monkeys encounter a leopard, they give a loud, barking alarm. On hearing this call, other nearby vervets run immediately into trees, where they are safe from a leopard's attack. In contrast, when vervets encounter an eagle they give a different alarm call that causes monkeys on the ground to look up into the air or run into bushes, where they are safe from an eagle's attack. Large African eagles like the crowned eagle (*Stephanoetus coronatus*) and the martial eagle (*Polemaetus bellicosus*) can take monkeys in trees, so this is not a safe refuge for vervets. Perhaps as a result, when monkeys in a tree hear an eagle alarm call they run out of the tree, onto the ground and into a bush. If vervets encounter a snake they give a third, acoustically distinct alarm call that causes nearby animals to stand on their hind legs and peer into the grass around them (Struhsaker 1967; Cheney and Seyfarth 1990).

The different responses of vervet monkeys could, of course, arise because in each case the animals see a different predator. To test this hypothesis we conducted playback experiments when no predators were present. For example, we waited until the members of one vervet group were foraging on an open plain and then, from a concealed loudspeaker, played a leopard alarm that had previously been recorded from a member of that group. The monkeys' reactions were filmed. Our experiments duplicated the responses observed under natural conditions, indicating that different alarm calls alone, even in the absence of a predator, provide the monkeys with sufficient information to make distinct and adaptive responses (for further details, see Seyfarth et al. 1980; Cheney and Seyfarth 1990, Chapters 4 and 5).

What goes on in a vervet monkey's mind when he gives or hears a leopard alarm call? The simplest explanation is that there is nothing "mental" at all about monkey vocalizations: They are just relatively inflexible responses to particular stimuli, like a cry of surprise given to someone who suddenly leaps out from a hiding place. Alternatively, a monkey might give an alarm call only after he has studied the situation carefully and taken into account a number of different factors. Calling might depend, for example, on whether a predator is hunting, whether there are other monkeys nearby, or whether there are *particular* other monkeys nearby, like close kin or mates. Finally, calling might even depend on the states of mind that the signaller attributes to others. Conceivably, before giving an alarm a monkey might ask herself, "Have other group members already seen the leopard? Have they responded appropriately? Wait a minute: Do I *want* others to know I've seen a leopard?"

The distinction between "true" communication and simpler, more reflexive calls that can nevertheless convey information had been considered by many different philosophers before Dennett. Grice (1957), for example, distinguished the "nonnatural" meaning of linguistic utterances, in which a speaker intends to modify the beliefs or behaviour of his audience, from the "natural" meaning of other signals, in which, for example, thunder and lightening mean that it's going to rain (see also Bennett 1976; Tiles 1987). According to Grice's definition, true communication does not occur unless both signaller and recipient take into account each other's states of mind. By this criterion, it is highly doubtful that *any* animal signals could ever be described as truly communicative.

Nevertheless, they might be. Keeping an open mind, how would we know if they were? Here is where Dennett has provided his greatest contribution to the study of animal behaviour. His "intentional stance" offers an analytical scheme that, in the hands of many investigators, has led to experiments that are beginning to clarify the mechanisms that underlie communication in animals. Thanks in large part to Dennett's work, we may ultimately achieve a better understanding of the most fundamental differences between animal communication and human language, and between animal and human cognition.

But before we summarize Dennett's method and some of the experiments it has inspired, we need a brief philosophical digression (it will be clear that we are ethologists, not philosophers). In philosophical terms, intentional phenomena are largely restricted to mental states, like beliefs, desires, and emotions (Dennett 1987). Intentional phenomena are always *about* some other thing, be it a physical stimulus or another mental state, and they probably constitute the major components of human thinking and language. Whenever an individual thinks, believes, wants, or fears something, he is said to be in an intentional state – from the Latin verb *intendo*, meaning *to point at* – because his thoughts, beliefs, or desires must by definition be about something

Unlike ordinary relational statements, intentional statements exhibit a specific logical property called referential opacity. If a statement is referentially opaque, there is no guarantee that "substituting equals for equals" preserves its truth value. Consider two words that are synonymous: In an ordinary, relational statement one of these words can be substituted for the other without damaging the whole statement. So, for example, since *vervet monkey* and *Cercopithecus aethiops* are synonymous, if the statement "The vervet monkey was eaten by a leopard" is true, we can infer that the statement "The *Cercopithecus aethiops* was eaten by a leopard" is also true. This is not necessarily the case for intentional statements. If a person doesn't know that *Cercopithecus aethiops* is the Latin name for vervet monkey, she may fear that the vervet monkey was eaten without feeling the same anxiety for *Cercopithecus aethiops*. There have been centuries of debate about the proper analysis of intentionality; before we dissolve into referential opacity ourselves we refer readers to Quine (1960), Fodor (1975), Searle (1983), and Dennett (1987).

In his analysis of vervet monkey alarm calls, Dennett begins by assuming that a vervet is an intentional system, capable of mental states like beliefs and desires. But what kind of beliefs and desires? At the simplest level, we must entertain the possibility that vervets are *zero-order intentional systems*, with no beliefs or desires at all. A zero-order explanation holds that vervet monkeys give alarm calls simply because they are frightened. Vervets experience different kinds of fear, each associated with a different predator. Each type of fear elicits a characteristic alarm call and a characteristic escape response. Zero-order explanations are explanations of behaviour with no intentional verb, and hence no presumption that animals engage in intentional activity like thinking or believing.

Alternatively, vervets might be *first-order intentional systems*, with beliefs and desires but no beliefs *about* beliefs. At this level, a vervet monkey gives leopard alarm calls because she *believes* that there is a leopard nearby or because she *wants* others to run into trees. First-order explanations presume that vervets do engage in intentional activity like thinking or believing, but restrict the array of things in the world that the vervet's thoughts or beliefs can be about. They presume that a vervet can have thoughts, beliefs, or fears about things like leopards and other vervets, but not about mental events like her audience's state of mind. If vervets are first-order intentional systems they have beliefs, but not beliefs about beliefs.

It is also possible that vervet monkeys are *second-*, *third-*, or even *higher-order intentional systems*, with some conception about both their own and other individuals' states of mind. A vervet monkey capable of second-order intentionality gives a leopard alarm call because she *wants* others to *believe* that there is a leopard nearby. Second-order explanations presume that vervets have mental states and that these mental states can be about the mental states of others.

At higher and increasingly baroque levels, both the signaller's and the audience's states of mind come into play. If a vervet is capable of third-order intentionality, she gives an alarm call because she *wants* others to *believe* that she *thinks* they should run into trees. Third-order explanations presume that vervets have mental states, that a signaller's mental state can be about the mental states of her listeners, and that the signaller knows that her listeners can be thinking about her mental state. As noted earlier, Grice (1957) and others have argued that linguistic communication requires at least third-order intentionality on the part of both signaller and recipient (see also Bennett 1976; Jackendoff 1994).

## DENNETT'S IMPACT

Dennett's article had an enormous impact on studies of animal communication, for several reasons. First and most important, it prompted investigators to carry out novel observations and experiments, and to reanalyse their data in ways they might not otherwise have considered. Much credit goes to Dennett for his easily accessible prose style (unusual among philosophers) and for his genuine interest in empirical tests of his ideas.

Second, Dennett's analytical method offered a means by which scientists could begin to quantify the cognitive mechanisms underlying communication in many different species. One might ask, for example, what is the simplest level of intentionality needed to explain the "deceptive" behaviour of an orchid or a scorpion fly, or the calling of a frog or a vervet monkey? Dennett set the stage for such comparisons by pointing out that one can ascribe a hypothetical level of intentionality to almost any object, whether animate or inanimate. Does a thermostat turn off the boiler because it *believes* that the room has reached a certain temperature (Dennett 1987, p. 22)? Does an orchid *want* a bee to distribute its pollen to other orchids? At first, it seems absurd to make such ascriptions. But the application of traditional scientific methods quickly does away with the absurdity (the thermostat and orchid are shown to be zero-order intentional systems), bringing us to problems and results that are by no means simple and straightforward. Does a chess-playing computer refrain from taking its (human) opponent's rook because it detects a strategy on the part of its opponent that, many moves into the future, will ultimately lead to the loss of its queen? Or is it simpler and more accurate just to say that the computer *knows* what its opponent *wants* to do? Does a chimpanzee act depressed because it truly empathizes with another? Below we briefly summarize some recent studies involving monkeys, apes, and children, many of which were inspired by Dennett's (1983) paper.

Third, Dennett's analytical method drew attention to the fact that in any communicative event the mechanisms underlying behaviour may be fundamentally different for caller and recipient. Once again, this was most clearly apparent in Dennett's examples of communication between humans and machines, or between infants and adults. Dawkins and Krebs (1978) were among the first to note that evolutionary interests between signaller and recipient might differ dramatically – recall the case of the frog and the bat. Dennett's analytical scheme raised the possibility that the behaviour of signallers and recipients might also be governed by entirely different mechanisms. Reviewing examples of communication in vervet monkeys and baboons (*Papio cynocephalus*), Cheney and Seyfarth (1998, p. 194) suggest that listeners extract rich, even semantic, information from calls given by signallers who may not, in the human sense, have intended to provide it.

Fourth, Dennett's intentional stance represented a novel approach to the comparative study of language and language-like communication in captive apes and children. Before Dennett's paper, most of the "ape language" studies had focussed almost entirely on syntax as the defining feature of language (see, for example, Gardner and Gardner 1969; Terrace 1979; and Savage-Rumbaugh 1986. The rather different research by Premack [1976] is discussed separately below). Because captive apes could readily be taught to use hand signs, computer keys, or plastic chips to represent objects, their ability to engage in semantic communication was widely accepted; whether or not they could combine these "words" to make sentences remained controversial. Syntax had therefore become the defining feature of human language. By contrast, Dennett's argument suggested that an animal's communication could be complex, semantic, and perhaps even syntactic and yet fail to meet language's standards on entirely different grounds. Instead of asking "Can an ape create a sentence?" (Terrace et al. 1979), we should instead ask whether any animal can recognize his companion's mental state and the effect of his communication on it. Cheney and Seyfarth (1998) suggest that the simultaneous absence of syntax and second-order intentionality in the communication of monkeys may not be an accident. Monkeys' inability to engage in syntactic communication may ultimately derive from their inability to recognize other animals' mental states.

Finally, Dennett's paper brought the ideas and tools of cognitive science – a field concerned almost exclusively with human cognition – to the field of ethology, and in so doing enriched both disciplines. Among ethologists, he refocused attention on the mechanisms underlying behaviour, while throwing off the rigid anti-mentalism of Skinnerian behaviourism. Among cognitive scientists, his explicitly comparative approach offered a reminder that brains had evolved in more than just the human species, and that reasoning and cognition can exist without language.

## OTHER SIGNIFICANT INFLUENCES

Although his contributions to ethology were undoubtedly original, it is important to recognize that Dennett was not alone in his emphasis on mental state attribution as a crucial component of communication. Credit must also be given to the philosophers whose work inspired Dennett (see the other chapters in this volume), and to psychologists David Premack, Heinz Wimmer, and Josef Perner, who carried out pioneering experiments on the attribution of mental states in chimpanzees and children in the late 1970s and early 1980s.

Premack and Woodruff (1978) conducted the first experiment designed explicitly to test whether or not chimpanzees can impute mental states to others. They showed Sarah, an adult chimpanzee, videotapes of a human trainer struggling to solve a variety of problems. The trainer, for example, was shown trying to operate a record player whose cord was not plugged into a wall socket. After each videotape, Sarah was given several photographs, one of which depicted the correct solution to the problem. In the most subtle tests, the possible solutions to the record player problem might include photographs of a cord that was plugged into the wall, a cord that was not plugged in, and a cord that had been cut. Sarah consistently chose the correct photograph. Interestingly, when tested with videotapes of a favoured and a less favoured trainer, Sarah chose correct solutions for the favoured trainer but incorrect ones for the trainer she did not like.

Premack and Woodruff interpreted Sarah's choice of the correct alternative as evidence that she recognized the videotape as representing a problem and inferred purpose – or in Dennett's terms, an intentional state like *wants* – to the trainer. The fact that Sarah picked out incorrect solutions for the unpopular trainer suggests that she was not simply choosing actions that would constitute the best solution for herself. Premack and Woodruff argued that even if Sarah's choices had simply reflected appropriate solutions for herself, some form of attribution would have to be invoked, since it is hard to imagine how she could recognize the correct solution without interpreting what the human was trying to do.

Although Sarah seemed to have little difficulty in attributing purpose to others, later experiments (Premack 1988) raised doubts about other aspects of the chimpanzees' theory of mind, particularly their ability to recognize false beliefs in others. The ability of chimpanzees to recognize the mental states of others remains controversial to this day (see below).

At roughly the same time, Heinz Wimmer and Josef Perner (1983) carried out what has since become a classic experiment on the development of a theory of mind in young children. Wimmer and Perner presented three- to nine-year-old subjects with scenarios in which they had to describe the knowledge of others. In one case, the children watched a puppet show in which a boy, Maxi, puts a piece of chocolate into a blue cupboard. Maxi then leaves the room, and in his absence his mother removes the chocolate from the blue cupboard and places it in a green one. The children were then asked where Maxi would look for the chocolate when he came back. Children under four years of age consistently indicated the green cupboard, the cupboard in which they themselves knew the chocolate to be located. In contrast, about half of the four- to six-year-old children, and over 80 percent of the six- to nine-year-old children, correctly pointed out that Maxi would still think that the chocolate was in the blue cupboard. The younger children's errors were not due to a failure of memory, because most of the children who gave an incorrect answer to the question nevertheless gave a correct answer when asked if they remembered where Maxi had put the chocolate. Rather, it seemed that children's ability to represent two incompatible beliefs does not become established until around the ages of four to six years.

## RECENT RESULTS

*Monkeys.* The alarm-calling of vervet monkeys cannot be described as a zero-order intentional system ("monkeys alarm because they are afraid") because monkeys do not always give alarm calls when they encounter a predator. If a lone vervet is pursued by a predator, he flees silently. When a group of vervets encounters a predator, not all individuals give alarm calls. And in experiments with captive vervets, adult females gave alarm calls to a predator at significantly higher rates when they were with their own offspring than when they were with an unrelated immature of the same age and sex (Cheney and Seyfarth 1990). At the same time, there is no support for the hypothesis that alarm calling by vervets constitutes a second-order intentional system ("monkeys alarm because they want others to know they have seen a predator"). Despite many experimental tests, there is no evidence that monkeys recognize mental states like ignorance in others and communicate with the goal of changing these mental states.

For example, although vervets, like many other animals, vary their rates of alarm calling depending upon the presence and composition of their audience, they do not act deliberately to inform ignorant individuals more than knowledgeable ones (Cheney and Seyfarth 1990). Similarly, they do not attempt to correct or rectify false beliefs in others, nor do they instruct others in the correct usage or response to calls (Seyfarth and Cheney 1986). Because vervets seem unable to distinguish between what they know and what others know, they may fail to recognize that ignorant individuals need to have events explained and described to them. As a result, they may not understand that there is a need to specify whether a leopard is in a tree or on the ground. Perhaps for the same reason, vervets and other monkeys do not comment on events of the past or signal about things in their absence.

A particularly good example of the lack of a theory of mind in monkeys comes from recent experiments on the "contact barks" of free-ranging baboons. In the Okavango Delta of Botswana, baboons often give loud barks when moving through wooded areas. Because several different individuals may be calling at roughly the same time, it often appears as if individuals are exchanging barks in order to inform each other of their location and to co-ordinate the group's movement. Field experiments, however, have shown that a baboon will not answer another animal's bark, even the bark of her own infant, unless she herself is peripheral or separated from the rest of the group. Mothers who hear the contact bark of their infant will not answer if they themselves are in the centre of the group progression and at no risk of becoming separated (Cheney et al. 1996; Rendall et al. 2000). In this and other cases, monkeys' calls appear to reflect the knowledge the signaller has rather than the knowledge the signaller intends her audience to acquire (Cheney and Seyfarth 1996). The baboons' communication is consistent with a description based on first-order intentionality; second-order intentionality is not required.

At the same time, it is important to note a striking difference in the meaning and function of these calls from the signaller's and the listener's perspective. Although calling baboons may not recognize the mental states of other animals and communicate with the goal of modifying them, their barks nonetheless function as if they were based on second-order intentionality because they permit listeners to deduce the group's location and direction of travel. Through experience, and perhaps by observing the behaviour of others, the listener is able to derive the call's meaning and function and learn how to respond adaptively to it. The listener extracts rich, even semantic, information from a signaller who may not, in the human sense, have intended to provide it. The communication of baboons is much more language-like from the listener's perspective than from the signaller's.

*Apes.* The evidence for second-order intentionality in apes is more controversial. While some investigators maintain that there are greater cognitive differences (specifically with reference to a theory of mind) between monkeys and apes than between apes and humans (Savage-Rumbaugh and Lewin 1994; Byrne 1995), it is also argued that no cognitive tests have as yet demonstrated a qualitative difference between monkeys and apes in the capacity to attribute mental states to others (Tomasello and Call 1997).

In captivity, there is some evidence that chimpanzees learn more easily than monkeys to recognize the goals and motives of others. For example, they are better than monkeys at assuming another individual's role in a co-operative task and at recognizing intentional gestures, such as pointing (Povinelli et al. 1990, 1992a, 1992b). They also seem better at emulating others. When watching a demonstrator use a tool, chimpanzees, unlike monkeys, readily learn the use and function of a tool. Unlike children, however, they do not copy the precise motor patterns or methods of the demonstrator (Nagell et al. 1993). As a result, it remains unclear whether the difference in performance between chimpanzees and monkeys stems from chimpanzees' greater capacity to comprehend the goals and intentions of others or from their proficiency in recognizing cause-effect relations (Tomasello et al. 1997; Limongelli et al. 1995; Povinelli and Eddy 1996; Tomasello 1996a; Tomasello and Call 1997; Povinelli 2000).

There is at present little evidence from natural populations of chimpanzees that apes take into account their audience's mental states when communicating with one another. For example, chimpanzees do not appear to adjust their loud calls to inform ignorant individuals about their own location or the location of food (Mitani and Nishida 1993; Clark and

Wrangham 1994; Mitani 1996). And although chimpanzees certainly differ from monkeys in the variety and frequency of tool use (McGrew 1994), there is no evidence that chimpanzees learn to use tools by actively imitating or instructing one another (Tomasello 1996b; Tomasello and Call 1997; Povinelli 2000). Finally, although there are more anecdotal examples of deception in apes than in monkeys (Byrne 1995), it is unclear whether this difference stems from apes' capacity to recognize the causal relation between behaviour and knowledge or from their greater ability to recognize and act on behavioural contingencies.

In a far-ranging series of experiments, Povinelli (2000) and Povinelli and Eddy (1996) tested whether chimpanzees "appreciate that visual perception subjectively connects organisms to the external world." They argue that to do so the chimpanzees "would have to appreciate that seeing refers to or is 'about' something – in other words, they must interpret seeing as an intentional event" (Povinelli and Eddy 1996, p. 120). Povinelli's evidence argues against such an interpretation.

In a typical experiment, for example, chimpanzees were first trained to use their natural begging gesture (an outstretched hand) to request food from a human trainer. Then an individual chimp was given the opportunity to beg from one of two trainers. One trainer was facing the subject and could plainly see him; the other trainer could not because her face was covered (or her eyes were covered, or she was facing in the opposite direction). Given this choice, chimps showed no difference in their preference for one trainer over another. By contrast, three-year-old children immediately gestured selectively to the person who could see them.

In contrast, other experiments suggest that chimpanzees may have some understanding about the relation between seeing and knowing, even if this understanding is more rudimentary than that of a young child. For example, Tomasello et al. (1998) demonstrated that many nonhuman primates will reliably follow the gaze direction of a human or a member of their own species. Chimpanzees, however, do not simply orient in the appropriate direction and search randomly for something interesting. Instead, they follow gaze direction to a specific geometric location, much as human infants do (Tomasello et al. 1999). Most recently, Hare et al. (2000) conducted an experiment in which a subordinate and a dominant chimpanzee were placed in a situation in which they competed over food. Under normal conditions, the dominant animal consistently obtained the food. Subordinates were often successful, however, if they themselves could see where the food was placed but the dominant animal could not. For example, when given the choice of two food items, only one of which the dominant could see, the subordinate consistently approached the food that was not visible to the dominant. Such results do not prove that chimpanzees impute mental states like ignorance to others, or that they recognize that other individuals' visual experiences are similar to their own. They do suggest, however, that chimpanzees know what others can and cannot see, and that "the behaviour of others is determined in some specific ways by what they do and do not have visual access to" (Hare et al. 2000, p. 784).

*Children.* The pioneering experiments of Wimmer and Perner (1983) prompted a virtual tsunami of experiments on the development of a theory of mind in children. Such an enormous literature is difficult to summarize. Given our previous discussion of "semantic" signals in monkeys and the relation between seeing and knowing in chimpanzees, here we simply highlight some recent work on these topics in young children. (See also Griffin and Baron-Cohen, this volume.)

Word learning in even very young children seems to be accompanied by primitive mental state attribution. Clearly, young children of one and two years of age do not have a fully developed theory of mind, in the sense that they attribute false beliefs to others (Astington et al. 1998; Wellman 1990; Perner 1991). However, by the age of one year, they already seem to understand that words can be mapped onto objects and actions in the world (Golinkoff et al. 1994; Hirsh-Pasek and Golinkoff 1996). This understanding seems to be accompanied by a form of 'social referencing,' in which the child uses other people's direction of gaze, gestures, and emotions to appraise a situation.

As early as six months of age, infants are capable of attending to their mothers' direction of gaze to infer where to look, and by the age of eighteen months they are able to guess both the direction and the location of an adult's focus of gaze, even when this is outside their own visual field (Butterworth and Jarrett 1991). Infants at this age also actively attend to the speaker's gaze and focus of attention when inferring the referent of the speaker's utterance (Baldwin 1993a, b), as if they have developed some tacit understanding that gaze and attention are a reflection of underlying knowledge (Tomasello 1996a).

Similarly, around the age of one year, infants begin to use gestures and sounds to recruit adults' attention. In pointing toward a desired object, they will often turn to the addressee as if to check that the message has been received, and they begin to repeat and alter sounds or gestures that have been interpreted incorrectly (Golinkoff 1986; Bretherton 1992). One-year-old children also seem capable of inferring the goals and intentions of adults, even when adults perform an intentional act incorrectly (Meltzoff 1995). Finally, by the age of two years, they begin to distinguish between ignorance and knowledge in others and adjust their speech accordingly (O'Neill 1996).

In sum, in marked contrast to chimpanzees, where the evidence is so mixed, young children clearly demonstrate that they view adults as intentional beings. They do so through imitation, declarative gestures, and speech. Children readily compare another's perceptual state with their own, and this comparison forms the basis of a social referencing system that is integral to early word learning.

It is interesting to note that, although the acquisition of knowledge through joint attention involves the ability to attend to gaze direction, this by itself is by no means sufficient. People with autism, for example, seldom point to others, monitor other peoples' gazes to gain information, or bring objects to other peoples' attention, even though they are capable of attending to other people's direction of gaze (Baron-Cohen 1995; Baron-Cohen et al. 1995). Gaze is recognized as a behavioural act, it seems, but not as a reflection of underlying beliefs and knowledge.

In this respect, monkeys seem very different from young children and more like many people with autism. Several neurological studies have suggested that monkeys and other mammals are very sensitive to eye contact and gaze (Perrett et al. 1987; Perrett & Emory 1994; Walsh and Perrett 1994). Under natural conditions, monkeys also readily follow the gazes of others. However, monkeys do not use gaze or gestures like pointing to attract other individuals' attention to themselves or to some third individual or object in the environment (Anderson et al. 1995, 1996). Similarly, although monkeys can be trained to point and to attend to pointing by humans, they appear to recognize pointing only as an indication of a predictable event, and not as a representation of intent. For example, a rhesus macaque that has been trained to point to acquire food will nonetheless fail to recognize the significance of pointing in others. Conversely, a monkey that has been taught to respond to a human's pointing will not himself gesture or point to acquire food (Povinelli et al. 1992b, Hess et al. 1993; see also Anderson et al. 1995, 1996). Finally, monkeys do not appear to make adjustments to messages that were received or interpreted inaccurately, except to escalate a display. They do not, for example, attempt to correct others or themselves (Cheney and Seyfarth 1990). Although results of experiments with apes are more equivocal (see review by Tomasello and Call 1997), there is no evidence that, under natural conditions, apes spontaneously point or use other gestures to attract ignorant individuals' attention or to indicate an object's location.

## CONCLUSION

Dennett's intentional stance prompted many to realize that, contrary to conventional wisdom, natural selection does not act entirely on outcomes. It also selects from among the mechanisms by which these outcomes are achieved. Evolution will favour male *Physalaemus* frogs whose calling reaches a sufficiently high level of intentionality to achieve their adaptive goal. If zero-order intentionality ("begin calling whenever the sun goes does down and the temperature is above a certain minimum") is sufficient to achieve an adaptive outcome for the caller, then no more complex mechanism will arise. Natural selection has no need for energetically expensive neural machinery that serves no beneficial function (Humphrey 1976). Likewise, if zero-order intentionality is all that listeners need to respond appropriately (for females "approach the call with the lowest pitch" and for males "avoid all calls with a pitch lower than your own"), then there will be no need for more elaborate perceptual mechanisms. Communicative systems with zero-order intentionality prove Skinner right: The mind is little more than a sensory transducer that does little to restructure or modify information as it passes from the caller's to the listener's brain.

But if there is an adaptive advantage to be gained from first-order intentionality ("begin calling only if you *think* a female is near, or if you *want* a female to approach"), this extra cognitive step will be favoured by natural selection, as indeed it has been in many species. Now, Skinnerian explanations (or at least their simplistic caricatures) are insufficient, and we face the challenge of elucidating the neural basis – and what we actually mean by – *thinks*, *wants*, or *believes*.

Phrased in this way, it is not hard to see that Dennett's intentional stance offers a working hypothesis for future research on the evolution of intelligence: Natural selection favours the lowest level of intentionality that is sufficient to do the job. For thermostats and plants, zero-order intentionality may be enough. But for many other creatures it surely will not. And once second-order intentionality ("Vocalize if you know that your companion thinks X") has been favoured by natural selection, because it gives individuals a reproductive advantage over others, a crucial Rubicon has been crossed and there is no longer any barrier in principle to the kind of rampant n-order intentionality we find in humans (see also Trivers 1971; Humphrey 1976). The challenge for ethologists is now to find, in the elementary features of social behaviour, the crucial evolutionary break point: a problem that requires second-order intentionality and cannot be solved any other way.

### References

Anderson, J. R., M. Montant, and D. Schmitt. (1996). Rhesus Monkeys Fail to Use Gaze Direction as an Experimenter-given Cue in an Object Choice Task. *Behavioral Processes* 37:47–55.

Anderson, J. R., P. Sallaberry, and H. Barbier. (1995). Use of Experimenter-given Cues during Object-choice Tasks by Capuchin Monkeys. *Animal Behavior* 49:201–8.

Astington, J. W., P. L. Harris, and D. R. Olson, eds. (1998). *Developing Theories of Mind.* Cambridge: Cambridge University Press.

Baldwin, D. (1993a). Early Referential Understanding: Infants' Ability to Recognize Referential acts for What They Are. *Developmental Psychology* 29:832–43.

Baldwin, D. (1993b). Infants' Ability to Consult the Speaker for Clues to Word Reference. *Journal of Child Language* 20:395–418.

Baron-Cohen, S. (1995). *Mindblindness: An Essay on Autism and Theory of Mind.* Cambridge, MA: MIT Press/A Bradford Book.

Baron-Cohen, S., R. Campbell, A. Karmiloff-Smith, and J. Grant. (1995). Are Children with Autism Blind to the Mentalistic Significance of Gaze? *British Journal of Developmental Psychology* 13:379–98.

Bennett, J. (1976). *Linguistic Behaviour.* Cambridge: Cambridge University Press.

Bretherton, I. (1992). Social Referencing, Intentional Communication, and the Interfacing of Minds in Infancy. In S. Feinman, ed., *Social Referencing and the Social Construction of Reality in Infancy.* New York: Plenum Press, 57–77.

Butterworth, G., and N. Jarrett. (1991). What Minds Have in Common. Space: Spatial Mechanisms Serving Joint Visual Attention in Infancy. *British Journal of Developmental Psychology* 9:55–72.

Byrne, R. W. (1995). *The Thinking Ape: Evolutionary Origins of Intelligence.* Oxford: Oxford University Press.

Capranica, R. R. (1977). Auditory Processing of Vocal Signals in Anurans. In D. H. Taylor and S. I. Guttman, eds., *Reproductive Biology of Amphibians.* New York: Plenum Publishing, 337–55.

Cheney, D. L., and R. M. Seyfarth. (1990). *How Monkeys See the World.* Chicago: University of Chicago Press.

Cheney, D. L., and R. M. Seyfarth. (1996). Function and Intention in the Calls of Nonhuman Primates. *Proceedings of the British Academy* 88:59–76.

Cheney, D. L., and R. M. Seyfarth. (1998). Why Animals Don't Have Language. In G. Peterson, ed., *The Tanner Lectures on Human Values, Vol. 19*. Salt Lake City: University of Utah Press, 173–209.

Cheney, D. L., R. M. Seyfarth, and R. A. Palombit. (1996). The Function and Mechanisms Underlying Baboon Contact Barks. *Animal Behavior* 52:507–18.

Clark, A. P., and R. W. Wrangham. (1994). Chimpanzee Arrival Pant-hoots: Do They Signify Food or Status? *International Journal of Primatology* 15:185–205.

Dawkins, R., and J. R. Krebs. (1978). Animal Signals: Information or Manipulation? In J. R. Krebs and N. B. Davies, eds., *Behavioural Ecology: An Evolutionary Approach*. Oxford: Blackwell Scientific, 282–309.

Dennett, D. (1971). Intentional Systems. *Journal of Philosophy* 68:68–87.

Dennett, D. (1978a). Beliefs about Beliefs. *Behavioral and Brain Sciences* 1:568–70.

Dennett, D. (1978b). *Brainstorms*. Cambridge, MA: MIT Press/A Bradford Book.

Dennett, D. (1983). Intentional Systems in Cognitive Ethology: The 'Panglossian paradigm' defended. *Behavioral and Brain Sciences* 6:343–55.

Dennett, D. (1987). *The Intentional Stance*. Cambridge, MA: MIT Press/A Bradford Book.

Fodor, J. (1975). *The Language of Thought*. Cambridge, MA: Harvard University Press.

Gardner, R. A., and B. T. Gardner. (1969). Teaching Sign Language to a Chimpanzee. *Science* 165:664–72.

Golinkoff, R. A. (1986). 'I Beg Your Pardon?': The Preverbal Negotiation of Failed Messages. *Journal of Child Language* 13:455–76.

Golinkoff, R. A., C. B. Mervis, and K. Hirsh-Pasek. (1994). Early Object Labels: The Case for Developmental Lexical Principles Framework. *Journal of Child Language* 21:125–55.

Grice, H. P. (1957). Meaning. *Philosophical Review* 66:377–88.

Hare, B., J. Call, B. Agnetta, and M. Tomasello. (2000). Chimpanzees Know What Conspecifics Do and Do Not See. *Animal Behavior* 59:771–85.

Hess, J., M. A. Novak, and D. J. Povinelli. (1993). 'Natural Pointing' in a Rhesus Monkey, But No Evidence of Empathy. *Animal Behavior* 46:1023–5.

Hinde, R. A. 1966, (1970). *Animal Behaviour: A Synthesis of Ethology and Comparative Psychology, 2nd edition*. New York: McGraw-Hill.

Hinde, R. A., and J. Stevenson-Hinde, eds. (1973). *Constraints on Learning: Limitations and Predispositions*. New York: Academic Press.

Hirsh-Pasek, K., and R. A. Golinkoff. (1996). *The Origins of Grammar: Evidence from Early Language Comprehension*. Cambridge, MA: MIT Press/A Bradford Book.

Humphrey, N. K. (1976). The Social Function of Intellect. In P. Bateson and R. A. Hinde, eds., *Growing Points in Ethology*. Cambridge: Cambridge University Press.

Jackendoff, R. (1994). *Patterns in the Mind*. New York: Basic Books.

Krebs, J. R., and N. B. Davies. (1993). *An Introduction to Behavioural Ecology, 3rd edition*. Oxford: Blackwell Scientific.

Krebs, J. R., and R. Dawkins. (1984). Animal Signals: Mind Reading and Manipulation. In J. R. Krebs and N. B. Davies, eds., *Behavioural Ecology: An Integrated Approach*. Oxford: Blackwell Scientific, 380–402.

Lewontin, R. C. (1972). Testing the Theory of Natural Selection. *Nature* 236:181–2.

Limongelli, L., S. T. Boysen, and E. Visalberghi. (1995). Comprehension of Cause-Effect Relations in a Tool-Using Task by Chimpanzees (*Pan Troglodytes*). *Journal of Comparative Psychology* 109:18–26.

Marler, P. R., and W. J. Hamilton III. (1966). *Mechanisms of Animal Behaviour*. New York: Wiley.

McGrew, W. C. (1994). Tools Compared: The Material of Culture. In R. W. Wrangham, W. C. McGrew, F. B. M. de Waal, and P. G. Heltne, eds., *Chimpanzee Cultures*. Cambridge, MA: Harvard University Press, 25–40.

Meltzoff, A. N. (1995). Understanding the Intentions of Others: Reenactment of Intended Acts by Eighteen-Month-Old Children. *Developmental Psychology* 31:838–50.

Mitani, J. (1996). Comparative Studies of African Ape Vocal Behaviour. In W. C. McGrew, L. F. Marchant, and T. Nishida, eds., *Great Ape Societies*. Cambridge: Cambridge University Press, 241–54.

Mitani, J., and T. Nishida. (1993). Contexts and Social Correlates of Long-Distance Calling by Male Chimpanzees. *Animal Behavior* 45:735–46.

Nagell, K., R. S. Olguin, and M. Tomasello. (1993). Processes of Social Learning in the Tool Use of Chimpanzees (*Pan Troglodytes*) and Human Children (*Homo Sapiens*). *Journal of Comparative Psychology* 107:174–86.

O'Neill, D. K. (1996). Two-Year-Old Children's Sensitivity to a Parent's Knowledge State When Making Requests. *Child Development* 67:659–77.

Perner, J. (1991). *Understanding the Representational Mind*. Cambridge, MA: MIT Press/A Bradford Book.

Perrett, D. I., A. J. Mistlin, and A. J. Chitty. (1987). Visual Neurons in Response to Faces. *Trends in Neurosciences* 10:358–64.

Perrett, D. I., and N. J. Emory. (1994). Understanding the Intentions of Others from Visual Signals: Neurophysiological Evidence. *Current Psychology of Cognition* 13:683–94.

Povinelli, D. J. (2000). *Folk Physics for Apes*. Oxford: Oxford University Press.

Povinelli, D. J., and T. J. Eddy. (1996). What Chimpanzees Know about Seeing. *Monographs: Society for Research in Child Development* 61:1–152.

Povinelli, D. J., K. E. Nelson, and S. T. Boysen. (1990). Inferences about Guessing and Knowing by Chimpanzees (*Pan Troglodytes*). *Journal of Comparative Psychology* 104:203–10.

Povinelli, D. J., K. E. Nelson, and S. T. Boysen. (1992a). Comprehension of Role Reversal in Chimpanzees: Evidence of Empathy? *Animal Behavior* 43:633–40.

Povinelli, D. J., K. A. Parks, and M. A. Novak. (1992b). Role Reversal by Rhesus Monkeys But No Evidence of Empathy. *Animal Behavior* 44:269–81.

Premack, D. (1976). *Intelligence in Ape and Man*. Hillsdale, NJ: Lawrence Erlbaum.

Premack, D. (1988). 'Does the Chimpanzee Have a Theory of Mind' Revisited. In R. W. Byrne and A. Whiten, eds., *Machiavellian Intelligence: Social Expertise and the Evolution of Intellect in Monkeys, Apes, and Humans*. Oxford: Oxford University Press, 160–79.

Premack, D., and G. Woodruff. (1978). Does the Chimpanzee Have a Theory of Mind? *Behavioral and Brain Sciences* 1:515–26.

Quine, W. V. O. (1960). *Word and Object*. Cambridge, MA: MIT Press.

Rendall, D., D. L. Cheney, and R. M. Seyfarth. (2000). Proximate Factors Mediating 'Contact' Calls in Adult Females and Their Infants. *Journal of Comparative Psychology* 114:36–46.

Romanes, G. (1882). *Animal Intelligence*. London: Kegan, Paul, Trench.

Rand, A. S., and M. J. Ryan. (1981). The Adaptive Significance of a Complex Vocal Repertoire in a Neotropical Frog. *Zietschrift für Tierpsychologie* 57:209–14.

Ryan, M. J. (1980). Female Mate Choice in a Neotropical Frog. *Science* 209:523–5.

Ryan, M. J. (1985). *The Tungara Frog: A Study in Sexual Selection and Communication*. Chicago: University of Chicago Press.

Ryan, M. J., M. D. Tuttle, and A. S. Rand. (1982). Bat Predation and Sexual Advertisement in a Neotropical Frog. *American Naturalist* 119:136–9.

Savage-Rumbaugh, E. S. (1986). *Ape Language: From Conditioned Response to Symbol*. New York: Columbia University Press.

Savage-Rumbaugh, E. S., and R. Lewin. (1994). *Kanzi: The Ape at the Brink of the Human Mind*. New York: Wiley.

Searle, J. R. (1983). *Intentionality: An Essay in the Philosophy of Mind*. Cambridge: Cambridge University Press.

Seligman, M. E. P., and J. L. Hager. (1972). *Biological Boundaries of Learning*. New York: Appleton Century Crofts.

Seyfarth, R. M., D. L. Cheney, and P. Marler. (1980). Monkey Responses to Three Different Alarm Calls: Evidence for Predator Classification and Semantic Communication. *Science* 210:801–3.

Seyfarth, R. M., and D. L. Cheney. (1986). Vocal Development in Vervet Monkeys. *Animal Behavior* 34:1640–58.

Skinner, B. F. (1957). *Verbal Behavior*. New York: Appleton Century Crofts.

Skinner, B. F. (1974). *About Behaviorism*. New York: Knopf.

Struhsaker, T. T. (1967). Auditory Communication among Vervet Monkeys. In S. A. Altmann, ed., *Social Communication Among Primates*. Chicago: University of Chicago Press.

Terrace, H. (1979). *Nim*. New York: Knopf.

Terrace, H., L. A. Pettito, R. J. Sanders, and T. Bever. (1979). Can an Ape Create a Sentence? *Science* 206:891–902.

Tiles, J. E. (1987). Meaning. In R. L. Gregory, ed., *The Oxford Companion to the Mind*. Oxford: Oxford University Press.

Thornhill, R. (1981). *Panorpa* (*Mecoptera: Panorpidae*) Scorpionflies: Systems for Understanding Resource-Defence Polygyny and Alternative Male Reproductive Efforts. *Annual Review of Ecology and Systematics* 12:355–86.

Tinbergen, N. (1963). On Aims and Methods of Ethology. *Zietschrift für Tierpsychologie* 20:410–33.

Tomasello, M. (1996a). Chimpanzee Social Cognition. *Monographs: Society for Research in Child Development* 61:161–73.

Tomasello, M. (1996b). Do Apes Ape? In C. M. Heyes and B. G. Galef, eds., *Social Learning in Animals: The Roots of Culture*. New York: Academic Press, 319–46.

Tomasello, M., and J. Call. (1997). *Primate Cognition*. Oxford: Oxford University Press.

Tomasello, M., M. Davis-Dasilva, L. Camak, and K. Bard. (1997). Observational Learning of Tool Use by Young Chimpanzees. *Human Evolution* 2:175–83.

Tomasello, M., J. Call, and B. Hare. (1998). Five Primate Species Follow the Visual Gaze of Conspecifics. *Animal Behavior* 55:1063–9.

Tomasello, M., B. Hare, and B. Agnetta. (1999). Chimpanzees Follow Gaze Direction Geometrically. *Animal Behavior* 58:769–77.

Trivers, R. L. (1971). The Evolution of Reciprocal Altruism. *Quarterly Review of Biology* 46:35–57.

Walsh, V., and D. I. Perrett. (1994). Visual Attention in the Occipitotemporal Processing Stream of the Macaque. *Cognitive Neuropsychology* 11:243–63.

Wellman, H. (1990). *The Child's Theory of Mind*. Cambridge, MA: MIT Press/A Bradford Book.

Wilson, E. O. (1975). *Sociobiology*. Cambridge, MA: Harvard University Press.

Wimmer, H., and J. Perner. (1983). Beliefs about Beliefs: Representation and Constraining Function of Wrong Beliefs in Young Children's Understanding of Deception. *Cognition* 13:103–28.

# 6 | Dennettian Behavioural Explanations and the Roles of the Social Sciences

## DON ROSS

Dennett is not usually included in lists of the major contributors to the philosophy of the social sciences, mostly for the perfectly good reason that he has written almost nothing that is explicitly about that subject or officially part of that literature. Nevertheless, his principal concerns – which are about the complex relations between intentions, thoughts, designs, functions and causes – are about as central to what troubles social-scientific methodologists as can be imagined. And these people are indeed troubled: Social scientists spend *far* more of their professional time reflecting on, doubting, tinkering with, defending and reformulating their methods of inquiry than do physical scientists. Almost all of this fretting is motivated, directly or indirectly, by the following general problem. When they're not merely collecting data (and scientists are hardly ever engaged in *mere* data collection, since what they want is *relevant* data, and relevance is a function of theoretical frameworks, hunches about real causal relations, and so forth), social scientists are mainly in the business of explaining human actions and/or institutional and cultural structures by reference to *intentions* and/or *functions*. As almost all have recognized, however, intentions and functions can only be assigned on the assumption of purposes (*somewhere*, even if not necessarily in the conscious designs of actors or those who fulfill functions). However, there can be no purposes, anywhere, unless there are, somewhere, both goals and mechanisms that maintain more or less rationally appropriate connections between goals and means. Rationality, it is widely noted, is a *normative* idea. And norms, we have been told since the early modern revolt against Aristotelean method, have no proper place in science. At this point, social scientists tend to be pulled in one of two directions. Some, embracing a very strong reading of the work of Thomas Kuhn (a reading disavowed by Kuhn himself, one should always add), try to preserve the 'scientific' status of social science by denying that *any* science is nonnormative. Others try to show that normative assumptions can be nonvicious as long as they're neither arbitrary nor directed by personal or cultural self-interest. Social scientists who take the first road thereby involve themselves in difficult, and controversial, exercises in the history of science, and typically must make their case against passionate opposition from natural scientists. The second path leads straight into dense thickets of epistemology. Once in these bushes, the social scientist will find that philosophers have, from the point of view of her desired goal, made things still more complicated.

The second kind of social scientist enters the philosophical inquiry here in hopes of finding valid arguments and concepts of explanation according to which her favored sorts of intentional explanations can be considered *objective*. But then she finds many philosophers doubting, with Gilbert Ryle (1949), that intentional explanations are even *causal*. Reasons, according to Ryle, are not causes. I strike the match because I want to light my cigar; but my mere wanting doesn't cause *anything*. Some physical events must go on somewhere in my nervous system to produce the appropriate hand and finger movements, which bring about the contact of the match-head and the box, which bring about the flame, and so on. Very well, then: Could my wanting be the cause of the nervous events? This idea lands us straight in a regress, since unless we are dualists we must suppose that the wanting, if it can be causally effective, must itself be a nervous event. Now, if we stick with our hope that the wanting can be a typical sort of cause, we find that we are multiplying nervous events to no gain, in frank violation of Occam's razor. In addition to this, the logic of reason-giving and of explanation by reasons differs from that of causation in all sorts of systematic ways. In the view of some philosophers, such as Paul Churchland (1979), the endless difficulties with which we struggle in trying to get reasons to do physical work should lead us to abandon attempts to explain by reference to reasons at all. Others, such as (lately) Jerry Fodor (see, e.g., Fodor 2000) tell us that it's just fundamentally mysterious.

Readers who have worked through the introduction to this volume will have encountered these difficulties already, and will know that Dennett's main project in the philosophy of mind has been to show how we can continue to take reasons seriously (along with their derivative concepts, the *intentional states* such as beliefs that $p$ and desires that $q$), even in scientific moods, without having to suppose that reasons are causes. Descriptions of actions and states in terms of reasons, Dennett argues, are ways of picking out *abstract patterns* (henceforth, following Dennett's usage, *abstracta*) in networks of causation, rather than attempts at isolating causes directly. *Some* chain of causation, to be sure, got my cigar lit; but lots of others could have done just as well. When you say that I struck the match because I wanted to have a few puffs, you are directing attention *away from*, rather than toward, the particular causal sequence that unfolded, and delivering the information that, given the *overall state of my person and its immediate environment at that time*, some one of the many possible sequences that would end in a smoking cigar was likely to happen. In itself, this claim is not somebody's normative judgment; it reports a *fact*, which you were in a position to state because you evidently had some relevant *information* despite (in all probability) having *no* relevant information about states of my nervous system fine enough to pick out hopes for a mouthful of aromatic smoke.

The metaphysics of mind behind this Dennettian story are, of course, much more complicated than the simple sketch above conveys, but here our concern is not with that subject but with the worries of our insecure social scientist. If she is reassured at finding that she can state facts even when speaking about reasoned actions, this will now be overborne by another, closely related, concern that the Dennettian answer will seem to have amplified. When Dennett maintains that in explaining by reference to reasons we are not trying to refer to chains of causation in nervous systems, he shifts almost *all* the weight of intention-attribution justification onto our grounds for thinking that the bearers of the attributed intentions are rational. In explaining my lighting of the match by appeal to my desire for the cigar, you must assume that I believe that lighting the match will produce a flame, and that I believe that a flame is what I need to get the cigar going, and that if I want to smoke my cigar I'll be able to spot the relevance of these beliefs and combine them into an appropriate plan of action, and so on. With breathless audacity for a careful, objective scientist you don't even consider a host of other possible explanations equally compatible with what you saw. ("He was hoping to trim his beard with the flame, but then the cigar in his mouth got in the way, and on its accidental lighting he found that it tasted pretty good and forgot about his beard and . . . etc.") You might even doubt that a cigar is a rational thing to want; and so you jump to the complex assumption that my rationality as you see it holds good until *just* a certain point because . . . well, because what *else* could a *generally* rational person be up to in putting an unlit cigar in his mouth and then striking a match? It will be seen that this doesn't look much at all like defensible scientific reasoning. If you're trying to be very self-consciously abstemious about making assumptions you could probe me with a question, of course, but in treating my response as evidence you must assume that I give true responses to questions unless I have some evident rationale (from your point of view) for lying, leading you back to just the sort of assumption you were trying to avoid. As countless philosophers of social science have stressed, once you have recourse to explanation by appeal to reasons you will not be able to escape the hermeneutic circle from interpretation to goal-attribution and back no matter how long and hard you follow your skeptical scruples.

This sort of concern really is a dominant problem in the epistemological foundations of social science, made especially acute by the fact that subjects of genuine social-scientific inquiry typically differ from the inquirers in ways much more radical than liking cigars when the inquirer doesn't. The anthropologist's subject from an exotic culture, or the historian's interpretive target who lived two hundred years ago, probably *will* connect certain patterns of belief, desire and action in unfamiliar ways; indeed, that is precisely what the social scientist is often hoping to *discover*, the very point of her enterprise. When Dennett tells her that the belief-desire framework ('folk psychology') is a rationalizing interpretive apparatus imposed by the interpreter for purposes of 'making sense' of behaviour, rather than a theory that tracks kinds of causal relations, independently of interpretation, she is apt to say that *that is precisely what she was afraid of.* And she will become almost sure that Dennett's philosophy provides the opposite of comfort to her enterprise when she notices the intellectual company he keeps.

As described in the introduction to this volume, Dennett's work provides crucial philosophical background to the attack by evolutionary psychologists on what Tooby and Cosmides (1992) call the Standard Social Science Model (SSSM). That attack has been uncompromising in its general verdict:

> [T]he content-independent psychology that provides the foundation for the Standard Social Science model is an impossible psychology. It could not have evolved; it requires an incoherent developmental biology; it cannot account for the observed problem-solving abilities of humans or the functional dimension of human behaviour; it cannot explain the recurrent patterns and characteristic contents of human mental life and behavior; it has repeatedly been empirically falsified; and it cannot even explain how humans learn their culture or their language. With the failure of Standard Model psychology, and the emergence of a domain-specific psychology, the remaining logic of the Standard Social Science Model also collapses. (Tooby and Cosmides 1992, p. 14)

The "remaining logic" to which Tooby and Cosmides refer here – although they are slightly coy about the point – is nothing less than the sustaining raison d'être of the disciplines of (at least) sociology and social anthropology as they are now practiced. It goes without saying that this has been controversial. A volume of essays intended for a popular audience (Rose and Rose 2000) has recently been devoted to attacking it. Here rhetoric and indignation dominate argument. Malik (2000) offers

another, much more responsible and conscientious, critique for nonspe-
cialists, while Fodor (2000) has contested the strong adaptationism needed
to drive Tooby's and Cosmides's claims. The issues raised by these criticisms, and their relationship to Dennett's arguments for methodological
adaptationism, are considered in detail in Chapter 10 of this volume. Here,
I am going to *assume* that Tooby and Cosmides (and their colleagues in
the evolutionary psychology program) are broadly correct in thinking that
there is *something* basically amiss in the 'official' theoretical foundations of
the social sciences (although I will not need to endorse their claim that these
problems seriously infect most actual, applied social-scientific study), and
then show how aspects of Dennett's work on intentionality and consciousness enrich and broaden their diagnosis of the trouble. The result, I will
suggest, does not imply the demise of the social sciences. Rather, it implies
their reconstitution as branches of just two: cognitive-evolutionary psychology and economics. That cognitive-evolutionary psychology (hence-
forward CEP) is an essential foundation for the study of social behavior
will be seen to follow immediately from my opening sketch of Tooby and
Cosmides's position, and will require no special new argument from me.
The continuing – indeed, deepened – importance of economics, however,
may seem more surprising. Tooby and Cosmides do, in fact, exempt micro-
economics from their general assault on the SSSM, but, as I will show, the
reason they imply for this exemption is not quite correct. When the better
reason is given, it will turn out that (mainstream) economics is not only
not condemned in association with the other social sciences as traditionally
practiced, but is in fact an essential complement to CEP. The philosophical
foundations on which this argument of mine will rest are due mainly to
Dennett, as I will explain.

## 1. COGNITIVE-EVOLUTIONARY PSYCHOLOGY AND THE STANDARD SOCIAL SCIENCE MODEL

The SSSM, as Tooby and Cosmides present it, may be sketched as follows.
Human individuals are endowed by their genetic heritage with a few highly
generic 'urges' (e.g., for food, sex, companionship, a range of preferred environmental temperatures, and so on) and an equally unspecialized set of
general learning capacities realized in their neural structures. The reper-
toires of much more specific goals and purposes they acquire after birth,
along with the special skills, bodies of factual knowledge and interpretive
practices necessary to try to achieve these goals and purposes, are then

learned. A certain amount of such learning can be done by the individual on her own; to cite the standard example, she can learn by her own private probing that hot oven elements had best not be touched. For the most part, however, such individual learning is both inefficient – because the number of hypotheses to be formulated and tested is too large – and too dangerous to be carried out by the person acting alone. (The best account of this set of points, although one consistent with CEP rather than with the SSSM, is in fact given by Dennett [1996].) Human organisms must therefore be molded into the fully purposive and skilled *persons* they (normally) become through cultural learning. But since nature provides only highly generic goals, and since even these (e.g., for sexual contacts) may be subverted culturally (e.g., by the cultivation of monastic impulses and institutions), the scope for variance with respect to behavioural patterns amongst cultures is enormous. We should therefore expect that as human communities spread and diversify, in their circumstances and then in their traditions, variance will grow and cross-cultural similarities will decrease. At the same time, cultures grow internally complex as they evolve, to the point at which the learning individual confronts not a 'given' world that her culture helps her to understand and manipulate, but a collectively *interpreted* world that she may understand (or misunderstand, or perhaps only *re*understand, depending on the radicalism of a particular social scientist's level of constructivism), in the way a reader treats a text (Wagner 1981; Geertz 1983). This picture is further complicated by the fact that most individuals, at least in modern societies, are born into not one culture but several, all operating cooperatively or competitively in various biologically arbitrary, and often politically contested, domains. Thus, a given person might simultaneously be raised in an Italian-American culture, a family military culture, a working class culture, a postmodern literary culture, a consumerist culture, and so on. The individual and her personal history of behaviors and relationships constitutes a knot in this complex cultural web, which can only be understood objectively by treating the various cultural constructions as more or less autonomous forces impinging on and interacting with one another. Understanding cultures in their symbolic senses is (roughly) the task of the social anthropologist, while understanding their interactions and political and economic dynamics is (roughly) the task of the sociologist.

I do not think that this sketch caricatures the SSSM; many social scientists hold the view as I have just described it quite explicitly. It is not monolithic among them, however. Some social scientists of course recognize that biological influences may exert a greater degree of influence on behaviors and capacities than was acknowledged during either the heyday of empiricist behaviorism or the early days of social constructivism (which tossed away behaviourism's realism and determinism but not its extreme psychological empiricism). These possible biological influences are commonly treated by social scientists as *constraints* on the learning potentials of individuals. However, they will then often point out (correctly, at least in this context) that constraints at the level of individual learning may be transcended at the level of *group* learning. To suppose that what is biologically natural to the untutored individual should be given precedence over the conclusions (empirical, interpretive, and moral) of cultural learning is, we are often told, equivalent to 'siding with our genes' against our own best, necessarily collective, accomplishments as a species and as communities within that species. As cultures develop in complexity, it is supposed, ever wider domains of behavior come to be 'controlled by' cultural forces *rather than* by biological ones. (This is often the only sort of a moral progress that relativistic social scientists will allow as possible.)

The view taken by Tooby and Cosmides and by numerous other researchers in the CEP tradition is that the picture of the human world as just described is almost entirely false or misleading, resting on fundamental ignorance and/or misunderstanding of the nature of both evolutionary processes and of cognitive structures. I will work back through the elements of the SSSM as sketched, showing briefly how, according to Tooby and Cosmides, initial errors of assumption cascade to produce an edifice of confusion.

First, they argue that the concept of a generic biological 'urge' makes neither evolutionary nor psychological sense. No mechanism in human (or feline, or insect) brains or DNA realizes a general urge even for reproduction (something often falsely cited as a central assumption of evolutionary theory). Evolution cannot produce such mechanisms since it is guided by no engineer with the foresight necessary to perceive and work toward such abstract goals. Instead, organisms that are better, probabilistically, at reproducing leave more copies of their own particular mechanisms for use by future generations. These mechanisms are organs – some, like fingers, literal machines in the seventeenth-century sense of the word, others, such as programmers for face recognition, machines in the more expansive twentieth-century sense – that serve the 'goal' of reproductive fitness only at one remove (at least one), by more proximately supporting the limited goals that define them as machines in the first place. That is, while there can be (and are) machines for picking up and manipulating delicate objects, and machines for identifying particular conspecific faces with particular personal concepts, there are no machines for 'leaving lots of descendants.'

A good way of seeing this distinction clearly is to express it in terms of what does and doesn't follow from manifest evolutionary success. There *is* a sense in which every individual alive today is a product of ancestors who were 'good at' leaving descendants. However, no inherited genetic structures code directly for any such capacity because it is not, and cannot be, the immediate product of any *mechanism*; and genes build only mechanisms, which may or may not subserve abstractly described functions depending on the characteristics of environments in which they find themselves. Thus, the fact that a present organism evidently had ancestors who were 'good at' reproducing does not imply that that organism is also 'good' in this respect, since her environment – including that part identified with her 'culture' – might no longer present her with opportunities in which the mechanisms with which she is genetically equipped can interact with one another to create copies. Someone whose cognitive routines make her good at attracting healthy sexual partners might use those same routines to convince the partners to use contraceptives. By contrast, someone whose fingers make her good at manipulation of delicate objects really is unambiguously good at such manipulation, even if new technology deprives the skill of its value. This distinction might initially appear purely scholastic, or as a dogmatic insistence on privileging one level of relationship between capacities and goals over another. The point of importance here, however, is this: Evolution, like a person herself, has 'purposes' only when viewed from the 'intentional stance' (see the Introduction to this volume, and Chapter 10). Machines, by contrast, have purposes visible from 'the design stance' alone. The difference this makes in practice is as follows. Intentional purposes are abstract goals that can be achieved in any of a number of ways. Design purposes, by contrast, are particular *means* of bringing certain causal processes through to fruition.

The damage done by confusion between intentional and design purposes in the foundations of the SSSM shows up most clearly and perniciously in the view of genetic inheritances as *constraints* (Tooby and Cosmides 1992, p. 36). Intentional purposes may genuinely be constraints, since in a world of scarce resources to be committed to one general goal is typically to eschew others; and this is exactly the sense of 'constraint' embedded in the description of genetic endowments from the standpoint of the SSSM as given above. By contrast, there is no sense in which having the capacity to pick up a pencil, or to recognize a face, is a constraint. (Of course, if you can pick up a pencil in one way perhaps you can't pick it up in another way; but a limitation on means rather than ends is *not* the sense of 'constraint' usually intended by social scientists writing about biological influences). The belief that genetic heritages build constraints as opposed to capacities licenses the following bad inference, found early in the sketch of the SSSM: Since the range of significant possible human goals does not seem to be very significantly constrained, the biological element in human behavior must be sharply limited, or, at least, strongly overridable. And if biological 'urges' are frequently overridden, what could be doing this overriding if not culture? ('Will' was once the most popular answer among philosophers; it is anything but among social scientists.) Note the way in which this inference converges on the SSSM by two possible paths: If genetic inheritances are constraints, then the range of cultural and individual variability suggests that they aren't very strong; and to the extent that they *are* strong in places, culture provides the key force that might 'oppose' them.

Before we return to the point, let us reapproach it from another angle. I said above that the view of biological humans as driven only by generic urges is implausible *both* from the evolutionary and the cognitive points of view. So far, however, we have considered only the first set of grounds for the implausibility. It leads fairly directly, however, to the second set. If evolutionary purposes are entirely general, then the evolved mechanisms by which individuals learn ways of achieving these goals must also be general. The empiricist psychology that underwrites the SSSM has thus devoted most of its energy, by methodological fiat, to searching for and studying the capacities of general-purpose learning systems. Tooby and Cosmides spend the majority of their long paper showing both that and why such systems cannot be the basis for complex behavior. General-purpose learning systems tend to be crippled by the absence of biases and specific, content-driven focus; they are not enhanced by such 'freedom.' As researchers in artificial intelligence painfully discovered, machines that can in principle learn anything cannot pick the practical needles from the logical haystacks they confront. They are rendered behaviourally stupid – unable, that is, to *do things*, as opposed to store facts – by the so-called frame problem. A system that does not find its world presorted into self-contained domains of relationships and strong initial selectivity on both the information that will be received and the packages into which it will be arranged, along with predetermined routines for using this information to reliably generate certain kinds of outputs, will often be incapable of either significant learning or coherent action unless that world is exceedingly simple and stable. (A clear, but entertaining and highly accessible, guide to the frame problem and its implications, is provided by Dennett [1984].) Many models in cognitive science – especially in the so-called Artificial Life research program (see Langton 1989) – thus seek to implement sophisticated learning capacities not by building general-purpose associative mechanisms, but by highly specialized input-output computers, usually called 'modules' in the trade.[1] Complex, often uncoordinated, interactions amongst these modules, it is claimed, produce much of the behavioral complexity and variability celebrated by adherents of the SSSM. Such complexity and variability, therefore, does not contradict the claim that much human behavior is produced by dedicated, highly domain-specialized modules; on the contrary, such complexity is predicted by modularity.

The advocate of the SSSM may try, at this point, to turn a premise used against her model into one that counts in its favor. If a general-purpose learning system cannot cope with an unsorted world, she may argue, and if people are naturally equipped only with such systems, then perhaps it is precisely the edifice of culture that is called on to impose the necessary order. Tooby and Cosmides, as one would expect, reject this response uncategorically. Some of their objections cite difficulties arising from data on infant, child, and adolescent development.[2] Here, I will pass over this aspect of the argument simply by noting that the data are not univocal. (See Karmiloff-Smith 1992.) Their more general objection is derived from a long-standing claim of Jerry Fodor's. A 'culture,' the argument goes, is, in the sense of the concept relevant to semantic learning, a set of conventions for associating certain sound-patterns with certain concepts (and, from there, with complex embedded networks of signification). In that case, Fodor wonders, how could a general-purpose learner infer the correct conventional associations unless it already possesses the concepts for which its culture provides symbols? This echoes an earlier worry due to Quine (1960). If knowledge of meaning must be built up recursively (that is, guided by reference to already established meanings), then how could the learning of conventions ever get *started* for a general learning-system that faces a world unsorted into pre-established conceptual spaces? Such a learner, Quine argues, lacks the "wedge into semantic ascent," that is, the ability to understand, either prelinguistically or at the level of fully digitalized conceptualization, what its elders are trying to tell it when they set about teaching it their associative conventions.

The flat rejection of the possibility of general learning that Tooby and Cosmides derive from such considerations[3] could (and should) be tempered by a more careful reading of Dennett. It rests crucially on the idea that a system's semantic knowledge is entirely 'in its head,' and then raises seemingly insuperable difficulties about what could put the semantics there if there was no internal semantic frame to begin with. In Dennett's view, however, when we focus on the purely internal mechanisms that drive a system's behavior – including its learning – we are engaged in what he calls 'sub-personal cognitive psychology' (henceforth SPCP) (Dennett 1981). There is no reason to suppose that the elements over which theories at this level will be built will be units familiar to folk psychology, such as beliefs or desires that $p$ or sentences asserting $p$ in some neural code, or their philosophical refinements, propositions and propositional attitudes. Indeed, the most promising proto-theories we presently find at this level, connectionist learning theory and neuropsychology, deal in vector-transformations across state spaces that find closer analogues in the physics of thermodynamics than in any hitherto conceptualized intensional psychology. (See Clark 1989 and Churchland 1995, respectively, for nontechnical introductions to the two proto-theories.) Full-fledged intensional semantics of the familiar sort emerges, according to Dennett, only when we step up to the more abstract level at which we seek to capture informational patterns that describe systematic *relations* amongst a system's goals, representations, and environment. We do this for the sake not of explaining the internal microcauses of the system's behavior, but for the sake of understanding the system's global capacities and dispositions in terms of recurrent patterns in its responses to environmentally posed problems that are characteristic of wider classes of intelligent systems of which the system in question seems to be a member. Here is the level of informational categorization at which we ascribe the kinds of content supported by cultural evolution. Dennett (1981) calls this 'intentional system (IS) theory.'

IS theory idealizes its subjects. That is, it is the perspective from which we ask what a system *ought* to do and to represent to itself *given that* it is (perfectly) designed to solve a particular class of problems. Now, we know that no systems (or, at least, none built by natural selection, with its absence of foresight) are in fact perfectly designed. Where cognitive capacities, including learning capacities, are concerned a basic limitation is the following: A system can't act on the basis of inferences, however rational, that would require the manipulation of information it can't acquire or compute. In this way, mechanisms identified by SPCP for a given class of systems force relaxations of the optimality assumptions in the IS models of that class. However, mechanisms are only identifiable *as* mechanisms given the prior specifications of some functions for them to perform, and this function-specification is done from the perspective of IS. According to Dennett, then, the fundamental methodology of the behavioral sciences works as follows. One begins by building an IS model of the target system. One does this by identifying the problems posed for it by its extracognitive environment, including its own morphology, which generates budget constraints (e.g., snakes can't follow the example of frogs and enhance their survival prospects by catching flies with their tongues), and then seeking 'whole organism level' functional models that simultaneously optimize the solutions to the problems given the constraints. (The technically minded might be helped here by thinking of this modeling as a kind of generalized linear programming.) The IS model will yield predictions of behavior that must then be tested against the target system's *actual* behavior in the field. Some discrepancies can and will typically be handled by adjusting the IS model itself, but many will require relaxation of the original optimality assumptions, specifically motivated by what SPCP modeling reveals about the information-processing mechanisms at the system's disposal. Ultimately, the system must not be assigned any cognitive capacities that could not be supported by a plausible mechanism. However, one must remember that mechanisms need not be capable of operating in isolation just as they do *in situ*, and that some information exploited by a system may be stored only virtually, in the form of redundancies created by patterns of causal and covariational reliability in the external environment.

This last point is especially relevant to the problems with Tooby's and Cosmides's campaign against general learning mechanisms, including cultural ones. It *may* be true that the brain cannot employ general learning mechanisms at the SPCP level of analysis. (This is a technical issue best studied using computation theory and the other methods of AI in the strictest sense of 'AI,' that is, *ex*cluding the 'whole organism' approach of artificial life.) However, if this *is* true, it does not imply that semantics specifiable only at the IS level could not be derived from relational patterns embedding subpersonal cognitive mechanisms in environments, including cultural environments. Consider the following example. In conversations with my mechanic, I can use the word 'carburetor' to both convey and receive plenty of useful information, despite the fact that I'm almost completely ignorant about how engines work and have no idea where the carburetor is or what it does. There are minimal requirements on my being able to do anything with the concept of a carburetor, but they're mostly negative: I could do nothing at all with the idea if I thought that carburetors were vegetables, or demons. Now, to ask a standard philosopher's question: Do I have the concept 'carburetor' or not? Clearly, I'm missing a great deal of the concept, but I don't have *nothing*; I really would be practically worse off if I thought that carburetors were demons. Notice, however, that this 'something' I have is almost all 'stored' in cultural information external to data-structures that could be recovered at the level of a subpersonal model of my information-processing abilities. I live in a culture that has the concept, and I know that

I do, and I can exploit this fact to achieve reference to whatever, as far as I can tell, inhabits the relevant black box. If everyone who knows where carburetors are and what they're for perished in a deadly plague among the automotively competent, the concept would die with them, leaving only an empty word as its vestigial trace. At that point, I and others like me really would have nothing in the carburetor-concept department, beyond a bit of lexical arcana historically related to it, despite the fact that, by hypothesis, nothing has changed in our individual cognitive capacities. I do not think that this variety of semantic parasitism on culturally stored competence is an unusual or deviant case; it is an instance of the standard one. This is one of the reasons why necessary-and-sufficient condition definitions are hard to produce and to make counterexample-proof, even of concepts whose use-conditions are fluently grasped in practice, and why Socrates, who insisted that all knowledge requires such definitions, can tie all of his interlocutors in knots.

Examples like this do *not* show that minds empty of structure could learn anything interesting. Cultures likely could not arise in communities of such minds, just as Tooby and Cosmides say (and as almost anyone, including diehard advocates of the SSSM, might admit). What such examples *are* supposed to suggest is that *not all semantic learning need map onto processes identifiable at the level of SPCP*. Indeed, if Dennett is right then at the IS level, from which the concepts associated with 'culture' are identified, subpersonal learning and computation *aren't what we're trying to talk about*. On this view, the question 'Can (do) people learn networks of culturally embedded concepts using the general processes of their brains, or using dedicated modules?' is a bad question, because people don't learn such concepts *just using their brains*. Whole-organisms-in-environments may well be general learning 'mechanisms' even if brains are not.

Despite their overstatement of the case against general-purpose learning, however, Tooby and Cosmides do not by any means write off the importance of environments for the development and manifestation of cognitive capacities. They take the mind/environment barrier to be sufficiently fluid that we should give up trying to understand the acquisition of complex capacities by asking how much of a given capacity is due to 'nature' and how much to 'nurture.' If a capacity is genuinely complex, they maintain, then this is evidence that it is the product of heavily prestructured input-output mechanisms that are built to accept and process only certain sorts of input. But, they add, input-output systems will not do anything interesting without the input. Therefore, an environment is as essential to cognitive development as are the mechanisms it tunes. In the case of a social animal such as a person, conspecifics provide the essential input for many crucial mechanisms, such as the 'folk psychology module' that causes children to naturally account for the actions of animate creatures in terms of unobservable beliefs and desires (and which, if impaired, may produce autism; see Baron-Cohen et al. [1985], and Chapter 4 of this volume). These conspecific influences can, after a certain stage of development, be implicated in almost *any* behavior or experience because (i) some modules are mechanisms for comparing the outputs of other modules [see Ross 1990, 1993a], but (ii), more significantly in the case of humans, acquisition of a shared digital encoding device – a public language – allows organisms to take already processed output from others (and from themselves) as input for further processing (Dennett 1991a). These wonderful loops are what make possible the vast collective enterprises, extending for (in principle) boundless distances through time and local space, in which people engage and which is the most distinctive behavioral capacity of the species.

Is the existence of this capacity not sufficient to get the SSSM off the ground after all? Perhaps the anthropologist and the sociologist must wait until an individual has acquired a language before they bring their interpretations and systems to bear on her behavior and on other interpretations of it (including, of course, the subject's own interpretations), but many important social scientists have seemed happy enough to grant this, since it resonates nicely with a predilection to see the culturally constructed world as a set of texts. Dennett has said a good deal that suggests this view. It is especially prominent in Dennett 1991a, where he provides a phylogenetic account of the self as a construction forced on every individual by the social environment, which modifies computational structures at the subpersonal level during ontogeny. The particular social requirement that forces each human organism to build a self is the need for a roughly consistent folk-psychological historical narrative that can be communicated to others, and this in turn is a product of our need to render our plans, experiences and justifications into public language for purposes of coordination. This view, however, is consistent with Tooby's and Cosmides's emphasis of the point that regardless of how prominent and ubiquitous socially processed information becomes in an environment, the inherited biological processing mechanisms do not stop operating and do not cease to be necessary for keeping all the socially constructed balls in the air. At the very least, the social scientist must abandon the perspective according to which social and cultural forces are causally autonomous and independent of the sorts of processes studied by CEP. Talk of this or that as a 'pure' social or cultural construct does not, on this view, make clear sense. Furthermore, the social scientist must resist the temptation to try to ask 'how much' of behavior is 'controlled' by culture and how much is 'controlled' by biological and psychological mechanisms, since it is environmental input that determines the output of the mechanisms, but the structure and nature of the mechanisms plays a crucial role in determining what happens to input and what gets taken as 'input' to particular cognitive procedures in the first place.

Tooby and Cosmides leave their criticism of the SSSM at roughly this point. In their view, a social scientist who grants the concessions just demanded has abandoned the SSSM, and can now usefully practice her anthropology or her sociology in a way that is integrated with CEP (and, by transitivity, with what CEP is in turn integrated with, which stretches through biology and neurophysiology all the way across the natural sciences). What I wish to do here is show how this picture is extended by what I will call *the Dennettian method* for behavioral explanation, and how this extension can help to resolve some impasses resulting from the subsequent criticisms to which Tooby's and Cosmides's critique has been exposed.

## 2. ADAPTATIONISM AND REVERSE ENGINEERING

Tooby's and Cosmides's attack on the SSSM has met with a rather furious response from some social scientists concerned to defend the autonomy of their disciplines. The idea that sociological and other social-scientific explanations are entirely independent of biology (and even psychology) goes back at least to Durkheim (1895), who was explicit and tendentious on the point. Rose and Rose (2000) have recently assembled a panel of (mostly) social scientists who argue this case in direct opposition to the claims of evolutionary psychologists. Most of these responses rely on a premise to the effect that Tooby and Cosmides require an implausibly strong *adaptationist* thesis. In Chapter 10, I outline a general reply to this charge that can be offered on the basis of Dennett's work. Here, I will summarize that reply only briefly, on my way to making a more positive point. There *is* a sense, I will show, in which social scientific explanations can be autonomous, at least in their construction (though not in their final refinements); but the only social science that consistently achieves autonomy in this appropriate sense is economics. Sociological and historical accounts can manage it to the extent that they are exercises in applied economics, or so I will argue.

First, however, a few words are required on the adaptationism issue. The classic criticism of adaptationism is given in Gould and Lewontin (1979), to which Dennett replies at length in both *The Intentional Stance* (1987) and *Darwin's Dangerous Idea* (1995). Gould and Lewontin stress the extent to which many products of evolution are side-effects, consequences of developmental constraints, or results of accidents. The shape of the human jaw is often cited as an example of a developmental side-effect: It is not a direct adaptation to any purpose, but a consequence of the evolution of human dentition. The asteroid explosion that was the probable cause of the extinction of the dinosaurs, and, hence, of the subsequent rise of the mammals, provides the most spectacular, and therefore standard, instance of an exogenous accident that substantially rerouted evolution's trajectory. According to Gould and Lewontin, to the extent that many evolutionary outcomes are products of such side-effects and accidents, rather than of natural selection, they are not adaptations, and we will fail to give accurate histories of them if we seek to explain them by trying to find their functions.

This criticism is generalized in much of the literature following a standard extended treatment given by Elliot Sober (1984). Natural selection is characterized as one of several *forces* driving evolution, along with others. One of these is *genetic drift*, the tendency of gene frequencies in populations to shift over time as consequences of accumulated accidents at the molecular level that are not filtered by any systematic selection pressures. Another is geographical change, which can erect or remove barriers between populations in ways which are, it is often claimed, unrelated to fitness. Finally, a number of forces at the molecular level are cited that are held to be relatively insensitive to selection pressures from outside the genome. (See Sigmund 1992 for a survey.) Within this framework, the arguments between adaptationists and their critics are then presented, often by both sides, as empirical debates over the *strength* of natural selection as an evolutionary force relative to the others. Defenders of the SSSM such as those appearing in Rose and Rose (2000) then argue that, where the phenomena typically studied by social scientists are concerned, intended and unintended cultural and social-structural forces operate with a strength that effectively swamps that of natural selection acting on psychological structures. (These critics often *also* feel it necessary to resist evolutionary models of cultural change such as those defended by Dawkins [1982] and Dennett [1995]. However, this is a logically distinct issue, since social sciences could still be autonomous even if the main causal and explanatory mechanism to which they appealed was cultural evolution.)

Dennett does not accept the premise within which this debate is framed, because his adaptationism is not empirical but *conceptual*. For Dennett, to organize the sequences of conceptions and births of organisms that make up the history of life into patterns of evolutionary development, in which organisms sort into populations within which gene frequencies can change, and into species such that we can study lines of descent from one to another, is to imply function in nature from the start. Specifically, we assume the intentional stance toward a mindless selection process, and the design stance toward its products. The use of these stances to identify abstract patterns in natural history is, for Dennett, logically identical to their use in establishing patterns of mental phenomena with which to characterize and explain the behavior of entities equipped with nervous systems. Just as we idealize the rationality of individual cognitive systems when we assume the intentional stance toward them, so we idealize the rationality of the evolutionary design process (although only in some respects, since we must ascribe no foresight to it) when we assume the intentional stance toward *it*. Now, in viewing each other as intentional systems we obviously don't thereby rule out accidents or unanticipated environmental contingencies that thwart plans and turn sound assumptions into disastrous mistakes. Similarly with the operation of IS reasoning in evolutionary theory: We can agree that dinosaurs were good designs for which a rich lineage of descendents could have been expected well into the past 65 million years given the standing probabilities on all relevant environmental and biological contingencies; but then something terrible happened and destroyed most of the design work. We distinguish this sort of case from one in which a species or group meets extinction because of design flaws; thus, for example, it is sometimes claimed that cheetahs are disappearing naturally because their genetic variability has been forced through an unsustainably small bottleneck. This is just the same distinction as the one we habitually draw between good plans of agents that go unexpectedly awry, and bad plans. Dennett thus need not deny – and certainly *does not* deny – that many events in the history of life are accidents, or products of causes visible from the physical stance such as genetic drift and systematic molecular processes. But he does not view these influences as causal forces *competing* with natural selection for influence, since they arise at a different level of explanatory organization. Most philosophers, and not just Dennettians, would agree that it is not fruitful to think of neuroelectrical activity as (in general) competing with thought to influence the behaviors and biographies of people, since neuroelectrical activity is a necessary part of the set of vehicles by which people think. Similarly, the myriad accidents of encounters, conceptions, infections, births, interactions with weather and natural disasters and so forth that constitute natural history, *with the web of statistical regularities they embed, and which the design stance permits us to notice and track,* are the main part of the set of vehicles by which natural selection runs its ongoing fitness tournament. Dennett's conflict with Gould and the other adaptationists is in the end, therefore, not empirical but philosophical.

This does not entirely answer the anti-adaptationist's objection, however. The critic of Tooby and Cosmides will still echo Gould in complaining that evolutionary psychologists assign functions to patterns of behavior that, if they are in fact side-effects of cultural or other social structures, may have none. In order to understand Dennett's answer to this worry, we must elaborate briefly on the epistemology of function-specification. A major recent advance in this area is due to Ruth Millikan (1984), who defines the notion of a 'proper function' and applies it specifically to aspects of language and cognition. We fix the proper function of an organ or behavioral disposition by asking the following counterfactual question: In the absence of which selection pressures would the organ or disposition have failed to evolve and/or be sustained? Note two questions we do *not* ask in fixing proper functions: (1) To what uses is the organ or disposition mainly put *now*?; and (2) What tasks are/were successfully accomplished by means of the organ or disposition most of the time? The motivation for eschewing (2) as a selector of proper functions is that some organs and dispositions, such as sperm cells, realize their function only occasionally; yet it is unquestionably the occasional successes that explain why sperm evolved and are maintained. With respect to the first excluded condition, the motivation is that we want our specification of functions to depend on facts rather than interpretations. It may happen, perhaps even often, that an organ is exapted under changing evolutionary circumstances and recruited to a new function. But this only constitutes a change in its *proper* function if in the absence of the exaptation the organ would disappear in the lineage. Dennett has been inclined to a less rigid interpretation of the role of exaptations in specifying proper functions (see Millikan 2000 and Dennett 2000), but in most other respects he has been pleased to welcome Millikan's work as a careful development of the consequences of his own. The importance of the notion for our purposes is that it enables us to identify *facts* (though these may or may not be available to us in any given case) against which we can test functional attributions made from the intentional and design stances; and this is crucial if we are to have principled ways of relaxing our idealizations against empirical evidence from a level of investigation analogous to that of SPCP in psychology.

The notion of a proper function also plays a crucial role in connecting Dennett's theory of individual intentionality with his interpretation of evolutionary theory, and is thus central to a Dennettian version of CEP.

According to Dennett (1987), an organism inherits its basic, and many of its specific, goals from the proper functions of its cognitive and other behavior-guiding mechanisms. (Of course, many complex goals may then go on to be developed by the organism, if it has a substantial brain, in interaction with its conspecifics on the platform provided by the inherited goals.) This leads him to speak of human intentionality as *derived* from the 'original' locus of intentionality in an unconscious 'agent,' natural selection itself. Many commentators have expressed discomfort with this fundamental separation between agency and consciousness, though Ross (1993b) defends and expands upon it. The point of it is mainly to emphasize that goals are not willed *de novo* by organisms, but themselves evolve both within *and* outside the organism's own learning history, and this is a claim that few cognitive scientists would dispute. Furthermore, since agents do not have access to some definitive 'register of intentions' in consciousness, they must consult behavioral and evolutionary evidence about themselves in interpreting their own goals and intentions; in this respect they are on all fours, epistemically, with outside observers.

Proper functions are sometimes easy to specify on the basis of straightforward inferences and a few behavioral or other facts. Thus we have no difficulty identifying the proper functions of a rattlesnake's fangs or a woman's mammary glands. Where organs have multiple uses the inferential task can be much more difficult. Thus, for example, we are unlikely to find the proper function of the elephant's trunk without careful attention to the fossil record, and even this may leave crucial evidence forever obscured from our view. We must also exercise care in individuating organs in the first place. It is not clear, for instance that it makes sense to ask for a proper function of the human brain, since it is likely an assemblage of *separately* selected mechanisms yoked together by morphological and developmental constraints. (It would *certainly* be a mistake to think of the mammalian brain stem and the neocortex as parts of one organ linked by a single proper function, since they evolved millennia apart and under significantly different selection pressures.) This is *part* of the basis for Dennett's skepticism about Millikan's uncompromising realism concerning the *determinateness* of proper functions. (Note that we can deny that evidence will absolutely *fix* proper functions without implying that their approximate identification is *independent* of evidence, which would destroy the point of postulating them.) Fortunately, as we will see shortly, we are not restricted to (possibly) lost evolutionary history and underspecified present behavioral patterns as our sole sources of evidence in proper-function specification. In any case, Dennett has been quite explicit about the appropriate procedure for understanding nature's more complex biological products. We must follow, he argues, the method of *reverse engineering*.

As Dennett (1994) begins by pointing out, reverse engineering is a practice familiar to actual human engineers, especially those who work in product design.

> When Raytheon wants to make an electric widget to compete with General Electric's widget, they buy several of GE's widgets, and analyze them: that's reverse engineering. They run them, benchmark them, x-ray them, take them apart, and subject every part of them to interpretive analysis: Why did GE make these wires so heavy? What are these extra ROM registers for? Is this a double layer of insulation and, if so, why did they bother with it? Notice that the reigning assumption is that all these 'why' questions have answers. Everything has a *raison d'être*, GE did nothing in vain.
>
> Of course if the wisdom of the reverse engineers includes a healthy helping of self-knowledge, they will recognize that this default assumption of optimality is too strong: sometimes engineers put stupid, pointless things in their designs, sometimes they forget to remove things that no longer have a function. Sometimes they overlook retrospectively obvious shortcuts. But still, optimality must be the default assumption; if the reverse engineers can't assume that there is a good rationale for the features they observe, they can't even begin their analysis. (Dennett 1998, p. 254)

Dennett advocates the same default assumption, and with the same motivation, for interpreters of nature's designs. Indeed, he stresses that where products of evolution are concerned the importance of reverse engineering is even greater. Because evolution has no foresight, it is more tolerant than human engineers of harmless unanticipated side-effects and interactions in its designs. This in turn, combined with its endless blind patience, allows it to stumble across occasional *beneficial* interactions, and makes it more likely to produce designs that have *multiple* functions. Forward engineering, in which biological products are viewed strictly from the physical instead of the design or intentional stances, is unlikely to arrive at these, since they are entirely path-dependent. Reverse engineering is therefore the key to discovering them.

It is important to be clear about the location of the necessary optimality assumption in reverse engineering of nature's products. We cannot assume that evolution is a *global* optimizer, since it has no overall goal against which optimality could be measured. Instead, we assume that it *locally* optimizes. That is, having gotten as far as the manufacture of a particular line of organisms, it seeks and then refines those features that tend to maximize the expected number of grandchildren in a randomly drawn hypothetical representative of the brand. (We must put matters this way because the only product-development work done at the level of the particular organism is roughly random; there is no optimizing activity in meiosis itself.) This does *not* imply that individual organisms will be maximizers of actual numbers of grandchildren, since, as noted earlier, evolution can design to that specification only at the abstract level of species-engineering; it builds no mechanisms for *direct* fitness-enhancement. The functions subserved at the level of individual organs and dispositions typically (although certainly not always) have instead to do with maximum expected prolongation of lifespan *given* sacrifices built at the level of species-design with respect to organs and dispositions associated with reproduction. Thus, for example, a male peacock is stuck with his long, dangerous (to himself) tail because his male ancestors would not have given rise to him had they not had such tails themselves to attract mates. And, of course, many animals have dispositions for individually costly fighting over sexual opportunities, dispositions to self-sacrifice for the sake of offspring, and so on. Again, however, these specifications are built *at the species level*. With respect to the level at which we 'reverse engineer' an animal's individual organs, we expect them to represent points along an overall budget curve that, in aggregate, is designed to serve the direct purpose of maximizing the animal's expected probability of surviving to and through its reproductive peak. (After that point, its apparent design reflects a 'designer' who increasingly ceases to care what happens to it.) We will partition the organism's organs and behavioral patterns into the most accurate ensemble of mechanisms for this analytic exercise just to the extent that we hit on the correct set of proper functions, and this requires attention to the history of its morphology as inferred from the fossil record and from fixing the organism's phylogenetic relationships. Pace what one would imagine from many of the anti-adaptationist critiques, empirical evidence is thus relevant and to be used even at this most abstract stage of theory construction following Dennett.

That said, the assumptions used in biological reverse engineering *are* abstract and *will* ignore many important details invisible from the design stance – as the anti-adaptationist critic will be only too quick to forcefully remind us. We have made no allowance as yet for effects of kin selection (which may cause some organisms to be designed to self-destruct in defense of close genetic relatives), or environmentally contingent variables that interact with fitness-enhancing design principles (such as the presence of malaria in the ancestral environment, which stabilizes a positive probability of sickle cell anemia in some populations of humans), or a host of other complications. But this, in an important sense, is the point. No biologist ever applies the *simple* optimality assumption because no biologist is *altogether* ignorant of particular complications in the evolutionary economy of the species she is studying. But to the extent that she is trying to learn about further complications of which she is yet unaware, what she will do is assume optimal design subject to the constraints she already knows about, and then *test* this assumption against behavioural, morphological, genetic, and other detailed evidence. The point of beginning with optimality assumptions in reverse engineering is to provide a clear baseline against which to discover and measure the extent to which evolutionary products are quirky; this is how we come to understand both what they do and the details of how they came to be. This whole procedure, beginning from optimizing IS theory, is what I am calling *the Dennettian method in behavioural explanation*. He would have us deploy it in every discipline concerned with behaviour, from entomology to social anthropology.

When we apply the reverse engineering method to minds and psycho-logical mechanisms, the optimal design default that we provisionally adopt is simply the rationality assumption of IS theory. What is meant here is *not* rationality in the sense often used by philosophers, which has its proximate origins in the work of Descartes and, especially, Kant. That is, we do not suppose that the mind arrives only or mainly at conclusions that accord with the consequents of sound deductive arguments. That is, in fact, an *irrational* way to go about practical thinking and planning, since it sacrifices productivity of inference for minimization of error. There is no clear rea-son as to why an organism would want to guide its behaviour this way, and there are excellent reasons for doubting that evolution's designs could pos-sibly arrive at this method directly. (Some of them, of course, all human, arrived at it *indirectly*; evolution made Kant possible, after all.) As Fodor (1983) pointed out, if 75 percent of the things rustling behind bushes in one's environment are rabbits and the other 25 percent are tigers, it may be better to be paranoid than scientific and to run from all rustles rather than wait for more reliable evidence. When we assume rationality as our first step in studying minds, what we instead suppose is that creatures are rational in the *economic* sense of the word. Specifically, we assume that they can discriminate between preferred states of the world and less preferred ones, can relate their possible actions to rough probabilities of outcomes in various circumstances, and will choose, all else being equal, those actions that raise the probabilities of desirable outcomes over those of less desir-able outcomes. We do not necessarily suppose that rational creatures can entertain and formulate these rules of rationality, only that their behaviour approximately accords with them. This sense of 'rationality' is not just *more or less* the economist's one; it is *exactly* the trio of assumptions that economists take as *definitive* of a rational economic agent. Like the biologist or evolutionary psychologist, the economist does not imagine that natural people are always, or even usually, identical with perfectly rational agents. But all three sorts of inquirers require specific, situated *evidence* about a particular kind of mind-endowed organism before *either* suspending or supplementing these assumptions. For Dennett, to be an organism whose control system is best reverse engineered from this starting point is *what it means* to be an intentional system, that is, a thing with a mind. Therefore, Dennettian intentional systems just *are* economic agents, and vice-versa.

This claim – my central one here – needs a good deal of further justification and elaboration. Let us first, though, be clear about what is at stake when we consider it. Economists have been at least as snooty about their disciplinary autonomy as other social scientists, and one might thus assume that the unifying program of CEP would imply changes in their methodology just as it does for sociologists. However, what I will now argue is that economics wins a kind of procedural autonomy – although not ultimate explanatory autonomy – insofar as it really is IS theory; and IS theory is, after all, distinct from SPCP, even if the two must be used in conjunction to deliver complete explanations of particular behavioral phenomena. To the extent that other social sciences apply the methods of economics, therefore, we will have identified a way in which these disciplines can be relatively autonomous while still contributing to CEP.

## 3. ECONOMICS AS INTENTIONAL-SYSTEMS THEORY

For much of its recent history, economics has simply been a formal elaboration of the strict implications of the three rationality conditions just described. What was crucially added around 1870, by (independently) William Stanley Jevons, Carl Menger, and Leon Walras, was the idea that, in conditions of scarcity, a rational agent that desires two or more goods $x$ and $y$ will be increasingly inclined to spend more resources on $y$ as his stock of $x$ increases and vice versa. This *marginal principle*, grounded in the logic of optimization rather than in any empirical claim about human behavior, allowed for the mathematical construction of an equilibrium concept as applied to a single agent – who will value both $x$ and $y$ at the prices that leave him indifferent between further units of either – and did not require a system of producers and consumers. Thus, as every economics undergraduate used to be taught, one can derive all of the fundamental economic concepts, including capital, interest, and labor, on Robinson Crusoe's island when he is by himself, in a situation where money would thus make no sense because there is no exchange.[4] The significance of Jevons's achievement – along with provision of the means for applying calculus to create static models of dynamic economic phenomena – was that it rooted economic analysis firmly in the logic of rational-agent analysis. Famously, this foundation has encouraged economists to endorse the principle of 'methodological individualism,' the view that all social-level phenomena should be constructed as aggregates of processes operating at the level of individuals. The centrality of Robinson Crusoe in economic pedagogy has made this particularly vivid, to the point where neoclassical micro-economics is sometimes referred to as 'Robinson Crusoe economics' by its anti-individualist critics. Tooby and Cosmides (1992, p. 47) follow rhetoric standard among economists themselves when they suggest that adherence to the principle has kept microeconomics insulated from the pernicious effects of the SSSM. I regard this analysis as seriously confused. As Elster (1985) demonstrates decisively, Marx was among the first explicit advocates of methodological individualism, but this did not prevent him from falling into many of the original and leading errors on which the SSSM is built. Neoclassical economists, with their philosophical predispositions centrally influenced by the empiricism of Hume and Mill, would likely have been just as susceptible to the seductions of the SSSM but for the fact that they wanted no part of the psychological hypotheses at its base. This was not because they particularly doubted the truth of these hypotheses, but because their tradition encouraged the view that their framework had no basis in *any* empirical psychology at all.

I think that the individualism issue is entirely a red herring, but a dangerous one from the point of view of getting clear on the real issues. Many commentators have of course supposed that since all groups decompose strictly into individuals, and since all social activity must be causally grounded in individual activity, all sociological claims simply reduce, at least ultimately, to psychological ones. Tooby and Cosmides, in sparing economists from their fire because their methodology is supposedly individualist, encourage critics to read them as holding this view, and few of their opponents as represented in Rose and Rose (2000) can resist the encouragement. (How much of the rhetorical advantage social theorists try to score by accusing their enemies of individualism arises from the fact that 'individualist,' in a largely unrelated meaning of the word, sounds *selfish*?) However, no serious researchers in the CEP school, and certainly not Dennett, actually hold the

opinion that methodological individualism implies the inappropriateness of
generalizations about the dynamics of groups and structures. Equally certainly, primitive individualism is incompatible with sound economic epistemology, for reasons that will be clear shortly, when we discuss the role of
game theory in economics. It is precisely the point of game-theoretic analyses that the explanations they give appeal to structural facts rather than to
individual intentions or actions. The clouds of rhetoric about individualism
in the economic methodology literature are, to judge by economists' *actual*
explanatory efforts over the years, performances in need of deconstruction.
This rhetoric is likely explained by appeal to a conjunction of three factors.
First, economists *teach* their fundamental concepts using perfectly competitive markets as the baseline case, and since in perfect competition interaction is irrelevant, its models can be scaled up from a one-person economy
without the introduction of new variables. Second, cases of breast-beating
about methodological individualism usually turn out, on careful analysis,
to be confused instances of demands for mechanisms in the context of
presupposed psychological frameworks that are simplistic; while such demands should be heeded, there are many sorts of mechanisms besides individual minds. Third, economists are rightly concerned to combat the
widespread view that successful collective action is mostly just a matter of
morality and willpower, and the demand for methodological individualism
is a straightforward way of emphasizing this. The point remains, however,
that economists have (at least in their applied studies) always been interested in markets that are not perfectly competitive, and that they have always
been ready to drop individualist scruples with alacrity when studying such
markets.

What actually held economists aloof from the specifically *psychological*
empiricism to which Tooby and Cosmides object in the SSSM is (ironically) another aspect of the extreme empiricism that drives the SSSM itself,
namely, a positivistic inclination to operate within a closed axiomatic framework that implied no reference to unobservable mental states. This became
explicit with the axiomatic foundational scheme for economic theory developed by Samuelson (1947), which was celebrated and widely accepted within
the profession mainly *because* it offered a picture of economics as purely
formal elaboration of the logic of maximization. Doubts about Samuelson's
foundational model are now frequently expressed as a result of discomfort
with his behaviorist motivations. I think these doubts are poorly motivated.
It is true that Samuelson considered respect for behaviorist principles an
essential legitimating condition for a science, and that in this he was mistaken. However, it is descriptively *true* that micro-economists observe a

methodological rule according to which their models may not rest upon contingent psychological hypotheses, and this rule *can* be (though too often is not) given an excellent justification: It permits economists to develop analyses that apply to *any* rational maximizers – bears, birds, bees, firms, or computers – and not merely to human organisms. Generality is an important scientific value, although one that is typically traded off against ease of applicability in particular situations.

I argued above that the explanatory targets of 'pure' IS theory, when we consistently unpack its Dennettian foundations, just are the rational agents familiar to economists. We can now reach that same conclusion again from the other direction, that is, from reflection on what economists do. An economic model at the micro level is simply a detailed elaboration of what is to be expected of an intentional agent – the sort of entity whose dispositions and behavioral tendencies are characterized by reference to its beliefs, desires, and capacities, but *without* reference to any causal mechanism implementing these intentional capacities at the level of SPCP – given a particular utility function (that is, an ordered schedule of preferences over states of the world) and a budget constraint. Samuelsonian edicts to the effect that the economist is not doing psychology can thus simply be reinterpreted as calls for the economist *not to engage in SPCP*, or, if you like, to stick to IS theory.

Of course, and as we have seen, CEP as a whole is not equivalent to IS theory by itself. If we observe the Dennettian method as it was elaborated above, we obtain a complete behavioral explanation only when we relax the optimizing assumptions made in our proper function specifications in IS analysis against the facts about causal mechanisms identified by SPCP. Now, a number of economists have recently started to recognize this point, although in a confused way. Thus, for example, Kreps (1990), in his very influential advanced text on micro-economic theory, reviews the empirical literature on human choice under uncertainty,[5] and concludes from it that the so-called pure theory of the consumer, which provides the basis for the standard economic analysis of demand (and of behavior in financial markets), is *not true*. On the basis of this reasoning, Kreps then goes on to hope that the axiomatic theory of preference, choice, and demand will be successfully revised so as to incorporate the systematic departures from rational optimization that psychologists are discovering to be characteristic in humans. According to the argument being advanced here, this advice combines a sound insight with a flawed epistemology that needs correction from the Dennettian method. The sound insight is that the results of pure IS analysis do indeed require comparison with results derived from SPCP if

they are to be used in furnishing adequate empirical predictions and complete explanations of the actual behavior of human consumers. The flawed
epistemology consists in the fact that it would destroy the point of IS analysis to try to incorporate tendencies peculiar to humans (or, for all we know,
to animals equipped with cortex more generally) directly inside the axioms
of that analysis itself. The nature of rational optimization has been studied
in a far more rigorous way by economists than by any school of thought
in cognitive science, precisely *because* economists have a tradition of ab-
stracting themselves wholly away from micro-causal psychological mechanisms. By the strictures of the Dennettian method, CEP *needs* economics to
make its baseline assumption of rationality sufficiently clear and contentful to be tested in particular cases. On this analysis, the relative autonomy
of economics is not merely *tolerated* by CEP but *required* for its optimal
progress. Equally, however, in trying to explain and predict actual economic
behavior, the economist, *as a participant in the larger program of CEP*, relies
on SPCP to discover the information-processing limitations, attentional biases, and dispositions to inferential error that create both competence and
performance differences between types of biological systems and rational
economic agents. Kreps's confused recognition of this fact comes danger-
ously close to the demand raised by some radical critics of economists' use
of rationality postulates (e.g., Lawson 1997) that economists should stop
modeling rational economic agents because psychological research shows
that people are not such agents. As Dennett's work shows us, evolutionary psychologists, the very experts on human departures from rationality,
begin with rational-agent analysis in order to have base cases for reverse
engineering. What economists *should* recognize and acknowledge is that
constructing a rational-agent model is merely the essential *first* step in
understanding an economic system whose participants are biological organisms. Complicating such models by adding the actual perceptual and
computational mechanisms discovered by SPCP is the equally essential
next step.[6]

I have so far addressed only methodological issues arising within *micro*-
economics. *Macro*-economists, who have never been as confident about
their splendid Samuelsonian isolation, are often inclined to see theoretical
sociology – interpreted as in the SSSM – as the empirical discipline that
is their natural partner at the level of modeling, explaining, and predicting
macro-level phenomena. This, I will now argue, arises from a failure in
some quarters to understand that the neoclassical framework incorporates
a lacuna at the level of interactive analysis, but one that can and should be
filled from *within* the domain of rational-agent modeling rather than from

without (as by input from sociologists). The next few pages will simply outline the way in which this is done. My aim, ultimately, is to show that just
as micro-economic theory amounts to the rigorous working-out of pure IS
theory at the level of *individual* agents, so macro-economic theory, if properly interpreted, constitutes the detailed logic of IS theory in application to
populations. This is something, as we will see, that Dennett and his fellow
advocates of CEP need.

Jevons's procedure for defining equilibrium resource allocations for a
single agent is just the right tool for modeling rationality *so long as* agents
face only *parametric* constraints on their optimization efforts. That is, so
long as Robinson Crusoe is alone on his island, deciding how much time
and energy to allocate amongst harvesting fruit, sleeping, daydreaming, and
investing in the construction of a fishing rod, then simple application of the
marginal principle will tell him (and the analyst) what he should do. This
changes as soon as Friday comes along because, unlike the fruit and the
weather, Friday will formulate his plans in anticipation of those he expects
from Robinson, and Robinson will in turn base his plans and expectations
on Friday's expectations of his plans and expectations, and so on. Keynes's
great breakthrough lay in his recognition of this, and the field of modern
macro-economics was born as a result; but Keynes lacked the mathematical resources to do anything with this insight except include expectations
about the actions of others amongst the fixed features of the world an
agent takes into account when maximizing. (This attitude is perpetuated,
not corrected, by the so-called rational expectations theory that has largely
supplanted the Keynesian foundational apparatus in macro-economics. See
Bicchieri [1993, Chapter 1] for a philosophical critique along these lines.)
Genuine interactive effects could not be modeled until the development of
game theory, which began with von Neumann and Morgenstern in 1944
but required many subsequent years of work to be fully serviceable as a
general-purpose analytical tool. Game theory has now thoroughly transformed micro-economics, but its extensions into macro-economics have
been uneven with respect to their underlying logical coherence. (See, again,
Bicchieri 1993, and also Ross and LaCasse 1995.)

Game theory has become best known outside of its main fields of application through the publicity acquired by one of its less typical products, the
so-called Prisoner's Dilemma (PD). Thus it is quite widely understood that
if, for example, a group of fishermen could all do best for themselves in the
long run by limiting their catches according to an agreed-on quota system,
thus allowing the fish stocks to replenish themselves, but if no single fisherman can deplete the stock significantly by himself, then rational action on

the part of each fisherman may lead them to disaster. If all except fisherman $i$ observe the agreement, then $i$ will maximize his utility by cheating and exceeding his quota. And if the others do not observe the agreement, then $i$ would be foolishly throwing away utility and being made a sucker if he did not cheat along with them. Thus, $i$ is best off cheating regardless of what the others do, and so should cheat. If all so reason – and they all rationally *should*, since they can each foresee that the others will – then the result is the destruction of their livelihood. Now, the PD does illustrate at least one common and (for present purposes) central implication of game theory, namely, that pursuit of rational maximization at the individual level often leads to entirely unintended consequences in circumstances where non-parametric (i.e., strategic, or interactive) dynamics dominate. But the odd feature of the PD, the fact that it leads to an unfortunate outcome when an unambiguously better one seems to be available, has led a stampede of commentators to chase after 'solutions' to its apparent challenge to the normative appropriateness of individual maximization. (See, e.g., Gauthier 1986 and the vast related literature). This may be an important application of game theory for moral philosophers (although, for reasons given in LaCasse and Ross 1998, I am extremely skeptical of this), but it is certainly not the locus of game theory's main significance in the philosophy of economics. We will better serve our purposes here, therefore, by taking as a sample game a situation that is socially and politically significant but less cute and bewitching in its logic.

Consider, then, a plausible (although not necessarily correct, and certainly oversimplified) analysis of the widely noted fissiparousness of the Canadian federation. Canada elects a Westminster-style federal parliament that is not balanced against a house that provides regionally equitable representation (as the U.S. Senate does). Canadian MPs are also bound by rigorous party discipline, so they cannot trade votes as in the American Congress. The result is that each Canadian elector $j$ has an equally weighted expression of ordinal preference over every issue from coast to coast, including issues over which $j$ may be almost, but not quite, indifferent because they mainly concern people in another region. A possible result of this setup is that people in less populous regions, such as the West, find themselves being continuously overruled on matters of special importance to them by majorities of almost-indifferent voters from other regions. Frustrated in many particular instances by their difficulties in manipulating the insensitive federal structure, Western voters will tend to put greater emphasis on political action at the level of their provincial governments. A result of this, which might be intended by almost no one, could be the gradual weakening of federal cohesion and unity, as federal politicians find it easiest to avoid cross-regional discord by letting provincial governments acquire ever wider powers through an incremental, unplanned accumulation of small precedents. If the end result were the breakup of a federation that had gradually lost its point through repeated failures of coordinated action, the *mistaken* inference might be made by commentators that Canadians valued their national unity, in some intentionalized sense, less than (say) French or Americans do. If we strictly rely *only* on the simple story just imagined, however, we can *see* that this intentionalization is a mistake because the mechanism that weakens the structure at no point depends on any fissiparous intentions on anyone's part; it is entirely a global-level consequence of the interactions of locally focused individual incentives with game-level *structures* that consistently channel actions in a direction that produces an unintended outcome.

More sophisticated and realistic examples of this sort can be found throughout the so-called public choice literature, which applies the methodology of game-theoretic micro-economics to political and social analysis (see Mueller 1997). While I endorse the public choice approach as a good instance of Dennettian method, I should make clear that I am *not* helping myself to the most controversial element found in some public choice theory, which is that narrowly selfish motivations generally dominate socially concerned ones. Whether this is generally true or false is another red herring: A community of Mother Theresas will tend to find themselves driven to the unintended consequences represented by the equilibria of games if they have different preferences as to which starving children should be fed first from a finite pool of resources. I have chosen to focus on a political example here because economists and others are well used to the idea that conventional market outcomes are generally products of uncoordinated actions; but in the widespread reluctance of many people to apply this same logic to behavior that is not strictly concerned with maximization of monetary income, we see a curious assumption to the effect that the properties of interactive behavioral structures suddenly change where pursuit of money is concerned. Certainly, nothing in the philosophical foundations of economics justifies this assumption, and many canonical texts in the history of economic methodology (e.g., Robbins 1936) explicitly deny it.

It is precisely because of its agnosticism about the objects of maximization that economics has been able to contribute its most outstanding instrument, game theory, to deepen the resources of evolutionary theory. Since the work of Maynard Smith (1982), dynamic game theory has featured indispensably in the standard toolkit of the evolutionary theorist.

(Skyrms [1996] provides a superb, and accessible, survey of this instrument at work.) In applying game theory to evolutionary processes, we drop the idea that agents can choose any of a number of strategies. Instead, we let strategies compete directly against one another for the privilege of leaving more copies of themselves in future games – that is, subsequent generations. In such games, lineages *learn* to play more optimally (relative to environments) as less successful strategies are culled in favor of better ones. The evolutionary theorist is less interested in the *statics* of a game – that is, in locating its equilibria in a single round – than in its *dynamics*, that is, in the development over time of the composition of strategies making up the population. The dynamic equilibrium concept is essentially different from the static one: It is a point at which the composition of strategies settles into a relatively stable state. These strategies may then be identified with evolved, selected behavioral dispositions.

This version of game theory, developed mainly by biologists, has been reimported into economics as a framework for studying the dynamics of markets. Firms and other cooperative associations, after all, may be expected to increase in profitability and perhaps in size, or to be driven to bankruptcy, or to settle at equilibrium levels, according to their responses to the pressures of market environments that include other firms. This insight was in fact anticipated by the great economic iconoclast Hayek (1948), and introduced into the theoretical mainstream by Nelson and Winter (1982). Extensive later developments, incorporating the framework of evolutionary game theory, are reviewed in Hodgson (1993). General mathematical models that apply equally to economic and biological domains may be found in Weibull (1996) and L. Samuelson (1998). The unification of this branch of economics – which, at least in micro-economics, is now less a 'branch' than it is the dominant theoretical approach – with its applications in biology, CEP, politics, and cultural studies is thus well on the road to formal completion.

Attention to these developments permits us to draw a striking point about the relationship between economics and Dennettian method. When the intentional stance is assumed toward Mother Nature and the design stance toward her products (which amount to the same thing) we are familiar with the scientific approach that results: adaptationist evolutionary biology. Some defense of this against its critics has already been suggested. When the same approach is taken toward *cultural* evolution the implied research program is one that has struck even otherwise sympathetic critics as much less plausible, namely, 'memetics.' In writing about the evolutionary dynamics of memes – units of cultural transmission, including such things as simple ideas, clichés, bits of melody, stereotypical techniques, and so on – Dennett has, like Dawkins (the originator of the idea) been mainly content to argue *that* these dynamics replicate those of natural selection, without trying to produce a rigorous protocol for *doing* memetic science or for telling good memetics from bad. This has encouraged skepticism even from such staunch friends of adaptationism as Maynard Smith (1995). Blackmore (1999) provides the richest survey to date of what a consistently memetic perspective might look like, but, again, makes no attempt at developing a method to go with the ontology; and this leads Malik (2000), a generally responsible critic, to feel entitled to simply dismiss Blackmore's perspective as "absurd." In general, it seems unlikely that memetics will be taken seriously until and unless someone can show how to turn it into an analytical technique that is constrained by some rigorous technical apparatus of its own. Now, what I suggest here is this: The technical apparatus we seek has been sitting under our noses all along. It is macro-economics underwritten by evolutionary game theory. Everything that both Dennett and Blackmore want to do with memes is accomplished by seeing them as strategies competing to out-replicate one another across successions of hosts. To be successful, these strategies must be supportable at equilibria given the difference they make to the expected payoffs of their carriers. As with genetic evolution, we should model these games and their equilibria by adopting the design stance toward memes and the complexes they form, and then we must have ways of relaxing the optimality assumptions built into the design stance through the use of an approach analogous to SPCP. For just as the history of gene frequencies is shaped by contingencies of geographical change, developmental canalization, and the other kinds of events discussed earlier, so the history of meme frequencies cannot be accurately predicted from the IS – that is, evolutionary macro-economics – alone. What I want to suggest is that narrative history and analytic sociology and social anthropology, so long as they observe Elster's dictum to posit no causation without plausible mechanisms, play the role of SPCP to macro-economics' IS-level analysis of social dynamics.

Let us consider one example to help get the feel of the proposal. A game-theoretic macro-economic account might have been able to predict that the triumphalist and militarist political memes of the Bolsheviks, which encouraged Lenin and Stalin and their followers to make literal war on all competing meme-complexes within the USSR, would fare well within that country and go to fixation despite the economic, psychological, and demographic disasters they caused for most of that country's population. However, the rationalizing account would probably also have predicted, incorrectly, that the meme-complex would be unlikely to spread beyond the borders of the first closed political unit in which it went to fixation, simply because observation of the disasters by those outside, where rival memes were not suppressed, would discourage their spread; and also because as the violent memes ceased to need to compete with others at home, they would become increasingly incompatible with memes governing normal apolitical life, thereby coming to sound increasingly strained and foreign to outside sensibilities. This is just what happened during the 1930s. Despite the massive loss of confidence in capitalism brought about by the depression, communism did not come close to capturing power in any second country,[7] was out-competed everywhere by fascism, and led moderate people to resist alliances with Stalin even as a means of securing protection against the vivid menace of Hitler. It is essentially rationalized memetic dynamics that enables us to explain – that is, see as a sustainable equilibrium – the situation in which the Moscow trials of 1938 could simultaneously seem comprehensible and even sensible within the Soviet Communist Party, and literally freakish to most outside spectators. However, these rationalized dynamics could *not* have predicted the series of accidents – invasion of Russia by a Germany that had, partly through its own improbably great military success, acquired an aura of outstanding evil, followed by heroic Soviet resistance that, at tremendous cost, broke the back of that evil – which injected dramatic plausibility into slogans that had seemed deranged and enabled the memes of the Bolsheviks to flourish across much of the world for decades longer. The point of the example is this: Without the rationalizing perspective the central explanatory questions we want answered by analysts of Stalin's regime – for example, "How *could* a large social and political structure *ever* have come to base itself on such palpably demented discourse as flowed out of the Moscow trials?" – do not even arise, let alone invite the serious effort now put into them. (See Getty and Naumov 1999 for the best illustration of this.) At the same time, anyone who tried to explain the fortunes of militarized socialism after 1945 without reference to the military and other contingencies of the immediately preceding years would stand no chance of giving us an adequate account.

To many, this sort of example will not seem connected to the traditional domain or form of macro-economics. This is largely because, prior to the advent of formal techniques for dynamic analysis, macro-economists could maintain mathematical rigor only by confining their attention to static analysis. As this source of pressure has diminished, we have seen the rapid rise of the so-called New Institutional Economics (North 1990), and the extension of that approach to problems of the sort just exemplified.

(See Bates et al. 1998 for further such examples, with detailed analyses actually shown and with accompanying meta-analytical discussion. They call their approach 'analytic narrative,' a usage I predict will become both widespread and standard.) This new emphasis on the contingent in macroeconomics is widely hailed by those who see it as returning both 'human' and 'realistic' dimensions to economics. However, in the present context we must also emphasize its other side, which is that it is deeply rationalistic in its epistemology and that it has recourse to the deliberate and self-conscious plans of agents only at the stage of correcting for the empirical oversimplifications introduced by its optimizing assumptions, just as CEP appeals to particular limitations on the rational powers of agents only when it starts to compare IS accounts with those furnished by SPCP. Anyone who finds memetics 'absurd' must, to be consistent, be prepared to say the same thing about much of the leading *actual* social history that is being done. To return to our example above, Stalin's deliberative agency is typically held to be the cause of many of his *particular* murders (in answering questions such as "Why so-and-so?"), but leading explanations of the fact that the system he led was so murderous in the first place are essentially memetic.

Macro-economists often defend the causal irrealism of their rationalizing assumptions by appeal to a different defense that is *not*, at least in general, licensed by CEP or by the Dennettian method. That is, they often assume that in situations where many agents interact, individual departures from rationality will tend to cancel out, so that predictions based on locating the equilibria of games can be used to make *direct* predictions about real situations. This confidence requires an assumption to the effect that all such departures are unsystematic and idiosyncratic accidents. Ironically, this attitude is least justified precisely where agents are *most* intelligent and complex – that is, most 'rational' in the old-fashioned sense of Descartes. Where very simple systems, such as wasps, are concerned, natural selection will tend to effectively eliminate dispositions to waste resources. Thus, given their limited utility functions and capacities, simple agents will tend to be nearly perfect maximizers so long as their ancestral environments have not altered too rapidly and the conditions in which they are observed are ecologically typical. Consider, by contrast, the usual paradigm environment in which human idiosyncrasies are often supposed to be similarly eliminated, that of the stock market. Here, irrational tendencies in behavior on the part of any one trader provide opportunities for exploitation by others, since any patterns not driven by common information will be interpreted as giving away private information, at which point the value of such information will be driven to 0 through consumption by all. This reasoning, which financial economists use to justify the common hypothesis that the long-run expected profit to any trader in stocks must be 0, depends on the assumption that all traders are sufficiently self-aware as to be able to *detect* any pattern, no matter how complex, that emerges from the accumulation of systematic psychological biases. Professional investors – and recently some economists, such as Lo et al. (2000) – are often highly skeptical about this hypothesis, and so tirelessly plumb market statistics for evidence of long-run systematicity. CEP suggests that this skepticism is well motivated. Stock markets do not resemble anything that existed in the human ancestral environment, so evolution could not have selected against irrational stock traders in the way that it selected against wasps who are inefficient sugar gatherers. It is an open empirical question as to whether there are systematic patterns in investor behavior, but I would not want to bet any good money against it.

This skepticism about perfect rationality in aggregate complex markets can be used as the basis for making a series of related points. First, the expectation that outcomes of interactions involving many agents should be efficient is a tendency derived from *parametric*, Robinson Crusoe–style, economics; it is quite foreign to game theory. The Prisoner's Dilemma is merely a (misleadingly) simple example of the fact that *there is no general reason at all* to expect the equilibria of games – even games played amongst perfectly rational individuals – to be efficient. Our fanciful example from Canadian politics illustrates this point less distractingly. Second, where individuals may be modeled as systematically *irrational*, based on empirical evidence discovered by SPCP, the relevant biases can and should be built into the agents' budget constraints, just as the biologist will do when she builds game-theoretic models of wasp behavior. Third, the economist must first predict equilibria in games that assume rational individuals, in order to be able to infer the sorts of patterns in departures from these equilibria that reveal biases. We will not discover possible biases that influence stock market patterns except by first studying market data in search of the patterns themselves, and these will be exposed only against the backdrop of the null hypothesis, that of the random walk. But, fourth, merely *spotting* a pattern in the data is never sufficient to generate confidence that it is real. Stock market history goes on, and any apparent pattern that is observed can be made consistent with the random walk hypothesis if our long run is long enough. Despite my skepticism about the truth of the random walk hypothesis, I would not choose stocks on the basis of belief in the celebrated 'Kondratiev' or other long waves that periodically tantalize the financial media. As discussed at length in Ross and Bennett (2001), the problem with these putative phenomena is that no one has ever so much as *suggested* a plausible *mechanism* that would explain them. Such a mechanism would have to be psychological, and, as a device systematically present and hitherto unrecognized in millions of traders, its basis would have to be evolutionary. The pattern of the Dennettian explanatory method thus emerges again.

I have been suggesting that the economist uses a pattern of reasoning sufficiently clear and distinctive as to deserve recognition as an *explanatory schema* (Kitcher 1981) in its own right; and I have then argued that this schema is essentially identical to the Dennettian method of behavioral explanation. (Historically, Dennett has nothing to do with the adoption of the schema by economists, so the justification and clarification he provides is purely retrospective. Economists could do much to clear their heads about their own methodology and its logical basis if they carefully read Dennett.) I thus think it appropriate to say that game-theoretic economics provides – along with work in cognitive ethology (see Chapter 5) – a paradigmatic instance of *Dennettian explanation* in action.

Getting to this point has involved us in reviewing a good deal of complex logical and historical material. We should therefore recapitulate here and summarize the logic of the economist's practice that I am calling 'Dennettian.' First, the careful economist does not take her models to be directly describing any internal psychological properties of biological organisms. Like any IS theorist, her task is to elaborate the logical implications of various optimality assumptions. These elaborations, however, allow her to reach well beyond simple descriptions of rational agents. Using game theory, she can study properties of complex systems in order to predict equilibria that are functions not of any intentions for the corresponding outcomes on the part of agents, but of systematic structural features relating the incentives, budgets, and capacities of interacting agents and aspects of their common environments. Such equilibria can then be compared with the outcomes of actual empirical interactions to infer properties of either agents or environments that cannot be predicted on the basis of theoretical abstraction alone. This in turn inspires the search for mechanisms that relate incentives, as purely nonpsychological descriptive elements on a par with utility functions and other economic *abstracta*, to psychological adaptations that instantiate behavioral dispositions and can actually cause things to happen. In effect, economic analysis predicts *possible* proper functions of behavioral dispositions by precisely locating and, ideally, measuring the advantages to utility they tend to confer. It is then the task of SPCP to confirm or reject these function-assignments on the basis of empirical evidence, and to substantiate them with mechanisms. The whole programme relies fundamentally on *methodological adaptationism* (= IS theory = reverse engineering), the conclusions of which must then be tested against micro-causal constraints drawn from the relevant domain (= SPCP in the case of explanations of individual behavior = analytic narratives in the case of explanations of structured social behavior); and that is what justifies calling it 'Dennettian.'

## 4. MACRO-REDUCTION

The implication of all this for social sciences other than economics is that they retain essential roles in the enterprise of explaining behavior, even (relatively) autonomous ones, without falling afoul of CEP, so long as this autonomy is not understood in the senses of Durkheim or of the SSSM, and so long as any functional structures they postulate are substantiated by plausible mechanisms. Most sociology, if 'most' is meant simply as a quantitative measure of professional person-hours, consists of historical, statistical, and anecdotal *description* of social patterns and structures, and as such stands to the economist's IS-level of modeling just as SPCP stands to IS theory in psychological explanation.

Some leading social scientists outside of economics have come to similar conclusions by slightly different routes of argument, although terminological differences may obscure this. Walking carefully through an example will be a useful concluding exercise for showing what is and is not at stake when we bring Dennettian method to bear on work from a mainstream discipline such as sociology. Consider, then, a widely cited recent exercise in semipopular sociology, Francis Fukuyama's *The Great Disruption* (1999). Fukuyama opens the book by placing himself in the main trajectory of theoretical sociology: He will, he says, show how seeing contemporary industrialized societies as being situated at a certain point along the transition from *Gemeinschaft* to *Gesellschaft* explains recent real and perceived erosions of community trust and family structures in those societies. However, as the argument develops this affinity turns out to be more generic and historical than logically substantive. Following a 140-page review of relevant data and sociological literature, Fukuyama steps back and comments on the methodological perspective from which he hopes to furnish new insights. An economic perspective, he tells us, will be inadequate in itself because it is likely to restrict its attention to rationally justifiable norms and rules, and because it will arbitrarily constrain its terms of explanation through adherence to methodological individualism. A narrow sociological view is also rejected as too partial, on grounds that it will treat all fundamental norms as arational, and so fail to address key questions either about the sustaining equilibrium conditions of sets of norms, or about the comparative efficiencies among them. Fukuyama then contends that these two individually inadequate perspectives can be rendered complementary, and jointly sufficient as an analytical framework, if they are understood as having common foundations in the conjunction of game theory and CEP. An approving summary of Cosmides's and Tooby's basic argument follows, and then Fukuyama returns to the subject matter of his application.

Substantively, then, Fukuyama proposes to engage in what I am calling Dennettian explanation.[8] What requires comment in the present context is Fukuyama's brief but overt philosophical digression (pp. 160–2) to the effect that the synthesis of game theory and CEP as the foundation of a more powerful social science shows that *Homo sociologus* is a better model of the human agent than *Homo economicus*. This, of course, puts the matter in exact opposition to my way of describing it. This will seem puzzling, given the absence of any significant disagreement between us on what best explanatory practice actually demands. However, the Dennettian perspective permits a diagnosis of what is going on here. Fukuyama's stated basis for finding *Homo economicus* inadequate *even where economic behavior is modeled game-theoretically* is the old charge of methodological individualism. Now, why does Fukuyama imagine that methodological individualism infects even game-theoretic economic models? Here is what he says: "Economists frequently express surprise that there is as much cooperation in the world as there is, since game theory suggests that cooperative solutions are often difficult to achieve.... Most non-economists would reply that cooperation occurs readily because people are naturally sociable, *and do not need to strategize extensively in order to find ways of working with one another*" (Fukuyama 1999, p. 162; emphasis mine). This remark indicates misapprehension of the Dennettian explanatory logic on which economists actually rely. That logic does *not* enjoin us to view explicit representations of complex strategies *by actual individuals* as causing system-level states such as cooperative equilibria. The reverse engineering embedded in evolutionary game-theoretic modeling predicts that such equilibria will arise if some causally efficacious mechanism or other permits transmission of information that enables noncooperators to be recognized and ostracized, and it is then up to CEP to tell us whether such mechanisms (in this case, modules for processing information about reliable behavioral correlates of dispositions to feign cooperativeness) actually exist. To think that economists must postulate agents who self-consciously represent the games they are playing is to confuse the optimizing hypothesis itself, made from the level of IS

theory, with the causal hypotheses from the level of SPCP that are subsequently compared with its predictions. Fukuyama recognizes that much
cooperative behavior *is* mysterious unless CEP can furnish evidence that
mechanisms exist that function so as to raise the price of cheating on agree-
ments, but he fails to see that the need for this particular evidence results
precisely *from* the prior application of economic logic. It does not confute
that logic in favor of an alternative approach.

My purpose here is not to quibble with Fukuyama over questions of
epistemology, since the issue makes, as we have seen, no difference to his
substantive account. If someone wishes to use a cumbersome phrase such as
'incentive-compatible-mechanism-sensitive-sociology' wherever I say 'applied economics' then I have no objection; and I suppose this would reas-
sure some sociologists who are anxious over the claim that their methodological foundations lie in economics (plus CEP); they could say instead,
if they liked, that game-theoretic foundations and sensitivities to institutional constraints have turned macro-economics into analytical sociology.
My usage here reflects a preference on my part for identifying the 'winner' in a disciplinary synthesis with whoever's characteristic *logic* is adopted,
rather than with who gets to affirm a particular empirical intuition. Lurking
close behind it, however, is a deep and very important philosophical issue
about how we should think about the relationships between disciplines in
general. Dennett (1981) himself raises the issue directly, in response to
Michael Friedman's claim that individual cognitive capacities should be
'macro-reduced' to social capacities, in contrast to the more traditional
micro-reductionist strategy of explaining social cognition in terms of individual cognition. Says Dennett in reply:

> With the idea of macro-reduction in psychology I largely agree, except that
> Friedman's identification of the macro level as explicitly social is only part
> of the story. The cognitive capacities of non-language-using animals (and
> Robinson Crusoes, if there are any) must also be accounted for, and not just
> in terms of an analogy with the practices of us language users. The macro
> level *up* to which we should relate microprocesses in the brain in order to
> understand them as psychological is more broadly the level of organism-
> environment interaction, development and evolution. That level includes
> social interaction as a particularly important part . . . , but still a proper part.
> (Dennett, 1981/1987, p. 65)

In these terms, what I am claiming here is that it is similarly more fruitful to
see sociological explanations as macro-reduced up to the level of the economic than to think of economic explanations as micro-reduced down to the

level of the sociological. This structural displacement of conventional ways of thinking about interdisciplinary relationships serves, I think, as a particularly vivid way of showing what is distinctive about taking a Dennettian methodological perspective to the social sciences, and so as a suitable point at which to conclude. It should help to convince us that, polemics about putatively obsolete disciplinary perspectives (e.g., Tooby and Cosmides in some moments) and defensive anxieties about reductionism and biological imperialism (e.g., Rose and Rose) notwithstanding, Dennett's work shows us how to take the 'unifying' agenda of CEP more seriously than the divisive tones in which it is sometimes expressed.[9]

### Notes

[1.] For a stimulating and historically crucial discussion of modules and modularity, see Fodor (1983). Garfield (1987) provides a survey of some early empirical investigations, though the trickle of results reported there has since become a flood. Ross (1990) gives an argument for radicalizing Fodor's version of the hypothesis, and this argument has since been echoed by many others in cognitive science. Fodor (2000) himself, however, rejects it.

[2.] See Carey (1985), Carey and Gelman (1991).

[3.] It should be noted that neither Fodor nor Quine derive Tooby's and Cosmides's conclusion from the arguments.

[4.] Later, welfare economists showed that Adam Smith's market equilibrium concept follows from Jevons's in the special case of perfect competition; but, contrary to a popular opinion, this is among the *results* of neoclassical theory, not part of its foundations.

[5.] See Kahneman et al. (1982) for the classic results. Hogarth and Reder (1986) provides theoretical discussion of these results from various perspectives. Thaler (1992) summarizes the whole literature to that point and evaluates its significance for economists. Gigerenzer et al. (1999) provide new research on the actual mechanisms serving optimization procedures in humans that can be used to complicate the inference engines presupposed in standard economic models.

[6.] Binmore (1994) is unusual among economists in seeming to see this point correctly, though without ever putting it explicitly. But Binmore has spent more time hanging around with evolutionary psychologists than have most of his colleagues.

[7.] Communists briefly seized power in Hungary in 1919, but this is too early to be relevant to my claim. Spain might be thought to represent a counterexample from the 1930s, since communists there were by 1938 able to inflict their usual hyper-violent control relatively unchecked over those parts of the country still in the hands of the Republican government. However, this wasn't endogenous; it resulted from the presence for military purposes of armed Soviet agents.

8. I will not try to pronounce on the extent to which he actually provides a consistently successful instance of such an explanation. For what my opinion is worth here, I think that the general account is very plausible; but the book is not intended as an academic treatise and so does not emphasize logical rigor.

9. I would like to thank Andy Brook and Nicoli Nattrass for their extremely helpful comments on an earlier draft of this paper; these produced very substantial changes. Thanks also to audiences at the University of Cape Town, Rhodes University, and the University of British Columbia for critical discussion.

## References

Baron-Cohen, S., A. Leslie, and U. Frith. (1985). Does the Autistic Child Have a Theory of Mind? *Cognition* 21:37–46.

Bates, R., A. Greif, M. Levi, J.-L. Rosenthal, and B. Wengast. (1998). *Analytic Narratives*. Princeton, NJ: Princeton University Press.

Bicchieri, C. (1993). *Rationality and Coordination*. Cambridge: Cambridge University Press.

Binmore, K. (1994). *Game Theory and the Social Contract, Volume One: Playing Fair.* Cambridge, MA: MIT Press.

Blackmore, S. (1999). *The Meme Machine*. Oxford: Oxford University Press.

Carey, S. (1985). *Conceptual Change in Childhood*. Cambridge, MA: MIT Press/Bradford.

Carey, S., and E. Gelman, eds. (1991). *The Epigenesis of Mind*. Hillsdale, NJ: Erlbaum.

Churchland, P. (1979). *Scientific Realism and the Plasticity of Mind*. Cambridge: Cambridge University Press.

Churchland, P. (1995). *The Engine of Reason, the Seat of the Soul*. Cambridge, MA: MIT Press/Bradford.

Clark, A. (1989). *Microcognition*. Cambridge, MA: MIT Press/Bradford.

Dawkins, R. (1982). *The Extended Phenotype*. Oxford: Oxford University Press.

Dawkins, R. (1989). *The Selfish Gene, 2nd edition*. Oxford: Oxford University Press.

Dennett, D. (1981). Three Kinds of Intentional Psychology. In R. Healey, ed., *Reduction, Time and Reality*. Cambridge: Cambridge University Press. Reprinted in Dennett (1987). (Citations in text are to the reprinted edition.)

Dennett, D. (1984). Cognitive Wheels: The Frame Problem in Artificial Intelligence. In C. Hookway, ed., *Minds, Machines and Evolution*. Cambridge: Cambridge University Press, 129–151. Reprinted in Dennett (1998).

Dennett, D. (1987). *The Intentional Stance*. Cambridge, MA: MIT Press/Bradford.

Dennett, D. (1991a). *Consciousness Explained*. Boston: Little, Brown.

Dennett, D. (1991b). Real Patterns. *Journal of Philosophy* 88:27–51.

Dennett, D. (1994). Cognitive Science as Reverse Engineering: Several Meanings of 'Top-down' and 'Bottom-up.' In D. Prawtiz, B. Skyrms, and D. Westerstahl, eds., *Logic, Methodology and Philosophy of Science*. Amsterdam: Elsevier Science BV, 679–89. Reprinted in Dennett (1998), 249–59.

Dennett, D. (1995). *Darwin's Dangerous Idea*. New York: Simon and Schuster.

Dennett, D. (1996). *Kinds of Minds*. New York: Basic Books.

Dennett, D. (1998). *Brainchildren*. Cambridge, MA: MIT Press/Bradford.

Dennett, D. (2000). With a Little Help From My Friends. In D. Ross, A. Brook, and D. Thompson, eds., *Dennett's Philosophy: A Comprehensive Assessment*. Cambridge, MA: MIT Press/Bradford, 327–88.

Durkheim, E. (1895/1962). *The Rules of the Sociological Method*. New York: Free Press.

Elster, J. (1985). *Making Sense of Marx*. Cambridge: Cambridge University Press.

Elster, J. (1998). A Plea for Mechanisms. In P. Hedström and R. Swedberg, eds., *Social Mechanisms*. Cambridge: Cambridge University Press, 45–73.

Fodor, J. (1983). *The Modularity of Mind*. Cambridge, MA: MIT Press/Bradford.

Fodor, J. (2000). *The Mind Doesn't Work That Way*. Cambridge, MA: MIT Press/Bradford.

Fukuyama, F. (1999). *The Great Disruption*. New York: Simon and Schuster.

Garfield, J., ed. (1987). *Modularity in Knowledge Representation and Natural-Language Understanding*. Cambridge, MA: MIT Press/Bradford.

Gauthier, D. (1986). *Morals By Agreement*. Oxford: Oxford University Press.

Geertz, C. (1983). *Local Knowledge: Further Essays in Interpretive Anthropology*. New York: Basic Books.

Getty, J. A., and O. Naumov. (1999). *The Road to Terror*. New Haven, CT: Yale University Press.

Gigerenzer, G., P. Todd, and the ABC Research Group. (1999). *Simple Heuristics That Make Us Smart*. Oxford: Oxford University Press.

Gould, S. J., and R. Lewontin. (1979). The Spandrels of San Marco and the Panglossian Paradigm: A Critique of the Adaptationist Program. *Proceedings of the Royal Society of London B: Biological Sciences* 205:581–98.

Hayek, F. (1948). *Individualism and Economic Order*. Chicago: University of Chicago Press.

Hodgson, G. (1993). *Economics and Evolution*. Oxford: Polity.

Hogarth, R., and M. Reder, eds. (1986). *Rational Choice*. Chicago: University of Chicago Press.

Jevons, W. S. (1871). *Theory of Political Economy*. London: Macmillan.

Kahneman, D., P. Slovic, and A. Tversky, eds. (1982). *Judgment Under Uncertainty: Heuristics and Biases*. Cambridge: Cambridge University Press.

Karmiloff-Smith, A. (1992). *Beyond Modularity*. Cambridge, MA: MIT Press/Bradford.

Kitcher, P. (1981). Explanatory Unification. *Philosophy of Science* 48:507–31.

Kreps, D. (1990). *A Course in Microeconomic Theory*. Princeton, NJ: Princeton University Press.

Langton, C., ed. (1989). *Artificial Life*. Redwood City, CA: Addison Wesley.

Lawson, T. (1997). *Economics and Reality*. London: Routledge.

LaCasse, C., and D. Ross. (1998). Morality's Last Chance. In P. Danielson, *Modelling Rationality, Morality and Evolution*. Oxford: Oxford University Press, 340–75.

Lo, A., H. Mamaysky, and J. Wang. (2000). Foundations of Technical Analysis: Computational Algorithms, Statistical Inference and Empirical Implementation. *Journal of Finance* 55:1705–70.

Malik, K. (2000). *Man, Beast and Zombie*. London: Weidenfeld and Nicolson.

Maynard Smith, J. (1982). *Evolution and the Theory of Games*. Cambridge: Cambridge University Press.

Maynard Smith, J. (1995). Genes, Memes and Minds. *New York Review of Books* 42(19):46–8.

Millikan, R. (1984). *Language, Thought and Other Biological Categories*. Cambridge, MA: MIT Press/Bradford.

Millikan, R. (2000). Reading Mother Nature's Mind. In D. Ross, A. Brook, and D. Thompson, eds., *Dennett's Philosophy: A Comprehensive Assessment*. Cambridge, MA: MIT Press/Bradford, 55–75.

Mueller, D., ed. (1997). *Perspectives on Public Choice*. Cambridge: Cambridge University Press.

Nelson, R., and S. Winter. (1982). *An Evolutionary Theory of Economic Change*. Cambridge, MA: Harvard University Press.

North, D. (1990). *Institutions, Institutional Change and Economic Performance*. Cambridge: Cambridge University Press.

Quine, W.V.O. (1960). *Word and Object*. Cambridge, MA: MIT Press.

Robbins, L. (1936). *An Essay on the Nature and Significance of Economic Science, 2nd edition*. London: Macmillan.

Rose, H., and S. Rose, eds. (2000). *Alas, Poor Darwin*. New York: Harmony.

Ross, D. (1990). Against Positing Central Systems in the Mind. *Philosophy of Science* 57:297–312.

Ross, D. (1993a). *Metaphor, Meaning and Cognition*. New York: Peter Lang.

Ross, D. (1993b). Dennett's Conceptual Reform. *Behaviour and Philosophy* 22:41–52.

Ross, D. (1995). Real Patterns and the Ontological Foundations of Microeconomics. *Economics and Philosophy* 11:113–36.

Ross, D. (2000). Rainforest Realism: A Dennettian Theory of Existence. In D. Ross, A. Brook, and D. Thompson, eds., *Dennett's Philosophy: A Comprehensive Assessment*. Cambridge, MA: MIT Press/Bradford, 147–68.

Ross, D., and F. Bennett. (2001). The Possibility of Economic Objectivity. In U. Maki, ed., *The Economic World-View*. Cambridge: Cambridge University Press.

Ross, D., and C. LaCasse. (1995). Toward a New Philosophy of Positive Economics. *Dialogue* 34:467–93.

Ryle, G. (1949). *The Concept of Mind*. London: Hutchinson.

Samuelson, L. (1997). *Evolutionary Games and Equilibrium Selection.* Cambridge, MA: MIT Press.

Samuelson, P. (1947). *Foundations of Economic Analysis.* Cambridge, MA: Harvard University Press.

Sigmund, K. (1992). *Games of Life.* Oxford: Oxford University Press.

Skyrms, B. (1996). *Evolution of the Social Contract.* Cambridge: Cambridge University Press.

Sober, E. (1984). *The Nature of Selection.* Cambridge, MA: MIT Press/Bradford.

Thaler, R. (1992). *The Winner's Curse.* New York: Free Press.

Tooby, J., and L. Cosmides. (1992). The Psychological Foundations of Culture. In J. Barkow, L. Cosmides, and J. Tooby, eds., *The Adapted Mind.* Oxford: Oxford University Press.

Wagner, R. (1981). *The Invention of Culture, rev. ed.* Chicago: University of Chicago Press.

Weibull, J. (1996). *Evolutionary Game Theory.* Cambridge, MA: MIT Press.

Wittgenstein, L. (1953). *Philosophical Investigations.* Oxford: Blackwell.

# TWO CONCERNS

Dennett's work on consciousness and mental content has given rise to two general concerns. One is over how his picture of the mind relates to language. The other is over how his work connects to neuroscience.

Andy Clark takes up the first concern. Here is how the concern arises. From the intentional stance, we can ascribe beliefs and desires to humans, dogs, insects, and even the lowly thermostat. However, Dennett also insists that human minds are special. They can organize information in ways that confer consciousness, free agency, purpose, self-control, and even a special capacity for suffering. Clark asks, does this dual perspective mask a deeper tension in Dennett's accounts of consciousness and personhood? Can human language and culture bear the heavy explanatory burden that Dennett places on them? Clark then relates Dennett's project to current debates concerning the degree of continuity in evolved cognitive strategies and the hybrid (biological and non-biological) nature of human minds and persons.

The second concern is over Dennett's a priorism, his insistence that we determine what to say about cognition by using general strategies for explaining behaviour. Akins takes up a version of this concern. Rather than the Churchland/Ramachandran concern about the relationship of mental content ascribed under constraints of rationality, capacity, environment, and history to actual brain activities (see the Introduction), Akins is interested in the relationship between this 'free floatingness' of ascribed content and our relative stability and fixedness as we appear to ourselves in self-awareness. Akins centres her essay on the question, 'So what really happens in vision?' and shows that, once you answer this crucial question in even a bit of detail, the problem evaporates – the way we appear to ourselves is an illusion. In fact, Dennett's model is turning out to be a good philosophical guidebook for neuroscience as it is actually unfolding.

# 7 | That Special Something: Dennett on the Making of Minds and Selves

*ANDY CLARK*

## INTRODUCTION

Dennett depicts human minds as both deeply different from, yet profoundly continuous with, the minds of other animals and simple agents. His treatments of mind, consciousness, free will, and human agency all reflect this distinctive dual perspective. There is, on the one hand, the (in)famous Intentional Stance, relative to which humans, dogs, insects, and even the lowly thermostat (e.g., Dennett 1998, p. 327) are all pronounced capable of believing and desiring in essentially the same theoretical sense. And there is, on the other hand, a noteworthy (and increasing) insistence that human minds are special in that they exhibit a distinctive kind of "informational organization": one that confers consciousness (Dennett 1998, p. 347), and creates the space for agency, purpose, self-control (Dennett 1984, p. 100), and "significant suffering" (Dennett 1998, p. 351).

What follows is a critical examination of this dual perspective, and of Dennett's account of the key factor that makes us special – human language and our immersion in the sea of culture (Dennett 1998, p. 146; 1996, p. 130; 2000, p. 7). In particular, I shall ask whether Dennett's dual perspective masks a deeper tension in his accounts of consciousness and personhood, and whether the appeal to the transformative power of human language and culture can bear the heavy explanatory burden Dennett places on it. These turn out to be significant challenges but ones that also help clarify the scope and power of this complex, multi-layered account.

I end by commenting briefly on the wider significance of Dennett's project as a major contribution to current debates concerning the continuity (or otherwise) of evolved cognitive strategies and the essentially hybrid (biological and non-biological) nature of human minds and persons.

## 1. THINKING UP THE SELF

I begin by very briefly rehearsing the main elements of Dennett's account of the emergence of our "kinds of minds." The story moves through several distinct stages. Ground Zero, for Dennett, is the presence of what might be called "minimally rational response." Many of the animals and artefacts around us are in some broad sense "well designed," and thus reward treatment as rational agents. Examples include the human, the racoon, and the thermostat. Such systems are the proper objects of Dennett's (in)famous "intentional stance" so well described in the Introduction to this volume.

Intentional systems, however, come in a variety of shapes and forms. In particular, Dennett likes to distinguish among what he nicely dubs "Darwinian," "Skinnerian," "Popperian," and "Gregorian" creatures. Darwinian creatures come in many forms. The most basic are the simple, hardwired variety, whose ecologically adjustable, survival-enhancing responses are fixed by evolution. Next up is the Skinnerian variety, able to learn new strategies and responses by the reinforcement (via reward) of behaviour. Simple connectionist networks (artificial neutral networks whose processing profiles are tuned by training and reinforcement) fall, Dennett comments, into this category (see Dennett 1996, p. 85), and exhibit a simple kind of learning that Dennett calls ABC learning (1996, p. 87). Popperian[1] creatures, however, are able to deploy an additional (and mighty handy) resource. Such creatures exploit a kind of inner model of their world, enabling them to try out moves in their imagination in advance of committing their physical bodies to the act. This strategy sounds fancy, but it is one deployed, Dennett suggests, by most animals whose sophistication exceeds that of the simple invertebrates (1996, p. 92). Minds like ours, Dennett finally suggests, use all the tricks just mentioned but add a final, language-and-culture based twist. For we are (in addition) Gregorian[2] creatures: creatures "whose inner environments are informed by the *designed* portions of the outer environment" (1996, p. 99). The idea here is that "tool use is a two-way sign of intelligence: not only does it *require* intelligence to recognize and maintain a tool (let only fabricate one) but a tool *confers* intelligence on those lucky enough to be given one" (1996, pp. 99–100).

Given a tool (e.g., the nautical compass described in detail in Hutchins [1995]) the problem space confronting the biological brain (in respect of some real-world problem) is radically transformed and (often) simplified. In just this vein, Richard Gregory (the psychologist from whom Gregorian creatures take their name – see note 2) paid special attention to the use of words, conceived as themselves a special class of "mind-tools." Mind-tools, in this sense, are any designed (or culturally inherited) constructs that help transform and simplify problem solving in the inner (mental) environment. The resources of public language, as just mentioned, constitute the original and most singularly potent such mind-tool. Brains equipped with such resources, and populated by a rich culturally accumulated stock of concepts and labels, become able (Dennett claims) to make a crucial cognitive leap. Where the Skinnerian creature is able to learn new behaviours, and the Popperian creature is able in addition to try out possible behaviours in mental simulation, the Gregorian creature becomes able to actively think about its own thinking. By turning the communicative and co-operative resources of public exchange and discussion in on themselves, such creatures are able to concern themselves with such questions as: "What is my reason for believing such and such?" "Is it a good reason?" "How sound is the evidence upon which I am about to act?" and so on. Such self-questioning (and the crucial attendant possibilities of improved "rational hygiene") becomes an option, Dennett believes, only when the agent's rationales can become objects *for* the agent: only when the agent has available "a representation of the reason [which may be] composed, designed, edited, revised, manipulated, endorsed" (Dennett 1996, p. 133). And the inherited mind-tools of public linguistic expression, it is argued, provide natural support for such objectification.

Much more, to be sure, needs to be said about the precise way in which this magic is supposed to be worked. But it is the larger picture that I want first to bring into focus. And what matters here is just that the Gregorian creatures, courtesy of their special fluency with mind tools, are able to:

> Take a big step towards a human level of mental adroitness, benefitting from the experience of others by exploiting the wisdom embodied in the mind tools that these others have invented, improved and transmitted: thereby they learn *how to think better about what they should think about next* – and so forth, *creating a tower of further internal reflections with no fixed or discernible limit.* (Dennett 1996, p. 101; emphasis mine)

In Dennett (1984), the same kind of story (of a cascade of cognitive innovations) is pursued, but with the special agenda of accounting for the gradual emergence of moral agency and self-hood. There, Dennett contrasts the Skinnerian and Popperian creatures (these labels, however, are drawn from the later works) with creatures exhibiting (in addition) "the open-ended capacity (requiring a language of self-description) for "radical self-evaluation" (Dennett 1984, p. 100). Such self-evaluation requires the explicit articulation of the values and ideals inherent in our actions and projects, and the development of deliberative skills that further enhance our capacity for controlled, value-reflecting action (1984, Chapter 4). Once again, it is the deployment of mind-tools, especially those bequeathed by the capacity to make our reasons explicit using words, that ushers human-like intelligence and agency into the natural order. The Gregorian creatures, and the Gregorian creatures alone, emerge as "loci of self-control, of talent, of decision-making. They have projects, interests and values they create in the course of their own self-evaluation and self-definition" (1984, p. 100).

Finally, notice that the very same story is used (in Dennett 1991, 1996, and elsewhere) to account for the emergence of consciousness itself. Indeed, consciousness and personhood, for Dennett, seem to go pretty much hand in hand, courtesy of the crucial role played by certain mind tools in each case. Thus we read that:

> In order to be conscious – in order to be the sort of thing it is like something to be – it is necessary to have a certain sort of informational organization that endows that thing with a wide set of cognitive powers (such as the powers of reflection and re-representation).

And this special kind of organization, Dennett clearly states, is:

> Not part of our innate "hard-wiring" but in surprisingly large measure an artifact of our immersion in human culture. (Both quotes from Dennett 1998, pp. 346–7)

Consciousness, personhood, moral responsibility, free will, and even real thinking (see, e.g., Dennett 1996, p. 130; 2000, p. 4) are thus all tied together, and ushered into the natural world by our peculiar fluency with mind tools, especially those linguiform resources with which we are able to turn reasons into objects for reflection and refinement. The liberal embrace of the Intentional Stance notwithstanding, human thought is thus marked out as deeply different from the cognitive capacities of other animals. It is different courtesy largely of the culturally incubated mind-tools whose transformative powers open up the space within which we actively construct the experiencing and responsible self. Belief is cheap, but Gregorian creatures have that special something that makes their mental lives unique.[3]

## 2. HOW MIGHT MIND-TOOLS DO THEIR WORK?

Let us call the matrix of special Gregorian features (consciousness, personhood, moral responsibility, free will, and "real thinking") "mindfulness."

What makes mindfulness possible, on Dennett's account, is, we saw, the operation of all those extra layers of mind-tools we humans have added to our basic evolutionary heritage. Such a view is highly attractive, and it is certainly one that I myself endorse (see, e.g., Clark 1997; Clark 2000, Chapter 8). But it raises a number of deep and difficult questions that none of us (or so I believe) has yet fully addressed. The hardest such question is also the simplest: How, *exactly*, do the mind tools work their magic?

This is clearly the crucial question. But when it comes to the crunch, neither Dennett nor I have much to offer beyond some impressionistic speculation. Dennett stresses the role of culturally inherited mind-tools in labelling, organizing, and controlling the inner environment of ideas and associations, and the importance of rendering explicit both knowledge and reasons for action.[4] And I have stressed the importance of harmonizing inner mental operations with external cognitive props and scaffolding, and the role of acquired linguistic labels in enhancing incremental learning.[5] At the heart of both these accounts lies a common factor: The idea of language (and public codes and foundations in general) as providing a new (and cheap!) realm of manipulable and re-recognizable objects on which to turn more evolutionary basic capacities of recognition, imagination, and learning. As Dennett nicely puts it:

> Once we have created labels and acquired the habit of attaching them to experienced circumstances, we have created a new class of objects that can themselves become the objects of all the pattern-recognition machinery, association-building machinery, and so forth. (Dennett 1996, pp. 150–1)

This process, Dennett claims, begins with our encounter with public language words, and our subsequent habits of inner rehearsal of "voiced concepts," and ends with the effective installation of a whole inner economy of (if you like) idea-processing technology:

> We build elaborate systems of mnemonic association – pointers, labels, chutes and ladders, hooks and chains...turning our brains into a huge structured network of competences. No evidence yet unearthed shows that any other animal does anything like that. (Dennett 1996, p. 152)

That all sounds right. But once again, the question looms: Just how, *exactly*, is all this supposed to work? For it is not (I claim) until we see (in much more detail) how it could all work that we can be in a position to judge just *how much* this kind of move can really buy us. Dennett plausibly suggests, for example, that it is only courtesy of our linguistic capacities that we can think certain thoughts. Examples include considering whether a certain visually identical penny is in fact the *very same* penny that someone brought with them to New York many years ago (Dennett 1996, p. 116) and the explicit representation of *reasons* (see Section 1 above; Dennett 1996, pp. 131–3). More generally, Dennett endorses the view (Clark and Karmiloff-Smith 1993) that there are large benefits to making explicit knowledge that is initially locked away in some special-purpose, context-dependent encoding, and he suggests that language is a crucial tool for such processes of explication (Dennett 1996, p. 132).

And once again, this all sounds promising. But the actual details remain uncomfortably vague. Why, for example, is the possession of linguistic mind-tools *necessary* for thinking the thought about the penny? Dennett seems to think this ("It doesn't take a rocket scientist to think such thoughts, but it does take a Gregorian creature who has language among its mind-tools" [1996, p. 117]). But it is not at all obvious why this should be so. The question of necessity (or lack of it) is, I concede, probably not crucial. Perhaps public language is not strictly necessary for such thinking but is instead the (contingent) route by which it is achieved in humans (see Clark 1996b). What looks more important, however, is the slightly weaker claim that such thinking requires the use of at least *some* kind of mind-tool capable of objectifying concepts and relations. This I in fact believe, but still cannot prove to my own satisfaction. One argument, roughly sketched, might be that certain kinds of abstract thought require the capacity to create and deploy what might be called "perceptually simple inner objects" as stand-ins for complex concepts, ideas, and relations. I know of one rather compelling demonstration of this, which I think is worth mentioning here, even though I have treated it at some length elsewhere (Clark 1998b). For it will help focus some further issues concerning the scope and power of Dennett's overall vision.

The example (Thompson, Oden, and Boyson 1997) involves a study of problem solving in chimps (*pan troglodytes*). What Thompson et al. show is that chimps trained to use an arbitrary plastic marker (a yellow triangle, say) to designate pairs of identical objects (such as two identical cups), and to use a different marker (a red circle, say) to designate pairs of different objects (such as a shoe and a cup), are then (and only then) able to learn to solve a specific new class of abstract problems. This is the class of problems – apparently quite intractable to chimps not provided with the token-based training – involving recognition of *higher-order* relations of sameness and difference. Thus presented with two (different) pairs of identical items (two shoes and two cups, say), the higher-order task is to judge the two pairs as exhibiting the *same* relation, that is, to judge that you have two instances of *sameness*. Some examples of such higher-order judgments (which even human subjects can find hard to master at first) are:

| Cup/Cup | Shoe/Shoe |
|---|---|
| = | two instances of first-order sameness |
| = | an instance of higher-order sameness |
| Cup/Shoe | Cup/Shoe |
| = | two instances of first-order difference |
| = | an instance of higher-order sameness |
| Cup/Shoe | Cup/Cup |
| = | one instance of first-order difference and |
|   | one of first-order sameness |
| = | an instance of higher-order difference |

The token-trained chimps' success at this difficult task, it is conjectured, is explained by their prior experience with external tokens. For such experience may enable the chimp, on confronting, for example, the pair of identical cups, to retrieve a mental representation of the sameness token (as it happens, a yellow triangle). Exposure to the two identical shoes will likewise cause retrieval of (a token of) that token. At that point, the complex higher-order task is effectively reduced to the simpler lower-order task of identifying (internal representations of) the two yellow plastic tokens as "the same."

*Experience* with external tags and labels thus enables the brain itself, by *representing* those tags and labels, to solve problems whose level of complexity and abstraction would otherwise leave us baffled. Learning a set of tags and labels (which we all do when we learn a language) is thus rather closely akin to acquiring a new perceptual modality. For like a perceptual modality, it renders certain features of our world concrete and salient, and allows us to target our thoughts (and learning algorithms) on a new domain of basic objects. This new domain compresses what were previously complex and unruly sensory patterns into simple objects. These simple objects can then be attended to in ways that quickly reveal further (otherwise hidden) patterns, as in the case of relations-between-relations. And, of course, the whole process is deeply iterative – we coin new words and labels to concretize regularities that we could only originally conceptualize thanks to a backdrop of other words and labels.

This example, then, shows us several things. It demonstrates, in a quite striking way, how the provision of concrete labels can indeed "turbo-charge" biologically basic modes of learning and comprehension. But it also suggests some of the apparent limitations of the larger story. For there is nothing about the "cognitive bonus" thus achieved that looks (superficially at least) to bear very deeply on the development of self-hood, or of the capacity for consciousness and "significant suffering." What we get is a useful account of how certain types of intelligence may bootstrap themselves to new levels if augmented with some additional resources. But can the appeal to mind-tools really illuminate the *rest* of the matrix of mindfulness: especially the key aspects of responsible agenthood and consciousness? And is there still some biological difference that enables us humans to repeatedly create and exploit so many mind-tools in the first place? Finally, if there *is* such a difference, how can we be sure that it is the use of the mind-tools, and not that difference itself, that is responsible for the bulk of the matrix of human mindfulness?

## 3. CAN TOOLS MAKE THE SELF?

A natural worry about the appeal to mind-tools in the *constitution* of the self arises from the surface grammar of tool talk. For tools, in normal parlance, need a user. Yet on Dennett's account the nearest thing to a user we ever get is a kind of "user-illusion," an illusion itself created by the operation of certain mind-tools (specifically, those of narrative). The idea (see Introduction, this volume, and Dennett 1991) is that our kind of conscious awareness depends rather directly on our culturally inculcated capacity to tell a story (to ourselves and others) concerning our own life, reasons and actions. It is the presence of this story that makes our pains and pleasures *ours*, our choices our own, and our experience the way it is. We are nothing more than a bag of user-less cognitive tools (some natural, some artefactual) held together by a kind of illusion-of-selfhood: an illusion rooted in the operation of the narrative-spinning capacity acquired courtesy of our facility and language. The story Dennett tells thus depicts our kind of consciousness as dependent on a narrative-spinning capacity that literally creates the self (or is it just the illusion of a self?) to which experiences and actions are referred.[6]

Once again, the question to press is simply "How?" How is it that the activity of spinning a narrative can bring into being a conscious self, a site of potentially "significant suffering?" It is tempting to think the proposal must be either false or circular. It would be circular if the narrative only *counted* when it was spun by a person: a pre-existing locus of awareness, understanding, and experience. It would be false if it were imagined that the mere activity of (seeming to) tell a story about one's life and one's reasons for actions was somehow sufficient to construct "our kind of consciousness" from the void.

Or would it? I take it that, in some fairly dramatic sense, Dennett really is claiming something like the latter. He really is claiming that the constructing of a narrative distils consciousness and agency from the matrix of survival-enhancing innovations that constitute the biological organism. But the story hereabouts strikes me as less compelling than the previous story (the one concerning a specific "cognitive bonus" bestowed by the culturally aided process of label production).

How might the spinning of a narrative (one that cannot be assumed to be *already* the narrative of a conscious agent) help bring minds like ours into being? Dennett offers a number of ideas none of which, I think, can quite carry the load. They include:

- The idea that linguistic formulation yields a kind of shallow determinacy of content that simple belief-like states lack.[7]

- The idea that linguistically rehearsed contents are especially well positioned to win the struggle for control of action.[8]

- The idea that any notion of a "point of view" depends on one story winning out over others, and that linguistic judgings are what allow such victories to occur.[9]

- The idea that certain kinds of morally significant self-control require the capacity to confront one's own beliefs and reasons for action, and that the linguistically supported objectification of our own mental states contributes deeply to this process.[10]

I suspect that the other contributors to this volume will have much to say about the first three of these ideas, so I shall restrict myself to one single comment. It is that even if all these points (the first three) are conceded, it remains unclear why conscious experience and "significant suffering" should depend on having these capacities in place. Certainly, neither determinacy of content nor linguistically based capacities of wielding local control seem to have much to do with qualitative experience. And even the third idea, concerning the construction of a "point of view," seems to be pointing to a feature of typical human consciousness that may well be unnecessary for pleasure, pain, and suffering.

I propose to dwell, however, only on the fourth suggestion: the idea that certain kinds of morally significant self-control depend crucially on something like a capacity to treat one's own thoughts, beliefs, and reasons as objects. For it is here, I believe, that we come closest to seeing some kind of conceptually deep connection between the operation of certain mind-tools and the presence of fully fledged human agency.

Dennett suggests that it is, in large part, our capacities of self-description that allow us to actively create ourselves as persons: "What you are is that agent whose life you can tell about" (Dennett 1996, p. 156). Such self-description is said to begin in early childhood, with fantasy self-descriptions such as "I am an ace fighter pilot," and carry on throughout life (hopefully, although perhaps not actually, with a greater grip on the facts). But to get a full sense of the potential role of such self-description in constituting knowing moral agency, we need to go back to Dennett's (1984) discussion of "self-made selves." The key idea here, which we already touched on in Section 1, is that the availability of a language of self-description opens up the morally crucial possibility of "radical self-evaluation." Dennett is here deeply influenced by Charles Taylor (see, e.g., Taylor 1976), who depicts such self-evaluation as involving first an attempt to formulate what was previously inchoate: a sense of what is important, and why it is important, that was previously merely implicit in the patterns of activity in which we engaged. And then a direct confrontation of that newly achieved articulation, during which we question, refine, affirm, or reject certain elements. It is in this way that (as Dennett glosses Taylor) "we create our values while creating ourselves" (Dennett 1984, p. 90).

Such special deliberative skills, Dennett suggests, enhance our potential for self-control and for the improvement and stabilization of character. And a self, for Dennett, is "above all, a locus of self-control" (1984, p. 81). We are thus presented with a cascade of types and levels of self-control somewhat analogous to the cascade of adaptive strategies rehearsed earlier. At the bottom level is the simple capacity to control the motions of one's own body. But the self emerges (if I read Dennett correctly) only when that control becomes in various ways self-conscious or transparent. Such a process reaches a kind of apex when the self-controlling agent can ask meta-level questions about their own general operating strategies, or styles, and assess how well these strategies and styles serve their desires and needs, and even (see Frankfurt 1971) whether their desires and needs are the ones they really want.

Such dizzy heights of self-control become available, Dennett claims, only once organisms acquire a language of self-description. And this is because:

> The aspirant to a high order of self-control must have the capacity to represent his current beliefs, desires, intentions and policies in a detached way, as objects for evaluation. (Dennett 1984, p. 86).

The equations at the heart of Dennett's account of the emergence of fully fledged human agency and self-hood thus look to be these:

Maximal Control = Maximal Self-Hood and Responsibility

Radical Re-evaluation = The Route to Maximal Control

If Radical Re-evaluation requires a language of self-description, then a link between fully fledged agency and the presence of some language-like resource seems indicated.

Considered as an account of the pre-conditions of morally responsible agency, this argument (or equation) has much to recommend it. Moreover, it comes closest to displaying a truly critical role for the mind-tools bequeathed to us by public language. True, it might be possible in principle to acquire and exploit a "language of self-description" even in the absence of public language or practices of abstract symbolic communication. But for human agency, it surely *is* the practice of public, language-dependent, criticism, and reflection that instills in us the kind of meta-reflective skills that Dennett and Taylor highlight. The "cognitive bonus" that language confers thus seems central not just to the incremental learning of abstract concepts (see Section 2) but also to the emergence of morally responsible agency (for further arguments to this effect, see Clark 1996a; 2000a).

And this, I think, is an intuitively appealing result. Nonlinguistic creatures are not prominent candidates for thick moral agency. Given a morally loaded concept of self-hood, they are likewise not likely to count as persons or selves (although weaker notions of personhood and self-hood may remain available). There is still nothing here, however, which speaks to the rather bulky remainder of our matrix of mindfulness: the presence of qualitative consciousness and the potential for significant suffering. To make the rest of the case requires one further move which I still find unwarranted, viz., to claim that *experiences need a thick subject*, that is, a subject whose capacities of self-knowledge and self-control lie at, or close to, the apex of deliberative reason described by Taylor. It is this last piece of the puzzle, the imagined link between qualitative consciousness, significant suffering, and the presence of a "*complex* subject to *whom* [things] matter" (Dennett 1998, p. 351, emphasis in original), that I still cannot seem to fit into place. As a result, the appeal to the transformative role of mind-tools (especially language) buys us a whole lot while (I suspect) not *quite* making the complete case that Dennett requires. The matrix of mindfulness has many parts, and the appeal to culturally incubated mind-tools may not fully illuminate the whole.[11]

## 4. ON BEING CYBORGS

Shortfalls aside, the appeal to culturally incubated mind-tools must surely play a crucial role in any account of what's *special* about human thought and reason. In this final section, I shall examine some of the bigger issues, opportunities, and problems that this looks likely to involve.

The most basic problem, of course, concerns the use and origin of the mind-tools themselves. Take, for example, Dennett's pre-eminent tool: the capacity to use words to label states of oneself and of the world. What does it take to acquire and exploit such a tool? The rats, hamsters, and snakes of the world cannot seem to acquire this skill to any significant degree, no matter how hard we humans try to inculcate it. Chimps and dolphins, it seems, do significantly better. But no other animal looks capable of acquiring a linguistic framework comparable in depth, breadth, and expressiveness to our own. Doesn't this suggest, rather strongly, that the crucial cognitive innovation (that special something) actually *precedes*, and in fact makes possible, the acquisition of human-style language and the subsequent cascade of designer mind-tools?

Well, yes and no. Consider a somewhat analogous (or so I claim) question. What is that special something that makes Granny's fruitcake so good? Let's rule out all the things that Granny's fruitcake has in common with other, demonstrably fruitcake-y yet not-half-so-good, confections. What, we want to know, is Granny's special trick? Here is an answer: Granny marinates her raisins in a special over-proof Jamaican rum, yielding an exceedingly heady product. But wait. Not just any old raisins will do. In fact, many of the raisins used by inferior cooks would be unable to benefit from the proprietary over-proof immersion, being too small, spindly, and burnt to absorb any significant amount of the Jamaican elixir.

So what *is* Granny's secret? Is it the rum or the raisins? The question is kind of silly. The difference in taste is attributable, let's suppose, to the rum. But the capacity to *take that difference on board* lies with the raisins. The case of language and mind-tools is, I suggest, perfectly parallel. The cognitive bonus that yields human levels of thought and reason may well be (as Dennett claims) largely due to what certain mind-tools do to, and with, the brain. But the capacity to acquire, develop, and exploit such mind-tools may well itself depend on some prior (perhaps small) neural innovation.

It seems rather likely, in fact, that there is a double biological difference at work here. First, there is the neural innovation that lets a recursive, recombinable public language get a grip. But second, there is an additional biological difference involving unusually extensive neural plasticity (centered on the cortex)[12] coupled with an extended period of sheltered learning and development (the extended human childhood). Thus, consider the evolutionary story sketched by Griffiths and Stotz (2000). These authors (who cite Furth 1987) suggest that "human evolution has given rise to a new stage of development: childhood." And childhood, they suggest, provides a window of learning in which "cultural scaffolding [can] change the dynamics of the cognitive system in a way that opens up new cognitive possibilities" (both quotes from Griffiths and Stotz 2000, p. 11). This whole account resonates deeply with the Dennettian ideas explained earlier. Thus the authors convincingly argue against what they term a "dualistic account of human biology and human culture" in which a process of biological evolution *first* produced the "anatomically modern human" and was *then* followed by the (on-going) process of cultural evolution. Such a picture invites us, they note, to conceive of a kind of true biological human nature underlying the culturally clothed product. But the project of investigating this naked biological nature, they argue, is "as misguided as seeking to investigate the true nature of an ant by removing the distorting influence of the nest!" (Griffiths and Stotz 2000, p. 10). By contrast, Griffiths and Stotz depict human nature as the complex product of a "developmental matrix" in which the influences of biology, artefact, and society are pretty well inextricably intertwined. They conclude, nicely in line with recent work on situated and embodied cognition (see Clark 1997), that:

> The individual representational system is part of a larger representational environment which extends far beyond the skin. Cognitive processes actually involve as components what are more traditionally conceived as the expressions of thought and the objects of thought. Situated cognition takes place within complex social structures which 'scaffold' the individual by means of artifactual, linguistic and institutional devices... culture makes humans as much as the reverse. (Griffiths and Stotz 2000, p. 45)

Notice, then, an intuitive but fallacious idea that we need to firmly reject. It is the idea that mind-tools cannot make us fundamentally more intelligent since we had to be *exactly that intelligent* to create them in the first place. Such an argument is multiply flawed. It is flawed because not all artefactual innovation is the result of deliberate design. It is flawed because multiple individual intelligences, spanning multiple generations, are involved in the production of the culturally inherited set of mind-tools. And it is flawed because even a tool that I myself design and use can do more than merely enhance my practical problem-solving ability. Experience in using such a tool can, over time (and especially during the sensitive periods of early development), alter the way my brain actually works, so as to yield a better brain-tool union. (This latter process, in which human brains alter to fit the tools created by [previous] human brains, I call "cognitive dove-tailing" – see Clark [1998a].)

All of which serves to reinforce the conclusions reached by Griffiths and Stotz. It is a mistake to posit a biologically fixed "human nature" with a simple "wrap-around" of tools and culture. For the tools and culture are as much determiners of our nature as products of it. Ours are especially plastic brains (see Note 12) whose biologically proper functioning has always involved the recruitment and exploitation of nonbiological props and scaffolds. More so than any other creature on the planet, we humans are *natural-born cyborgs*, tweaked and primed so as to participate in cognitive and computational architectures whose bounds far exceed those of skin and skull.

In his own pursuit of such themes, Dennett has tended to stress the transformative effects of the cultural, linguistic, and artefactual surround on the brain (the creation of the "user-illusion," for instance, is the creation of an *internal* kind of "informational unification" – see Dennett 1998, pp. 346–7). I have tended, by contrast, to stress the new dove-tailed wholes comprising brains, bodies, and complexes of external props and scaffolding (see, e.g., Clark 1997, Chapter 9). These two (entirely compatible) perspectives converge, of course, in the developmental matrix highlighted by Griffiths and Stotz. I think it remains an open question, however, just how extensive and important a role is played by the "internalization" of mind-tools, as against a process (falling somewhat short of full internalization) in which the brain adapts so as to better use and exploit tools that remain firmly located in the external environment (see, e.g., Hutchins 1995 for a wonderful exploration of this scenario).

Let me end, however, by flagging just one more issue – one that suggests a possible tension within Dennett's overall picture. The issue concerns the cognitive continuity between human minds and the minds of other (non-Gregorian) animals. Just how special *are* human minds in the earth-bound natural order? At times, and increasingly so in recent years, Dennett seems to think our minds are very special indeed. He writes, for example, that:

> Chimpanzees may well be incapable of *thinking about thinking*. They may, indeed, not really be capable of thinking at all (in some florid but important sense of thinking). (Dennett 2000, p. 20)

Or again, consider the claim about consciousness:

> My claim is not that other species lack our kind of *self*-consciousness. . . . I am
> claiming that what must be added to mere responsivity, mere discrimination,
> to count as consciousness *at all* is an organization that is not ubiquitous
> among sentient organisms. (Dennett 1998, p. 347)

And again:

> It may not be able to talk, but surely it thinks! – one of the main aims of this
> book has been to shake your confidence in this familiar reaction. (Dennett
> 1996, p. 159)

In all these quotes (and there are many more) Dennett seems to be
linking real thinking to the presence of the kind of description language
necessary for the project of radical self-evaluation and meta-level reasoning. Yet elsewhere (sometimes on the very same page) we encounter what
appears to be a much more liberal story:

> What structural and processing differences make different animals capable
> of having more sophisticated beliefs? . . . there are many, many differences,
> almost all of them theoretically interesting, but none of them, in my opinion,
> marking a well-motivated chasm between the mere mindless behavers and
> the genuine rational agents. (Dennett 1998, p. 331)

Or on the matter of consciousness:

> The very idea of there being a dividing line between those creature "it is
> like something to be" and mere "automata" begins to look like an artifact
> of our traditional presumptions. (Dennett 1998, p. 349)

Granted, there are many careful phrasings in Dennett's corpus that
allow these two perspectives (roughly, one of cognitive continuity and one of
cognitive discontinuity) to exist side by side. For example, there is said to be
a continuity of belief-states and a discontinuity at the level of linguistically
infected "opinions" (see Dennett 1998, Chapter 4). But there seems (to me
at least) to be a deeper tension here that cannot really be massaged away by
the careful use of words. Sometimes, Dennett tries to reject the very issue
that I am here (with some trepidation) raising, as when he writes:

> At what point in evolutionary history did real reason-appreciators, real
> selves, make their appearance? Don't ask . . . it is a fool's errand to try to
> identify a first or most simple instance of the "real" thing. (Dennett 1998,
> p. 362)

But while I agree that firm dividing lines and clear first instances are often (indeed typically) not to be found, it does not follow that there are no profound organizational differences which demarcate (even with vague mid-points) the true selves and reason-appreciators from the rest. Indeed (and this is why the tension still strikes me as potentially important), Dennett himself, as we just saw, often seems to assert as much – and recall also his (1984) discussion of the construction of the morally responsible self via the linguistically mediated installation of habits of self-criticism and self-evaluation (as discussed in Section 1 above). Yet in this latter case, at least, Dennett is never tempted to speak elusively of "our kind of morality," or to deny the existence of a firm (even if fuzzy-at-the-edges) distinction between the radical self-evaluators and the rest. In short, I suspect that Dennett really needs to make a hard call in the case of thinking itself, and to decide whether the presence of various linguistically mediated transformations and enhancements does or does not mark a truly deep discontinuity in the space of mind-designs.

The question may perhaps be put like this: Just how *important* are opinions? How important, cognitively speaking, are the special linguistic mind-tool-generated states underlying our capacities of self-evaluation and meta-deliberation? My own hunch is that these capacities are crucial neither for the genesis of 'real' thought, nor for consciousness. But that once present, they make a large difference to the space of learnable concepts and hence to the space of possible mental contents. In sometimes speaking of "our kind of thinking" (Dennett 1996, p. 130) or "our kind of consciousness" (Dennett 1998, p. 346), Dennett elides the difference between the types of contents of thoughts and experiences, and the very presence of thinkings and experiencings. This helps mask the tension. But it will not, I suspect, make it go away.

It is, of course, part of Dennett's even *larger* project to re-cast many major issues as (precisely) turning on the *contents* of representational states rather than the presence or absence of the "mythic light bulb of consciousness" (Dennett 1998, p. 349). So one way to interpret my portrayal of an apparent tension would be to try to cast it as a simple failure to appreciate this major element of the story. But that, I suspect, is a little too fast. For even if it is (if you like) *content all the way down*, it remains possible that the appreciation of reasons requires the capacity to entertain and manipulate specific kinds of content that are (absolutely) beyond the reach of other animals, while the contentful states necessary for the presence of qualitative consciousness and simple thoughtfulness do not.

As I finish writing these words, I find myself unsure whether the tension I seem to detect is real, or if real, important. For without a doubt any decent scientific image of mind must be an image of multiple, criss-crossing continuities and discontinuities. What matters most, and where Dennett truly excels, is in the careful elaboration of the warp and weave of multiple design elements, both inner and outer, and of their roles in generating the patterns of whole-agent behaviour that inform our intuitive understandings of minds and selves. By this unusual (philosophically speaking) means, Dennett hopes to show us who and what we are. He hopes to show us what makes us special, while reminding us that we are neither miraculous, nor fundamentally disjoint from the rest of nature's adaptive engines. We, too, are bags of user-less survival tools. But in our case, there is the additional shimmer of the user-illusion and the potent capacity – in cultural, linguistic, and artefactual context – to engage in biologically novel acts of self-evaluation and self-definition. We are about as natural as a Palm Pilot on a sunny day, and as special, and mundane, as any new technology built on a platform of old parts. In pursuing such a delicate balance between pride and humility, and in displaying the essentially hybrid (biological/nonbiological) nature of human minds and persons, Dennett sets a rich and complex agenda: One whose full cultural, scientific, and philosophical implications remain as unclear as they are visibly fundamental.

### Notes

1. So-called because it was Karl Popper who memorably described certain cognitive designs as allowing "our hypotheses to die in our stead" (see Dennett 1996, p. 88).

2. So-called after the psychologist, Richard Gregory, whose work stresses the role of designed artefacts in actively enhancing intelligence (see Gregory 1981, p. 311ff.; Dennett 1996, p. 99).

3. See, for example, Dennett 1996, p. 162, for a clear statement of the uniqueness claim, and of the idea that the Gregorian creatures have crossed a genuine threshold in cognitive space.

4. See especially Dennett 1996, Chapters 4–6.

5. See especially Clark 1997, Chapters 9 and 10; Clark 1998b.

6. See, for example, Dennett 1998, p. 351, and Dennett 1996, pp. 156–7.

7. E.g., Dennett 1998, pp. 89–90.

8. E.g., Dennett 1996, p. 155.

9. E.g., Dennett 1998, p. 348.

[10.] E.g., Dennett 1984, pp. 86, 90.

[11.] For my own recent, and quite Dennettian, attempt to complete the puzzle, see Clark 2000a.

[12.] See recent work on "neutral constructivism," for example, Quartz and Sejnowski 1997; Quartz 1999.

## References

Clark, A. (1996a). Connectionism, Moral Cognition and Collaborative Problem Solving. In L. May, M. Friedman, and A. Clark, eds., *Minds and Morals*. Cambridge, MA: MIT Press/A Bradford Book, 109–28.

Clark, A. (1996b) Linguistic Anchors in the Sea of Thought. *Pragmatics and Cognition* 4(1):93–103.

Clark, A. (1997). *Being There: Putting Brain, Body and World Together Again*. Cambridge, MA: MIT Press/A Bradford Book.

Clark, A. (1998a). Where Brain, Body and World Collide. *Daedalus* 127(2):257–80.

Clark, A. (1998b). Magic Words: How Language Augments Human Computation. In J. Boucher and P. Carruthers, eds., *Language and Thought*. Cambridge: Cambridge University Press, 162–83.

Clark, A., (2000). A Case Where Access Implies Qualia? *Analysis* 60(1):30–38.

Clark, A. (2000a). Word and Action. In R. Campbell and B. Hunter, eds., *Moral Epistemology Naturalized: Canadian Journal of Philosophy. Supplement* 26:267–90.

Clark, A. (2000b). *Mindware: An Introduction to the Philosophy of Cognitive Science*. New York: Oxford University Press.

Clark, A., and A. Karmiloff-Smith. (1993). The Cognizers Innards: A Philosophical and Psychological Perspective on the Development of Thought. *Mind and Language* 8(4):487–519.

Dennett, D. (1984). *Elbow Room*. Cambridge, MA: MIT Press/A Bradford Book.

Dennett, D. (1991). *Consciousness Explained*. New York: Little Brown & Co.

Dennett, D. (1996). *Kinds of Minds*. New York: Basic Books.

Dennett, D. (1998). *Brainchildren: Essays on Designing Minds*. Cambridge, MA: MIT Press/A Bradford Book.

Dennett, D. (2000). Making Tools for Thinking. In D. Sperber, ed., *Metarepresentations*. Oxford: Oxford University Press, 17–29.

Frankfurt, H. (1971). Freedom of the Will and the Concept of a Person. *Journal of Philosophy* 68:5–20.

Furth, H. (1987). *Knowledge as Desire: An Essay on Freud and Piaget*. New York: Columbia University Press.

Gregory, R. (1981). *Mind In Science: A History of Explanations in Psychology*. Cambridge: Cambridge University Press.

Griffiths, P. E., and K. Stotz. (2000). How the mind grows: A developmental perspective on the biology of cognition. *Synthese* 122(1–2):29–51.

Hutchins, E. (1995). *Cognition in the Wild.* Cambridge, MA: MIT Press/Bradford.

Quartz, S., and T. Sejnowski. (1997). The Neural Basis of Cognitive Development: A Constructivist Manifesto. *Behavioral and Brain Sciences* 20:537–56.

Quartz, S. (1999). The Constructivist Brain. *Trends in Cognitive Sciences* 3(2): 48–57.

Taylor, C. (1976). Responsibility for the Self. In A. Rorty, ed., *The Identities of Persons.* Berkeley: University of California Press.

Thompson, R., D. Oden, and S. Boyson. (1999). Language-naive Chimpanzees Judge Relations Between Relations in a Conceptual Matching-to-sample Task. *Journal of Experimental Psychology: Animal Behavior Processes* 23:31–43.

# 8 | A Question of Content

KATHLEEN AKINS

## PART I

### 1. Introduction

The topic of this essay is, or is supposed to be, the influence of Daniel Dennett's philosophy of mind on neuroscience. Since I do not have a straightforward answer to the question, "What has Dennett contributed to the neurosciences?," I am going to start off with a *different* question, one that I stand some chance of answering, and then with that answer in hand, I will circle back around to the original question in Part II. In other words, I am going to take (what I hope will be) the scenic route. (Got it?)

The question with which I will begin, then, the 'different question,' is one that almost every philosophy of mind student has asked since the publication of *Consciousness Explained (CE)*. Why does Dennett think that our folk attributions of perceptual states, attributions made from the intentional stance, do not merely *describe* the propositional contents of the subject's conscious perceptions? *CE* makes clear that, for Dennett, there are neural representations 'in there' (after all, Dennett is not *that* kind of behaviourist) and that the contents of these representations somehow determine how we consciously experience the world. You see the world as you do because certain visual 'specialists' within the visual system have determined that the world is a certain way. But if so, it would seem to follow that at least, we must know how the world seems. If so, then surely *we* are capable of making accurate (self-) attributions of our own perceptual beliefs. So why does Dennett think that not even we, as conscious subjects, get it right? This is an extremely good question. Before taking it up, however, let me make the put the question in philosophical context.

### 2. A Cartesian Stalking-horse

Like Ryle before him, the principal motivation of Dennett's view of mind is a negative thesis about what the mind *could not possibly be*, namely Ryle's

Ghost in the Machine or Dennett's Cartesian theatre. On the strongest version of this view, no doubt a view that not even Descartes espoused, the mind is portrayed as like a stage on which the self-luminous denizens of consciousness parade for an audience of one, the ever present, all-seeing Self. Famously, on this view, the mind has immediate, infallible, and incorrigible access to the passing mental stream. First, the contents of the mind are, as Ryle would have put it, 'phosphorescent.' Insofar as one has a conscious mental state, one knows one has it, without inference, attention or any other quasi-perceptual process of 'illumination.' There are no phenomenal events – could not be any phenomenal events – which dance in the dark unknown and unappreciated by the Theatre's audience. For conscious events, to be is to be perceived.

Second, because the mind's access to the stage is unmediated there are no quasi-perceptual processes that might 'go wrong.' A conscious event cannot be misperceived or unrecognized for what it is. If I see a tree before me, then I know that I do so, and moreover, I know that I seem to see *a tree* (although, of course, I may be wrong about the state of the external world, whether or not there is a tree before me). In the same way that the mind could not fail to notice a conscious event as it passed by, it cannot fail to apprehend the phenomenal events as they really are. Our access to conscious mental events is infallible.

Third, because there is but one Self to a theatre, a person's access to the conscious contents of his or her mind is unique. My access to the events of your mind is mediated necessarily by both our bodies. I can only infer, on the basis of what you say – or more generally what you do – which conscious states lie within and the same is true for your knowledge of me. Hence, no one can know better than the Self the nature of its own conscious experience. Self-knowledge, in this limited sense, is incorrigible.

All of the above, I hope, is a familiar portrait of the 'Cartesian' view or at least familiar enough from its detractors' descriptions. One more piece needs to be added, however. Because Dennett's positive view of consciousness is largely a theory about *perceptual* consciousness – even more specifically, about visual consciousness – something needs to be said about the role of perceptual states in the Cartesian theatre of mind. Unfortunately, insofar as I know, Dennett has not given a sustained description of the 'Cartesian' view of perception that he is targeting. The target arises piecemeal in Dennett's writing. Substance dualism aside, though, Descartes' view of perception (as opposed to a Cartesian view) has many of the features of contemporary materialist theories of perception against which Dennett is reacting. So, for our present expository purposes (and with apologies to Descartes for the historical vilification) it should do.

On Descartes' view of perception, neural events in the brain 'occasion' phenomenal sensory events, sensations that in and of themselves tell the Self almost nothing about the states of the world which caused them. That is, *some* of these states may be pleasant or unpleasant, a 'content' that informs the Self that the cause of the sensation is either harmful to or good for body. Take the case of a scratched toe. Damage to the body results in a phenomenal state, that of pain, a sensation that is intrinsically unpleasant. Hence, it warns the Self not of a particular kind of bodily damage per se, say, puncture, nor of damage to a particular part of the body, say the toe, nor of *damage to the surface* of the body. An unpleasant sensation serves only to warn the Self *that* the cause is, in some unspecified way, harmful. The same holds true for some noxious tastes and odours, unpleasant temperature sensations, and so on. To put this another way, apart from the contents of pleasantness or unpleasantness, the qualitative properties of sensations, *what they are like*, exhausts their 'content,' what they tell you about the world. By comparing sensations, one with another, you can come to know *something* about their causes in virtue of their qualitative similarities. For example, given three sensations, a 'blue' sensation, a 'yellow' sensation, and a 'red' sensation, by comparing these sensations to each other and to the multitude of other sensory sensations before you, you could come to realize, that these sensations are of the same type ('visual' or 'colour' sensations). You could also infer that the *causes* of the yellow sensation and red sensation are more similar to each other than to the cause of the blue sensation because yellow is more similar to red than to blue qua phenomenal property. But all of this is inferred knowledge, made on the basis of qualitative similarity. More generally, on Descartes' theory of perception, on the basis of its innate understanding of the general properties of the physical world and the particular facts of the sensory array before it, the mind infers the presence of the properties and events that might inhabit the world beyond it. The mind must *infer*, for example, that it is my toe that seems to be hurt, that my right leg seems to be crossed over the left, that there seems to be a wooden table before me, and so on. And then, with these inferential conclusions before it, the mind *judges* whether or not these states of affairs actually obtain, whether the content of the inferential conclusions is true *of the world*. So judged, we come to have conscious perceptions of the properties and events of the world external to the mind.

One feature of Descartes' view of perception is worth special note in this context, namely the role of 'pure sensations' – or rather the two distinct roles that *qualia* are made to play. As I said above, sensations are the phenomenal *inputs* to the mind, the raw materials of (perceptual) cognition. They are the purely qualitative (and sometime evaluative) states, *qualia*, which the physical senses deliver up to the mind for the scrutiny of its rational capacities – for the mind to categorize, make inferences about and from, and perhaps to like or dislike according to the idiosyncratic nature of the subject. (Some likes and dislikes are merely a matter of personal preference. For example, I may love broccoli and George Bush Sr. may hate it, but the 'awfulness' of broccoli-for-Bush is not a property it has in virtue of God's goodness.) That said, our sensory perceptions of the world, of tables and chairs and the bodies we possess, have purely qualitative aspects to them as well. For example, while the mind can infer from the sensory array, the size, shape, and position of objects within the visual field, our sensations of colour tell us nothing about the particular surface properties of objects. In Descartes' terms, God has constructed our sensory processes such that we can tell from certain sensations only *that* a particular property of the world has caused them, not *what* the particular cause is. To infer that the daffodils in the vase *are* yellow is to mistake a phenomenal property for a physical one. Strictly speaking, daffodils are *not* yellow (because yellow is a phenomenal property), even though the fact that they appear so does indicate something about the surface properties of daffodils, we know not what. Thus, our fully formed, intentional perceptions also have qualitative 'aspects,' the second role of *qualia* within the theory.

In Descartes' theory of perception, then, *qualia* play a dual role: They are both the *inputs* to higher-level perceptual processes and the qualitative aspects of the *output* of perceptual processes, of intentional perceptions per se. Dennett would argue, I expect, that the *qualia* play a dual role in our contemporary understanding of perception. Certainly we speak of, say, the taste of Marmite qua a part of the sensory experience of eating bread and Marmite, a part that we can isolate and 'examine' as 'the exact taste' of Marmite. In the same breath, however, we will speak of the memory of one's very first taste of Marmite, and how *that* taste affects or compares with the experience of Marmite we have at present. We speak as if what is stored is a purely qualitative sensation that can later be used, say to assess one's current perception of Marmite on toast. (Is today's Marmite on toast, for example, up to the standards of that very first bite?) So the tensions implicit in Descartes' 'antiquated' theory can plausibly be said to continue on in contemporary theory.

This, at least in rough outline, is the Cartesian stalking-horse.

## 3. The First Move

As I understand it, Dennett's philosophical project is this. Dennett wants to develop a positive, stable theory of the mind by steering clear of the reefs and shoals of the Cartesian view, while incorporating the 'landings' supplied by the cognitive sciences within his charted route. To put this another way, he sees quite clearly where most of the Cartesian hazards lie, what he has to avoid. He has also some (but fewer) positive landmarks to visit, 'stops' from neurophysiology, social psychology, and on to evolutionary theories about the brain that he should include. Still, those constraints leave a lot of open water. What is far less clear is which route, of the indefinite number of possible routes the landmarks leave open, he should take. This is why I suspect (and please excuse both the metaphor and the pun) so many people have found Dennett's theory of mind a 'moving target.' It seems that way because it *is* that way. From Dennett's perspective, there is nothing wrong with deviating from one's stated route given a good reason – that is, an unexpected (Cartesian) hazard or an unforeseen need for a (empirical) pit stop. After all, just how else would a person navigate? ("Officer, I ran into the pedestrian because he was there and because I had not planned to avoid him.")

Famously, both Ryle and Dennett make the same crucial – and irrevocable – first move. The problem, as both Dennett and Ryle understand it, is that psychological states, the garden variety beliefs, desires, and emotions that we attribute to ourselves and others, are not (as Ryle so often said) either conscious *or* unconscious states. Strictly speaking, psychological 'states' are not states in the mind/brain at all: They are behavioural dispositions (Ryle 1949) or "patterns of behaviour" (Dennett 1991b). We, as practitioners of folk psychology, may well suppose that our attributions of propositional attitudes serve to pick out or refer to particular mental/neural events, tokens of the appropriate type, in a subject's mental/neural economy. But if we do so, we are in the grip of a systematic misunderstanding of both what we do (Dennett) and what we say (Ryle) through such attributions. Rather, according to Dennett, both folk psychology and its more sophisticated cousin, the Intentional Stance, are "best viewed as a rationalistic calculus of interpretation and prediction – an idealizing, abstract, instrumentalistic interpretation method that has evolved because it works and works because we have evolved" (Dennett 1987b). We begin our predictions by looking at the organism's behaviour and ascribing to it the beliefs it ought to have given its particular needs for information and its perceptual history. We ascribe to it the desires it *ought to have* – its primary needs being those for procreation and survival, its secondary needs being whatever conditions are required to survive and procreate. Finally, we deduce what the organism *ought to do* (or ought to have done) to satisfy its desires relative to those beliefs given the constraints of rationality. Thus we use intentional attributions to predict and "retrospect" (Ryle 1949, pp. 166–7) the actions of intentional systems without recourse to any knowledge of the (astoundingly) complex causal processes within the mind/brain. This is *in fact* how we make intentional attributions and the reason why we do so – and we should not suppose in light of this predictive success that we have gained any great insight into the concrete workings, the neural processes, that result in human action.

Let me stop for a moment to highlight just how radical this first move is. Unlike tables or chairs or the average kumquat, we – you and I and most of the rest of the species homo sapiens – *are* conscious entities, beings with full and rich phenomenal lives. This is not something that either Dennett or Ryle denies. What is radical about the first move, then, is not that the theory portrays us as zombies, poor old automatons without two conscious states to rub together. What is radical about the move is how little it leaves us vis-à-vis what we thought we understood about ourselves and about our perceptual relations to the world. To put this another way, what the Cartesian view of mind makes possible is a very neat and orderly epistemic portrayal of what goes on 'both within and without.' One begins with the realist assumption of a 'set' ontology, of the world with all of its objects, events, and properties neatly delineated, at the ready for us the fair perceivers. Now our perceptual systems given to us by God (or evolution) allow us to infer our way from sensory input to what lies beyond the mind/brain. If everything is working correctly (and as Descartes often reminds us, it will work correctly only if we too are working hard), we will have reliable information about how the world lies. So, for example, if you are standing looking at a plate of kumquats the sensory input from your eyes will eventuate in a conscious perception of that fruit, perhaps with a content <Lo! Kumquats!>. With the perception of kumquats before you, you can now think about those kumquats. You can wonder how much the kumquats cost, who bought them, or what they really are (i.e., are they really just very tiny oranges?). Moreover, given the "phosphorescent" nature of all conscious events, you know what you think and you can *express* your perceptual belief to others should you be so moved. You as the speaker of the English language can express it with the sentence, "Lo! Kumquats!" Of course, if a thought can be *expressed* by means of an utterance, then it can also be *described* in the same way. Using the appropriate sentence, I can refer to or pick out your perceptual thought by means of a belief attribution with the appropriate propositional content. All of which, as I said above, yields a very orderly view: (a) our perceptions reflect the properties of world; (b) our utterances express the propositional contents of our conscious perceptions; and (c) our attributions of psychological states refer to those perceptual states by means of their propositional contents. The mind may be necessarily private on the Cartesian view, but fortunately through the grace of God (or evolution), we gain a window on the world and the minds of others via perception and language.

The classic behaviourist move attempts to annihilate this tidy picture. Our intentional practices give us no reason to think that our attributions pick out, by means of their content, specific conscious (or unconscious) states. Nor do we have any reason to think that our utterances are *caused by* these conscious states, and hence that our utterances express their contents (see Brook, this volume). Nor can we adopt, without critical examination, the Cartesian picture of perception. According to Dennett, when we attribute beliefs to an intentional system, including perceptual beliefs, we do so according to what beliefs the system *ought* to have, relative to its informational needs and perceptual history. When a fly buzzes by a frog, the frog ought to believe that a fly, as opposed to a lead pellet, is present. But to attribute a belief about a *fly* leaves open a rather wide range of possibilities of how – or even *if* – the property of being a fly is represented by the frog's brain/visual system. The intentional stance works just insofar as the frog behaves *as if* it sees the fly. The same point holds, *mutatis mutandi*, for the attribution of *any* intentional state to any intentional system. Given a 'correct' attribution of an intentional state (i.e., one that works) is an entirely open question 'what goes on within,' whether the neural capacities of the species are genuinely representational (whatever that might mean) or merely 'contentful' or 'informational' in some other sense. Moreover, it is an entirely open question what kind of causal relations the organism's conscious states bear to the world beyond it, to its perceptual capacities in general, and to its other behaviours. To put this another way, there is no reason to think, on the basis of an attribution of a perceptual state, that we are referring to or picking out particular conscious states, the 'end products' of a process that begins when we open our eyes and stare out at the world – that is, that we refer to an event of this kind when we say, for example, "She sees a plate of kumquats." Seen this way, the behaviourist strategy is a truly radical first move.

We are now almost back to the question with which this paper began, namely, "Why does Dennett think that the contents of conscious perceptual states will not 'line up' with the content of the attributions of perceptual beliefs that we make from the Intentional Stance?" Note that the behaviourists' 'first move' does *not* give us the strong negative thesis that Dennett wants: It does not prove that the two kinds of contents will not align. What he gains from the first move is really only an open question, the very possibility of nonalignment as it were: 'Will they or won't they?' To show that the two kinds of content will not align, a different sort of argument needs to be made.[1] In particular, for a strong argument, what Dennett needs is a positive view about the nature of neural content, the nature of perceptual processes as well as a theory about the relation between conscious perceptual states and perceptual processing. Of course, it is these views that are going to be primarily of interest to the neuroscience community, and so I will turn to them now.

## 4. Neural Content

Where Ryle and Dennett part company is over the issue of 'what goes on inside?' Ryle was disinclined to sanction anything that looked vaguely Cartesian, of course, including all talk of representations, conscious perceptions, and inferential processes (although, touchingly, Ryle often admits that he does not know what to say, *really*, about perceptual phenomenology). In stark contrast, Dennett begins with the assumption that 'subpersonal' neural states can also be said to have 'content', but of course not the (bad) propositional content of folk beliefs and desires. He says in "Styles of Mental Representation" (1987d), that subpersonal psychology "will be 'cognitive' in that it will describe processes of information-transformation among content-laden items – mental representations – but their style will not look or behave like sentences manipulated in a language of thought" (p. 235).

As a subpersonal psychologist, Dennett is a 'pure laine' computationalist: Brain-states are computational states. To determine the content of a subpersonal functional/computational state one must engage in a process of holistic interpretation: One must look at the role of the state in the overall cognitive economy of the organism, its contribution to overall function. Says Dennett: "It is only the globally defined role of such a state (the role that is characterized in terms of rules of operation the whole system 'follows' when it goes into that state) that fixes its information or external semantic properties" (1987d, p. 224). Most important, brains, like any computational devise are mere *syntactic engines*. Says Dennett:

> the brain, as physiology or plain commonsense shows us, is just a syntactic engine; all it can do is discriminate its inputs by their structural, temporal and physical features and let its entirely mechanical activities be governed by these 'syntactic' features of its inputs. That's all brains *can do*. . . . If you want to get semantics out of syntax . . . in the end all one can hope to produce (all natural selection can have produced) are systems that *seem* to discriminate meanings by actually discriminating things (tokens of no doubt wildly disjunctive types) that co-vary reliably with meanings. (1987e, p. 61)

In virtue of evolution, certain computational states have come to function within the computational system as if they had meanings of a certain kind. Hence, most of the time (insofar as both evolution and the organism's environment have settled on a mutual solution for the moment) we will be able to assign neural content by appeal to function. But this is all there is to a neural state's having meaning to or for a system. At bottom, there are no facts of the matter about neural contents in exactly the same way that there are no facts of the matter about the semantics of linguistic utterances (à la Quine) or facts of the matter about the intentional states of whole persons (à la Dennett). There are only better or worse holistic *interpretations*. Neural content, *like all content*, is mere *as if* content (see 1978b, 1978c).

Most important, we should not mistake our privileged positions as external interpreters of function for "the organism's being in a position to know or to recognize or to intuit or to introspect that fact from the inside" (1987f, p. 304). To put this another way, says Dennett: "Brains . . . do not assign content to their own events in the way observers might: brains fix the content of their internal events in the act of reacting as they do" (1987e, p. 63).

## 5. Visual Processing: Shoals and Rip Tides

In 1978e, Dennett presented a thought experiment of the following kind. You wake up to find yourself locked in a windowless room, all alone but for a desk, the chair on which you sit, and, covering one large wall, something that looks for the all the world like a control panel (think here of your first experience of the cockpit of a 747). Lo and behold, it *is* a control panel. A note, left on the desk, tells you that you are trapped in the control room of a giant robot, on whose activities your life now depends. 'Your' robot inhabits a world of physical events and objects, some nasty and some nice, or so you are told, and your job is to 'steer' the robot safely through it all (whatever 'all' is) using the control panel in front of you. There are thousands of 'input' lights and 'output' switches on the control panel. The problem is that they have *no labels*.

Dennett argues from this thought experiment that if an unlabelled control panel were your *only* access to the 'your' environment and motor capacities, you would never learn to perform the Cartesian deduction (or inferential) task. Says Dennett (private correspondence) "you don't have the leverage without the labels . . . even if you have 'OUCH' and 'YUM,'" that is, some kind of evaluative labels affixed through the beneficence of God or whomever has so kindly placed you there. Were this the predicament of the human neonate, neither motor control nor perceptual understanding would ever get off the ground. Dennett goes on, "The only way you could survive is if the system is to some degree pre-labelled or, more realistically, some of the input-output linkages are already made for you." Here Dennett voices a familiar enough philosophical complaint: The inputs to perception could not be purely qualitative states.

As might be guessed, Dennett does not believe in *qualia* qua the *outputs* or products of perceptual processes either. There are no *qualia* served up by the senses on the stage of consciousness, to be liked or disliked, judged, examined, stored in memory, or used for other cognitive purposes by the Self. However it may seem to you from the first-person point of view, there is no qualitative state '*the* taste of my first bite of Marmite.' There is no taste that you immediately dislike, that you judge to be suis generis in your gustatory experience, that you can examine at leisure for its various qualitative parts ("what, exactly, *was* that?") or that you can store in memory in anticipation of future Marmite encounters. More subtly, by Dennett's lights, our intentional perceptual experiences do not have 'qualitative aspects' at all. Because the inputs to perceptual processes are not phenomenal states (à la the Empiricists), there are – can not be – phenomenal 'survivors' of the perceptual process (there being none to begin with). Hence, there are no qualitative states in the phenomenology of my intentional perceptual experience which, through a suitable act of concentration, I can access by abstraction. Explaining this will take a little work.

Let me begin with a classic misunderstanding about vision, one that inevitably arises in undergraduate classes, in either the neurophysiology of vision or computational approaches to vision. Take Marr's (1982) computational theory of vision. Recall that according to Marr's theory there are four levels of representation in image processing. First, an image represents light intensity at points in the retinal image. Second, the Primal Sketch makes explicit intensity changes and their spatial organization. Third, the 2.5-D sketch represents edges, depth, and orientation information. Fourth, the 3-D Model represents shapes and their spatial organization in terms of stick figures and volumetric primitives (e.g., generalized cylinders). As soon as one begins to explain the Primal Sketch, however, a very large number of introductory students will look deeply puzzled. "Why do we have do *anything* to the digital photograph?" some students immediately ask, "Why do we have to make the contrast information *explicit* when it is already clearly visible?"

Other students will find Marr's methodology more or less comprehensible, at least until the very last step. As a model for scene segmentation or discerning depth information, that is, Marr's theory may look reasonably plausible. Where most students balk is later, at the suggestion that something like Marr's model is – or even could possibly be – a good model for human visual perception. That is, as a model of what our visual systems eventually do – namely produce conscious visual phenomenology – Marr's representational scheme seems strange at best. When you look out the window to the forest before you, you do not *see* little dots and arrows affixed to 'cartoon' outlines of the trees (the primitives of the 2.5-D sketch) nor do you *see* stick figures or generalized cylinders (the primitives of shape recognition). Our visual experience insofar as it is 'like' anything within the model seems more 'like' the photographic image, a kind of 'pixel-by-pixel' depiction of the scene. Yet, in Marr's model, pixel-by-pixel intensity information is eliminated by the second stage of processing, the Primal Sketch. Starting with the photographic image, the more levels of representation completed – each one serving to make explicit more information – the less 'like' our visual phenomenology the representation seems to become. So how could a visual perception be produced by *that*? In both cases – for the student who refuses to leave behind the digital image and the one who is unwilling to take the final step – a number of confusions are at play, each of which will emerge in the explication of Dennett's positive theses below.

Dennett's central claim about visual perception is just this: *It is NOT the function of perceptual systems to produce our conscious perceptual experiences.* For example, given the visual experience you are having right now, as you read from this printed page, it may *seem* to you that *this* – your visual phenomenology of the page in all its complexity – is just what vision is for. With this image 'in mind,' you can *see* the letters on the page, see the structure of each individual letter. Perhaps you will use that information to identify the font or typeface. You can also use it to *read* and *comprehend* the text. You can form beliefs about what typeface has been used, which words appear on the page and what the text says. And, of course, in virtue of seeing the page, you can flip it over and lay it face down on your desk. On the basis of your conscious perception, you can 'act with respect to' the page. That is, as the end product of (no doubt) many complex unconscious processes, a conscious visual perception can be used for an indefinite number of cognitive and motor activities – to turn one's attention toward a salient part of the visual landscape, to visually guide one's actions, or to form inferences about the nature of the visual scene. Or so it seems. Dennett's claim is that this common understanding of vision is wrong. It is merely an entrenched *illusion* engendered by your first-person point of view. As such, it embodies any number of confusions.

First of all, it is a mistake to think that visual processes produce a single static representation, one that the mind's eye then uses to discern, as needed, the relevant details of the visual world. Just as one serially examines, say, an architect's plans for a building, looking first at the site placement, then at the general layout, followed by the dimensions of individual rooms, place-ment of stairways and so on, the mind's eye scans the static visual image for relevant information. This is the first and most obvious mistake of the introductory student, the student who refuses to move past the digital/retinal image. The student mistakes the visual phenomenology that arises out of looking at a static digital image for that which is presented to the mind's eye: a static phenomenal 'visual field.' Hence, there is no need to *extract* information from the digital image, thinks the student, because the digital/retinal image itself just *is* the kind of static 'presentation' required by the mind's eye. Of course, you cannot interpret an architect's plans without some prior knowledge of the conventions of drafting, but with that in hand, you can infer what you need to know. In this, the student shares much with Descartes. The mind's eye must come equipped with some kind of knowl-edge about the nature of the external world in order to interpret the static phenomenal array.[2] But you do not need, first, to transpose each element of the plan into a different format. Why would one *re-represent* that which is already represented?

Second, what makes the visual image so tempting qua phenomenologi-cal presentation to the mind's eye is that the image is, well, an *image*. Because what we see when we look at a photograph of a kumquat is somehow similar to what we see when we look at the kumquat itself, this tempts the unwary into the belief that vision, and hence the representations that support vision, must somehow be 'imagistic,' just as photographs are. Of course, explicitly, very few people would assent to the most naïve view of visual processing or neural representation in general. No one thinks that the only way to represent an oval-shaped, orange kumquat is with an oval-shaped, orange kumquat – or even with an oval-shaped, orange *plastic* kumquat (Akins 1996). And of course, given the very limited means that brains have to encode information, by frequency encoding, spatial encoding, and population encoding of various kinds, visual representations are unlikely to be 'picture-like' in any straightforward sense.

Still, if you start from the other end, if you think about neural representations beginning with what we *see* – our visual world in all its complexity – as opposed to concentrating on the representational relations between neural states and what they represent, the 'naïve' view is far more compelling. That is, if you think of vision as producing a static phenomenal image, then you need not be terribly naïve to think that what underlies that experience is, well, a static *neural* image (at least in some sense of the phrase). Certainly this is one reason why the student who willingly follows Marr through each level of representation may still balk at accepting the whole as a model of human vision. That is, most students understand immediately that information about the visual world must be extracted from the intensity information of the digital image before it can be used. They start to worry, however, about what the whole process actually buys us. Why is it – *how could it be?* – that anything like Marr's model supports visual experience? For all that Marr's 3-D model may help us to *identify* the shape of, say, a horse, it seems hard to imagine that a 3-D model of a horse has anything to do with my present conscious perception of the horse before me – that is, my perception of a noncylindrical genuinely horsey horse. The underlying structure must be *something like* the perception of the horse I actually have. But unfortunately, this way of thinking takes one right back to where few of us have wanted to go – namely to a naïve theory of perception, the view that properties of our visual phenomenology can result from only 'like' properties of the representational vehicles. This is the second mistake of the introductory student, the naïve view of perception.

Dennett's response to this intuition is distinctly 'hardline.' Indeed it is Berkeley's line *tout court*. The brain does not represent states of the world with neural 'pigment' nor are phenomenal states composed of qualitative 'figment.' For example, an orange kumquat need not be represented in the brain by an orange neural state, and seeing an orange kumquat is not a case of having a kumquat appear 'orange-ishly,' of having in mind some 'orange figment.' As Berkeley was at pains to teach us (for rather different reasons!), phenomenal properties are not 'like' physical properties if by 'like' one means 'qualitatively similar.' The very idea is incoherent.[3] Only an idea could be 'like' or qualitatively similar to another idea, said Berkeley (and Descartes agreed). Add, now, the further proviso that 'qualitative similarity' does not involve *qualia*, and Dennett would also agree. Entirely.

Finally, there is a third intuition at play in the students' reluctance – the intuition that visual perceptions qua static images are 'complete.' I will not pretend that I can give anything but a very rough sense of what this means, but perhaps it will suffice to say something like this. A perception must be 'complete' in the sense that it should contain all of the visual detail that the mind's eye comes to infer or notice or act on. That is, insofar as the static image is the *input* to the mind's eye, the fuel for the inferential engine as it were, then it must be capable of sustaining our actual cognitive/motor activities. The image must contain enough 'visual detail' within itself to guide action, or sustain inferences about the identities of visually present objects, or determine the typeface on a page, and so on. So, if you see the horse's glossy chestnut coat, that information about the texture and colour of the horse's coat must be *there for the taking*, as Dennett would say. This intuition as well as the one above, that genuine perceptions must be underwritten by imagistic vehicles, is what confounds the more sophisticated student. Although he or she realizes that the digital/retinal image could not guide activity in and of itself, what makes for conscious experience is yet another question. And Marr's 'sketchy' 3-D model, while both static and imagistic (in some sense), looks like a rather poor possibility for this role. Hence the sophisticated student's reluctance to take the final step.

So, the function of vision is not to produce a conscious state, a static, 'complete' visual image. But if not that, then what? Ah, Dennett would say, but that is the crux of the matter. *There is no 'what,' no single product of vision, much less a single conscious product.* What we must take on board – *really* take on board – is that for any species with a lens and retina, the *only* image in vision as a whole is the retinal image, an ever-changing complex mosaic of light. And like any proximal stimulus, visual or otherwise, it is of no use to the organism in and of itself. Insofar as evolution manages to exploit the various properties of a retinal image – its changing patterns of light wavelength and intensity – within the behavioural economy of a particular species, can it *become* useful. To put this another way, we have to remember that the march of evolution is a march *away* from the retinal image. If the behavioural/cognitive economy of a species is large and diverse, so, too, will be the ways in which the visual system exploits the retinal image. But we make a (large) mistake when we equate this fact with a march toward a *reconstruction* of the image or toward a representational format suitable for producing 'figment.'

## 6. Visual Processing: First Sightings

So what really happens in vision? Insofar as I can discern, once the negative debris is cleared away, Dennett's theory of vision has very few premises. What the human visual system is attempting to do – like any sensory system at all – is to make use of the properties of the proximal stimulus, the retinal image. It does so through using a series of 'visual specialists,' parallel, multi-track processes, each of which serves to 'fix a content,' 'make a discrimination,' or 'perform a micro-taking.' Starting with the receptors themselves (which act as the first filters of the retinal image), down through the three types of neurons of the human retina and ending with the ganglion cells, the retina itself serves as the first visual 'specialist.' It does not 'render' the retinal image into a digital code, with a description of the wavelength and intensity of light at each point on the retina, as the metaphor of the image suggests. Rather, it sends the brain an intricate mosaic of luminance and wavelength contrast information, across a wide range of spatial resolutions. Then, in series of cascading events, second-tier cortical and subcortical 'specialists' (those downstream from the ganglion cells) make discriminations using the ganglion cell signals. In turn, these second-tier discriminations are passed along to other specialists, which make further discriminations, and pass along their fixations to yet other specialists . . . and so on in a cascade of content fixations. (Note that by using the term 'cascade,' I do not mean to imply that the effects of micro-taking only go in one direction, i.e., away from the sensory periphery. The effects can flow upstream and downstream, as well as laterally.)

As Dennett will admit, exactly what happens next – what happens to the outputs of the visual specialists – is a very good question. In simple visual systems, such as in the visual system of the frog, one class of retinal ganglion cells responds to small dark spots moving across the retina. It is the spatial and temporal pattern of this population of 'fly' detectors that signals the fly's direction of movement across the frog's retina. Together, the ganglion cells encode, in egocentric space, spatial properties of the distal world, and it is this population response that initiates and guides the appropriate behavioural response: The tongue swipes toward the location of the fly encoded in egocentric tongue-swiping space. For many visual systems, the loop between input and output is really this short. One can virtually read off from the pattern discriminations made by the ganglion cells, the motor uses of those signals. Of course, even a frog tongue-swiper might be a bit more complicated than this, depending on how 'fail-safe' the system actually is. For example, it may be that the frog can correct his tongue motion in mid-swipe in reaction to a change in the flight trajectory of the fly – a move that would require a translation of fly flying co-ordinates into tongue position co-ordinates and vice versa. But such 'tricks' still make for a reasonably simple input-output loop – a short hop from 'discriminations' to behaviour.

The human visual system is not a 'short loop' system of course. We, unlike the frogs, see a stable world of objects, properties, and events, and our visual systems must support this perceived ontology. We use our representations of the world to predict future events, reminisce about the past, draw complex inferences, or just muse on the passing scene. As yet, we do not know how this occurs. What Dennett is betting is that two positive empirical theses will turn out to be true. First, all visual systems, our own and the frog's included, will be shown to have the following property in common: All have evolved for the visual guidance of behaviour. Whatever 'discriminations' are made by the human visual system, that is, they must still subserve our repertoire of behaviours, both motor and cognitive. And however vast and complex that repertoire might seem to be, like the frog, it is still tightly constrained, both in the present, by our bodies and the environment, and historically, through evolution.

To put this another way, the type of specialists on board any visual system – the kind of 'micro-takings' made – is the result of a complicated, historical process, driven at each step by a process of mutual constraint satisfaction. Each specialist is the product of the co-evolution of the species' behavioural repertoire/motor systems and its sensory systems taken together, and a particular (co-evolving) environment. For example, flies being what they are, the pattern of light produced as a fly goes by, is a small convex moving edge – a pattern of light that also makes possible the computation of the fly's position and trajectory. But if during the evolution of frogs, the most abundant of flies had large, slowly oscillating wings, the ganglion cells of the frog might now respond to a different pattern, say a small flicker of movement at a certain frequency. Now, while a discrimination of visual flutter might have worked well to identify or pinpoint the fly, it might not have lent itself very easily to 'on the fly' (sorry) predation. In that event, a very different kind of motion computation might have come into existence, either as a separate class of ganglion cells or further downstream in the frog's (limited) visual system – and so on throughout the remainder (limited) of the frog's cascade of vision specialists.

This same lesson, believes Dennett, continues to hold true of our own visual system, only more so given what profoundly visual creatures we are. Even though we now represent a world of stable and changing objects, properties, and events, our visual system evolved to guide behaviour and continues to do so. Hence, it is likely that the cascade of human 'visual specialists' and the 'micro-takings' they make, continues to reflect its history of evolution. What the neurosciences will show is that our army of visual specialists has not been co-opted into the production of static 'master' representations, the kind of 'complete,' 'detailed,' 'unified' images of the visual scene that our first-person experience makes plausible. Rather, we, as a species, have found a way to represent a stable, coherent world of objects and properties and yet our visual system has nonetheless retained its army of specialists.

Second, neuroscience will show that *primate vision works on a need-to-know basis, to a large extent constructing its representations as required.* In primate vision, the structure of the retina represents a necessary informational trade-off, between spatial resolution and high sensitivity. Without the spatial resolution, we could not see the fine-grained spatial features of objects, such as object texture, recognize faces or make fine-grained judgments about object location. Without the high luminance sensitivity, we would loose the ability to see under less than ideal light conditions, to see objects in the light of dawn and dusk, in shadows and so on. Hence the organization of the primate retina, into a central, very small area of densely packed, 'high resolution' cells – the fovea – and the large surrounding retinal area, which, through cell convergence, sums the spatial results of many different cells. In this way, the parafoveal region increases its sensitivity to light but loses spatial resolution. As a result of this evolutionary compromise, primates make eye movements. We (or, for the most part, our visual system) rapidly move the fovea from point to point in visual space, foveating first on one small area of the visual world (3° of visual angle or the width of your thumb held at arm's length), then on another. To do object recognition or texture resolution, to see fine-grained depth or motion information the eye must fixate the appropriate portion of the world with the centre of each eye's visual field. Hence, as a result of this arrangement, the visual system must construct much of its understanding of the visual scene serially, from a sequence of very small (relative to the visual field as whole) high-resolution encodings.

What we do know about the eye movements of primates is that our eyes do not 'scan' the scene in the same way a computer refreshes a screen, for example, by starting at the top left corner, back and forth, back and forth, back and forth, until the entire screen has been covered. Rather, our eyes move in specific patterns of saccadic movement, directed by the particular features of the visual scene itself. For example, when looking at a human face, we make eye movements largely in the triangular region between the eyes, the nose and the mouth, while giving scant attention to the jaw-line, hair, and so on. Our eyes are 'entrained' by objects/properties of interest. Perhaps then primate vision does not even try to construct a representation of all the events and properties before it. That is, given that for the most part, the visual world is stable and unchanging, there is no reason why the visual system must store within itself all of the detail of the external world. It can operate on a 'piecemeal' basis, moving from point to point according to current interest – according to what specific visual specialists want to know, or what seems worth exploring on first glance, or what other neural specialists might be asking. All the system would need is some very rough information about the general lay of the land, and some cue(s) that inform the system if anything within the visual field moves/changes. If so, then in a blink of the eye (actually, much faster than a blink of the eye), it can turn its attention where needed.

In light of these two empirical assumptions, the central question Dennett tries to answer is this: How is the illusion sustained? Why do we seem to have a 'complete,' 'unified,' static 'image' of the scene before us?

First and most centrally, says Dennett, we should not forget *that vision looks out not in*. What we (humans) see is *the world as represented* – with the properties we represent it as having. Insofar as the phenomenology of vision gives us any insight into the processes of vision, it is not through the examination of the phenomenological properties of visual experience per se. We do not inspect *qualia* or the qualitative aspects of visual experience (for there are none). Rather we can only do what we always do: We can look at *the world* and say how the world seems to us under various visual conditions. We can say, for example, whether this illuminated matte surface looks the same colour as the sample directly beside it. We can say whether an illusory contour appears in front of or behind the point of fixation. In other words, we can do no more than use the standard methods of psychophysics to test what we can and cannot see.

Second, given the actual nature of our visual experience, the human visual system must be able to individuate events, order them in time, assign a coherent set of properties to a single object and understand an object's/event's/property's coherent and orderly progress through space and time. To do so surely requires an enormous integration of information about objects qua objects, events qua events, and properties qua properties. But this does not mean that the representational vehicles that make possible this kind of perception must be 'like' what they represent – the vehicles qua vehicles need not be physically unified, or make progress through neural space and time in the appropriately ordered fashioned, and so on. To believe as much is to cling to the naïve theory. Insofar as we perceive orderly events, coherent objects, or stable properties, there must be an explanation of how our perceptions come to have that content. But being aware of this kind of content is consistent with any number of representational formats or systems.

Third, insofar as the specialists of vision 'fix' external properties of the world via properties of the retinal image, their states do not discriminate particulars per se (even though, through clever contrivance, such discriminations may allow the visual system to track or follow individuals). That is, even at the lowest levels of visual processing, the system both encodes and makes inferences about the general properties of the visual scene, which it can then use to direct visual attention. For example, a specialist might signal "there is a large-ish dark something about *there*," "there was a small movement in peripheral vision," or "something of high spectral contrast is over there," or even "there goes a familiar but not identifiable biological motion," and so on. If low level vision does carry general information, it follows that the visual system can represent the properties of objects *as determinate, without representing those objects as having any particular determinate properties*. Take the example above, of a visual state that carried the information "there is something of high spectral contrast over there." Here, it need not be the case that the precise hue or saturation of the object has been determined anywhere within the colour system. Perhaps *all* that exists is the information that there is something of a bright determinate colour or other. Alternatively, the system might represent the object as being a very bright, determinate shade of red, without computing, anywhere in the system, exactly what shade of red that might be. What the visual system can safely assume about the world, in other words, is that 'everything is what it is and not another thing.' The world (at least on the space/time scale on human vision) is fully determinate. So whatever generalizations the visual system fastens on, the system can rest assured that those generalizations are grounded in determinate properties of the world. One has only to look.

The illusion of 'taking in the world at a glance' – of seeming to see, as fully determinate, the properties of the visual scene before you – is maintained, for one, because we simply see the determinate properties of the world when we look for them. A brightly coloured object in the undergrowth catches my attention and now I see it as a discarded shirt, bundled into a particular shape. I pick up the newspaper and glance at the front page and now clearly see the front photo, a portrait of an ex-president who never came to like broccoli. For the most part, when particular properties of the visual scene are required, they are retrieved by a series of unconscious saccadic eye movements, *movements made, for the most part, without any conscious recognition that the requisite information has been missing*. Moreover, if the content of visual information is abstract, then, as I said above, we need not represent the particular properties of the world in order to represent the world as containing determinate properties. I see the shirt as bright and as determinately coloured, but not as red; alternatively I see the shirt as a bright determinate red, but without actually seeing what determinate shade of red that might be. Again, if the question arises, "But I wonder if that is the deep scarlet shirt that blew off my clothesline?," it can be quickly answered – by foveating the shirt and calculating its colour. The abstract nature of visual content leaves open the possibility that, at first glance, the shirt was not seen as *red* at all. As Dennett puts it (ever so nicely):

> It seemed to him as if . . . his mind – his visual field – were filled with intricate details of gold-green buds and wiggling branches, but although this is how it seemed, this was an illusion. No such 'plenum' ever came into his mind; the plenum remained out in the world where it didn't have to be *represented*, but could just *be*. When we marvel in those moments of heightened self-consciousness, at the glorious richness of our conscious experience, the richness we marvel at is actually the richness of the world outside, in all its ravishing detail. It does not 'enter' our conscious minds, but is simply available. (1991a, pp. 407–8)

### 7. Answering The 'Different' Question

We are now almost back to a point where we can address the students' question with which this essay began. So far I have outlined Dennett's theory of neural content in general, as well as his views about both the nature of mammalian visual processing and the kinds of neural contents involved in those processes. I have said very little about Dennett's theory of consciousness per se. Indeed, the only thing I have done was to hint, implicitly, at one of Dennett's central tenets about consciousness, namely that it is the contents of neural states that inform consciousness, not the physical properties of their representational vehicles. Still, even when made explicit, that statement is not very helpful. What is Dennett's view about how consciousness comes to be? What is Dennett's view about why we have the conscious visual events we do and not some others – that is, why is some neural content conscious? Again, Dennett's answer is dead simple. Information becomes conscious when it is shared (in some as-yet-unspecified way) with other neural specialists, specialists from other sensory modalities, motor special-ists, 'cognitive' specialists – indeed, whatever kinds of neural specialists there turn out to be. Perhaps one might put it this way: In the very act of informa-tion becoming available, conscious content comes into being. It is therefore incorrect to say that consciousness is what makes possible the use of certain information – as if a large spotlight picks out, shines on, a previously dark representation in the brain, illuminating its content for all the other spe-cialists to see and hence send for. Consciousness does not have a function in this sense. Dennett has also stressed (1991a) that at least in principle, any kind of neural contents could enter into our stream of consciousness. That is, because Dennett does not want to posit a conceptual/perceptual divide, or a distinction between 'conceptual' and 'subconceptual' neural content, there can be no divide, along these lines, between contents that can and cannot become part of the stream of consciousness. All neural contents are potentially conscious, at least insofar as they can be shared in the appro-priate way. Exactly what more Dennett wants to say about consciousness is not clear to me but fortunately, for our purposes, even these few words suffice.

We can now provide for Dennett an answer – or two answers – to the question with which we began, namely: Why does Dennett think that the contents of conscious experience will not map nicely onto the contents of our intentional ascriptions? Why do the perceptual beliefs made from the Intentional Stance not describe the contents of our perceptual phe-nomenology? After all, it would not be surprising if other people were not able to describe the contents of your conscious experiences very accurately. But among the attributions of intentional states are self-attributions. Surely I know what I see! For one, as I said above, our visual system sustains the illusion that, at any given moment, we have within us a representation of the visual world in all its detail. This illusion is made possible by three things: the directionality of vision (we look out not in); the general and abstract nature of visual contents; and the visual system's ability to answer questions (posed by specialists) usually before we realize that the questions have been asked. If the Cartesian picture of the mind were true, that is, you would be able to examine the phenomenal contents of visual experience, and the illusion could not be sustained. If you wanted to know something about the contents of your visual perceptions, for example, "Do I really see the determinate colour of that shirt before me?," the answer would be available by introspection. You could just 'see' whether the shirt was represented as 'some bright colour of high contrast with its background' or whether the shirt was represented as 'bright fuschia.' But given that vision looks out, you cannot examine your phenomenology itself (whatever that would be) only the properties of the external world as they are represented. Aha! Then why not just look out at the shirt? The problem is this. Whenever you ask the question, "What kind of visual detail is being represented?," you will see just the detail you thought you might. You will see the fuschia shirt as fuschia. The visual detail is produced on demand. So looking out at the world is not of any use, at least not if you want to know what it was you just saw a moment ago. Finally, you cannot even notice in passing that this or that complex detail was available to you or missing – or not with any certainty. You may be fooled, in retrospect, by the general and/or abstract contents of perception. Certainly you saw *something* – more specifically, something to do with the colour of the shirt – but what? You will never be certain whether you really saw the shirt's determinate colour a moment ago, or whether you just now moved your eyes in order to determine its colour. For the most part, in the ordinary run of events, we do not have a very good handle on the contents of our visual representations in virtue of first person experience. So there is no real reason to think that even our own self-attributions of propositional attitudes somehow 'get at' the true content of our perceptual states.

There is another more important reason, hinted at above. Recall from the Introduction that the Intentional Stance is an 'idealized rationalistic calculus,' the purpose of which is the prediction and explanation of action. It is an interpretative strategy, based on what an organism *ought to* believe and desire, all things being equal, that allows us to ascribe propositional attitudes to the whole organism – neural content be damned.

As I said above, when a fly buzzes by a frog, the frog ought to believe that a fly, as opposed to a lead pellet, is present. But to attribute a belief about a *fly* leaves open a rather wide range of possibilities of how – or even *if* – the property of being a fly is represented by the frog's brain/visual system. The intentional stance works just insofar as the frog behaves *as if* it sees the fly. As we also saw above, the frog's visual system 'fixes' flies in virtue of one class of ganglion cells that respond to dark, convex, moving edges. We, too, 'fix' flies (not to mention Doritos and salsa), but not through a gang of specialist ganglion cells. What lies between the eyes and tongues of the two species is very different indeed and so too ought the contents of those neural events be distinct. To put the point more generally, each visual system embodies its own particular cascade of specialized visual 'discriminations'; conscious visual perception occurs whenever these discriminations are shared among specialists in just the right way. But if so then the conscious visual experience of two species (say of two mammals) ought to differ in nontrivial ways. Again, we can say that the frog sees the fly just insofar as he behaves *as if* he sees the fly – and that a frog surely does. But so do we.

These, then, are two positive reasons, rooted in Dennett's empirical theories of vision, which predict that there shall not be an 'assignation of contents.'[4] The Intentional Stance will not meet up with neural contents within the stream of consciousness.

## PART II

### 1. Introduction

The conclusions in Part I may seem to be very small ones indeed, certainly ones that Dennett himself could safely acknowledge and incorporate into his repertoire – and I think they would be, were it not for one thing: Dennett's suggestions about vision are turning out to be entirely too prescient. Our most recent neurophysiology of vision suggests that our visual system engages in a drastic division of computational labour, the wholesale subcontracting of visual tasks. This is both good news and, well, 'interesting' news for Dennett. The good news is that Dennett's negative views about the mind will probably turn out to be largely correct: The Cartesian picture of mind is about to come up against hard empirical evidence. The 'interesting' news for Dennett, however, is that this new way of looking at visual function will bring with it many new questions about the functions of the visual specialists, the 'discriminations' they make, and the kinds of informational exchanges that occur between them. My guess is that characterizing what every specialist does as a 'content discrimination' or 'fixation' will turn out to be too theoretically impoverished for our theory of visual function, and hence too impoverished to play the required role in Dennett's (or anyone's) theory of consciousness. While Dennett may just turn out to be right about the nature of visual processing, we will come to see that most of the interesting questions about neural content have yet to be answered. In what follows, I will try to say why I think this is so.

### 2. Coming Full Circle

Let me begin by talking about sensory 'subcontracting' and why it is so ubiquitous. First of all any sensory system must negotiate the purely formal considerations around the possibility and feasibility of computational functions in a real time system. When, in the course of day, you see a car drive by, a pedestrian cross the street, a beetle scurry across the floor, or your own hand as it grasps the door handle, what you see, consciously, are a variety of objects – a car, a person, a beetle, a hand – instantiating a common property, namely, *motion*. These motions are, however, relevantly different: pedestrians stroll, beetles scuttle, hands rotate, and cars flash by. Hence, an algorithm that works to discern one kind of motion may not work for any of the others. Consider rigid motion (a moving car) versus nonrigid motion (a hand as it grasps the door knob). Given an image of a car moving relative to a stationary background, it can be assumed that for any point A in the car's image, if A moves from one point to another, then all of its nearest neighbours will be translated in space *mutatis mutandis* (as you go, so go your neighbours). In nonrigid motion, the nearest neighbours of a given point, A, need not retain their positions relative to A across time (think here of how your open hand contracts as it rotates and grasps the door knob). Scene segmentation involving nonrigid or 'biological' motion is an inherently more difficult computational task, one that cannot be performed using the simple algorithms of rigid motion. Of course, it may be possible to devise algorithms that work for both rigid and nonrigid motion but in a real time system, where speed is of the essence, such dual-purpose algorithms may not be feasible. A computational division of labour may well make sense: that is, use the faster, more economical algorithm when possible; when not, employ the slower, more computationally demanding strategy. Hence a variety of computational strategies for a 'single' property, motion.

Dividing (what we see as unified) events into various subcomponents is also entirely common in the visual system. For example, when a marble rolls from A to B in a linear motion, we see, in some sense or other, a seamless event – the motion of the marble through space from A to B. But again, qua event, the processes of early vision subdivide this task: There are separate processes, each using different aspects of the visual stimulus, which compute the onset of motion, direction of motion, its speed or velocity, and its trajectory. These are, then, dissociable mechanisms – it is possible, in theory if not always in practice, to provide a stimulus that will drive one mechanism without affecting the others. Thus, in colour and motion experiments, one can use stimuli that will trigger the 'onset of motion' specialist but not the mechanisms for the calculation of velocity or trajectory. Such stimuli will cause the subject to perceive that a coloured grating has moved, even though the subject is unable to say in what direction or how quickly it moved. Similarly, using another display, one will see the grating as moving in a particular direction, for example, to the right, but not see it as moving at any steady or discernible velocity (sometimes the grating appears to 'hop'). Here, we can see the utility of representing, separately, the various aspects of an object's motion in terms of the different kinds of behaviours that the different components of the event might guide or trigger. For example, a very fast motion detector can be used to capture visual attention or initiate a saccadic eye movement to that point of interest, to where the motion of the marble has begun. A slower 'direction' mechanism might initiate a tracking motion of the eyes (e.g., start the eyes moving to the left so that they can foveate on the marble itself). Finally, a much more complicated and hence slower 'trajectory' mechanism might provide the 'endpoint' for a visual saccade, that is, it might tell the eyes where they ought to land in order to see the properties of the now stationary marble. If there are many different reactions that could be initiated by a single event – a marble moving through space from A to B – there is a clear utility in subdividing the task, representing different properties of that event in response to particular motor needs.

Another kind of visual subcontracting is nicely illustrated by the multiple systems of depth perception. Depth information is essential to vision as a whole given the nature of the task, of determining from a two-dimensional image what lies in a three-dimensional world. We use depth information to discern figure from ground in scene segmentation and to discern other properties of objects, such as location, shape, and texture. We use depth information to differentiate (through depth-ordering cues) motion in the retinal image from the motion of surfaces in the world. We use depth cues to see motion toward us or away from us, motion we would not otherwise be able to see. Now, as any classic text in psychology will tell you, the primate visual system uses a number of different strategies for computing depth: Depth can be discerned from pictorial cues, occlusion cues, stereopsis, stereodepth-in-motion, motion parallax, and relative size, among other cues. These are computations that, for the most part, make use of different properties of the visual scene/image, thereby extending the range of conditions under which depth can be discerned. For example, the computation of depth by stereopsis is possible because of the small distance between our eyes. If you look at one point in visual space, the images of most other points will be slightly displaced on the two retinae, relative to one another. So, given two fixed points in the external world at different depths, the relative displacement of their left and right retinal images can be used to compute their relative depths. Depth from stereo-motion, by contrast, depends on the relative motion of the left and right images. When an object, directly in front of you, moves toward you, the left and right retinal images move outward at the same velocity and the image expands in size; when the object moves away, the left and right images move inward and they contract. More generally, the direction of motion in depth can be computed by two different functions: by the ratio of the velocities of the left and right retinal images and by the rate of change of image size, relative to the speed of translational motion. Yet a fourth computation for depth perception depends on parallax motion. When you move your head back and forth parallel to the plane of fixation, the retinal images of any objects behind the fixation plane will move in the same direction as your head; the images of objects in the front of that plane will be displaced in the opposite direction. For example, suppose you are looking at a vase of flowers on a table. In front of the vase (nearest you) is a water glass. Sitting opposite you at the table, behind the vase, is another person. Move your head to the right. Here the image of glass will move left; the image of your table companion will move right.

Note that the four different computations for depth probably use at least four different kinds of image properties: relative displacement of the left and right images, the ratio of velocities for the left and right image, the change of image size relative to translation motion, and direction of image motion relative to fixed point. As such, each will be possible when and only when the retinal images have these properties. For example, stereopsis will not work when the left and right images are not adequately displaced, that is, when the two fixed points are quite far away. You can not use stereopsis to determine which building in the distant skyline is in front of another (although you can use occlusion cues). Similarly, if you are blind in one eye, you cannot compute stereo-depth from motion, but given your single field of vision, you could use motion parallax (take note all one-eyed philosophers). Classic textbooks on psychology usually cite this reason as the evolutionary rationalization of the brain's multiple depth mechanisms: No matter what the nature of the visual scene, the visual system will almost always be able to compute whatever depth information is needed, using one depth system or another. Multiple representations offer the visual system a 'fail safe' system for a very important property of the environment, depth.

While the above is no doubt true, what interests me here is not merely that depth is used in so many computational/visual tasks but that depth information is used to perform an indefinite number of motor tasks – to put on our socks, tie our shoelaces, walk over uneven ground, kick a soccer ball, skim past the goal posts, and on and on. Importantly, different types of action require different representations of depth information.

Let me give two examples, that of depth from stereopsis and depth from stereomotion. What the psychophysics of stereopsis have shown is that depth perception of this type is maximally sensitive at the fixation plane and falls off rapidly both before and after. This is a system, in other words, which provides depth information about objects, not relative to the viewer, but relative to a fixed plane – depth information that rapidly diminishes in accuracy the further in front of or behind the fixed plane an object moves. This is a system suited to a particular kind of motor task, of manual movements relative to a fixed point, say, to threading a needle, plucking a Cheerio off the floor, picking grapes from the vine, and so on.

One hypothesis about how the brain performs 'fine stereopsis' or makes fine-grained static disparity judgments is Richards's Pool Hypothesis. According to this theory, stereo-depth is computed by three separate pools of neurons: one pool sensitive to objects in front of the plane of fixation (the plane on which the eyes are focused), one to objects behind the plane, and the third to near objects around the plane itself. On this view, the 'near' and 'far' pools act in an antagonistic fashion, such that the perceived depth results from the relative activity of the two pools; the third pool serves to enhance depth acuity at or near the fixation plane. In 1981, Poggio and Talbot reported finding two classes of neurons in both V1 and V2 of macaque monkeys, just as predicted by Richards's Pool Hypothesis: a class of neurons sharply tuned for near-zero disparity (i.e., for points very near the plane of fixation) and a class of reciprocally activated 'near' and 'far' cells. Impressively, the tuning characteristics of the two populations were reasonably well matched to our judgments of depth – or to put this another way, what the cells do, as a population, is surprisingly similar to what we do when making fine disparity judgments. Despite this correlation, however, Poggio's strong conclusion (1984; Poggio and Talbot 1981) that the depth cells of V1 alone are responsible for perceived depth by stereopsis was probably premature. Recent experiments (Cumming and Parker 2000) suggest that the depth cells of V1 signal only local disparity while perceived depth also depends on more spatially distant cues. In a sense, though, this was to be expected. That is, insofar as there are distinct 'depth specialists' in cortex, it would be surprising to find one of them in V1, the first cortical visual area after the retina. More realistically, the depth neurons in V1 form a preliminary stage to perceived depth, a process completed in extrastriate cortex.

To catch a ball or bat a badminton birdie, however, the visual system must judge the depth of a moving object, the ball relative to oneself or the birdie relative to the racket. As explained above, the received view, at least until the mid-1990s, was that depth from motion was computed by two independent systems, one that uses change in image size relative to the speed of translational motion and the other of which uses the relative velocities of the two images. Exactly how motion in depth is actually discerned is now a matter of some debate but there is at least some agreement about the psychophysical facts about motion-in-depth. We can model our capacity to perceive motion-in-depth in terms of four channels: two channels for objects behind the plane of fixation, one for rightward motion and one for leftward motion; and another two channels for objects in front of the fixation plane, again for leftward and rightward motion. On this hypothesis here is a nonlinear polar representation of visual space, of depth relative to the viewer's face, with the lion's share of representational space devoted to the cone of directions that intersect the head. Again, the rationale for this representational scheme is intuitively obvious – we are most 'interested' in objects that are quickly approaching our heads. Intuitively, that is, it is the baseball that's going to hit you smack in the face that is interesting, not the ball about to clear your left shoulder – and the representational system reflects this fact. Suggestively, the same class of 'far' and 'near' neurons in V1 (mentioned above) also subdivide into two more classes of neurons, those tuned to leftward motion and those tuned to rightward motion. Again, as in the case of static stereopsis, the direction-sensitive neurons are unlikely candidates for the specialists that compute motion-in-depth computations, although they may well be the first specialists to contribute to that (or those) computation(s) performed further downstream.

What the above two examples illustrate is just why different actions will require different encodings of the same objective property. What those examples do not give is any indication of the extraordinary heterogeneity of the depth systems that will be required for motor control. To illustrate this point, I can think of no better way than merely to present the abstract of a recent review article on the depth perception systems involved in hand control in parietal cortex alone. What matters here is not whether the reader understands where the various parietal regions are, or can keep straight which is which (I cannot), or understands all of the terms in the nomenclature of depth perception. It does not even matter whether the research conclusions summarized in this review are correct (for I suspect that some of these conclusions exceed the experimental evidence as I understand it). Still, for a sense of the sheer complexity of the situation, the following ought to prove illuminating. Without further ado, then, the abstract of "The parietal association cortex in depth perception and visual control of hand action":

> Recent neurophysiological studies in alert monkeys have revealed that the
> parietal association cortex plays a crucial role in depth perception and vi-
> sually guided hand movement. The following five classes of parietal neu-
> rons covering various aspects of these functions have been identified: (1)
> depth-selective visual-fixation (VF) neurons of the inferior parietal lob-
> ule (IPL), representing egocentric distance; (2) depth-movement sensitive
> (DMS) neurons of V5A and the ventral intraparietal (VIP) area represent-
> ing direction of linear movement in 3-D space; (3) depth-rotation-sensitive
> (RS) neurons of V5A and the posterior parietal (PP) area representing di-
> rection of rotary movement in space; (4) visually responsive manipulation-
> related neurons (visual-dominant or visual-and-motor type) of the anterior
> intraparietal (AIP) area, representing 3-D shape or orientation (or both)
> of objects for manipulation; and (5) axis-orientation-selective (AOS) and
> surface-orientation-selective (SOS) neurons in the caudal intraparietal sul-
> cus (cIPS) sensitive to binocular disparity and representing the 3-D orien-
> tation of the longitudinal axes and flat surfaces, respectively. Some AOS and
> SOS neurons are selective in both orientation and shape. Thus the dorsal
> visual pathway is divided into at least two subsystems, V5A, PP and VIP
> areas for motion vision and V6, LIP and cIPS areas for coding position and
> 3-D features. The cIPS sends the signals of 3-D features of objects to the
> AIP area, which is reciprocally connected to the ventral premotor (F5) area
> and plays an essential role in matching hand orientation and shaping with
> 3-D objects for manipulation. (Sakata, Tiara, Kusunoki, and Tanaka 1998,
> p. 350)

I take it that my central point about depth perception is now obvious:
Given the multiple processes involved in depth perception, it is misleading
to say that there is 'a' depth system doing 'depth detection' or 'depth discrimination.' There is no single depth mechanism the function of which
is to represent depth information. Nor is there likely to be any 'canonical'
form of depth representation, one that mirrors, faithfully, the objective
spatial relations between objects in the world and hence that anchors our
conception of objective depth relations. Rather, by using a variety of mechanisms for discerning depth and a variety of representational formats, the
depth systems, taken together, make possible the efficient control of diverse
visually guided motor behaviours as well as whatever cognitive 'behaviours'
that make use of visual depth information. *And somehow*, in all this, our
conception/perception of the objective spatial relations that hold between
us and the objects before us is anchored as well.

From the above examples alone, there are at least three very deep puzzles about how the contents of the 'specialists' are unified (or at least seem to be) in conscious experience that Dennett must explain before any theory of consciousness is possible. (And as Dennett well knows, if you are not going to explain them, you must at least explain them away.)

(i) When you see a car drive by, a pedestrian cross the street, a beetle scurry across the floor, or your hand as it grasps the door handle, you see a variety of different motions, no doubt each 'underwritten' by a different computational mechanism. Yet nonetheless you see each motion as *motion*, as an event of the same type. You see an object make a change in space over time. But how, in Kantian terminology, does 'subsumption under a concept' work? What does 'recognition as an instance of a type' amount to in modern neural terms?

(ii) When you see the marble, as it rolls from A to B, you perceive its movement as a single, seamless event despite the multiple mechanisms which must sustain this perception. In all likelihood, the onset of motion, its direction, velocity, and trajectory are all encoded separately, by mechanisms with different times of onset, temporal duration, and sensitivities. From your viewpoint, as a conscious subject, all this is news to you. You just see the marble roll from A to B.

This would seem to be a quite different type of 'unification' than the one above, in (i), however. For one, while it may be possible, by means of clever psychophysical experiments, to tease apart the independent mechanisms at work for motion onset, velocity, and so on, it may not be possible for the observer likewise to 'tease apart' the 'informational contribution' of these mechanisms in conscious experience. You will readily admit, when a car zooms by, that *that* was motion; you will readily admit, when you see your cat chased up a tree, that *that* was motion. And if you are a shrewd psychophysicist, one day you may even be able to sort these different perceptions of motion into distinct categories, categories defined by the distinct motion specialists that underlie them. But there is something rather more 'subpersonal' about the mechanisms that underlie the perception of each 'movement event.' You acknowledge, of course, that the movement of the marble has a beginning and an end, and that the marble moves at a certain velocity throughout, first accelerating and then decelerating to a stop. But there could be (and indeed almost surely are) many more specialists at work in your perception of that single event. If so, you would simply have to take the psychophysicist at his or her word. That you cannot necessarily recognize the effects of these specialists in consciousness experience *as* particular effects of a certain kind does not impugn the psychophysicists' results. The psychophysicist need only show that without the mechanism at issue, you cannot perform the appropriate judgments about the movement of the marble, and that, moreover, in an 'A or B' forced choice test, you can reliably indicate the difference between how the motion seems with and without the mechanisms at issue. The same conclusion holds, I suspect, for much of what goes on in, say, shape perception and object recognition.

(iii)   The example of depth perception furnishes us with yet another puzzle about the unity of perceptual content. Over the course of a few moments, during the course of any visually guided task, say threading a needle, numerous different mechanisms of depth and spatial perception will be involved, each using different representational formats. You see the depth of the thread relative to the needle as the thread goes in and out of focus, using depth from stereopsis. You also see the needle and thread as but two objects in the room, as occupying fixed positions relative to other objects. For example, behind the needle and thread, across the room and out of focus, is the television; in front of the needle and thread are your equally 'fuzzy' moving arms. These facts you know from motion parallax. (Or to put this in a less misleading way, if you concentrate first on the foreground and then on the background while holding steady the needle as your fixation point, this is what you know from motion parallax.) No doubt, occlusion cues tell you that the wicker chair stands behind your hands and the needle and the television across the room. And so on, for the many different depth processes. What seems striking to me is that, despite the plethora of depth mechanisms, each with a distinct associated phenomenology, you nonetheless maintain some conception of the needle and thread as being, at a given moment, in a single objective position. I see the thread weave in and out of focus as I move it about, but I do not conceive of the thread as having moved so far away I can no longer see it, as having backed up into the television. We do not mistake the contributions, the form and spatial resolution, of, say, depth from stereopsis for that of, say, depth from parallax motion. We seem to move effortlessly between them, hardly ever noticing where one leaves off and another begins. Instead, what we tend to notice are only the rare occasions when such transitions fail (e.g., when one looks through a screen door and the standard cues for stereopsis are degraded). So what makes the depth systems co-operate so seamlessly? What makes it possible for us to move back and forth between distinct – and some people might say incommensurate – representational systems?

It is also interesting that we do not focus on the contributions of one depth mechanism as providing *the* objective spatial properties of the world. From your point of view, the information that you get about depth as you thread the needle might be roughly characterized as coming in the following 'gradations': 'way out – nowhere near the needle,' 'ballpark,' 'homing in,' or 'on target!' This does not shake your sense of spatial objectivity, however. The fine spatial resolution around the fixation point of static depth from stereopsis does not 'trick' you into thinking that somehow objective space itself is more 'fine-grained' around the needle. In some sense or other, we 'see' the deliverances of those mechanisms as being *in alignment with* the objective spatial relations of the visual scene as we understand them. Depth from stereopsis informs our spatial perception (as, no doubt, do a myriad of other spatial mechanisms), but does not impugn its objectivity. So how exactly does *this* work? What maintains our sense of spatial unity and objectivity in the face of representational heterogeneity – hence, in the face of a heterogeneity of both content and phenomenology? Good question.

Or rather one good question among many – the many one would need to solve in order to connect content with consciousness. What this new understanding of vision results in, I suspect, is a plethora of questions about content – about how the 'subpersonal' processes of the specialists eventuates in 'our' visual experience.

## 3. About *Qualia*

And what, one may ask, happened to *qualia*? Recall, from Part I, that Dennett's view is that there are no *qualia*: There are no 'purely qualitative' inputs to perceptual processes and no 'purely qualitative aspects' of perceptions either. Assuming that Dennett's example of the robot has been convincing (or that most people no longer believe that the inputs to perception could be qualitative states), certainly it seems to many of us that our conscious visual perceptions have qualitative aspects to them. I see the hyacinths on my desk as a particular buttery yellow and I smell that almost overpowering, sweet, slightly spicy fragrance that marks that species of flower. If those are not 'qualitative' aspects of visual experience, then what are they? I want to take up this question to show how the questions about neural content posed above may well offer Dennett some new avenues for explaining (away) *qualia*.

Dennett's standard answer to the question "what are *qualia*?" is this:

> Sensory qualities are nothing other than the dispositional properties of
> cerebral states to produce certain further effects in the very observers whose
> states they are. (1998, p. 146)

As Andrew Brook points out (this volume), this answer works reasonably
well for some cases but not very well at all for others. Take, for example,
Dennett's explanation of what happens to a subject's phenomenology when
he or she is fitted with inverting goggles, goggles that reverse the retinal
image from left to right, and invert the retinal image to 'right side up' (oddly
enough, the retinal image is normally 'upside down'). At first, subjects report
just what you would expect, that they see the world as upside down and
reversed left to right. After adaptation, subjects report that the world has
once again regained its 'right side up-ness.' In between, pre-adaptation,
subjects do not know quite what to say about their experience. As Dennett
points out, if you conceive of the output of visual perception as a static
image, then you will ask this: "*Have they adapted by turning their experiential
world back right side up, or by getting used to their experiential world upside
down?*" (1991a, p. 397). The problem is that neither option explains the subject's pre-adaptive experience. It is hard to say what could be happening to
a single visual image such that the world appears neither right side up
nor upside down, or why the question would start to seem senseless (as it
does) by the mid-point of adaptation. On the view of vision as governed
by multiple specialists, however, this is just what one would expect: one by
one, the multitude of visual/motor specialists adjust and co-ordinate their
outputs until finally the goggle wearer is able to get around the world much
as before. If there is no single 'product' of vision, but rather individual
answers and changing coalitions that control behaviour, then behaviour
ought to follow the adaptation of individual specialists and coalitions, that
is, behaviour ought to improve over time, in a series of leaps and plateaus.

What Dennett does not explain about the example is the subject's pre-
adaptive phenomenology, or more accurately, why the subject cannot seem
to get a grip on the phenomenology of his or her partly adapted visual
system in order to explain it. The suggestion made at the end of Part I
about why self-attributions of conscious content are not to be trusted given
both the abstract and 'need-to-know' nature of visual perception does not
apply here. The problem is not so much that the subject's descriptions
are inaccurate (although they may be) but that the subject cannot settle
on *any* description that seems reasonable. Perhaps Dennett might say in
response that the subject is too much in the grip of the Cartesian metaphor

(of the static image) and hence for this reason does not have the resources to describe a world that is neither right side up nor upside down. This is one possibility. Then again, Dennett might say that there is no reason to think that, in the midst of adaptation, the responses of the specialists will necessarily cohere or be consistent with one another. In Dennettian terms, when the question is asked, "Are the kumquats on the plate?," there could be a chorus of answers: "No, they're *under* the plate!," "No, they're *on* the plate!!," "No, *under* the plate!!!," "Which kumquats are you talking about – the ones under the table?," and "How should I know?" Hence, it would not be surprising if the subject were confused about just how the world seemed. This is another explanation. Still, Dennett needs to solve this puzzle in some way or other. Why is it that the subject, by concentrating on the properties of the *world*, cannot accurately describe which dispositions have/have not been adjusted?

Dennett's answer to the problem of qualia looks even less plausible vis-à-vis the classic philosophical cases of 'pure' *qualia* – for tastes, sounds, colours, and so on. If my experience of 'buttery yellow' is merely 'a complex of dispositions,' then exactly what dispositions make up this complex? Here, the problem is this: The only dispositions that readily come to mind are *reactions to* a particular qualitative experience – what we would say or do in response to a visual experience of the appropriate qualitative kind. Thus, on seeing the buttery yellow hyacinths, you might exclaim about their colour, wonder why you ever started buying margarine, recall a dress you had as a child, or suddenly remember that you have forgotten the birthday of your mother (who loves yellow hyacinths). This is what comes about when your experience of the hyacinths has a 'buttery yellow' aspect. But how could the dispositions to behave in response to *qualia* literally *be* the qualitative experiences that cause them? Nor does the example give us any reason to think that qualitative experiences, in and of themselves, could not play the causal roles that folk psychology suggests. For 'classic *qualia*,' Dennett's theory is really quite puzzling.

What Dennett can gain from the wholesale 'subcontracting' of visual specialists is a way to address these two puzzles – of why we lack access to various parts of our visual experience (the case of the inverted goggles) and how it might be that 'real' *qualia* can be explained in terms of dispositions (the case of buttery yellow). Once one acknowledges that the ontology of the perceived world is not mirrored by the ontology of visual processing – that what appear to us as singular properties, objects, and events in the world are unlikely to be discerned by single specialists – Dennett gains a very useful distinction.

On the one hand, there is that which makes certain information conscious – call it 'shared' information. In a parallel computational system such as vision that works (at least in part) through mutual constraint satisfaction, the 'answers' of any modules must be 'share-able' with at least some of the other modules. For example, if an object actually has moved from left to right, and if the luminance contrast of the object with its background has changed, then the spectral contrast ought to have changed as well (because objects that differ in luminance almost always differ in spectral reflectance). So spectral contrast information and luminance contrast information ought to be available, at the beck and call of different specialists including those that perform motion analysis of various types.

On the other hand, given both the disjoint and heterogeneous outputs of the various specialists, plus the fact that we manage to see a world of orderly and unified objects, properties, and events, there must be some way – some ways – in which this is accomplished. Somehow out of the labour of many specialists, we come to have a perceptual ontology, one that is distinct from the outputs of the specialists per se. We come to see unified objects with a multitude of properties, to see coherent events in orderly succession, to understand the properties of world as objective or as independent of our particular perceptual presentations. Now, no doubt these various processes of 'unification' require that information be exchanged between modules. If so, the means by which we come to gain our perceptual ontology will result in conscious experience. Still, there is no reason to think that all information exchanged between modules is for the purposes of unification. For example, when the linear motion module requests luminance contrast information, it may do so in order to compute linear motion, not in order to unify the luminance properties of the moving object with its property of motion. So a distinction seems in the offing: There is (very likely) a difference between the general processes in virtue of which information is shared between specialists and whatever specific processes result in the perceived world's ontology.

What the distinction gains Dennett is a way to explain why various aspects of conscious visual experience seem to be 'purely' qualitative and why we have such a difficult time explaining just those (and pathological) aspects of our own experience. Start again with Dennett's view that we look out not in. Insofar as we have any access to our phenomenology, it is through looking at *the world* and saying how the world seems to us under various visual conditions. I move my head back and forth, this way and that way, I rotate the object so that the light strikes it at various angles, in order to see what is the case. Suppose then that there is distinction between those processes that make information a part of conscious experience and those which serve to 'carve' the world into ontologically sound divisions. When we look out at the world, the content of conscious experience is determined by the multitude of on-going processes through which information is shared. Yet when we try to see *what* is in the world, when we ask ourselves *what* we are looking at, we can see the world only in terms of our perceptual ontology, only by using whatever capacities make it possible to 'carve up' the world into objects, properties, and events. What arises, then, is a profoundly non-Kantian possibility: *There may be a difference between that which informs our visual phenomenology of the world and that which we can grasp qua properties of the world.* There may be a distinction between the (conscious) discriminations that visual specialists make and the properties *we* can see in the world. If so, we will be able to understand our visual phenomenology of the external world only insofar as we can corral the (conscious) discriminations of the specialists into a stable ontology – here, an ontology of the external world, not of phenomenal experience. Our access to our own phenomenology is available to us only *through* our intentional perceptions of the world, through the properties we see as existing in the external visual world. And here, at last, is the punch line: There is nothing to guarantee that we can (or can learn to) corral *all* of the discriminations made by the visual system that affect our visual phenomenology into perceived properties of the world.

Let me go back to the examples of 'subcontracting,' in particular the example of depth processing from motion parallax. When told how motion parallax works, most people find the story quite surprising (certainly I did). It is just not self-evident to most people what will happen to the visual image when fixation is maintained and the head moved – that images in the background will move with the head, and that images in the foreground will move in the opposite direction. What makes motion parallax a nice example, is that the subject can come to understand how the 'subpersonal' visual process works through demonstration. If you fixate on the window frame, and squint the right way, the distant mountains will 'move' with your head, while the flowers on the window sill will 'move' in the opposite direction. In some sense, you see how motion parallax works. Note however that, through squinting, the subject is not gaining access to the retinal image or indeed to any image at all. Rather, normally, when the visual system discerns depth through parallax motion, the image motion, insofar as it can be co-ordinated with head movement, is discounted. Stationary objects in the visual scene are seen as stationary. When one 'squints' in order to understand motion parallax, your visual system manages to do what you might have done by drawing a picture – you are able to understand the optics of the situation.[5] While you can still feel your head moving, and while you know that, say, the mountains are *not* moving in objective space, nonetheless you

are able to see the mountains 'as appearing to slide back and forth.' That
the mountains are not actually sliding – that the motion is not veridical –
is a part of your phenomenology. But then, so too are the mountains qua
mountains. You have not, through some miracle, managed to attend to your
retinal image qua a retinal image. You are still looking out not in. Nor, in
all likelihood, have you managed to access the inner workings of whatever
'subpersonal' specialist performs depth from motion parallax. It is entirely
possible, that is, that a person who, through some deficit, did not have
depth from motion parallax might nonetheless be able to 'see' what optical
facts make motion parallax possible in the ordinary case. What you have
managed to do is to see the mountains 'move,' by accessing information
about image movement and using it in whatever processes normally result
in intentional visual perception.

For the subject who wears inverted goggles, the situation is quite different. When the goggles are first put on, there is a handy way to re-conceive
of his or her visual experience – "It is just like the world was upside down."
As the sensory/motor adaptations – realignments – come into being, one
by one, however, the subject will have no method in general with which
to re-conceive of his or her visual experience in terms of perceived properties of the world. No doubt if we knew more about how the processes
of adaptation, and, in addition, more about the normal processes of vision,
the psychophysicist might be able to make some helpful suggestions (as in
the case of parallax motion). But again, there is no reason to think that the
adaptive processes can be made to neatly mimic any aspects of the normal
phenomenology of seeing the world. (Very similar points could be made,
I think, about attempting to recognize the multiple processes that underlie
the normal perception of a marble moving from A to B.)

There is obviously an enormous amount more that needs to be said
about this suggestion but perhaps enough has been said to say a little about
the 'hard case,' the classic cases of *qualia*. First, as I said above, when we try
to imagine how *qualia* could be complexes of dispositions, all that comes
to mind are our reactions to a qualitative experience – for example, the
experience of 'buttery yellow' reminds me of how much I dislike margarine.
What the discussion of subcontracting makes clear is that properties we perceive as unified need not be 'underwritten' by a single kind of information,
by the output of a single specialist. We know, that is, that the perception of
a marble rolling from A to B is 'underwritten' by the results of numerous
specialists – of movement onset, velocity through luminance processing, velocity through spectral processing, of trajectory, and so on. We also know
that these individual components of the perception probably have quite
distinct causal effects or uses. A very fast motion detector could be used to

capture visual attention or initiate a saccadic eye movement to that point of interest; a slower 'direction' mechanism might initiate a tracking motion of the eyes and so on. But if we could find this out about motion perception, so, too, could we find this out about any of the other *qualia* that have historically plagued philosophical discussion. There is no reason why colours, pains, and so on could not be similarly 'decomposed' into perceptual parts (see Akins and Hahn, in progress) and hence into complexes of causal dispositions, each without mention of a 'purely qualitative aspect' as cause or effect at all. Such a decomposition is just what would show that felt *qualia* are, in fact, exactly analogous to the feeling of upside down-ness, to the 'qualitative experiences' induced by inverting goggles. If the phenomenology of 'upside down-ness' is no barrier to explaining consciousness then neither should be the phenomenology of pain or colour.[6]

Second, the theory would explain just why *qualia* seem both complex and ineffable, why we have so little access to, say, colours, other than to speak in terms of 'the very blue' of the teapot before me now. We know, for example, that it is very easy for a normal trichromatic observer to discern that one colour is different than another colour sample, when both samples are of identical hue and saturation. It is impossible to tell, however, which of the two samples is brighter. Similarly, given two colour samples that differ in either hue or saturation, it is extremely difficult – in some cases impossible – to tell along which dimension the difference occurs. But if the samples are put side by side, that there is a difference is entirely obvious. In other words, in colour perception, there seem to be any number of factors that make a difference to how the colour of an object or surface is seen. Yet, it does not follow that we can differentiate or categorize the phenomenal differences, or at least not in virtue of merely looking at the colour sample. This inability to delineate, say, brightness in vision as an independent property of a surface under normal viewing conditions is what makes colours seem both complex and 'ungraspable.' We can detect differences in surface brightness. Our phenomenology is affected by that discrimination. But under normal conditions, we cannot see brightness qua a distinct stable property of coloured opaque surfaces.

Certainly it seems to me that this is one route that Dennett could go to further dismantle the Cartesian theatre. Whether or not he will go that route is an open question.

## 4. Conclusion: Dennett and Neuroscience

Were I to don a fortuneteller's garb, I would say that Dennett's negative views, his arguments against the Cartesian theatre, will come to be acknowledged as largely correct. Indeed, already so many of Dennett's criticisms have been so thoroughly incorporated that no one seems to remember having ever held the criticized views, for example, the naïve view of perception. Of his positive views, my guess is this: In retrospect, they will be seen to have been profoundly prescient, at least in outline form. This is not a view I held fifteen years ago. In fact, it is a view I have come to only gradually over the last decade, largely in virtue of the last six years or so of neuroscience research. What explicit effect Dennett will have on the actual course of neuroscientific progress – what role he will play as an acknowledged intellectual force in the community – is another question. At this point, what Dennett lacks – what we all lack, philosophers and neuroscientists alike – is a substantive theory of neural content/representation. At least as I understand much of the recent neuroscience, *most* of the interesting questions about neural content have yet to be asked, much less answered. So, the question of Dennett's influence on the neurosciences is not unrelated to the question of the influence of the neurosciences on *him*. Should Dennett join the party, and I certainly hope that he will, his influence may well be profound.

### Notes

1. Throughout his work (e.g., "Language and Understanding" in *Content and Consciousness* [1969], "How to Change Your Mind" in *Brainstorms* [1978a]), Dennett has stressed the role of verbal expression in how we understand (or misunderstand) our 'thoughts.' Very briefly, Dennett suggests that when we 'express our thoughts' with sentences of a public language, this fosters the illusion that the *causes* of our self-attributions are both sentence-like in syntax (i.e., compositional) and sentence-like in meaning (i.e., endowed with whatever 'firm edges' of semantic content that a public language provides). Says Dennett:

> [O]ne point here is paramount: while it is certainly true that there is in general no better way to tell what someone (oneself included) thinks than seeing what he says, if one views the clues one gets thereby on the model of say, the publication of a poem or the release (by the Vatican library) of a heretofore sequestered volume, one may well be making a mistake along the lines of supposing that a head cold is composed of a large set of internal sneezes, some of which escape. The self-questioning process that individuates belief expressions so crisply need not be revealing any psychologically important underlying individuation (or beliefs, presumably) but be just an artifact of the environmental demand for a peculiar sort of act. (1987c, p. 115)

The request for a statement of belief from the subject merely *precipitates assent to a public sentence*. We choose a sentence to which, on the whole, we can assent, now that we stop to consider the linguistic options. But this choice says little about its causes.

Following Churchland, Dennett asserts that "the process that produces the data of folk psychology, we claim, is one in which the multidimensional complexities of the underlying processes are projected *through linguistic behaviour*, which creates an appearance of definiteness and precision" (1991b). What folk practice reveals, however, is that in some sense we do not take belief ascriptions 'at their word.' We presuppose that the content specified is merely 'rough and ready' content, that revisions, emendations, or even 'ad hoc' restrictions made by the subject are all fair game, a standard part of self attribution. Whatever the merits of this line of argument (and I myself think it has merit), the evidence is 'circumstantial' at best. These are arguments that show only what could be the case or what neural causes are consistent with our actual practices of belief attribution.

2. Dennett's point above is that these kinds of knowledge are not analogical. That is, what the architect knows is which icons represent which features of the world. But on Descartes' view, the innate knowledge of the mind is confined to the essence of material objects, not what properties of objects are correlated with what qualitative aspects of the phenomenal array.

3. Dennett does not deny that neural representations could be 'picture-like.' Finding an orange plastic kumquat in visual cortex is a logical possibility. But Berkeley's point, and Dennett's, is about the relation between phenomenal events and neural representations, as opposed to neural representations and their objects.

4. This goes back to an old joke between Dennett and myself. When I worked for Dan at Tufts, it became very clear to him that most of my vocabulary had been learned not from conversation but from reading. Hence, much of what I 'knew' about the English language was not quite right. One day, Dan discovered that I had made it to the age of twenty-seven with the unshaken belief that the word 'assignation' meant roughly 'an assignment to or attribution of.' Thus, much of my dissertation had been devoted to what I called 'the assignation of contents' – you know, what was involved in an assignation, under what conditions they occurred, what 'the experts' had to contribute, and other such standard philosophy of mind fare. Needless to say, Dan being Dan, found this exceedingly amusing – and no less so when I demanded that he look it up 'assignation' in the Oxford English Dictionary. What can I say? There are no assignations of content, not even in the stream of consciousness.

5. I owe this point to Martin Hahn.

6. This is, in fact, what Dennett attempted to do with some success in an early paper, "Why You Can't Make a Computer That Feels Pain" (1978d).

## References

Akins, K. 1996. Lost the Plot? Reconstructing Daniel Dennett's Multiple Drafts Theory of Consciousness. *Mind and Language* II:1–43.

Akins, K., and M. Hahn. More Than Mere Colouring. In progress.

Cumming and Parker. 2000. Local Disparity Not Perceived Depth Is Signalled by Binocular Neurons in Cortical Area V1 of the Macaque. *The Journal of Neuroscience*, June 15, 20(12):4758–67.

Dennett, D. 1969. *Content and Consciousness*. London: Routledge and Kegan Paul.

Dennett, D. 1978a. *Brainstorms*. Montgomery, VT: Bradford Books.

Dennett, D. 1978b. Brain Writing and Mind Reading. In Dennett 1978a.

Dennett, D. 1978c. The Abilities of Men and Machines. In Dennett 1978a.

Dennett, D. 1978d. Why You Can't Make a Computer that Feels Pain. In Dennett 1978a.

Dennett, D. 1978e . Current Issues in Philosophy of Mind. *American Philosophical Quarterly* 5:249–61.

Dennett, D. 1987a. *The Intentional Stance*. Cambridge, MA: MIT Press /A Bradford Book.

Dennett, D. 1987b. True Believers. In Dennett 1987a.

Dennett, D. 1987c. When Frogs (and Others) Make Mistakes. In Dennett 1987a.

Dennett, D. 1987d. Styles of Mental Representation. In Dennett 1987a.

Dennett, D. 1987e. Three Kinds of Intentional Psychology. In Dennett 1987a.

Dennett, D. 1987f. Evolution, Error and Intentionality. In Dennett 1987a.

Dennett, D. 1991a. *Consciousness Explained*. Boston: Little Brown & Co.

Dennett, D. 1991b. Real Patterns. *Journal of Philosophy* 88:27–51.

Dennett, D. 1998. Real Consciousness. In his *Brainchildren*. Cambridge, MA: MIT Press/A Bradford Book, 131–9.

Marr, D. 1982. *Vision*. San Francisco: Freeman Pub.

Poggio, G. F., and W. H. Talbot. 1981. Mechanism of static and dynamic stereopsis in foveal cortex of the rhesus monkey. *Journal of Physiology* 315:469–92.

Poggio, G. F., 1984. Processing of stereoscopic information in monkey visual cortex. In G. M. Edelman, W. E. Gall, and W. M. Cowan, eds., *Dynamic Aspects of Neocortical Function*. New York: Wiley, 613–35.

Regan, D., J. P. Frisby, G. Poggio, C. M. Schor, and C. W. Tyler. The Perception of Stereodepth and Stereo-motion: Cortical Mechanisms. In L. Spillman and J. S. Werner, eds., *Visual Perception: The Neurophysiological Foundations*. San Diego: Academic Press, 317–47.

Prince, S., A. Pointon, B. Cumming, and A. Parker. The Precision of Single Neuron Responses in Cortical Area V1 during Stereoscopic Depth Judgements. *Journal of Neuroscience* 20(9):3387–400.

Ryle, G. 1949. *The Concept of Mind*. London: Hutchinson.

Sakata, H., M. Taira, M. Kusunoki, A. Murata, and Y. Tanaka. 1998. The Parietal Association Cortex in Depth Perception and Visual Control of Hand Action. *Trends in Neuroscience* 21(2):350–7.

# ARTIFICIAL INTELLIGENCE
# AND EVOLUTIONARY THEORY

We have explored the nature of Dennett's contribution to consciousness studies and the explanation of child, animal, and adult social behaviour, and we have looked at two deep running concerns with his contributions in both areas. In this final section, we will explore two more areas of Dennett's influence. One is artificial intelligence research. The other is theory of evolution.

Dennett has been writing on artificial intelligence for thirty years and has generally been sympathetic to the idea that genuine intelligence and even consciousness can and probably will be achieved in systems built very differently from the human organism, systems built out of silicon chips or neural network nodes for example. Yorick Wilks, chair of a major school of computer science and an internationally known artificial intelligence researcher, casts a rather jaundiced eye over Dennett's work in this area. Wilks's view is that many of Dennett's claims are not taken seriously by AI researchers, a leading example being his well-known distinction between what the brain can process (physically expressed differences sometimes called syntax, in a vastly extended sense of that term) and what it cannot (meaning, informational content). Furthermore, says Wilks, Dennett is far more optimistic than researchers actually doing the work. Wilks's diagnosis of these problems is that they reflect a deep-running gap in cognitive science. Cognitive science lacks clear canons for determining when claims made in it are justified and when they are not.

Dennett's role in the progress of evolutionary theory has taken a remarkable turn in the past few years. Few major scientific debates can ever have been conducted in the popular press as much as this one, or with as bad a ratio of light to emotional heat. Much of the dispute has centred on Dennett's views on the evolutionary foundations of consciousness. Don Ross surveys the battlefield and urges that both Dennett's opponents and popular commentators on the dispute have seriously misunderstood him. In particular, they fail to understand how his position grows out of his prior theory of intentionality (the term is defined in the Introduction). One commentator who *has* understand what is at stake is Jerry Fodor. Fodor wants to reject Dennett's picture of intentionality and understands that to do so he must reject Dennett's picture of natural selection and evolutionary development generally. This is what motivates him to reject the latter. Ross then sketches a response that Dennett could make to Fodor.

# 9    Dennett and Artificial Intelligence: On the Same Side, and If So, Of What?

*YORICK WILKS*

## 1. INTRODUCTION

Some twenty years ago, I sat next to a distinguished colleague and friend who was already well known in artificial intelligence (AI), at a meeting in a Dutch seaside research institute while Daniel Dennett was speaking; as I put my hand up afterwards to ask a question, my friend dug me firmly in the ribs and hissed, "Don't attack him, he's on our side."

I have thought about this remark since, and wondered to what extent he is, or ever was, on our side, which I then took to mean a philosopher well disposed toward the AI program in general terms, one of explicating and understanding human mental function in terms of machine function. Of course, philosophers are not normally on anyone's side but their own: Any critical position they adopt with respect to a form of scientific or engineering activity is purely personal and in pursuit of their own goals. Dennett's goals are complex and have shifted over time, particularly with his growing interest in Darwin in recent years (1995), a topic easier to relate to recent developments in AI, in particular connectionism, evolutionary computation, and so-called Alife. However, I shall restrict my remarks to Dennett's period of explicit and declared interest in what he himself has called GOFAI (Good Old-Fashioned AI). What I think my colleague had in mind in Holland was probably twofold:

(i)  that Dennett's apparent approbation of folk-psychological explanations of human behaviour is at least consistent with the AI program where that level and style of explanation was exactly what symbolic AI (i.e., pre-connectionist/Alife AI) sought to model in machines, often with the subsidiary aim of modelling and explaining human behaviour.

(ii)  that Dennett's use of flowcharts and process-talk in his discussions of phenomena like consciousness showed that he, too, accepted and understood the purpose of some form of AI- or machine-metaphor in the explanation of mental function.

I believe the first of these is correct, at least in the sense of a weak consistency of aims, and it is quite different from the position those who argue that mental explanations must be, in the end, physiological and involve the brain (Churchland and Ramachandran 1993). Many AI researchers (see below) would also assent to that last proposition, although it has nothing to do with their professional activities. A third point of agreement, my friend might well have added, would be joint opposition to those, like Searle, who accept the primacy of brain talk while showing no interest in it, and who also believe AI explanations fundamentally flawed (1988). The problem with Searle, in the Dennettian terms of this essay, is that his arguments are largely in terms of a quite specific kind of folk psychology (namely, Intentionality) which he thinks Dennett and AI fail, in their different ways, to do justice to. I shall argue below that there is no real difference here, but more a dispute about taste in folk psychology styles, and that if, as Searle claims, AIers and Dennett are all just behaviourists at heart, then so is he, because there is, in a certain sense, nothing else to be until brain physiology finally delivers.

Dennett is undoubtedly one of the most entertaining and deservedly popular philosophers of our age but, from an AI point of view, he is no more than an agreeable fellow traveller as far the language of explanations are concerned: one consistent with the AI program, although offering nothing particular to it, since, like all science and engineering, its evaluation criteria are empirical not philosophical. As to the particular issue of consciousness, I think his views are less rich and structured than AI is capable of offering and that his famous demonstration of the relative emptiness of consciousness is more a challenge to AI than any kind of agreement.

## 2. WHAT AI IS AND DOES

Many AI workers are, by and large, naïve materialists and mechanists, so that, for them, mental processes are no more than software running on organic hardware. For them such a position hardly needs to be justified, but is simply an unprovable assumption that allows them to get on with the job of constructing mechanical analogues or simulations of ourselves, who are, in Minsky's memorable phrase, 'meat machines.' This assumption is essentially what Searle called 'strong AI' (1988), but the activity that follows from such researchers is no different in kind from the research of those, probably the more reflective, who hold some form of 'weak AI': an essentially instrumentalist, as-if, view rather like (ii) above.

The point here is that these metaphysical assumptions by AIers are essentially idle: They do not affect their work, any more than physicists who take strongly realist views of their theories do a different physics from others. This may be a normal situation in the sciences, where very general assumptions allow experimental, as opposed to philosophical, work to proceed, but do not constrain the activity much. Yet, AI is not an experimental science but an engineering technique or, if you want something more dignified, a practical task in the alchemical tradition (a point Dreyfus made long ago [1979]), and its suggestiveness for investigating the nature of mental function rests largely on that fact.

When Turing originally suggested we might as well speak of such a successful machine as thinking by polite convention, just as, "instead of arguing continually . . . , it is usual to have a polite convention that everybody thinks" (1950), he was a clearly on the weak, ascriptivist, wing of the subject, whereas Minsky has tended to be at the strong end:

> When a man M answers questions about the world we attribute his ability to some internal mechanism W* (a model of world W) inside of M. It would be most convenient if we could discern physically within M two separate regions W* and M-W*, such that W* 'really contains' the knowledge and M-W*contains only general purpose machinery for coding questions, decoding answers and general administrative work. However, one cannot really expect to find in an intelligent machine a clear separation between coding and knowledge structures, either anatomically or functionally, because, for example, some 'knowledge' is likely to be used in the encoding and interpretation processes. (Minsky 1968, p. 426)

None of this is philosophical argument, just the adoption of a position on the issues; In Minsky's case, the philosophical question of whether there are hidden mechanisms that explain mind, and so on, never arises, because their existence is assumed from the outset without discussion. The passage will remind some readers of Chomsky's palmier days, in linguistics rather than AI, when he would begin arguments with "Obviously, everyone has internalised a grammar" (Chomsky 1965, p. 8).

## 2.1. Modularity

Let us turn to AI practice and the sorts of in-house speculation it has given rise to. Modern computer programs, especially those in AI, are normally written as interconnecting subparts or modules, rather than as linear seamless wholes. Modules, in this sense, do not have access during execution to the contents of other modules and, in Carl Hewitt of MIT's immortal words, "Modules shouldn't be able to dicker around with the insides of their neighbours" (1972). In Winograd's (1972) language understanding program, for example, there was a syntax analysis module and a semantics analysis module: These could demand answers from each other to specific questions about the structures of sentences but could not get at how the other one found out whatever it did. Herb Simon argued (1969, p. 115) that evolution would prefer structures that are decomposable in this way, and that modularity may be expected in "genetic programs." Simon considered the commercial viability of two watchmakers, one of whom put watches together out of finished subassemblies that cannot fall apart, and another who assembled each watch from its basic parts and risked the whole thing falling to pieces if dropped. It is obvious that the first watchmaker, with 'modules' of watches, will do better.

It was such an idea of modularity that Minsky intended in the passage quoted above, and he has suggested at various times that an organism would be more efficient, in terms of its ability to survive, if it had, as a separate module, a model of itself, one that might of course be totally false as to the facts of the self's reality. But alcoholics who believe themselves to be alcoholics probably survive better than those who believe themselves to be merely social drinkers. An accessible model of the self is clearly one of the first places that one might look for analogues of consciousness in a machine system.

Later (1975), Minsky has revived these notions, explicitly drawing analogies with the sorts of modularity to be found in the writings of Freud, with his triple of Ego, Id, Super-ego. Leibniz, in his Monadology, perhaps the first work on modules, claimed that an appropriate machine analogue of the human individual should have, among its modules, a 'supreme organizer.' This module would, Minsky suggests, alone have access to the model of how it itself related to all the other, lower, modules, and it might be expected to have some property of the type we refer to as consciousness or self-consciousness. This additional property, Minsky argued, could have a functional or evolutionary explanation, of the sort suggested for the property of modularity by Simon, so that the potentially 'conscious' supreme organizing module would therefore be in a position to debug (in the sense of altering it or patching it up in such a way that it works) or repair the connections of the lower modules amongst themselves or to itself. In order to preserve modularity, this power could not, of course, extend to repairing the modules themselves, for that is just the sort of tinkering that a principle of modularity would rule out.

Personally, I find it hard to connect the commonsense and traditional properties of consciousness (vague as they may be), with the notions of repair and debugging, fundamental as those are to any account of intelligent mechanisms. Consider, for example, that certain yogis appear, on all the evidence, to be able to take control of their physiological functions (heart beat rate, digestion, etc.) utterly inaccessible to most of us. They can, if these claims are true, debug their 'digestive program,' or slow their hearts considerably. But would we want to say that these abilities, striking though they are, have any particular connection with consciousness? If a yogi could tell us, at any given moment, what his digestive organs were doing in chemical terms, and some constant monitoring apparatus attached to his intestines confirmed everything he said, then we might want to admit that he could be conscious of them, for the performance would seem to show just that immediate awareness of goings on that we think of as intuitively necessary for a conscious process. But that is not debugging or repair (the things Minsky was referring to), for we would be impressed in this way by a yogi who changed his digestive processes. But we would be equally impressed, I suspect, by another yogi who could alter these processes in his intestines on a word of command but made no claims to know what was going on down there from moment to moment. These are simply different powers, but only one of them seems connected with consciousness, and not the one Minsky described.

An important point here that I shall want to return to later is a tension in Minsky's accounts between an emphasis on hierarchical organization (the supreme organizer, or Simon's modular watchmaker would be examples of that), and another, quite different one, on heterarchical organization. This latter notion has never been made very clear, but it was one much promoted by Minsky in the late 1960s and it enormously influenced, for example, Winograd's view of the organization of a language understanding system. Its essence was that there need be no permanent upper node of a system, as there always is in a hierarchical system, but that different nodes at different 'levels' could take control at different times. This was a more democratic view of organization, both socially and metaphysically, and one closer to Aristotle and Leibniz, for whom every entity, however lowly, had its degree of consciousness.

Minsky's "supreme organizer" view must be hierarchical, for that organizer alone has the model of its relation to other modules, and it must therefore always be in control, because no other module has a model of relationships that would allow it to be only sometimes in control, in the way a heterarchical view requires. Whether or not this control and its prerequisite knowledge remain as properties of a single 'command' module, or shift about heterarchically, are both forms of what I shall later want to call a 'light up' view of consciousness: As in a pinball machine, different areas light up at different times depending on the state of the game.

## 2.2. Implementation Independence

It is a well-known fact that the same computer program can be run on different machines, not only different tokens of machines but different types, where that extends to machines working with quite different physical processes. The Java language was written precisely to express this platform-independent aspect of programs. This is what is referred to when one speaks of the implementation of a program being machine-independent, and it is part of the conventional distinction between hardware (i.e., machines) and software (i.e., programs). That there is a conventional element in the distinction, making it less than perfectly clear, is shown by the fact that procedures expressed as programs can also be expressed by the hardware structure of machines itself. For decades, the principal programming language of AI was LISP, which has been in existence for about forty years, yet hardwired LISP-machines have been built, ones in which the LISP programs were more straightforwardly isomorphic with the operations of the hardware. Everyone agreed that hardwired machines are faster, but what one loses with them is portability: the ability to run programs in many languages on a single machine, and a program in one language on many different sorts of machine.

It is this portability aspect of programs, and the conventional hardware-software distinction that goes with it, that interested many of those concerned with the relation of brains to minds: There was an easy temptation to exploit the hardware-software distinction as a model of the brain-mind distinction leading, of course, to a portable notion of mind, one that many have always found attractive on theological grounds. Support for it came from the observation that both the brain and the conventional digital computer (i.e., one hardwired only for its machine code) seem to be surprisingly homogeneous in their internal structure, which led to remarks like Newell's (1973) "Intelligent behaviour demands only a few very general features in the underlying mechanism."

Since the early 1980s, the rise of the neural net/connectionist view within AI has made these views much less fashionable. One may well wonder how both groups, neural nets and GOFAI, could proceed on the assumption that the bottom level of their architectures was like the brain in some sense; to which the answer is that at the lowest level of logic gates, neural net, and conventional von Neumann machines are not really distinct.

Connectionism promotes the notion of implementation dependence on a particular neural net architecture; nonetheless, implementation independence has had a powerful effect on AI thinking about metaphysical problems, and has been behind McCarthy's insistence that AI must be defined as the study of intelligent mechanisms independent of their implementation in machines or brains, and hence to a denial that AI is, in any strong sense, about machines at all. The point can be seen best by contrast: in the uniform rejection, by anyone acquainted with the practice of programming, of Fodor's claim (1975) that the principal interpretations or models, in the logical sense, of programs are actual hardware items and states.

On this claim rests his whole theory of mental language, and yet it cannot be true for, if it were, there would be no serious portability of software, as between, say, machines of radically different architectures.

The purpose of this section has been to demonstrate, if only by example, the antiquity of AI speculation about the significance of its own structures, such as modules and platform independence, a notion very close to that of virtual machine, later taken up by Dennett. It is important to stress this since one could get the impression from works like (Dennett 1991) that modularity and virtual machine were notions that arose within philosophy, and whose consequences for the modelling of mind had never been considered by the engineers who invented them.

## 3. DENNETT'S POSITION

Dennett's interest in AI seems to have been fired by the upsurge of activity at MIT, CMU, and Stanford in the late 1960s and early 1970s, the period of Marvin Minsky's heyday, of David Levy's bet on the future of machine chess with AI leaders, of McCarthy and Hayes (1969) language of 'fluents,' the first attempt to formalise a language of rational mental activity, and so on. Talk of the beliefs of thermostats was commonplace then, and certainly not derived from philosophers' commentaries, as our editors seem to believe. The Microplanner language at MIT took goal-proving as its main primitive and became the basis for complex early models in planning, robotics, and language behaviour.

It is not my task here to settle the issue of whether or not Dennett is a behaviourist in any interesting sense: Churchland and Ramachandran (1993) and Searle (1997) consider he is, but the introductory chapter to this book seems to argue he is not, although noting that he himself seems unsure (1997, p. 16). The mere ascription of a word cannot be of any ultimate importance in a debate with scientific pretensions, but it is symptomatic of

Dennett's protean style that observers can be unsure after all this time and so many books, and a measure of how he avoids the search for clarity normally thought necessary to philosophers, in the Anglo-Saxon tradition at least, in favour of the story-telling mode that has brought great sales and fame.

Of course Dennett is a behaviourist, and for the straightforward summary reasons Churchland gives: He has simply avoided radical behaviourism (that there are no mental phenomena) in favour of a version of Ryle's logical behaviourism, in which a certain kind of mentalist talk is allowed but assigned no real significance, no correspondence to the brain, or to anything else outside itself. For Dennett, folk psychology has given a richer content and anecdotal structure to a dull Rylean category of discourse, but one not different in kind from what McGinn sharpens up as 'mental logicism' (1993), 'which takes a belief to be nothing other than a realized logical structure' (p. 86).

What has so confused the issue is that Dennett has also penetrated that boundary that held traditional behaviourists in check and made them so disliked by neuroscientists: namely, the skull. Behaviourists were once methodologically defined as brain researchers who didn't want to get their fingers wet. By taking up the AI metaphor and speculating about inner mechanisms, Dennett has gone where behaviourists had not traditionally gone (although, see below, one could say Skinner did exactly that), metaphorically at least, that is, into the head. He thus joined the Cognitive Scientists – and that is not intended as a compliment, see below, Section 5 – and proceeded to extend and massage the classic AI procedural models of mental function, whose only justification was that they led directly to actual computer programs that performed, on certain assumptions, in certain ways related to human mental function. Nothing followed from AI research about the brain or mind, of course, which is why AIers were able, when Searle made his distinction, to take up positions as either Strong AIers or Weak AIers, since these positions were private, like religion or political party membership, and had no relationship to their working lives. Both groups were happy to offer suggestive procedural models that some other kind of scientist, neural-, or psycho- might take further. That left behind a third group in AI: those with no professed interest at all in human functioning, but only in solving problems with machines: a group that was quite numerous and actually provided some of the best models of human function (e.g. Hewitt 1972 on modular architectures and goal-driven languages). Their explanatory intentions had no effect on the relevance of their models.

Thus explaining Dennett's overall position got much harder, when, in addition to his own form of Rylean behaviourism, he also adopted the

Strong AI position: walking straight into Searle's line of fire. As a salesman, he may have known exactly what he was doing, but for a philosopher that was a dangerous spot to be in: No one, and certainly no one who is basically a logical behaviourist, can assert with strong AI that mental functioning is no more than the implementation of some program. He had gone where a behaviourist, or an intentional ascriptivist, simply cannot go in making claims, since the Strong AI position inevitably identifies mental phenomena directly with implemented programs and so with brain-states; it is thus a realist position of sorts (even though the phenomena it identifies may not be what other realists wanted to save!) and Dennett does sometimes seem to have adopted precisely this form of realism, as in (Dennett 1987, quoted in Millikan 1993):

> I am as staunch a realist as anyone about the information-storing elements in the brain . . . to which our intentional interpretations are anchored. I just doubt . . . that those elements, once individuated, will be recognizable as the beliefs we purport to distinguish in folk psychology.

He may be right but this view is, on its face, incompatible with any form of ascriptivism that either denies there are mental phenomena (radical behaviourism) or is agnostic about their existence (logical behaviourism and Weak AI). Dennett is only agnostic about any correspondence between the two independent languages he wishes to go on using.

Dennett believes he has eased any resulting tension, between behaviour-talk and would-be-internal-structure-talk, by arguing that (external, third-person) ascriptions of mental properties can be directly linked to whatever mental properties a human or machine might assign to itself, and has done so by a range of ingenious arguments designed to reduce the content of mental states, by questioning the authority of the first-person subject over access to content, whether of perceptions or the content of consciousness. This is to attack Searle where it hurts him, since the latter's intrinsicality-of-content claim for mental states depends precisely on such authority, but Dennett's move does nothing logically to close the first-third person gap and nothing, in the end, can. By contrast, Dennett has made a substantial concession to Searle's position by even discussing first-person evidence; the incompatibility I claim to exist between Dennett's semibehaviourism and semiphysicalism does not need to mention first-person evidence at all.

It will always come down to a matter of what counts as data for science, and here Dennett and Searle seem to differ when Dennett is eschewing first-person data, rather than just seeking to reduce its content (which is what he actually spends much of his arguments doing). For the AI researcher,

there is no problem of principle here at all, since his task is one of engineering not science, and he will be as pleased if his mechanisms provide suggestive metaphors for first-person experiences (see below for an example)
as for third-person ascriptions to behaviour or to inner mechanisms. My
point is that an AI researcher can be both a Weak AI behaviourist and a
Strong AI physicalist without contradiction; but Dennett cannot be both,
as he has imposed constraints on himself about the admissibility of certain
kinds of description and their interpretation, a thing scientists and engineers
rarely do.

A slightly depressing aspect of this argument, along with its apparent
immortality, is that many of the distinctions on which it rests can only be
matters of degree. I argued many decades ago (Wilks 1967) and nothing has
changed my view since, that much of Chomsky's assault on Skinner (as a pure
radical behaviourist, which is to say, an explainer of a different type from
himself) was disingenuous because the two were proposing mechanisms
of different degrees of complexity: Skinner was, like Dennett, a nonstan-
dard behaviourist because he not only described behaviour but proposed a
simple explanatory neural mechanism, the stimulus/response cycle, while
Chomsky, as we all know, wanted something more complex though not, as
time has shown, all that much more complex. Certainly Chomsky's critique
of Skinner was never in terms of Skinner's inability to deal with intentional
concepts. Chomsky would have no truck with those, then or now.

The dispute about whether Strong AI is plausible gains strength (on the
Searle side) from the poverty of performance by modern computers: But
we cannot be sure what future machines may be like, and in (Wilks 1975)
I suggested possible, and plausible, machine behaviours that might make
us doubt, what everyone now seems to assume, that the person outside the
computer has the authority to declare what the computer is doing internally.
We can be pretty sure that this authority will slip with time. Indeed, this has
started already, and it may eventually adhere to the machine itself, which will
inevitably change the nature of these discussions in ways we cannot now
predict. Let us turn, very briefly, to some of Dennett's uses of particular
computational metaphors.

### 3.1. Consciousness

Dennett (1978, Chapter 9) set out to "sketch a theory of consciousness
that can be continuous with and help unify current cognitivist theories of
perception, problem solving and language use." Since then, his stories have
expanded and deepened but the strategy remains the same: to argue from

intuitive examples and psychological results that very little is in fact available to consciousness: that it is essentially vacuous. His most striking example is a result of Lackner and Garrett: Subjects heard sentences like "He put out the lantern to signal the attack" (which is ambiguous between 'place outside' and 'extinguish'). One group received just the sentence, while another group heard 'disambiguating input' through their other ear: which is to say, an additional sentence such as 'He extinguished the lantern'. Naturally enough, this group interpreted the first sentence appropriately but were unable to report what they heard through the unattended channel. In other words, they were not at all conscious of the information that had solved the problem for them. The heart of Dennett's case is that we just get the results of mental processes. We are conscious, in general, of some of our memory, and of what we say, but we are much the same position as any other observer.

A principal feature of Dennett's position is that we invent features of our unconscious apparatus, which may have no connection with the actual thoughts we have, any more than had Hume's perceptions of causation with perceptions of causes. This is an observation in line with Dennett's general theory of psychological predicates, and consistent with, for example, Minsky's notion of self-model that we discussed earlier. What Dennett calls our 'folk' theories of the contents of consciousness may be as wildly false to the facts as are our folk theories of grammar to the language that we actually speak.

None of this shows that the folk theories, even if false, are not well and truly in consciousness; indeed, if they were not one could not truly be said to be working with a false theory of the mind, unless theory became no more than a structure of unconscious assumptions. So the observations about folk theories of consciousness, although interesting, do not show consciousness to be more impoverished than we had earlier thought, for fictions are as good as fillers of consciousness as are truths.

The difficulty I have with Dennett's ideas of consciousness has to do with the fact that he makes use of implausible computational metaphors. At this stage in his argument, he produced a flowchart (see Figure 9.1).

He never actually says which parts of his 'diagram' of the mind are in consciousness, and his view is consistent with consciousness being

(A)  the control 'box,'

(B)  sometimes one box and sometimes another (very like the "heterarchical aspect" of Minsky's views I described earlier), or

(C)  some elements of what passes down the communication channels, which shows as the lines between the boxes.

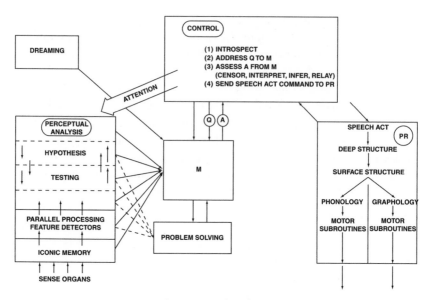

**Figure 9.1**  Flowchart.

View (C) is supported by his claims that we are conscious of some memories (those brought to INTROSPECTION in the 'control box,' for example) and some of the commands to say things (as in deliberately saying something, as distinct from finding ourselves saying it), which would be messages from the 'control box' to PR, the 'public relations box,' named by analogy with the White House public relations chief, who is simply handed a piece of paper telling him what to say, but not to think about.

I have no quarrel with interpretation (C) and think it probably consistent with my suggestions elsewhere (1984) that the notion of the "highest level of program" is the best available explication of consciousness. But Dennett has chosen, perhaps unnecessarily for his argument, a flowchart explication, which is inherently a static, rather than a process view of the mind. It is no accident that people in AI rarely draw flowcharts, and it is a cliché of programming in higher level languages like LISP (or so called object orientated languages in general) that if one finds oneself drawing a flowchart, one has not understood how the language works. Saying that is not really evidence of any kind (and may merely annoy those who program in other kinds of programming language and do use flowcharts!), but it does bring out the point that thinking about modules does not require thinking with flowcharts and that they are probably a very bad model for mental phenomena, largely because they are nonprocess models, while appearing to represent processes.

My more detailed disagreement here with Dennett is that if he intends interpretations (A) or (B), then those are inferior explications of consciousness, reducing it to a process involving notions like translation of content between differing representation languages: (B) because it lacks the 'unity' requirement that we feel consciousness must have, and (A) because it seems in some way arbitrary, just as did Minsky's supreme organizing module. After all, why should it be that particular one? Given the richness of interconnections between the boxes, surely any one of them could be the conscious one, so we would need more justification for choosing any particular one.

All this is quite close to the question of localization in brain physiology (as it was central to phrenology in the nineteenth century!): Can mental function be associated with a particular place in the brain? This is a lively issue where the brain is concerned, but not for the digital computer as we currently know it because, depending on how you interpret a computer's operations, information can be thought of as being anywhere at all in the machine (i.e., not localized in the sense of being associated with a particular place in it), or all operations of the machine can be thought of as going on in one very small and specific place. Neither of these views is of much interest for brain scientists seeking suggestive computer models, and it has been one of the appealing features of the alternative neural net model that one cannot usefully speak of localization within that paradigm.

We can think of different modules from Dennett's flowchart as functioning in the same place in a computer, just as we can think of different levels of translation of programming language as being carried out in the same place in the machine. Nonetheless, the flowchart-cum-module model is much more open to interpretation in terms of localization, because both are normally explained and displayed spatially. Therefore any explication of consciousness in those terms will tend to be a localized model, or what one could call a pinball-machine view of consciousness, one that seems to me implausible, because we have no reason to believe different parts of the mind or brain 'light up' and 'become conscious' at different stages of the game.

### 3.2. Multiple Drafts and Stacks

The problem with 'multiple drafts,' as with so much of Dennett's use of computer and process terminology, is that he does not exploit it at all to advantage but uses it only as a superficial metaphor. Contrast here the use of computational terms by linguists, who have shown far more penetration; one way of stating the central issue in language representation of the last twenty or so years is, can the syntactic processes necessary to use a language plausibly and accurately be modelled with a single push-down stack (onto which syntactic components can be stored like a plate stack in a restaurant, the last one comes off first and so on, such that you can never get at a hidden plate without removing those on top one at a time)? The alternative position is that two such stacks are required, with a second on which to stack the 'discards,' while one ferrets in the main stack.

Put crudely, and without any more technicality, the difference between one and two stacks is very close to the difference between those representations that Chomsky (1965) famously declared to be inadequate for language processing and those, which he called transformational grammars, that were. The stacks are not really a metaphor here but a real device, whose simplicity is deceptive; it was necessary to bring up obscure aspects of Dutch to show that the single stack may not be sufficient for virtually all languages.

My aim here is not to divert attention from the mind to language, but to show how a computational model can really work to explain cognitive phenomena. One finds little of this in Dennett, in spite of his addiction to the style. In his multiple drafts discussion, for example, the key point of the metaphor is to justify a view of mental content, and especially conscious content, as being like multiple drafts of a document scattered about, but 'in no one place' (Dennett 1991, p. 135, a complete change from the *Brainstorms* model of consciousness). Various unspecified processes edit drafts but 'detections or discriminations only have to be made once' and there is no 'master' discriminator where drafts are compiled and checked against each other, as authors do with real drafts, which rather undercuts the function of the basic metaphor. All this is to help free us of the Cartesian theatre picture, which is still 'entrenched' (1991, p. 111).

We have been liberated so many times from the Cartesian theatre, at least since Hume, that it is difficult to believe it can still be entrenched like some animist religion. Psychological and physiological evidence can be brought to bear in support of the 'no revisions' position, but can be equally firmly disputed, often by practitioners of the relevant science (e.g., Churchland and Ramachandran 1993). My worries about all this are different: First, that Dennett's metaphor serves his purpose rather badly, since 'drafts' inevitably suggest collation of contents, and whether or not a discrimination can be revised does not tell against that suggestion, but only against a view of collation where any item whatever can be revised. It is easy to conceive of editing models where certain discriminations or changes must always override any other evidence with which they appear to clash in 'other drafts.'

One sees what Dennett wants, and it is very much the 'heterarchical' model of control that Minsky argued for (1968) but that was never given any convincing form, and certainly not in (Winograd 1972) or (Hewitt 1972), whatever their authors' intentions in that regard. Second, the real problem under Dennett's metaphor is that it is just that when what it needs for plausibility is a process to make it explicit (as in the case of stacks in syntax) and without which it remains open to opposing interpretations.

## 3.3. Virtual Machines

The Virtual Machine (VM) is another rich and potentially stimulating metaphor for consciousness that it is also not clear that Dennett (1987, p. 230 and 1991, p. 216ff.) can make plausible and concrete, but here the reason is different, since the VM is a well-known concept in computing and in AI since Marr (1982). It is basically the notion that an algorithm, such as addition, can be considered as a single, abstract, entity, independently of the lower level, but in some sense equivalent, mechanisms of its implementation (e.g., in this case addition registers or the movements of an abacus). This abstract algorithm, or virtual machine, was behind McCarthy's desire to express intelligence as a process independently of its implementation in humans, machines, or animals (cf. McCarthy and Hayes 1969). It is also very much the same as the issue of the independence of the highest level of a program representation from its lower level translations and implementations, Section 2 above and discussed in connection with consciousness in Wilks (1984). But there is nothing specific about VM for the purpose of this analogy, nor anything that makes it more appealing than any other form of software execution as a mental model. It is not plausible to imagine that a machine can be 'thinking within its VM' any more than with any other software execution, since a VM is no less grounded in machine states than any other process when it is actually implemented. This may be the key point that Dennett misses. Whatever metaphorical benefit a VM conveys comes from discussion of software independent of its hardware. The metaphor here is not lacking procedural form, but is rather everywhere in talk about computers and of little concrete use.

## 4. MUTUAL INFLUENCES

Dennett's views of the function of 'folk notions' like intention is a central one for him, and one that goes back in an apostolic succession of teachers

from Dennett through Ryle to Wittgenstein, and to the latter's notion
of languages, in the sense of special languages or games, that constituted
specific areas of expertise, reasoning, and explanation. There is clearly a
special language of sorts for explaining human behaviour in terms of goals,
intention, beliefs, and desires, one that may be culturally local to some
degree, but as a whole is the only way in which humans can explain and judge
the behaviour of others and themselves. This is not a matter of philosophy
but of everyday life, from the courts to romantic advice in weekly magazines.
We have no alternative language with which to talk about, judge, and explain
our behaviour, and remain, as a species, somewhat resistant to the intrusions
of causal explanations of human action beyond simple ones like duress,
drugs, alcohol, and well-understood medical conditions.

Dennett has rightly drawn attention to the way we transfer such language to discussing the behaviour of animals and machines: It is natural to
talk of chess machines as 'intending to pin a rook' rather than calling on a
long series of causal or design factors from the program. In fact, such causal
conversation about the course of a game would not be possible, even if one
understood the program perfectly; it is simply a matter of the shorthand
required to talk to each other in a finite time, the very one that intentional
talk provides. One cannot converse about one's gestures by describing one's
hand movements in terms of muscles and nerves either, unless giving a medical demonstration, and this has nothing at all to do with the metaphysics of
mind but of information compression. It is perfectly expressed by modern
notion of 'level' in programming languages, one in which vast amounts of
detail of the operation of a machine's registers can be captured by a single expression at the 'top level' in a language like LISP. So much of folk
psychology, then, is a programmatic shorthand for conveying information
in time, and is no more mysterious than the fact that setting the washer at
number 2 gives rise to one set of complex washing actions, and 3 gives rise to
a quite different set, more appropriate, perhaps, for today's soiled diapers.
However, two important points of principle remain to be made here.

### 4.1. The Philosophical Point

As almost all parties in this dispute would agree, intentional talk about
people or machines does not, of itself, involve any commitments about
the 'realism' of such claims: The average person may now speak as unself-
consciously of his bank machine not wanting to give him more than $50
a day as he does of his bank manager doing the same. Many do not now
feel the ascriptions to be very different, perhaps, but could be persuaded

otherwise with appeals to the warm family-oriented humanity of the latter compared with the former, and so on. Dennett is surely right that the whole business is largely one of 'as if' (as the nineteenth-century version of his views were called by Vaihinger [1920]), and having a satisfactory story that sometimes works as well for both, apparently different, kinds of entity.

Beyond that well-known observation, it may be hard for an AI researcher to see as much difference between the views of Dennett and Searle, as they still evidently do and continue to do after the hundreds of thousands of words they have exchanged. Both agree that the brain is a machine and that therefore there are machines that have beliefs and intentions and are conscious. The differences seem to be the following, at least to this bystander.

Searle insists that mental states, whatever they are, have intrinsic content, whereas Dennett insists that content is ascribed, in the manner described above, and is subject to any degree of revision, and hence cannot be intrinsic. As the old rhyme had it: "He saw a hippopotamus/upon the mantelpiece/but looked again and saw it was/his uncle's mother's niece" (or something along those lines). This seeing cannot have been intrinsically hippopotamus-like, Dennett would remind us, because if it had been it could not then have become niece-like, while being the same mental state.

Those with pre-Dennettian philosophical memories know that this is little more than tired old phenomenalism of the mid-twentieth century, which led inevitably to a separation between an 'intrinsic' core of what were called 'sense-data' that the two seeings share, and an overlay of different interpretations that they do not. This certainly corresponds to what we know of computer vision and physiology, and the matter should by now have become a scientific one and have passed out of the clutches of philosophers entirely. Dennett is right about the possibility of revision and Searle is right about some irreducibility but it is not of a kind that will do much for what he wants, but more like (in the limit) the old Russellian backstop of knowledge as 'red-here-now' (1947/1994).

No serious person can possibly imagine that there is anything in the brain remotely like the computer programs we now have, so the whole basis of the strong AI claim is absurd, if interpreted in those terms. Moreover, Searle's own favourite argument against Strong AI is also technically weak as has been pointed out many times (including Wilks 1981): He claims that programs can only be syntactic and anything equivalent to them in the brain must be semantic in nature, or grounded, as some put it. This whole line of argument, deployed also by Fodor (1983) to somewhat different ends, makes no impact on computer scientists at all, who know full well that the semantics and syntax of programs are both entirely formal issues having nothing to with grounding, or reference to real world or brain elements as objects. The syntax and semantics of programs are expressed in very similar terms and no one could found a philosophical theory of brain function or mind on the difference between them.

The muddle, then, is a product of Dennett's swashbuckling bravado, foolishness some would say, in wading into Searle's trap by assenting to a claim (Strong AI) in a way that few in the AI business would do. But, putting all that aside, the difference between the two protagonists cannot be great: When Dennett says that Searle's first-person intuitions about consciousness and mental states cannot be basis of science, he is probably right, but that does not make them less important, nor less interesting for AI, which is not science but a complex engineering enterprise and that may yet succeed in simulating both. One may simulate what one cannot explain.

For Searle, it must be said that he is right when he claims that Dennett is, in a sense, not interested in mental life beyond a certain level (perhaps that of scientific data): But AIers, like Searle, do remain interested in it, very much so, and I have suggested possibilities of structural or programmatic metaphors (1984) for such phenomena from AI that I find more persuasive than anything Dennett has yet offered.

### 4.2. The Engineering Issue

A fairly unphilosophical use of intentional (or 'telic,' as some would now prefer) terminology (e.g., goals, motives, intentions, etc., of human actions) has been standard in GOFAI since the early 1970s, and Schank and Abelson (1977) must take much of the credit for promulgating this form of structural modelling to experimental and cognitive psychologists. The analysis and modelling of goal-driven behaviour more generally came from planning research in AI, and Winograd (1972) was the first to link that tradition explicitly to language behaviour and action in the world. It is important to stress that moment in AI history, because it would be easy to think from the examples used by Dennett, and other philosophical observers of AI, that chess modelling is the place to discuss the attribution of goals as alternatives to 'causal' accounts of machine and human behaviour. This is wrong in two ways: first, as I noted, because the domain of language use and action seems more natural in that it is superficially closer to general human behaviour (we all talk, few play chess) and, second, that telic explanations are not now fashionable in the design or discussion of chess programs, which have largely gone over from the use of deep search algorithms to the use of large data memories of previous games, combined with pattern matching to find the game positions of the past closest to the present, and to compare the possible outcomes again those of the past. Given the behaviour of chess masters like Fischer, who read old games compulsively, there is some reason to think this is close to the best human strategies, and has indeed produced the Deep Blue strategy that beat a world grand master for the first time.

It should not be thought for a moment that AIers are all agreed on how to proceed so as to engineer human behaviour and mental functioning. The field is still clearly divided at the moment and, as I noted earlier, between GOFAI, based on symbolic structures and von Neumann computation in a broad sense, and the revived doctrine of connectionism or neural nets, formerly known as cybernetics. Along with many commentators and observers, Dennett has picked up and used aspects of both trends in AI.

This notion of 'picking up' on AI is an important one, and must be mentioned here because of the explicit theme of this book, as set out in the introduction, namely that Dennett has had some influence on the course of AI research and development. To my knowledge, he has never made any such claim himself, though his reference in (Dennett 1997) to his actually doing Strong AI does seem to more than hint at it (p. 119). My own view is quite the opposite: Computation, in the broadest sense, and AI in particular in the cognitive areas we are discussing, has itself been the source of virtually all the explanatory metaphors of our time. Moreover, these metaphors are the more helpful and revealing, the closer they are to the actual procedural practice of the subject, for example, such notions as stacks, recursions, and virtual machines are far more productive notions than flowcharts and diagrams. It is one of the weaknesses of Schank's undoubted influence on the cognitive psychology of the 1970s that his notions of conceptual dependency and scripts were essentially static and diagrammatic, when compared with, say, Minsky's procedural notion of frame.

In a famous debate contribution, Feigenbaum once challenged cognitive psychologists to say what, if any, explanatory mechanism and metaphors they had that had not been derived from AI. I think this is a broadly correct observation, one confirmed by the science chitchat of our times, where computational explanation has effectively ousted the psychoanalytic, a genuinely pre-AI phenomenon albeit influential on it, as Minsky conceded. All this is a most important corrective to what I still think of a 'the white-coated lab assistant' view of AI, where some see its researchers as carrying out programming experiments to test more abstract theories conceived elsewhere, in linguistics, philosophy, or psychology. In the case of linguistics, anyone with any knowledge of AI only has to look at the work of, say, Sperber and Wilson (1986), to see that the reverse is the case, as it almost always is.

This reader of Dennett, for one, simply cannot accept that Dennett "charted a course beyond . . . empiricism" (Introduction). On the contrary, Dennett has, beneath the sugar of the stories and the jokes, kept the old discussions of phenomenalism and behaviourism firmly in play, and far from rejecting empiricism (in the sense of either of those doctrines), he remains firmly attached to them, treating his own folk-psychology explanations as no different from Ryle's, and his internal/structural additions as a form of mechanism that is, if not behaviourist, certainly not anything that any realist wants. As I asked in the last section, how can he pose as a behaviourist/ascriptivist and as a physicalist/mechanist at the same time; how does he not see that these are conflicting modes of talk and explanation?

## 5. THE CURIOUS POSITION OF COGNITIVE SCIENCE

In conclusion, something must be said about the nature of Cognitive Science, of which it used to be said that it was whatever Jerry Fodor was up to, but I think Dennett could now lay claim to some of that réclame. In its optimistic, far-off, interdisciplinary beginnings, everyone agreed not to notice the following inconvenient fact: Sciences, like all disciplines, tend to be defined in large part by their justification conditions. Neuroscience had observational data, psychology another kind of data, etc. AI built structured models that could be tested in principle against a range of data, physical or psychological, but whose justification was ultimately computer performance. Philosophy was constituted by reasonably well-understood justification criteria in terms of argument and the nature of evidence.

What has actually happened has been the creation of a generation of academic discourse, Cognitive Science, often stimulating, sometimes saleable, but which is not responsible to any justification area in particular, and hence to none. Linguistics has been a nice example of how to migrate around justification areas, and Chomsky set a bad example early on with his rejection of real language data in favour of 'informed native speaker intuitions.' Nonetheless, linguistics has found itself again in a return to data, both from exotic languages as well as the familiar in the form of computer accessible language data on a large scale.

Dennett refuses to play the traditional way and resorts to games and stories, perhaps imagining himself in the tradition of Wittgenstein, a notoriously hard act to follow. But this has left him without an intellectual base, and there is simply no way of knowing whether what he says is justified or not, only whether it stimulates. He grabs at AI metaphors but with no procedural or structural traditions to underpin them, just as Sperber and Wilson have done in their new linguistics, a development often referred to in Dennett's books, and in my view what links them to him is this potential the Cognitive Science movement has realised: the ability to rise above individual disciplines into an airy region with no real criteria for the judgment of what is said and claimed, while appearing very up-to-date in the use of metaphors from other subjects, metaphors that are imperfectly understood by one's target audience.

## References

Chomsky, N. (1965). *Aspects of the Theory of Syntax*. Cambridge, MA: MIT Press.

Churchland, P. S., and V. S., Ramachandran. (1993). Filling in: why Dennett is wrong. In Dahlbom, 1993.

Dahlbom, B., ed. (1993). *Dennett and his Critics*. Oxford: Blackwell Publishers.

Dennett, D. (1978). *Brainstorms*. Montgomery, VT: Bradford Books.

Dennett, D. (1987). *The Intentional Stance*. Cambridge, MA: MIT Press/Bradford.

Dennett, D. (1991). *Consciousness Explained*. New York: Little, Brown and Co.

Dennett, D. (1995). *Darwin's Dangerous Idea*. New York: Simon and Schuster.

Dennett, D. (1997). Response to Searle. In Searle 1997.

Dreyfus, H. (1979). *What Computers Can't Do*, 2nd ed. New York: Harper and Row.

Fodor, J. (1975). *The Language of Thought*. Sussex: Harvester Books.

Fodor, J. (1983). *The Modularity of Mind*. Cambridge, MA: MIT Press/Bradford.

Hewitt, C. (1972). Goal-driven Processing. In A. Rustin, ed., *Natural Language Processing*. New York: Algorithmics Press, 331–50.

Marr, D. (1982). *Vision*. San Francisco, CA: W. H. Freeman.

McCarthy, J., and P. J. Hayes. (1969). Some Philosophical Problems from the Standpoint of Artificial Intelligence. In B. Meltzer and D. Michie, eds., *Machine Intelligence*. Edinburgh: Edinburgh University Press, 463–502.

McGinn, C. (1993). Logic, Minds and Mathematics. In Dahlbom 1993.

Millikan, R. (1993). On Mentalese Orthography. In Dahlbom 1993.

Minsky, M., ed. (1968). Matter, Mind and Models. In M. Minsky, ed., *Semantic Information Processing*. Cambridge, MA.: The MIT Press, 425–32.

Minsky, M. (1975). *A Framework for Representing Knowledge*. Memo 3306, MIT AI Lab., Cambridge, MA.

Newell, A. (1973). Production Systems. In W. G. Chase, ed., *Visual Information Processing*. New York: Academic Press, 463–526.

Russell, B. (1947/1994). *Human Knowledge, Its Scope and Limits*. London: Routledge.

Schank, R. and R. Abelson. (1977). *Scripts, Plans and Goals*. Hillsdale, NJ: Erlbaum.

Searle, J. (1988). The Realistic Stance. *Behavioral and Brain Sciences* 11:527–9.

Searle, J. (1997). *The Mystery of Consciousness.* London: Granta Books.

Simon, H. (1969). The Architecture of Complexity. In his *The Sciences of the Artificial.* Cambridge, MA: MIT Press, 193–229.

Sperber, D., and D. Wilson. (1986). *Relevance: A Theory of Communication.* Cambridge, MA: Harvard University Press.

Turing, A. (1950). Computing Machinery and Intelligence. *Mind* 59:433–60.

Vaihinger, H. (1920). *Ist die Philosophie des Als Ob Skeptizismus?* Vaihinger u. Schmidt.

Wilks, Y. (1967). Review of Chomsky's Current Issues in Linguistic Theory. *Linguistics* 33:95–101.

Wilks, Y. (1975). Putnam and Clarke and Body and Mind. *British Journal for the Philosophy of Science* 26:213–25.

Wilks, Y. (1982). Searle's Straw Man. In *Behavioural and Brain Sciences* 5:344–5.

Wilks, Y. (1984). Machines and Consciousness. In C. Hookway, ed., *Minds, Machines and Evolution.* Cambridge: Cambridge University Press, 105–280.

Winograd, T. (1972). *Understanding Natural Language.* New York: Academic Press.

# 10 | Dennett and the Darwin Wars
## DON ROSS

Based on the distribution of his professional time over the related topics that occupy his attention, one would have expected with virtual certainty, until recently, that Dennett's most significant influence outside of philosophy would have been on either artificial intelligence or consciousness research. That may still be true in the long run, but since the loud fracas in the popular press that followed the publication of *Darwin's Dangerous Idea* (1995), it is false for the moment. In 1995, John Maynard Smith published a very favourable commentary on *DDI* in *The New York Review of Books*. Along the way, he took a surprisingly strong side-swipe at Stephen Jay Gould, writing that in the opinion of un-named evolutionary biologists, Gould is "a man whose ideas are so confused as to be hardly worth bothering with." Gould was quite evidently hurt, and let the pain show in an intervention of his own in the same magazine two years later (Gould 1997a). He characterized Maynard Smith as one might a formerly loving parent who one still respects immensely but who has turned inexplicably vicious. This sort of twist needs an explanation, and Gould finds the following one, posed in a rhetorical question: "Has he been caught up in apocalyptic ultra-Darwinian fervour?" Then, in a second installment a month later, Gould (1997b) turned the invective he may have been unable to bring himself to throw at Maynard Smith on Dennett. An argued case was hard to discern in *DDI*, he claimed, "amid the slurs and sneers." Dennett (1997) replied with considerable firmness, but avoided further escalation of the war of hot soundbites. Gould (1997c) declined the invitation to a more gracious tone, and larded his counterreply with the following phrases: "contentless commentary," "an uncomprehending Dennett," "a [reply] that does little more than grouse," "a protective wall of unbreakable a priori conclusions." In the middle of all this, Robert Wright took a somewhat embarrassing (to himself) little shot at Gould of his own, which earned him the most savage verbal blitzkrieg unloaded on any of the combatants. Then Cosmides and Tooby sent *their* attack on Gould to the *NYRB*, and this would have raised the temperature still *further*, if that is possible, had not the magazine at that point decided to return its attention to gentler and more familiar jousts, like Norman Schwarzkopf versus Saddam Hussein.

This is just terrible, of course. Scientists really are not supposed to carry on like this; so surely something of immense importance must be at stake. Well, as I will suggest below, there might be; but it has surprisingly little to do with evolutionary theory directly. There were of course some personal incidents along the road to war that made it all possible, but none are worthy of public, let alone scholarly, attention. If you are a *serious* student of these things, then you are best advised to just ignore all this shouting, because it's a red herring, and it will not lead you to the genuinely interesting issues in the new arguments over adaptationism, issues that the *NYRB* brou-ha-ha never so much as alludes to.

But, first, on just how well known for the wrong reasons this has made Dennett. The intensity of the fireworks of course attracted the media. Since 1999, no fewer than three popular books (Brown 1999; Malik 2000; Rose and Rose 2000) have appeared that aim to guide the perplexed through the strategies and motives of both sides in these so-called Darwin wars (Brown's phrase, and his title). In each of them Dennett has figured prominently, usually pictured figuratively beside Richard Dawkins on one of the combatant bridges, facing Gould and Richard Lewontin on the other, and beset by the small boats of affronted humanists. Although I know of no proper poll that might verify this, as a result of all these battle reports Dennett almost certainly now stands with or just behind Russell and Wittgenstein as the most famous professional philosopher of the century. Being famous *for* ideas, however, is almost never the same thing as having one's ideas be famous. Many who have read of Dennett, and who hold opinions about him, likely associate him with just three doctrines: that natural selection acidizes morality, that thermostats have beliefs and desires, and that people are not conscious. The anti-humanist's anti-humanist, it would seem.

Of course, I can safely assume that all readers of this book are better informed than that, and so I need not embark on the wearying exercise of trying to earnestly correct Dennett's popular critics on the question of whether he is some sort of ethical demon. Nor will I try to diagnose the deeper social reasons for this explosion of wrought interest, partly because these reasons surely aren't actually all that deep. Many people, both outside *and* inside the academy, clearly think that much of moral import hangs on the significance and interpretation of evolution in the wider human self-conception, thus confirming, at least in their perceptions, Dennett's view of Darwin's idea as dangerous. But neither Dennett nor any of the other serious participants in the debate think that Darwinism implies moral nihilism; and I am happy to endorse pretty much everything Dennett says on the subject in Chapters 16 and 17 of *DDI*, to which precisely *none* of the popular critics has ever replied in detail. Until they do, I'm not sure that much more needs to be said about the subject.

What I'm going to argue here instead is this. People cannot get to the bottom of these Darwin wars merely by trying to understand the biology. (And trying to understand the sociology, or the social psychology, likely doesn't help at all, though I'll leave that point.) Their substance will continue to baffle anyone who doesn't grasp the details of some quite tricky and technical philosophical issues lying beneath them. I emphasize 'tricky and technical'; I am *not* here referring to the obvious pop-philosophical questions about the place of morality in a world of selfish genes and memes (etc.). I am instead talking about some arcane issues surrounding the logic of conceptual reference, issues that, although professional philosophers lose sleep over them, do *not* attract the attention of the media.

Some readers will no doubt roll their eyes when a philosopher announces that he's about to reveal the fundamental importance of pure philosophy to a scientific and/or religious-sociological debate (whichever of those one thinks the latest hollering about evolution represents). I work in an economics department, though. More to the point, my published opinions on most philosophical and scientific subjects have followed Dennett's very closely for over a decade; and yet the claim that questions of analytic philosophy are crucial to the enterprise of understanding the role of mind in nature actually expresses a very *un*-Dennettian idea that I am surprised to find myself having. Dennett has often expressed reservations about the relevance of technical philosophy to science (see, e.g., Dennett 1994) and so, of course, have many scientists; so, for that matter, have I. But my reading of the most careful and conscientious of the popular commentaries, Kenan Malik's *Man, Beast and Zombie* (2000) has led me to change my mind, at least in this instance. Malik, unlike several of the authors in Rose and Rose (2000), understands that evolutionary psychology, like any other scientific approach, can and has been done both well and badly, and he recognizes that Dennett's suggested method of explanation by reverse engineering (see Chapter 6) does *not* constitute a license to spin just-so stories at will or to reduce all human behaviour to genetics. At the end of the day, however, Malik's tone concerning evolutionary psychology is very sharply critical, because he thinks that evolutionary psychologists must deny the causal significance of consciousness; and he arrives at *this* conclusion by entirely misunderstanding the philosophical motivations behind Dennett's work on that subject. By contrast, Fodor (1996), in *his* review of *DDI*, sees through to the core of the philosophical issue exactly. If one answers Fodor, one has answered Malik, or so I will maintain.

Before I turn to Malik, let me begin by noting that he is not the first popular commentator on the Darwin wars to lose the plot just at the point where the philosophical issues get deep. Andrew Brown's *The Darwin Wars* (1999) attempts to explain the ferocity of the *NYRB* polemics from a pretense of journalistic neutrality that Malik does not profess (but comes closer to actually achieving). If Brown were either a science-basher or a gushing enthusiast, we would know how to predict his story, especially given that he frames it as a conflict between 'Gouldians' and 'Dawkinisians.' Science-bashers loathe Dawkins and are apt to embrace Gould on the principle of My Enemy's Enemy; scientistic enthusiasts are equally prone to admire Dawkins for his stinging thrusts against *their* ideological foes. In this sort of pure battle of attitudes, actual questions of scientific content don't much matter. Brown's epistemological stance, however, is respectful and reasonable on the surface – just what most of us *say* we'd like 'our' public, or our students, to be – and confoundingly *weird* under a bit of critical inspection. On the one hand, Brown never introduces a combatant without some sentences of praise for his or her skill and intellect. Thus, "there are very few who can have succeeded as well as Dawkins does in opening up an entirely new way to ask questions about the world. More than any other author I know of, he makes vivid the central scientific idea that there are good logical reasons for things to happen one way rather than another and that we can, if we try, discover them" (1999, p. 25). There is "an astonishing thing" about "Gould as a show-off," namely that "he gets his facts right; and he combines this accuracy with a voracious sympathy for his subjects" (p. 59). Dennett "writes with tremendous vigour about important things," and "like Dawkins, he has the quality of making the world a more interesting place than it was before you read him" (p. 153). Midgley has "a capacity for scrupulous examination of a question" that is "equalled only by her gift for an eviscerating phrase" (p. 83). If these praise-songs read exclusively like blurbs for dramatic performers, that is probably misleading. Note that Gould is being toasted in the quotation above for an essentially scientific virtue. There is no doubt that Brown admires science and admires good (or, at least, famous) scientists *for* doing science well. On the other hand, it is jarring when Brown, the journalist, repeatedly calls them sharply to the bar of his own authority on 'common sense.' Thus, when Dawkins calls whole organisms "robots" from the gene's perspective, but then cautions that real robots are not like Hollywood androids, Brown sniffs that "Dawkins's nerdy enthusiasms have got the better of him here." "Who is he," asks Brown as champion of the person on the street, "to tell us what the erroneous associations of the word 'robot' are?" (p. 40). Dennett's 'universal [Darwinian] acid' is similarly rebuked in a sentence; the explicator of science, even if he is a professional philosopher, is required to respect the plain person's philosophical intuitions, not universally acidize them. Interestingly, no 'Gouldians' are at any point called on this carpet, which is why, after many pages of studied neutrality on Brown's part, they emerge as the party that Merits Your Vote by the end. I think that this particular route to a verdict is telling us something significant about the relationship between philosophy and popular science.

Brown is, as he says in the book, mainly a journalist of religion. He is also, he tells us, an "atheist" who finds it "depressing" that people think they can help others by praying for them (p. 180). Helena Cronin reminds Brown of a Christian fundamentalist cousin of his, and he says he likes this quality in both of them. As an aside, he admits that "[O]f course, there is an important difference. What my relative believes about the world is generally false, whereas what Helena believes is generally true" (p. 149). By now, I hope that my intent in calling Brown's epistemology "weird" (at least to a philosopher) has become evident. Truth is one of a number of likable things (along with fundamentalistic attitudes!), and scientists deserve respect for pursuing it. But broad democratic sympathy is at least as likable a thing, so much so that it precludes scientists from rubbishing commonly held views and favoured metaphors, at least when they are addressing the general public. Thus, Gould deserves the hometown support in the end because he (unlike Dawkins or Dennett) does just what Brown, the atheist, presumably must strive for in commenting on the eccentric doctrines of believers, that is, self-consciously sympathizes with the position of the epistemically benighted. Indeed, if there is a leading 'hero' in Brown's tale it is, of all people, Mary Midgley. The reasons for this, and what Brown forgives her as a result of them, are highly revealing.

Brown spends his first eight chapters surveying, in a mostly chronological and philosophically muddled way, the units-of-selection controversy, the debates over adaptationism, the shameful antics at Harvard after Wilson published *Sociobiology*, and the recent rise of evolutionary psychology. As scholarly history this is shallow, heroically troped, and wholly innocent of philosophical sophistication; but Brown is clearly working with a will to be fair.[1] His various misinterpretations all appear to be accidents, and both of his constructed teams of warriors suffer their share of these. This seems to be Brown the journalist-of-belief putting scientists in the roles of his more familiar subjects. It leads me to conclude that if I read Brown on religion, I wouldn't trust him on questions of theology, but I'd be prepared to learn interesting things about the personalities of various sorts of theologs. The main reason why a novice in evolutionary theory would learn little science from Brown isn't related to his philosophical simplifications and mistakes. Rather, Brown never attempts systematic exposition in the first place; he discusses issues of scientific interpretation only where he must do so in order to substantiate a claim that someone has attacked a straw version of someone else's view. (For example, his discussion of analytical versus functional individuation of genes [pp. 31–6] is directed against clumsy misinterpretations of Dawkins by his critics, and is much later [p. 86] picked up again and cited against Midgley's [1979] scientifically embarrassing diatribe at *The Selfish Gene*. Brown's science journalism here is generally good.) It would therefore be beside the point of Brown's enterprise for someone to mount detailed criticism of Brown's philosophy *of biology*. However, his wider [implicit] general epistemological stance is very much to the point, since it motivates and drives his entire stance.

What is supposed to mainly emerge from Brown's tour of the battlefield is that good scientists invite misinterpretations when they lose control of their metaphors. Brown refers to these metaphorical excursions as 'bad philosophy,' and he is particularly quick to judgment when he finds Dawkins and others claiming that what he sees as *obvious* metaphors (e.g., of organisms as 'survival machines' for genes [Brown 1999, p. 93]) are to be taken literally. Brown simply assumes that it is the task of 'philosophy' to elaborate on and preserve the Sellarsian manifest image, which in his hands is really just Dr. Johnson's tiresome 'common sense.' Brown should perhaps have been more worried than he is by his admitted failure to be able to understand Dennett's *Consciousness Explained* (1991a) (Brown 1999, p. 153). He sees that Dennett's project there is that of "exorcising the ghost from the machine" by demolishing, rather than repairing, the folk conception of consciousness. However, it doesn't occur to him that any philosophical attack on a morally significant conceptualization could ever amount to something besides simple-minded eliminative reductionism. As a result, he subjects Dennett to a two-page string of nonsequiturs in objection. If you succeed in building a machine that has free will, he announces "free will is what you have built" (Brown 1999, p. 154). Dennett would happily agree with this, adding that that is his *point*. (Similarly, for Dennett: If you build a complicated *enough* thermostat, one that can start to revise its goals and its means to them, then it would have *real* beliefs, not just some android imitation of them.) Brown, however, says that in that case "the ghost is back in the machine." We have already discovered by this point, in Brown's discussion of Dawkins's debate with Midgley, that his 'ghost' is anything that motivates *emotionally*. Although Brown agrees that emotions must have biological explanations and causal instantiations at the neural level, he sees their motivational force as somehow refuting 'genetic determinism.' *This* nonsequitur appears to result from Brown's being unable to conceive of any sort of causation except mechanical causation. Thus, both genetic influences and emotions are potential causes of behaviour, and if some particular bit of behaviour requires the second among its causes it can't be caused, under an alternative description, by the first. Reconciling this position with a sort of folk naturalism then requires metaphysical emergentism. Thus, Brown says, "It doesn't matter whether this effect [free will] has been produced without God or by a Darwinian process. All working biologists agree that intelligence, curiosity, free will and so on are produced by the normal, law-bound, *mechanical* [emphasis mine] processes of the world. The important point made by Dennett's opponents is that once these properties have emerged, they exist" (1999, p. 154). I don't think that there is much gain to be had in trying to associate this "important point" with any of the presently contending philosophical positions on the metaphysics of mind; Brown simply doesn't know enough about the issues or the alternatives to intend a sophisticated position here. What he clearly doesn't see is that 'common sense' has at least as serious a problem with mental causation as does Dennett's evolutionary naturalism, or even the kind of simple-minded genetic determinism that Brown thinks Dennett espouses and that he takes Dawkins to be suggesting when the latter says that his 'robot' metaphors are literally true.

This fundamental confusion about the nature of contemporary philosophy infects Brown's understanding of the controversies over adaptationism. Brown understands well enough the Gouldian objection that some products of evolution are spandrels, and that resort to unconstrained adaptationist explanation would turn evolutionary biology and psychology into free speculation. What Brown does *not* understand is that the debate between the Gouldians and the Dawkinsians as it erupted into the pages of the *NYRB* is *epistemological*, not *metaphysical*. Brown seems slightly puzzled by the fact that all parties to the debate agree both that some outcomes are adaptations and that environmental contingency plays an important role in evolution. Unable to find a clear fact of the matter that is at stake in the 'wars,' Brown must conclude that the contest is either over the reductive elimination of human purposes and moral motivations, or is *just* a politically inspired contest for the dominant metaphor. The key points of dispute, which concern issues of biological epistemology, are thus completely absent from Brown's story. The truth is, roughly, that adaptationists do biology by assuming that natural selection is a rational maximizer and then inferring the important contingent causal factors by comparing the predictions obtained using that assumption with the actual evolutionary outcomes. Gouldians, by contrast, are more traditionally empiricist, willing to risk the loss of some explanatory power in return for a smaller risk of confusing grand hypotheses for facts. This debate is real enough, to be sure, and important both biologically and philosophically (as I will presently show). But its two sides imply *nothing* distinctive from each other about the 'existence' of free will or of moral properties. Someone might, I guess, take a Gouldian approach that is so radical as to deny that *any* explanation of a behavioural adaptation could ever be reasonably complete *and* insist that to demonstrate a behaviour's rationality shows that its morality is spurious or redundant. That, at least, is what you'd need to do in order to read Dennett and Dawkins as threats to social morality, and then read Gould as guarding it against them. I suppose that in a world of ultra-radical and philosophically confused Gouldians it would be a bit easier to be a political egalitarian. But, then, sufficient philosophical confusion makes anything you like easier.

In fact, Brown really *does* seem to fear that adaptive explanations undermine the significance of morality. Thus, after an extended meditation endorsing the ethical compatibility (although, interestingly, *not* the metaphysical or epistemic compatibility) of religion and science generally, he says that "Anyone who believes in the importance of justice and mercy must be worried by Darwinism. . . . The mixture of kin selection and game theory . . . really does provide explanations for how cooperative behaviour can arise in the world, how it can spread, and how we can be born with all our good and tender instincts. . . . This raises again the horrible question of why all these instincts should have appeared in a world that is bound to frustrate them. [This 'why' alludes to the problem of evil, not to our capacity for scientific understanding.] To that extent there is some truth in the agreement between Darwinians and their opponents that Darwinism is necessarily opposed to Christian certainties" (1999, p. 191). As a dramatic device to frame his narrative, Brown suggests that the psychological trauma behind George Price's 1974 suicide stemmed from his recognition that "though his equation [for the degree of relatedness at which genetic altruism is an equilibrium strategy, something Brown never quite explains for his readers] showed that truly self-sacrificing behaviour can exist among animals, and even among humans, it also seemed to show that there is nothing noble in it" (p. 2). What does Brown mean by 'noble' here? At first, he seems to be alluding to the Kantian test of an action's morality: "What Price saw was that a world in which unselfishness really is rewarded can be even more horrible than one in which only the ruthless survive. The torment is that we want to be genuinely unselfish: gratuitously good.... Some part of everyone wants to make the leap that Jesus made in the parable of the Good Samaritan" (p. 9). Now, if what 'real' morality demands is *Kantian* morality, that is, morality that must motivate in a direction contrary to that of *practical* reason, then evolutionary game theory will indeed undermine it – although so will plain economic game theory unrelated to biology, as shown in a formal proof given by LaCasse and Ross (1998). However, a few pages after the remark quoted above, Brown changes his diagnosis. "The tormenting reflection," he says, "is not that altruism is a con in the obvious, vulgar sense that it is 'really' selfish or that it 'really' advances our interests." Rather, the problem is that if the emotions that underwrite *felt*, sentimental inclinations to altruism are evolved dispositions, they will not be perfectly reliable! "Our emotional constitution does more than direct us. It also orients us. It also tells us what our goals are: Wanting to behave well, or lovingly, is one of the things that tell us what good behaviour or love is. That is why it can seem so threatening that these desires have evolved fallibly, for if our wants and dispositions are as much a product of Darwinian forces as are our eyes, perhaps our instinct for what is goodness, or love, will be as fallible as our eyesight" (1999, pp. 10–11). So: What Darwinism threatens is confidence that we could infallibly track a domain of independently existing moral facts. These, then, are the 'noble' "Christian certainties" threatened by Darwinism. Although naturalistic moral realists would question the extent of this threat, many philosophers would not. But to make it go away would require more than the rejection of adaptationism, genetic determinism, and the other excesses associated by Brown with the Dawkinisians; one would have to deny evolution by natural selection altogether. Since Gould no more wants any part of that than his opponents do, it is not at all evident what Brown's Christian fear has to do with what is at stake in the 'Darwin wars.'

The diagnosis, it turns out, is existential. Brown's earnest neutrality between the sides in his battle finally gives way to a more confident and personal tone when, in Chapter 9, he contrasts the anti-religious polemics of Dawkins and Nick Humphrey with Gould's and Lewontin's sympathetic understanding of religion, including even fundamentalist creationism.[2] Brown strongly endorses such sympathies; indeed, he goes much further. We are told that "a statement which asserts a historical falsehood may none the less encode an emotional truth" (1999, p. 169). The idea of a 'historically false emotional truth' is puzzling to say the least, but it turns out to be a (historical) truth *about* emotional demands. (These demands are evidently not felt by everyone: Brown the atheist presumably resists them, as do all the characters in Brown's story except Price.) People must, we are told, take the universe personally. "And if we must take the universe personally, it is probably wiser and saner to believe and hope in resurrections than to rush around, crying 'We're all doomed!'" (1999, p. 169). At this point, Brown cites two "important" points due to Midgley. First: "Possibly, for human beings, the only alternative to thinking of the universe as, in some vast and remote way, purposive and benign, is to think of it as purposive and radically malignant. It may simply not be within our capacity – except of course by just avoiding thought – to think of it as having no purpose or direction whatever. And since the notion that it is radically malignant is a crazy one, benignity seems to be the only usable option." Midgley's 'crazy' here must of course mean *practically* crazy, since, pace Descartes, it is no less *rationally* crazy to imagine supreme governance by devils than by good gods. Here, then, is the voice of 'common sense' filtered through the philosopher's reflections and reaffirmed in only slightly more sophisticated tones. Midgley's "second important point" is extremely hard to distinguish from her first one: "Our view of the universe is not characterized by God-like detachment and can't be. Like the Christian God, people who think themselves above the universe constantly find themselves dragged back in to take sides in the struggles between hope and despair; and it matters which side we take" (1999, pp. 170–1, quoting Midgley 1986, p. 136). Thus reassured by Midgley's vapid eloquence, Brown now finally warms against the Dawkinsians: "Dawkins, Dennett and . . . Nicholas Humphrey talk about the [religious] 'memes' they disapprove of in exactly the same way that fundamentalists talk about 'demons'. In both cases, their opponents' ideas are dismissed as the result, quite literally, of possession. If this is your point of entry into their ideas, it makes it hard to take seriously anything else they have to say, which is unfortunate" (1999, p. 171).

The attitude suggested by Midgley's remarks, as endorsed by Brown, is 'philosophical' in one very popular, and deplorable, meaning of the term: It seeks to comfort the doubtful. And, of course, neither Dawkins nor Dennett is involved in *that* project (except where the doubts are themselves products of seeing the inconsistencies in comfortable but tired metaphysical pictures; I am thinking here of Dennett's arguments on free will as given in Dennett [1984]). For that matter, neither are Gould or Lewontin, who, in different contexts of orthodoxy on different questions, are prepared to be just as iconoclastic. Brown's partiality for what he sees as Midgley's sound moderation, which surfaces at various points in his book – we are even asked to imagine her "picking her way through the confusions of the world in her large, sensible shoes" (1999, p. 83) – explains his inability to *quite believe* that Dawkins means to be taken literally, and his complete incomprehension of Dennett. It does not seem to cast doubt, in Brown's eyes, on Midgley's competence as a participant in the disputes in the philosophy of biology when he must recognize that, in her 1979 attack on Dawkins, she "gets selfish gene theory, as a piece of biology, about as wrong as it can possibly be got" and "persistently failed to understand the concept of the analytic gene" (1999, p. 86). This fails to be devastating for Brown only because he thinks that philosophers have responsibilities fundamentally different from those of scientists. In particular, they must stand guard over everyday usage. And this is what Midgley does, rightly (in Brown's view) refusing to let Dawkins have the adjective 'selfish' for mindless entities. Brown glosses Dawkins's response in defence of his phrase as a case of "failing to see that philosophy mattered" (p. 92). 'Failing to see that *philosophy* mattered?' Given this conception of philosophy, it comes as no surprise that Brown thinks (p. 153) that Dennett's position on consciousness can be refuted simply by saying that it leads him to assert that "thermostats have beliefs." Imagine!

I suspect that many nonprofessional readers of Brown's will allow him his role as the spokesman for their 'common sense.' It leaves the scientists to their pursuit of truths in their restricted domains, so long as they leave the ordinary meanings of words like 'robot' and 'selfish' – and, much more important, their associated concepts – unexamined and unchanged. It spares the nonreligious from the discomfort of supposing that their believing fellow citizens live by 'moral certainties' that are at best groundless and at worst unhinged. It leaves a fuzzy space for fuzzy intuitions about free will. It allows people to agree with Gould, and with the current politically preferred view, that genetic determinism, whatever exactly it means, is both nasty and scientifically unsanctioned. And it implies, in a firmly democratic way, that everyone is a competent philosopher (except, it seems, Dennett and those scientists who stray outside their domain), their intuitions being merely less articulate than Midgley's. I do not think that Brown is *trying* to pander to know-nothingism in this book; his great *effort* to be both fair and morally serious is too evident for that. He is right that the 'Darwin wars,' at least as he imagines them, are products of philosophical confusion. But this confusion is, first and foremost *his*, and it is confusion *about* the very point and nature of philosophical inquiry. Pace Wittgenstein, it is *not* the task of philosophy to "leave everything as it is"; folk concepts often start to claw the air and generate logical confusions when scientific advances or other historically novel human experiences lead us to apply them in domains wider than those of their original application.

Such is the case with the concept of 'consciousness.' Its study has often been regarded as the most profoundly difficult domain of philosophical investigation for four interrelated reasons. First, it raises epistemological puzzles about how the 'intrinsically' subjective could be studied objectively. Second, the particular qualitative contents of sensations, such as the redness of red, do not seem to admit of any justification, which makes them difficult to assimilate into the essentially normative project of epistemology. Third, these contents have an apparent unity that is often taken to be essential to their identity, and this seems inexplicable from the standpoint of traditional causal theories of perception. Fourth, we can evidently be motivated by conscious ideas of things that do not and cannot exist, which introduces all of the traditional philosophical puzzles about intentionality into the subject, compounded by the fact that it would be circular to invoke deliberate acts of construction into the explanation of what is supposed to be the causal and logical prerequisite for deliberation in the first place. These conundrums were always implicit *somewhere* in epistemology, but it is the progress of science that has attached them all to the concept of 'consciousness.' Aristotle, who treated 'consciousness' as approximately synonymous with 'awareness,' was troubled only by the third problem. Once Descartes split the mind into active and passive faculties, *and* insisted on a mechanical account of the latter, the other three difficulties arose. They then became progressively more intractable as psychologists, over the subsequent years, postponed all of their more serious ontological problems by dumping them into a vestigial 'mystery' of consciousness, which was to be solved at the end of the discipline's development. Dennett's (1991a) study of consciousness is launched from the recognition that the concept had thus been loaded with more philosophical weight than *any* essentially folk notion could bear, and that the folk notion therefore needs to be replaced by a more sophisticated *family* of concepts that would permit analysis of the *relations* between them, if the long-deferred 'end of psychology' is to be brought any closer.

This is obviously not the place for a(nother) detailed account and defence of Dennett's theory of consciousness. (See Ross 1993, 1994, and forthcoming, for the gist of what I have to say on that subject.) Here, it will suffice to make two points. First, Dennett's famous denial of the existence of qualia is part of this effort of analysis; it is *not* the (absurd) claim that people have no sensations. *Qualia* is a technical concept of philosophers' invention, denoting a mental entity that is essentially private, ineffable, intrinsic, and directly or immediately apprehensible in consciousness. In denying that there are any such things, Dennett's claim is that no particular sensation, or report of a sensation, or experience of a sensation, or whatever in this neighbourhood of entities your favourite epistemology of mind and perception allows you to talk about, has all of these properties simultaneously and as conditions on its individuation. You might agree or disagree with this view according to your take on quite intricate philosophical arguments; but you do not refute it by asserting that you have feelings and that Dennett must be a zombie. Second, Dennett's work on consciousness was built on the foundation, many years in construction, of his distinctive and ingenious theory of intentionality. Among the popular commentators, only Malik seems to have any awareness of this. (Midgley, being a philosopher by trade, *must* be aware of it, but from her contribution to Rose and Rose (2000), one would never so gather. She encourages an extraordinary amount of outright interpretive error in one short essay, assimilating reductionism and atomism in both early modern and contemporary thought, then mislocating what is at issue between Hume and Kant so she can saddle Dennett with the astonishing label of 'reductionist,' his famous anti-reductionist statement in 'Real Patterns' (Dennett 1991b) notwithstanding. If this is what we're to get from the professionals, please give us the popularizers!)

Malik both appreciates that philosophical issues around consciousness matter to the evaluation of Dennett's adaptationism, and that Dennett's theory of intentionality is a basis for his theory of consciousness. He accurately presents Dennett's arguments against the possibility of a zombie (a being who is behaviourally indistinguishable from a conscious human but who is not conscious), and then goes on to draw exactly the right conclusion:

> Any entity that could pass the Turing test would, Dennett believes, 'operate under the (mis?)apprehension that it was conscious. In other words, it would be the victim of an illusion.' What illusion? The same illusion that makes humans think we are conscious and intrinsically intentional. Any machine, therefore, that was behaviourally complex enough to represent its own internal states, and to pass the Turing test, would necessarily be conscious and necessarily be able to ascribe meaning as well as humans could.... [A]ny machine that was sufficiently behaviourally complex would be conscious, have a mind, and be able to read meaning into symbols. (Malik 2000, p. 306)

Malik immediately glosses this by saying that "Dennett challenges Searle by arguing that there is no such thing as true intentionality, or true meaning." This is certainly *not* what Dennett argues or concludes. (See, again, Dennett 1991b, and also Dennett 1981, where Dennett works hard to make clear that his project is to show us how we *can* be realists about intentionality and meaning. Some philosophers doubt that he succeeds at this; but that is not the same thing as thinking, like Malik, that he argues for conclusions opposite to those he actually intends.) However, Malik then turns straight around and gets the gloss just right: "The only distinction is between derived intentionality – and derived intentionality that gives the illusion of being intrinsic intentionality." Yes; *precisely*. Not only does Malik seem to understand Dennett's point, he agrees with it: "Dennett's is a highly sophisticated argument. I think he is right in arguing that there is no such thing as 'intrinsic' intentionality" (2000, p. 306).

This is all very promising. But then, just thirty pages later, Malik swerves off the road. "Dennett," he says, "seems to accept that humans are conscious, but considers this consciousness to have no qualitative aspect over and above the physical actions of the neurons. This may be consciousness, Dan, but not as we experience it" (2000, p. 336). This, as I've said, is simply a misunderstanding on Malik's part: He has mistaken Dennett's denial of existence to *qualia* as a denial of there being 'ways things seem to us' (Dennett's own preferred phrase for the subjective aspects of conscious states). The confusion is explicit a page later when Malik says that "it may be true, as Dennett says, that there is nothing 'intrinsic' about neuronal states that constitute the way things look to us. But this does not mean there is not a way things look to us that is subjective and private" (p. 337). Dennett does not deny that there is such a thing as subjective experience, or that the subjective qualities of such experiences are generally private to their experiencers (until and unless they report them to others); this is precisely the state of affairs that *Consciousness Explained* is supposed to explain (and that it must, on pain of circularity, avoid doing by reference to *fundamentally* subjective explanans).

As I will show in a moment, I think it is quite easy to find what has led Malik astray here. First, however, let us observe the dizzying rush of further, and highly portentous, argument to which his mistake leads. First, having 'discovered' Dennett to be holding a ridiculous view, Malik must wonder what pressure could force him into it. This he identifies in Dennett's assumption that there must be a 'mechanical' account of mind. 'Mechanical' here turns out to be a severely un-apt, in historical terms (has Malik been reading Midgley?), label for what Malik means, which is any perspective on human intentionality and motivation that takes a third-person point of view, thereby regarding people as "just animals and machines – as Beasts and Zombies" (p. 337). Then we are told that this is the mistake made by evolutionary psychology, which forces the view that human behaviour and belief is just a causal product of interactions between genes and environments. Since 'mechanism' has been declared false, it follows that evolutionary psychology tells an incomplete story about the mind and about humans generally. The gears then shift, and in Malik's closing chapter he diagnoses the popularity of such stories in terms of political developments that have made people, in the decades since World War II, feel insecure about their own moral responsibility. The concluding plea for liberal humanist values that ensues is eloquent, forceful, and highly recommended; but that the call for it has been prompted by a supposed mistake of Dennett's is a bit amazing. (If you're looking for another sophisticated call to the humanist barricades after being roused by Malik, you could do a lot worse than the closing chapters of *DDI*.)

I've said that I'm not going to talk (here) about the relationship between Darwinism and the high moral zeitgeist, so let's put this aside. Malik is right to sense a close connection between Dennett's views on intentionality and consciousness and the themes of evolutionary psychology, but the basis on which he draws this connection is hopelessly confused. As I indicated above, it is not hard to see where Malik's logic slips. It turns out that when he endorses Dennett's denial of intrinsic intentionality, he has misunderstood what Dennett means by 'intrinsic.' He concludes his review of the Dennett/Searle debate over intrinsic intentionality with the following comment:

> Searle's problem is that his theory has, in fact, the same form as those of Dennett and the artificial intelligentsia: both sides assume that meaning, understanding, mental states and consciousness are all located in our heads. Dennett claims that it is located in the software, Searle that it is located in our hardware.... I believe that both sides are wrong for the same reason: they both assume that the mind lies inside our heads. (2000, p. 309)

This alerts us to what is going on when Malik supposes that Dennett eliminates qualitative experience in favour of "actions of the neurons." It prompts him, at this point, to sail off into a defence of the idea that individuation of intentional content requires reference to states of the wider environment. This, basically, is an affirmation of semantic externalism along with the stronger sort of 'extended mind' hypothesis that has been defended by a number of philosophers, most clearly and eloquently Andy Clark (1997). Malik's notes and references betray no awareness of this literature. Since Malik shows himself to be an able thinker, I am happy to believe that he arrived at the idea independently; but lack of familiarity with its genesis in academic philosophy would account for his failure to realize that Dennett is its basic author! In *Consciousness Explained*, Dennett argues that 'selves' are narrative constructions arising from and constrained by networks of social and other environmental relations. As Clark (this volume) makes clear, Dennett is thus the main proximate *source* of the view Malik chides him for ignoring. For Dennett, the folk-psychological idiom that anchors our pre-scientific notion of intentionality must not be taken to be describing brain-states, or *any other objects of purely 'inner' reference*, because the job of the intentional stance is to track persistent patterns that triangulate motivation, representation, and environment. Malik, therefore, is here criticizing the position of 'Dennett' by urging an alternative view that is mainly due to Dennett! What this reveals, of course, is his misunderstanding of the actual Dennett. Given this confusion, he can read Dennett's 'intrinsic' as meaning roughly 'self-caused' *on any given occasion*, and so as then denying that anyone ever intentionally causes anything. But this is not, and cannot possibly be, what Dennett intends.

In claiming that intentionality is 'derived,' Dennett is *not* maintaining that *particular*, present intentional states are never occurrences of novel meaning and significance, and for just the reason Malik says: Individuals constantly confront, are shaped by, and make sense of environmental complexes and contingencies that are genuinely new under the sun. What Dennett means is that the purposiveness that makes meaningfulness *in general* possible, that gives rise to the logical possibility of intentional systems in the first place, is historically and ontogenetically located in the process of natural selection. Because natural selection really is selection *for* capacities that serve purposes, it brings teleology into the world. This natural teleology is then the basic logical standard against which meaningfulness can evolve and, ultimately, be co-opted into the *personal* purposes of agents. This point has nothing to do with whether minds are identical to, or reducible to, the software (*and* neuronal hardware) on which, according to Dennett, their activity is *causally* dependent. This is the direct basis for Dennett's (as opposed to Dawkins's) version of adaptationism. Minds – intentional systems – arise *because* (both logically and historically) they are adaptations generated in the evolution by natural selection of nervous systems and of organisms situated in environments more generally. This relatively deep philosophical point is entirely missed by Malik, and by Brown, and so in the end the Dennettian basis for adaptationism in his theories of intentionality and consciousness simply escapes them, and makes his general stance in the Darwin wars ultimately baffling to them. There is a significant irony here. Both, in effect, criticize evolutionary psychologists and biologists for being shallow and/or incompetent philosophers. Neither, in saying this, understands what deep and/or competent philosophy really is. As Malik and Brown would agree, as indeed they stress to the point of obsession, the existence of meaning in the world is a profoundly hard and important question, harder, in fact, than they suppose. Dennett's work is among the two or three most serious carefully developed attempts to *answer* it, not some sort of apology for 'greedy reductionists' (Dennett's phrase) who seek to sidestep it.

Fodor (1996) sees this point exactly, and rightly makes it the focus of his response to *DDI*. As Fodor says "Dennett offers a sketch of a metaphysical construction in which the (neo)-Darwinian account of adaptation is supposed to ground a theory of natural teleology; and this theory of natural teleology is in turn supposed to ground an account of the meaning of symbols and of the intentionality of minds. This program is, of course, enormously ambitious, much more so than adaptationism per se" (Fodor 1996/1998, p. 171). Yes, indeed; to turn Gould's central organizing thrust from his *NYRB* intervention directly back against him, there are "more things in heaven and earth" going on than Gould and the other nonphilosophical critics dream of, and one of them is the need for an explanation of the metaphysics of intentionality that technically works.

Fodor, of course, doubts that Dennett's does. His skepticism arises at all points of the enterprise:

> My own view is that adaptationism probably isn't true; and that even if it is true there probably isn't any notion of natural teleology worth having; and that even if adaptationism is true and there is a notion of natural teleology worth having, the latter isn't grounded in the former; and that even if adaptation grounds a theory of natural teleology, natural teleology has nothing much to do with the metaphysics of meaning. (Fodor 1996/1998, p. 171)

Since this is an essay about how to understand – and how not to understand – Dennett's place in the Darwin wars, and not a philosophical essay on the metaphysics of intentionality, it is not the place for me to attempt a response to Fodor's (several) criticisms. I will say just enough about them to give the flavour of the issues – issues, again, of which the popular literature hasn't a clue – and of the kind of problem on which resolution of them must turn.

Fodor's comments on adaptationism itself distinguish between *methodological* adaptationism and what might best be called *ontological* adaptationism. The former is the view, discussed in Chapter 6, that to understand complex evolved organs or adaptations you need to engage in reverse engineering, and then test the results of that process against all the relevant empirical evidence you can get your hands on. That is, it is a thesis about how to do behavioural science (see Chapter 6). Ontological adaptationism, by contrast, is the thesis that, as a matter of fact, most of the features of present organisms were mainly produced by natural selection. Fodor is unsure about whether Dennett intends only methodological adaptationism, or both it and the ontological version. That Dennett defends, and requires, the first is not at issue. But Fodor finds some passages in *DDI* that he reads as implying that that is *all* Dennett needs, and other passages that seem to affirm ontological adaptationism. Against the latter view, Fodor reiterates arguments that are basically due to Gould and his colleagues, to the effect that many evolutionary developments are products of various forms of canalization in morphology rather than competition amongst designs that are generated pseudo-randomly.

The explanation for what Fodor regards as indecision on Dennett's part as between these two versions of adaptationism is, in fact, that Dennett doesn't allow for a clear distinction between them to begin with. This results from his broadly verificationist attitude toward explanation and causation. Dumouchel (2000) poses the question for Dennett as to whether all of natural selection's 'good tricks' (Dennett's term for optimal patterns in design space on which natural selection will tend to converge from any of a variety of contingent starting points) would not turn out to have been 'forced moves' if only we knew enough about the circumstances and constraints under which phylogenetic developments occurred. This would be a world in which Gould's radical contingency *from the design stance* was satisfied trivially because that stance turned out to be redundant given enough information visible *from the physical stance*; Stuart Kauffman (1993) has sometimes argued that this possible world is the actual one. What is interesting in the present context is that Dennett, in his reply to Dumouchel (Dennett 2000, pp. 336–41), considers the significance of this possibility only in epistemological terms. Essentially, he gives the answer one would expect from 'Real Patterns' (Dennett 1991b): The design stance, the perspective from which evolution is understood as development driven by natural selection, tracks statistical patterns that would emerge only on examination of many possible trajectories. This implies that Dumouchel's question only arises for Dennett as one about evolution *as it strikes an explainer from a perspective other than the physical stance*. This in turn strongly suggests that Fodor is arguing entirely at cross-purposes with Dennett because the latter *does not view natural selection, or any of the standard Gouldian and Kauffmanesque alternatives, as causal forces in the first place*.

This is not a very surprising view for an empiricist – and Dennett, student of Quine and of Ryle, certainly is an empiricist – to take: The causal events in the history of phylogeny are just the actual conceptions and births of organisms, and whatever causal processes directly drive events of meiosis.

Natural selection is then the organizing principle, *just conceptually equivalent to* taking the design stance toward evolution, from which explanatory patterns that would otherwise be invisible emerge from this biographical data about organisms. To put this another way, the relationship between actual conceptions and births in the history of life and instances of selection is exactly analogous to the relationship between brain events and intentional states for Dennett, that is, not a relation between tokens and types but between *illata* and *abstracta*.[3] (That is, a sequence of actual organisms is what we just 'find' in the data; natural selection is what emerges when we sort these data into interesting and abstract patterns from a perspective.) Since Dennett insists (as Fodor notes) that the logic of the design stance is literally identical as applied to engineered artefacts and to nature's products, and is not just a matter of analogy or family resemblance, this is what we should expect. Note that it provides Dennett with a perfectly general, entirely philosophical answer to Gould: Regardless of how many evolutionary products *could* be viewed as spandrels, this perspective *by definition* tracks no general patterns, since spandrels are by their nature local and particular. And in this case catastrophes (such as the asteroid that killed the dinosaurs), another favourite Gouldian worry, are not explanatory posits of the same logical type as instances of natural selection, since the former, but not the latter, are *illata* like conceptions and births. Thus, for Dennett, as for Gould, a terrible accident really *was* the cause of the mass dinosaur deaths 65 million years ago; but we understand this event as a crucial turning point in the history of life, giving the mammals room to flourish and diversify, only once we have organized that history by reference to natural competition and selection.

  This response to Fodor's objection to adaptationism in fact provides the key to answering Fodor's other main complaint (and the one Fodor clearly regards as most serious). Suppose it is conceded for purposes of argument, says Fodor, that the SELECTION FOR concept introduces intentionality into the natural domain because, like BELIEVES THAT and DESIRES THAT, it gives us intentionality, that is, opaque contexts of reference. (That is, "just as you can believe that *P* and not believe that *Q* even though *P* iff *Q*, so a creature might be selected for being *F* and not for being *G* even though all and only the *F*'s are *G*'s" [Fodor 1996/1998, 176–7].) In that case, Fodor goes on, Dennett's attempt to use the design stance toward natural selection as a basis for naturalizing intentionality generally relies on a claim to the effect that the SELECTION FOR concept is relevantly similar to the SELECTION FOR WITH SOMETHING IN MIND concept. But, Fodor argues, this approach is "hopeless" because

Mother Nature's myopia is so extreme. She is not only blind to future consequences of her design decisions, but to every nonactual possibility in design space, *and* to every actual thing or event that does not actually causally interact with the events relevant to selection. As Fodor summarizes the point, "Mother Nature never prefers any *F*'s to any *G*'s *except on grounds of (direct or indirect) causal interactions that the F's and G's actually have with the selection process*" (Fodor 1996/1998, p. 183). And this, Fodor goes on "looks like a whopping difference between Mother Nature and us." Since, for Fodor, the *main* puzzle connected with attempts to naturalize intentionality is the possibility it introduces of reference to nonactual or merely ideal objects (Plato's basic worry, of course), the SELECTING FOR that Mother Nature does is absolutely the wrong sort of notion for illuminating the intentionality characteristic of minds. This should hardly be surprising, Fodor concludes, since natural selection doesn't have a mind; *"there isn't any Mother Nature"* (Fodor 1996/1998, p. 186).

Notice, however, that once again Fodor is begging the question – the very same question as before – against the entire Dennettian ontology of mind. He is assuming that the primary interesting property of intentions is that they cause things (which is the context in which it's puzzling that, e.g., thoughts about Tarzan, who does not exist, have causal consequences distinct from thoughts about Johnny Weismuller, who does). And in that case *of course* Mother Nature's plans and preferences aren't interesting, since Mother Nature has no plans or preferences except in retrospect, and so there's no puzzle about how they cause things; they don't. But here we find a passage in which Fodor gives the whole game away. It is worth quoting in its entirety:

> But, you might reasonably wish to argue, this can't be a problem for Dennett's kind of reductionism [*sic*] unless it's a problem for *everybody's* kind of reductionism. For, you might reasonably wish to continue to argue, if *nothing* can be the effect of a merely Ideal cause, then, a fortiori, thoughts, decisions and actions can't be the effects of merely Ideal causes. And similarly for other intentional goings on. Remember that Brentano thought that the intentionality of the attitudes shows that naturalism can't be true; and Quine thinks that naturalism shows that the attitudes can't be intentional; and the Churchlands think . . . that the intentionality of the attitudes shows that there can't be any attitudes. In short, if there's an argument that Mother Nature is blind to merely possible outcomes, then there must be the same argument that you and I are blind to merely possible outcomes. So either Dennett wins or everybody loses. (Fodor 1996/1998, p. 184)

But *of course* from Dennett's point of view either he wins or everybody loses! His 'stance' stance with respect to intentionality is precisely supposed to be a way of avoiding the desperate conclusions of Brentano and Quine and the Churchlands (not to mention Fodor). And the key, central thrust of that position is that you get into these binds if you think that intentions are micro-causal forces at the level of *illata*, or if, like Churchland and Quine, you think that since they aren't that, then they can't exist. At the heart of Dennett's philosophy is the view that intentions (and various other things, like centres of gravity) can exist as real patterns without having to be token-identical to any billiard balls in systems of Humean causal relations. Your intentions and mine *don't*, for Dennett, cause anything below their own level of *abstracta*,[4] *and so, sure enough, neither do Mother Nature's. Yes, her plans and purposes are visible only in retrospect, but so are yours and mine*, because they show up only in the narratives that we and others tell when the intentional stance is taken toward us, by ourselves and/or by others. The intentional and the design stances really do work exactly the same way wherever they are applied.

Fodor, of course, won't buy a word of this, because the only project in town so far as he is concerned is the project of saving naïve causal realism with respect to psychological states. However, going into *that* argument would carry us all the way back through the past thirty years of general argument in the philosophy of mind. This very fact should, I think, make the case I set out to demonstrate in this chapter. The best grounds for adaptationism do not lie in bare biology – although the fact that biologists constantly reason by reverse engineering is a necessary condition for adaptationism's plausibility – or in the fact that by presupposing it we can spin nifty stories in evolutionary psychology. That's what you would gather from the popular arguments, but it *isn't true*. The scientific project involved in taking the design stance toward natural selection is, as Fodor says, logically stronger than mere adaptationism, which it obviously implies. If you want to understand why we should be engaged in that project, you need to study some complicated philosophy. And stop shouting.[5]

### Notes

[1.] This cannot be said of the packaging of Brown's book. Its back jacket features quotations of the violent *NYRB* soundbites by participants in the 'Darwin wars' about each other – Maynard Smith on Gould and Gould on Dennett – and ends at the bottom with the following: "'I wouldn't admit it if Andrew Brown were my friend. What a sleazy bit of trash journalism.' – DANIEL DENNETT." This is itself sleazy. For one thing, in the context of the accompanying quotes it makes Brown appear to be a participant in, rather than a spectator of, the elevated mudslinging. Much worse, Dennett's remark was not inspired by any of Brown's judgments on biological controversies, but by a tasteless comment of his about the personal lives of Dawkins and Gould. Worse still, the quote from Dennett is taken not from a public source but from a private e-mail message, and was printed here without Dennett's consent. I don't know how much control Brown had over the marketing people at Simon and Schuster; but this triply mendacious attempt to portray a 'Darwin warrior' as unreasonably ferocious is seriously at odds with Brown's celebration of the virtues of ecumenical sympathy in his text.

[2.] It must be noted here that the *way* in which Gould and Lewontin sympathize with believers is highly condescending to them. The religious, on their (Marxist) view, are victims of class exclusion, against which they retaliate with cranky, individualistic Protestantism. Is this *really* more sympathetic than the attitude of Dawkins, who is at least willing to credit believers with responsibility for their own (wrong) beliefs?

[3.] This is not how I would want to put the matter; see Ross (2000). However, my preferred way of conceptualizing this (in terms of mathematical information theory) is intended to capture everything that Dennett's *illata/abstracta* distinction is used to do, but without the implicit appeal to distinct 'levels of being.' In the present context, then, I can talk about *illata* and *abstracta* with the caveat that in a more extensional mode of address I would translate such talk into my own preferred idiom.

[4.] Note that if they *did*, then this would imply emergentism, and physics wouldn't be causally closed. Fodor would *really* hate that! (I owe this point to David Spurrett.)

[5.] I would like to thank Andy Brook and Dan Dennett for their helpful comments on an earlier draft of this chapter.

### References

Brown, A. (1999). *The Darwin Wars*. New York: Simon and Schuster.

Clark, A. (1997). *Being There*. Cambridge, MA: MIT Press/A Bradford Book.

Clark, A. (This volume). That Special Something: Dennett on the Making of Minds and Selves.

Dennett, D. (1981). True Believers. In A. Heath, ed., *Scientific Explanation*. Oxford: Oxford University Press, 53–75.

Dennett, D. (1984). *Elbow Room*. Cambridge, MA: MIT Press/A Bradford Book.

Dennett, D. (1991a). *Consciousness Explained*. Boston: Little, Brown & Co.

Dennett, D. (1991b). Real Patterns. *Journal of Philosophy* 88:27–51.

Dennett, D. (1994). Self-Portrait. In S. Guttenplan, ed., *A Companion to the Philosophy of Mind*. Oxford: Blackwell, 236–44.

Dennett, D. (1995). *Darwin's Dangerous Idea*. New York: Simon and Schuster.

Dennett, D. (1997). Letter to the Editor. *New York Review of Books* 44(13):46–8.

Dennett, D. (2000). With a Little Help From My Friends. In D. Ross, A. Brook, and D. Thompson, eds., *Dennett's Philosophy: A Comprehensive Assessment.* Cambridge, MA: MIT Press/A Bradford Book, 327–88.

Dumouchel, P. (2000). Good Tricks and Forced Moves, or the Antinomy of Natural Reason. In D. Ross et al. 2000, 41–54.

Fodor, J. (1996). Deconstructing Dennett's Darwin. *Mind and Language* 11:246–62. (Reprinted in Fodor, J. 1998. *In Critical Condition*, Cambridge, MA: MIT Press/A Bradford Book, 171–87; all page references in the text are to this source.)

Gould, S. J. (1997a). Darwinian Fundamentalism. *New York Review of Books* 44(10):34–7.

Gould, S. J. (1997b). Evolution: The Pleasures of Pluralism. *New York Review of Books* 44(11):47–52.

Gould, S. J. (1997c). Letter to the Editor. *New York Review of Books* 44(13):48–9.

Kauffman, S. (1993). *The Origins of Order: Self-Organization and Selection in Evolution.* Oxford: Oxford University Press.

LaCasse, C., and D. Ross. (1998). Morality's Last Chance. In P. Danielson, ed., *Modelling Rationality, Morality and Evolution.* Oxford: Oxford University Press, 340–75.

Malik, K. (2000). *Man, Beast and Zombie.* London: Weidenfeld and Nicolson.

Midgley, M. (1979). Gene Juggling. *Philosophy* 54:439–58.

Midgley, M. (1986). *Evolution as a Religion.* London: Routledge.

Rose, H., and S. Rose, eds. (2000). *Alas, Poor Darwin.* New York: Harmony.

Ross, D. (1993). Quining Qualia Quine's Way. *Dialogue* 32:439–59.

Ross, D. (1994). Dennett's Conceptual Reform. *Behaviour and Philosophy* 22:41–52.

Ross, D., A. Brook, and D. Thompson, eds. (2000). *Dennett's Philosophy: A Comprehensive Assessment.* Cambridge, MA: MIT Press/A Bradford Book.

Ross, D. (2000). Rainforest Realism: A Dennettian Theory of Existence. In D. Ross et al., 147–68.

Ross, D. (forthcoming). Chalmers's Naturalistic Dualism: A Case Study in the Irrelevance of the Mind-Body Problem to the Scientific Study of Consciousness. In C. Ernelling and D. Johnson, eds., *The Mind as Scientific Object.* Oxford: Oxford University Press.

Smith, J. M. (1995). Genes, Memes and Minds. *New York Review of Books* 42(19):46–8.

# Brief Annotated Bibliography
of Works by and About Daniel Dennett

## BOOKS BY DANIEL DENNETT

Virtually all of Dennett's important papers are collected in one of the following volumes. These books contain a complete picture of his highly distinctive point of view and it is not strictly necessary (although it is endlessly interesting) to consult his hundreds of publications in the professional literature. For writings on a particular topic, consult the references given at the end of the appropriate chapter of this volume.

*Content and Consciousness*. London: Routledge and Kegan Paul, 1969. Second edition, with new Preface, 1986.

> Dennett's first book on the nature of mind, in which most of the themes from his later work are anticipated in preliminary (often quite sketchy) form.

*Brainstorms*. Montgomery, VT: Bradford Books, 1978. Second edition, Cambridge, MA: MIT Press/A Bradford Book, 1981. Third edition, Harmondsworth: Penguin, 1999.

> A collection of Dennett's philosophical essays from the 1970s, including work on the nature of mental content, artificial intelligence, conscious experience, and differences between mere intentionality and full personhood.

*Elbow Room: The Varieties of Free Will Worth Wanting*. Cambridge, MA: MIT Press/A Bradford Book, 1984.

> A series of lectures originally given at Oxford arguing that the free will/determinism problem is, in most of its standard formulations, an artefact of an antiquated and confused conception of mind and intentionality.

*The Intentional Stance*. Cambridge, MA: MIT Press/A Bradford Book, 1987.

> Essays mostly from the 1980s on the nature of intentionality, the fixation of content in mental representations, and the evolutionary foundations of mind.

*Consciousness Explained*. Boston: Little, Brown, 1991.

> As the title implies, Dennett's mature theory of consciousness.

*Darwin's Dangerous Idea*. New York: Simon and Schuster, 1995.

> An extended essay on the philosophical interpretation of Darwinism, and on its implications for the human self-conception, views of the nature of mind, and public morality.

*Kinds of Minds*. New York: Basic Books, 1996.

> A shorter popular essay on the evolutionary origins of intentionality in general, and of the different sorts of cognitive structures – including the human one – found in nature.

*Brainchildren*. Cambridge, MA: MIT Press/A Bradford Book, 1998.

> A large collection of Dennett's essays, mainly from the 1990s, on a variety of topics including interpretations of his own earlier work, answers to his critics on consciousness, artificial intelligence, artificial life, cognitive ethology, and the nature of moral argument. Contains a candid and fascinating intellectual self-portrait.

### BOOKS ABOUT DANIEL DENNETT

There have been literally thousands of papers in the professional literature on Dennett's work. By contrast, there is not yet one single-authored book on his work. The following collections of paper are representative of the best in the critical literature. The volume edited by Ross, Brook, and Thompson aims at comprehensiveness.

*Daniel C. Dennett et les stratégies intentionelles*. Denis Fisette, ed. Montréal: Presse du Université du Québec à Montréal, 1992.

> A collection of critical essays by and for philosophers, concentrating primarily on *The Intentional Stance*.

*Dennett and His Critics.* Bo Dahlbom, ed. Oxford: Blackwell, 1993.

> A collection of critical essays by and for philosophers, concentrating primarily (though not exclusively) on *Consciousness Explained.* Includes replies by Dennett.

Two numbers of *Philosophical Topics* 22 (numbers 1 and 2) were devoted to critical studies of Dennett's work. He wrote a vigorous reply, "Get real. Reply to fourteen essays."

*Dennett's Philosophy: A Comprehensive Assessment.* Don Ross, Andrew Brook, and David Thompson, eds. Cambridge, MA: MIT Press/A Bradford Book, 2000.

> A collection of critical essays organized around evaluation of the extent to which Dennett's corpus of work on various subjects constitutes a coherent whole and a distinctive philosophical viewpoint. Includes an extended, sympathetic reply by Dennett, "With a little help from my friends."

# Index